BALL REDBOOK

18th Edition

VOLUME 1
GREENHOUSES AND EQUIPMENT

Edited by Chris Beytes

BALL PUBLISHING

Ball Publishing
622 Town Road
West Chicago, Illinois 60185
www.ballpublishing.com

Ball Publishing would like to thank the following people and companies who contributed photography to this volume: H.E. Anderson, Blackmore Company, Bouldin & Lawson, Cravo Equipment, Dramm Corporation, Jaderloon, Nexus Greenhouse Systems, PanAmerican Seed, Private Gardens, C. Raker & Sons, Rough Brothers, TrueLeaf Technologies, Flier Systems, Westbrook Greenhouse Systems, and Jim Willmott.

Cover designed by Christine Truesdale.
Cover photography by Mark Widhalm, copyright © 2011 Ball Publishing. All rights reserved.
Interior designed by Bay Graphics, Walworth, Wisconsin.
Edited by Rick Blanchette.
Printed by Walsworth Print Group, Marceline, Missouri.

Library of Congress Cataloging-in-Publication Data

Ball redbook. — 18th ed.
     v.
   Includes index.
   Contents: v. 1. Greenhouses and equipment / edited by Chris Beytes — v. 2. Crop production / edited by Jim Nau.
   ISBN-13: 978-1-883052-67-6 (v. 1)
   ISBN-10: 1-883052-67-X
   ISBN-13: 978-1-883052-68-3 (v. 2)
  1. Floriculture. 2. Plants, Ornamental. 3. Ornamental plant industry. I. Beytes, Chris, 1960– II. Nau, Jim, 1958–
  SB405.B254 2011
  635.9—dc23
                        2011035401

ISBN: 978-1-883052-67-6
Printed in the United States of America.
1   2011

Dedication

This eighteenth edition, published on the eve of the *RedBook's* eightieth anniversary, is dedicated to its founder, George J. Ball, and to his son Vic. It was George's vision that created what are today the Ball Horticultural Company, *Grower Talks* magazine, and the *Ball RedBook.* For his entire career until his death in 1997, Vic Ball was the industry's champion of education, communication, and sharing. We at Ball Publishing are proud to continue the journey along the path that these two pioneers blazed for us all. As George wrote, circa 1930, "Our books and trade papers are the most powerful source of information and exchange of ideas that we have." We believe that still holds true in 2011, even as "books and trade papers" are augmented by the Internet and all that it offers.

Contents

Preface

Most growers worldwide would agree that if they could only have one book on their office shelf, it would be the *Ball RedBook*.

The first edition of the *Ball RedBook*, published in 1932, sold for twenty cents, and was titled *Ball Red Book, Miscellaneous Flower Seed Crops*. George J. Ball penned the manuscript in longhand. At that time, almost all growers produced cut flowers, and most were also florists. That first edition featured cutting-edge crop culture on cut flowers such as asters (*Callistephus*), stock (*Matthiola*), snapdragons (*Antirrhinum*), larkspur (*Consolida*), calendula, sweet peas (*Lathyrus*), mignonette (*Reseda odorata*), zinnias, *Clarkia* (*Godetia*), centaurea, gerbera, *Didiscus,* and *Scabiosa.* The only bedding plants were petunias, candytuft (*Iberis*), marigolds (*Tagetes*), and lupine.

In today's floriculture industry, the bread-and-butter commodity cut flower production has moved offshore to Colombia and Ecuador, and most greenhouse producers focus on producing high-value, quick-turning bedding plants, perennials, foliage, and flowering pot plants. There are niche growers producing cut flowers, and, interestingly, many of the crops written about in the first *Ball RedBook* are viable, profitable cut flowers today. Incidentally, updated crop culture for most of these crops appears in this eighteenth edition.

As the industry changed, so has the *Ball RedBook*. Vic Ball took over the *RedBook* editing duties from his father and improved it with each subsequent edition. Over the years, the size of the book has increased to accommodate an expanding list of crops grown from seed and cuttings.

The *Ball RedBook* also has always touched on the technology side of the industry, with Vic sharing the contents of his notebooks filled with comments from growers all over the United States, Canada, and Europe on new ideas such as hydroponics, Dutch trays, roll-out bedding plants, open-roof greenhouses, round-robin production systems, transplanters, and more. There was no innovation that excited growers about which Vic Ball wasn't interested. His passion for encouraging innovation among growers and sharing information about growers was boundless. Vic was an inspiration to those of us who were fortunate to work with him and to every grower he encountered. Vic served as editor of the sixteenth edition of the *RedBook* and passed away in 1997, shortly after it was published.

When we published the seventeenth edition in 2003, we expanded the book into two volumes in order to devote even more pages to the topics of greenhouse production and crop culture. *Volume 1: Greenhouses and Equipment*, and *Volume 2: Crop Production*. Each volume is complete in its own right as a stand-alone book. Together, however, the volumes include enough practical information to set anyone interested in becoming a greenhouse grower on the road to success. Existing growers who have relied on the *Ball RedBook* as their "first consulted" reference text will find the volumes to be an invaluable resource.

This eighteenth edition continues the tradition of excellence set by the previous seventeen editions. Long-time *GrowerTalks* editor Chris Beytes again handled the editing duties on Volume 1, while Jim Nau, Greenhouses and Gardens Manager for Ball Horticultural Company, tackled Volume 2. An experienced horticulturist with several books to his credit, including the *Ball Culture Guide* and *Ball Perennial Manual*, Jim worked tirelessly for over a year to update the volume with many new crops.

Volume 1: Greenhouses and Equipment covers the basics of greenhouse structures and the tools needed to produce and market quality crops. This latest edition includes updated sections on open-roof greenhouse technology, water sanitation, "lean flow," sustainability, robotics, and alternative energy such as biomass boilers, solar and wind power.

Volume 2: Crop Production covers the basics of floricultural production in the greenhouse. Written in laymen's terms, the book is divided into two parts. Part 1 presents the basics of growing—including broad topics such as water, media, nutrition, temperature, light, and postharvest, as well as applied subjects such insect and disease control and growth regulators—all in grower-friendly text and graphics. Part 2 is a cultural encyclopedia of every important greenhouse crop, from annuals to cut flowers, perennials and potted plants. Dozens of contributors lent their expertise to its pages. There, you'll find propagation, growing on, pest control, troubleshooting, and postharvest information presented in an easy-to-use format.

We hope you find the *Ball RedBook* to be helpful, useful, and inspirational. Now, as Vic would have said, *"Let's go!"*

Chris Beytes

Jim Nau

Acknowledgments

In the seventeenth edition, I wrote a long-winded acknowledgement. This time, I'll cut to the chase and offer humble thanks to those who make this book possible:

First, the small-but-fierce Ball Publishing staff, who ran the company while I sweated over the book. Kim Brown and my right-hand-man, Associate Publisher Paul Black, the colorful sales duo who kept the advertising flowing in to pay the bills; Jennifer Zurko and Ellen Wells, who produce most of the magazine editorial each month; Melissa Parrish and Adriana Heikkila, who daily exceed the expectations of our readers and advertisers; Production Manager Kathy Wootton, who coordinated the making of this book in stellar fashion; and Christine Truesdale, our talented Creative Director who thought she'd signed on to design magazines.

I also want to thank all those who contributed to this book:

Bryce Anderson, Carlin Horticultural Supplies
Gary Baze, Golden Pacific Structures
Kurt Becker, Dramm Corporation
Steve Biles, TTA USA
Nora Catlin, Cornell Cooperative Extension
Tami Churchill, AmeriLux International
Raymond A. Cloyd, Kansas State University
Doug Cole, D.S. Cole Growers
Gerson "Gary" Cortés, FlowVision LLC
Al Denning, Rapid Automated Systems
Quinn Denning, Rapid Automated Systems
John DeVries, Rijk Zwaan Seeds
Kurt Dramm, Dramm Corporation
Ratus Fischer, Fischer EcoWorks
Jim Fowler, Bouldin & Lawson LLC
Bob Frye, The Plantation
Gene A. Giacomelli, Arizona State University
Mike Gooder, Plantpeddler
Don Grey, Freelance writer
Sara Grosser, Rough Brothers Inc.
P. Allen Hammer, Dummen USA
Edwin Hoenderdos, HOVE International Inc.
Thad Humphrey, TrueLeaf Technologies
Hans Izeboud, Flier Systems BV
Paul Jacobson, Green.tek Inc.
Paul T. Karlovich, C. Raker and Sons Inc.
Will Knowles, Welby Gardens
Robert Lando, AgriNomix
Peter Ling, Ohio State University

Chris Lundgren, Cherry Creek Systems
Neil Mattson, Cornell University
Kurt Parbst, Ludvig Svensson Inc.
Tim Raker, C. Raker and Sons Inc.
Jim Rearden, TrueLeaf Technologies
Ted Short, Ohio State University
David R. Steiner, Blackmore Company
Peter Stuyt, Total Energy Group
Bill Swanekamp, Kube-Pak Corporation
Scott S. Thompson, X.S. Smith Inc.
Jake Van Wingerden, Tidal Creek Growers
Arch Vermeer, Westbrook Greenhouse Systems
Richard Vollebregt, Cravo Equipment Ltd.
Joe B. Ware, Bouldin & Lawson LLC (deceased)
Jeff Warschauer, Nexus Corporation
Jennifer Duffield White, Editor-at-Large, GrowerTalks
Paul Whiting, Bouldin & Lawson LLC
Jim Willmott, U.S. Botanic Gardens
Doug Winterbottom, Greenhouse Technology Inc.
Bruce Zierk, Midwest GROmaster
Al Zylstra, DRAMMWater

Also, a special thanks to my boss, Director of Marketing Diane Hund, who both encourages and challenges me. She continues to push all of us to keep Ball Publishing—and the Ball RedBook—the leader in the industry.

And finally, Anna Ball, granddaughter of George J. Ball and every bit the champion of education, learning, and sharing that he was. Thank you, Anna, for allowing Ball Publishing to do what we do.

Chris Beytes
West Chicago, Illinois

1

Greenhouse Structures

What Is a Greenhouse?

P. Allen Hammer

What is a greenhouse? A typical dictionary definition may simply read, "a building having glass walls and roof, for the production of plants." Most greenhouse owners and growers, however, would argue that this definition is much too simple because it excludes greenhouses covered with various plastic glazing materials. As you read and use the *RedBook,* it will become apparent to you, too, that it takes a much broader definition of greenhouses to define the growing structures used in floriculture production.

Controlling the Environment

Greenhouses are considered "intensive" agricultural production. Intensive agriculture requires large inputs of labor and capital per unit of land to produce crops with high value per unit of land. That's opposed to "extensive" agriculture, which requires large inputs of land per unit of labor and capital with low crop value per unit of land. That is the major difference between field production and greenhouse production.

But before we more accurately define a modern greenhouse, it's important to understand a critical concept: controlled environment.

In nearly all horticulture production, we control the environment by using a structure along with other mechanical additions (e.g., heat) to create the modified environment. Although we have the engineering expertise to create a fully controlled environment for plant growing—up to and including artificial sunlight—the high cost of building and operating such an environment makes it unprofitable in most production. The exception has been in tissue-culture and seed-germination chambers, but those chambers contain high-value output per square foot of growing space and require less artificial light inputs.

Figure 1-1. With the right equipment, the modern greenhouse allows the grower year-round precision control over the environment.

The USDA Report No. 89, A Global Review of Greenhouse Food Production (Washington, D.C.: U.S. Government Printing Office, 1973), provides a more accurate definition of a greenhouse, "A greenhouse is a frame or inflated structure covered with a transparent or translucent material in which crops may be grown under conditions of at least partially controlled environment, and which is large enough to allow a person to walk within them and carry out cultural operations." This definition would include unheated structures with a roof that keeps rain off the crop and helps maintain warmer night temperatures as well as shade structures used to reduce wind and light.

Greenhouses use solar radiation as their primary source of "light," which is the most expensive input to try to add artificially. An important part of the greenhouse definition to me is the phrase "transparent or translucent" glazing because it includes all the commonly used coverings: poly, rigid plastic, glass, retractable-roof coverings, and shadecloth.

The sophistication of a particular greenhouse is often related to the climate in which it is constructed. Greenhouses located in the southern United States, for instance, often have less environmental control capability than those located in the north. However, this trend continues to change. Most greenhouses built in the last five years, regardless of location, are equipped with some form of computer system that operates the greenhouse's heating, ventilation, and cooling equipment with great precision. This is because the demands for better product quality and more precise timing have become increasingly important to growers in order to meet market demands.

The Greenhouse Effect

A discussion of greenhouses wouldn't be complete without a mention of the term "greenhouse effect." The terms "global warming" and "greenhouse effect" continue to be in the world news. Many misunderstand these terms, and global warming is often incorrectly associated with greenhouses because of the term "greenhouse effect."

The "greenhouse effect" is the possible warming of our planet because of increased levels of carbon dioxide and other so-called "greenhouse gases" in the earth's atmosphere. These gases occur naturally in the atmosphere as well as being released into the atmosphere from human activities—cars, factories, and so forth. For example, carbon dioxide is transparent to solar radiation but is opaque to long-wave (heat) radiation coming from the earth's surface. The carbon dioxide traps the heat near the earth's surface exactly like the glass does in a greenhouse. This is where the term "greenhouse effect" originated. Increased carbon-dioxide levels in the atmosphere are created by burning solid wastes and fossil fuels, not from greenhouse production. (It's interesting that this term doesn't technically apply to a polyethylene plastic-covered greenhouse because plastic is transparent to long-wave radiation. That's the reason infrared inhibitors have been added to plastic glazing used for greenhouses and the reason heat-retention curtains can be important in plastic greenhouses. Engineers have attempted to create the greenhouse effect with plastic glazing.)

Regardless of how a greenhouse is defined, floriculture crop production most often occurs in a modified environment. The future will no doubt require even better environmental control. Greenhouses will continue to be used and will become increasingly sophisticated because even under the best of natural climates, floriculture production requires modification to the environment.

Freestanding Greenhouses

Scott S. Thompson

A freestanding greenhouse is just what the name implies: a structure that's not attached to another structure. It may be a simple arch shape with no sidewall, have sidewalls just a few feet high, or have sidewalls 8–10' (2.4–3.0 m) high. This is in contrast to the other common greenhouse design—the gutter-connected house—in which numerous houses, or "bays," are connected together to create one large greenhouse.

A Little History

"I just want to say one word to you. Just one word. Plastics." No, that's not something my father once told me, but a line I heard in the movie theater while watching Dustin Hoffman get career advice while being chased around the pool by Mrs. Robinson in the 1960s classic *The Graduate*. Synthetic plastics, specifically polyethylene film, or "poly" as it's called in the trade, helped create the modern bedding plant industry and was the driving force behind modern freestanding greenhouse design.

Before World War II, all greenhouses were built of wood, iron, or steel and were covered or "glazed" with glass. World War II forced the aerospace and shipbuilding industries to develop lighter and stronger products to supplement steel as a raw material for the defense of our country. Advances in plastics technology spawned a tremendous variety of new market opportunities in diverse businesses, including agriculture and horticulture.

Figure 1-2. Before World War II, all greenhouses were built of wood, iron, or steel. This one is circa 1911.

Prior to the development of sheet plastics, greenhouse structures were designed and built for glass covering. With the advent of polyethylene plastic sheeting, farmers, florists, and nurserymen could now use this new "slat film" to cover existing small, wooden cold frames that were once glazed with more expensive, fragile, and heavy glass. Although the poly was thin, short-lived, and only available in narrow 2' (61 cm) or 3' (91 cm) widths, it allowed new growers to get into the business with a minimum of time, effort, and capital. However, the continued success of poly demanded production of wider, longer-lasting films. The original 3' (91 cm) wide material only lasted three or four months, depending upon the region of the country in which it was installed. At the time there were no ultraviolet (UV) inhibitors in the film, resulting in a quick breakdown of polymers, elasticity, and strength.

As poly became available in greater widths, greenhouse builders developed frames made of materials other than wood, such as steel, to offer a product that rivaled wood in size, shape, and strength, but cost less and required considerably less maintenance over the useful life of the structure. This also offered an alternative to costly steel-and-glass structures. Potential greenhouse construction costs could be cut from $4.00–7.00/ft.^{2} ($43.00–75.00/m^2) for glass to as little as $0.80–1.50 ($8.50–24.00/m^2) for steel frames covered with poly.

The first design profiles were crude and basic, but effective. Weather and wind were figured in the concepts, but at the time the actual considerations for stress and durability were new and untested. The only real data was for Quonset or arch-style roofline buildings covered with corrugated steel, or tent construction, which is still considered temporary. The Quonset (named for the city in Rhode Island near which the original military buildings were manufactured) was fairly easy to fabricate and cover; however, the available poly covering was still only wide enough to go partially across the frame. Cover separation had to be incorporated with the frame design to allow for completion of the securing process. This required the addition of a framing member rigid enough to span the rafter bows and to create an opportunity to either nail or staple the poly to this framework. These buildings were typically either a one- or two-piece construction with widths from 14–30' (4.3–9.1 m) and lengths of up to 200' (61 m). The structures

had posts or stakes driven 2' (61 cm) or 3' (91 cm) into the ground, depending on the size and location of the greenhouse. These developments resulted in an entirely new steel greenhouse design for the market to consider. However, lumber was still necessary in the framework to secure the poly covering.

Enter aluminum. The design staffs of greenhouse manufacturing companies worked closely and quickly with construction supervisors and other skilled craftsman in the building community to develop realistic ways to consider incorporating a positive and secure system to fasten the poly. The ability to reuse the fastening system would help offset the increased costs associated with a two-piece aluminum poly "lock." The first covering systems were mechanically based, with bolted or screwed base pieces used to cover the top of the greenhouses with poly. The covers were secured with rods that clamped them in place, allowing the poly to cover the walls down to the ground. Now covers could be installed quicker and easier. Also, for energy conservation purposes, builders began using two layers of film, inflating the layers with a small "squirrel cage" blower, creating the effect of insulation similar to a giant storm window. The poly fasteners could secure either one or two layers. (This same technology was also adapted to gutter-connected houses.)

Figure 1-3. Typical freestanding greenhouses.

The freestanding poly greenhouses could now be built, covered, and put to use in a matter of days, compared to weeks or months for a glass-covered greenhouse. The basic uses for these greenhouses were similar, but there now seemed to be a greater emphasis on using the structures for starting material from seed, such as starter plants for vegetable field crops, as well as for overwintering woody and perennial nursery crops. Bedding plant and potted plant growers who were using glass greenhouses began experimenting with growing their crops in the new poly structures. Immediately it was determined that the plastic-and-steel structures had many advantages over the glass-covered structures. The plastic greenhouses were considerably tighter than glass houses, which had laps between the panes that leaked air. The solar gain was equal to or greater than glass (even with approximately 15% less light transmission), and they held temperature much longer. These environment changes were now creating distinctly different reasons to use greenhouses for a variety of cultural applications. A whole new growing environment was available for various plant material and to traditional growers as well as the new breed of poly-greenhouse growers.

This tighter greenhouse environment now required more control. Glass greenhouses had for decades been heated with huge boilers that burned coal, oil, and natural gas to create steam or hot water, and were ventilated naturally by convection through the roof and sides. Experienced greenhouse builders had already been providing alternative heating and ventilation equipment (similar to what was being used successfully in livestock buildings) to glass greenhouse owners, specifically institutional and research facilities, who demanded the ability to create climate zones within their greenhouses. Freestanding poly greenhouses could be heated by small, oil-, gas-, or LP-fueled forced-air heaters. Ventilation was also done mechanically, with intake shutters or louvers on the intake end and electric exhaust fans on the outlet end.

Traditional glass growers were now thrown a huge curveball as new production greenhouses could be built and start producing plants almost immediately. This dramatically increased the amount of players in the market and decreased the time it took to produce plants for market. The same types of plant material could be grown in a shorter period of time for less capital outlay while still generating the same market price. The commercial greenhouse production market was changed forever.

Continuous Refinement

In the years since the first freestanding poly-covered greenhouses were built, the greatest changes have been in the development of the plastic coverings. Longer life, greater widths, condensation and heat-conserving additives, shading enhancements, and rigid plastic panels rather than sheets or rolls are all choices that

growers need to consider when deciding on cover. For a time, polyester-based fiberglass reinforced paneling (FRP) was popular. Glass growers could transition to the freestanding FRP greenhouse with less culture shock than switching between glass and poly. Glass growers who wanted freestanding buildings could build a house covered with the corrugated fiberglass sheets at dramatically reduced costs and not deal with the labor hassles of recovering with film every two or three years. However, the love affair with FRP ended when it was discovered how easily and quickly fiberglass burned, destroying entire ranges instantly.

There have been continuing refinements in a variety of other areas: stronger, lighter, and more corrosion-resistant framing materials, as well as wider, taller, and longer building profiles. In addition, improvements have been made in the development of more user-friendly hardware connections and in integration of environmental controls, including temperature, humidity, light levels, irrigation, and weather forecasting.

Because of increasing energy costs, freestanding greenhouse designers have recently adapted the natural ventilation used by wide-span glass greenhouse producers. These designs incorporate the use of roll-up sides and roofs, hand cranks, or automatic gearboxes, which allow air to flow passively through the house at a fraction of the energy cost of fans.

Pros and Cons

Several major issues arise when considering whether to build freestanding greenhouses versus gutter-connected structures, including land-value and tax implications, production planning, the crop type, the labor involved, utility costs, and time to build.

- Freestanding greenhouses still offer the lowest investment dollars per square foot of facility space. However, heating and ventilation costs can be higher, as each house needs its own heating and ventilation equipment.
- Labor and mechanization costs are usually higher in individual houses compared with gutter-connected buildings once your business approaches 1/2 acre (0.2 ha) in covered production area, as it's difficult (although not impossible) to use automation such as monorails, conveyors, or movable tables to move product.
- Freestanding houses take up more space than gutter-connected houses, as you need to leave space

Figure 1-4. Each freestanding house needs its own heating and ventilation equipment.

between each house. If useable building space on your site is at a premium, by the time the plan is properly laid out with all the required outbuildings, along with all the bells and whistles you might want inside the greenhouses, the initial benefits of low-cost individual houses may diminish compared with a gutter-connected house.

- If you need a sophisticated level of environment control and automation within your greenhouse for the crops you plan to grow, for example with bedding plant plugs, you may want to consider a gutter-connected structure.
- With freestanding houses, if you have an insect or disease problem in one house, you can easily keep the problem isolated.
- Freestanding houses can be relocated on your property more easily than a gutter-connected house if your land-use plans change.

Many growers have been very successful using low-cost freestanding houses for the bulk of their production. Several of the nation's largest growers, such as Harts Nursery of Jefferson, Oregon, utilize hundreds of freestanding houses to produce bedding plants. These buildings offer speed, flexibility, and few complications.

Gutter-Connected Greenhouses

Sara Grosser

As mentioned in the previous section, you have to consider many factors when selecting a greenhouse structure, including the crops to be produced, use of space, and expansion plans. Originally successful with vegetable and cut flower crops, the gutter-connected greenhouse offers today's grower a practical solution to each of these factors.

A gutter-connected greenhouse is defined as two or more greenhouse structures joined together at a common intermediate gutter where adjacent arches or slopes begin and end. Each greenhouse section is called a "bay."

Styles of Gutter-Connected Houses

There are several design styles for gutter-connected greenhouses, including A-frame/even-span, arch/gothic, sawtooth, Venlo, and open-roof.

Arch/gothic

The most economical greenhouse structure available is the arch/gothic house. The roof profile of the arch house is a simple curve, while the gothic roof curves to a slight point at the center. Construction of the arch/gothic house varies by manufacturer. Several construct the house with a webbed truss in the peak, while others provide a bar joist below the gutter height. A simpler design available in regions with low snow loads utilizes a simple crossbar from gutter post to gutter post.

The slope of the arch allows highly uniform light transmission and decreases interior condensation. Glazing options for the arch house include double poly, polycarbonate, and glass. Arch/gothic-style houses can be either naturally or mechanically ventilated. Some manufacturers offer the option of bowed sidewalls on arch houses. This gives you some extra growing space without the need for an additional run of gutter posts, as well as providing additional stability to the range.

Figure 1-5. This gutter-connected house uses the arch/gothic roof design.

Sizes and costs vary with manufacturer; however, the most common standard widths for gutter-connected houses include 20.5' (6.2 m), 22' (6.7 m), 24' (7.3 m), 30' (9.1 m), and 36' (11 m). Cost depends greatly on equipment and glazing selected. Typical equipment includes benching, forced-air unit heaters, single roof vent, side or gable vent, and doors. The cost for a greenhouse incorporating this equipment as well as double-poly roof glazing and 8 mm polycarbonate side and end glazing ranges from $6.00 to 9.00/ft.² ($64.50–96.75/m²).

Open-roof

The open-roof greenhouse offers maximum natural light and ventilation to the greenhouse crop. Similar in construction to that of the Venlo, the open-roof is constructed of two or more roof peaks per greenhouse bay. Each roof section is hinged at the gutter and is connected to a rack-and-pinion or push-pull drive system. Computer-controlled motors push the roof sections open, in effect making the entire roof into a vent. (Retractable-roof houses, which use a curtain-style fabric roof, are covered in the next section.)

Because it allows you to essentially grow your crops "outdoors" when the roof is open, this design provides a superior environment for hardening and conditioning crops, resulting in less shipping damage, improved longevity on the retail bench, and better performance in the garden. This also eliminates the labor of moving plants to a special hardening-off area.

Roof glazing options include glass, polycarbonate, acrylic, and double poly. Because of the relatively high cost of the structure, glass is the preferred covering. If you choose a plastic glazing material (polycarbonate and acrylic in particular) confirm that the covering has a UV inhibitor on both sides, as both sides are exposed to UV rays when open.

Sizes are typically the same as for Venlo houses and cost largely depends on the equipment selected. Typical equipment includes benching, forced-air unit heaters, roof motors, side or gable vent, and doors. With this equipment, double-poly roof glazing, and 8 mm polycarbonate side and end glazing, cost is approximately $7.00–12.00/ft.² ($75.25–129.00/m²).

A-frame

The A-frame, also referred to as an even-span structure, represents a traditional greenhouse design, with a peaked roof of two equal-length slopes. The A-frame is constructed of trusses in the shape of an elongated A (thus the name) either welded or bolted together and affixed to gutter posts spaced 10' (3 m) or 12' (3.7 m) on center. Additional members, referred to as purlins or girts, are placed perpendicular to the trusses along the slope.

The pitched roof (often 6/12 pitch) is the perfect angle to facilitate winter light transmission, increase interior condensate control, and shed snow. This pitch also provides increased air volume and hence less temperature fluctuation, which results in easier environmental control, ideal growing conditions for crops, and improved comfort for employees and customers. The A-frame is available in a variety of widths.

Easily equipped with roof vents as well as side and gable vents, natural ventilation is the common choice among growers and retailers; however, mechanical ventilation is readily installed.

Roof glazing options for the A-frame include polycarbonate, acrylic, glass, and insulated opaque panels (used over work areas or in retail settings). Double poly is less commonly used on A-frame houses.

The most common standard widths and equipment options are the same as with the arch/gothic design, although A-frame houses, because of the strength of the truss, can go as wide as 42' (12.8 m). Similar to arch/gothic houses, cost greatly depends on equipment selected, which again is similar to arch/gothic houses, except that double roof vents can be installed for improved natural ventilation. Cost is approximately $8.00–12.00/ft.² ($86.00–129.00/m²).

Atrium

A new design in the market, the atrium-style house is an adaptation of the A-frame. Roof pitch, glazing, and widths remain the same as those found with the A-frame. The only difference is the placement and configuration of roof vents. The roof vents on an A-frame hinge at the peak of the structure, while the roof vents on an atrium-style house hinge on the slope below the peak (the hinge is at the bottom of the vent rather than the top). Because of the vent design, some industry specialists have referred to it as a hybrid—combining the design (and select benefits) of an A-frame and open-roof into one structure.

Sawtooth

The sawtooth design is constructed with one roof slope having a vertical side, all above the gutter. Depending on manufacturer, the roof can be either arched or straight. The vertical side of the roof permits a great amount of natural ventilation as the vent opening is at the peak of the house, allowing the warmer air to rise and escape. Louvers or roll-up

Figure 1-6. The sawtooth design provides good natural ventilation. For this reason, it's often found in warm climates.

Figure 1-7. Notice the numerous, small roof peaks on this Venlo-style greenhouse.

curtains at the top of each vertical wall can be closed when the house needs to be heated. The placement of this vent also allows for dehumidification and ventilation when snow is in the gutter. Sawtooth greenhouses are often naturally ventilated.

Like the A-frame, the sawtooth is constructed of trusses welded or bolted together and affixed to gutter posts spaced 10' (3 m) or 12' (3.7 m) on center. Purlins or girts are placed perpendicular to the trusses along the slope.

Roof glazing for the straight sawtooth design is polycarbonate, while the arch design facilitates the use of polycarbonate or double poly.

Common standard widths include 24' (7.3 m) and 30' (9.1 m). Cost depends greatly on equipment selected. Typical equipment includes benching, forced air unit heaters, roof vent, side or gable vent, and doors. With this equipment and 8-mm polycarbonate roof, side and end glazing, cost is comparable to the arch/gothic design, at approximately \$6.00–9.00/ft.^{2} (\$64.50–96.75/m^2).

Venlo

The European-originated Venlo house, named for the city of Venlo in the Netherlands, is constructed of two to four small roof peaks per bay, with a bar joist affixed to gutter posts spaced 10' (3 m) or 12' (3.7 m) on center. Short posts extend from this bar joist to support intermediate gutters. The Venlo was designed to use single panes of glass from the peak to the gutter rather than lapped glass, and uses no purlins or girts in the roof structure, thereby maximizing energy efficiency and light transmission into the structure.

The typical Venlo utilizes natural ventilation, as the panel vents on each roof slope provide adequate air movement when paired with side and/or gable vents. The unique design of the vent system uses only two motors for an entire range, with one motor operating all the vents that face the same direction.

With the roof glazed exclusively in glass, the Venlo offers maximum light to the greenhouse crop—especially important in low-light northern regions and on crops that require maximum light. However, the need for an internal shade system does exist, as heat buildup will occur as a result of prolonged intense sunlight.

Sizes and costs vary with manufacturer; however, the most common standard widths include 20.5' (6.2 m), 24' (7.3 m), 36' (11 m), and 41' (12.5 m).

Because many of these designs originated with European manufacturers, sizes are often given in meters. Cost depends greatly on equipment selected. Typical equipment includes benching, forced-air unit heaters, roof vents, side or gable vent, interior shade system, and doors. With this equipment, glass roof glazing, and 8 mm polycarbonate side and end glazing, cost is approximately $7.00–11.00/ft.^{2} ($75.25–118.25/m^2).

Height

The height of all these structures is measured by gutter height (the distance from the ground to the bottom of the gutter). Typically, the higher the gutter, the better the environment within the greenhouse, both for the plants and the employees. Taller greenhouses allow for a larger air mass within the structure, resulting in simpler, more efficient climate control, as well as greater options in crop handling and automation. Today, average greenhouse height is 12–14' (3.7–4.3 m), with some soaring to 18' (5.5 m) or more, especially in greenhouses used for collecting and shipping plant material, where tall shipping carts and overhead table return systems need to be accommodated.

Figure 1-8. Tall gutter height provides a larger air mass, which helps maintain a good growing environment. The height also allows room for equipment and plants overhead.

Depending on the type of structure, the gutter height may be different than the height under the truss or joist because in some designs—such as Venlo and open-roof—the bottom of the truss or joist is placed below the gutter. For example, a structure may have a gutter height of 12' (3.7 m), with the bottom of the joist 9' (2.7 m) above grade, therefore giving 9' (2.7 m) of clearance. Check with your greenhouse manufacturer to determine design.

Pros and Cons

Gutter-connected houses are gaining in popularity because of the many advantages they provide over freestanding houses. Following are some of the key advantages and disadvantages to using gutter-connected houses.

Advantages
- Better control of the environment. Increased air volume results in less fluctuation in temperature. Small greenhouses have a large exposed surface area relative to their floor size through which heat is lost or gained, therefore the air temperature changes quickly in a small greenhouse.
- Lower heating costs. Less total covering surface relative to their floor area means less heat is lost. In addition, one heating system can be used to heat an entire range.
- More efficient use of land. Space isn't lost to aisles between freestanding greenhouses.
- Greater internal space utilization. Area isn't lost to the sloping walls such as those found in Quonset-type houses.
- Ease of expansion. Additional structures can easily be annexed for more rows of gutter posts. An existing sidewall or gable can be removed or left in place to provide partition between zones.
- Flexibility of zones. Partition walls can be installed to create separate zones.
- Increased use of automation. The space within the structure allows for the installation of booms, hanging basket systems, hot water heating, and shade systems.
- Labor savings increase. Employees don't need to exit and enter individual greenhouses to work with crops. In addition, the gutter-connected greenhouse range more readily allows the use of equipment such as lifts, carts, and monorails.
- Ability to move plant material within the range without exposure to outside winter air. Gutter-connect greenhouses have even been built large enough to accommodate a tractor-trailer for loading.

Disadvantages
- Greenhouse is all one zone. The lack of partition walls can restrict the ability to manage many different crops simultaneously.
- High initial cost.

- Increased disease and insect spread. No physical barriers exist to contain pests.
- Warm and cold areas may develop. Gutter-connected greenhouses' large area can create stagnant air pockets, especially when HAF fans aren't used. (See chapter 7.)
- Snow may build up in gutters. Although snow will melt when the greenhouse is heated, the situation should be monitored to avoid structural damage.

How High?

Chris Beytes

During the energy crisis of the 1970s, greenhouse manufacturers, in an effort to reduce heating costs, built very low structures, thinking this would reduce the amount of space that needed to be heated, thus minimizing heating fuel expenditures. Some gutters were barely 6' (1.8 m) high, leading to numerous bruised foreheads.

As energy costs moderated, growers who wanted space overhead for growing hanging baskets (and no doubt tired of banging their heads) began asking for taller houses. Typical gutter heights reached 9' (2.7 m), 10' (3 m), and then 12' (3.7 m) by the late 1980s. At the same time, equipment companies began developing automation—such as boom irrigation, hanging basket systems, shade and energy curtains, and internal transport systems—that required space above the crop for installation. Gutter heights climbed to 14–16' (4.3–4.9 m) to make room for this equipment.

During this upward expansion, growers learned that rather than making the environment more difficult to control or more expensive to heat, the large air mass inside the house acted like a giant sponge, holding a more consistent temperature for a longer period of time compared with shorter greenhouses, in which temperatures would quickly fluctuate. Also, energy curtains could be used to reduce the amount of heated space. Thanks to technology, today's 16' (4.9 m) tall greenhouse is more efficient and more useful than were those old head-knocker structures of the '70s, and most North American growers are asking for greenhouses in the 14–16' (4.3–4.9 m) range.

In northern European countries such as the Netherlands, they have taken greenhouse height well beyond this. Why? Again, climate control (a larger air mass holds a more consistent temperature), but also light diffusion. The higher the structure, the more the light has a chance to scatter and even out before it reaches the crop. Holland is a low-light country, and they want to get as much natural light to the crop as possible.

Also, to maximize space due to high land costs, most Dutch growers now have plant growing areas above their potting and packing areas. This requires even more greenhouse height, so some Dutch greenhouses now reach or exceed 29.5' (9 m).

The main construction consideration with a tall house is stability. Posts and other components need to be beefier to resist high wind and snow loads. But overall, adding additional height doesn't add much cost to the construction of a greenhouse, since it doesn't change the overall size or footprint.

Going Up?*

Chris Beytes

How tall should your next greenhouse be? Is there an optimum height for your greenhouse? We asked nine greenhouse experts for their views and recommendations.

How high?

"I like a 14' (4.3 m) house," says Gord Van Egmond, who handles U.S. sales for Westbrook Greenhouse Systems. "For the average grower, with one shade system, maybe two, and the average equipment overhead, it's nice." He adds that 15 or 16' (4.6–4.9) is a bonus, "but 14' (4.3 m) is plenty."

Scott Thompson, vice president of X.S. Smith, concurs. "What we see more of than anything else is 14' (4.3 m), both for production and for retail applications."

Matt Stuppy, president of Stuppy Greenhouse Manufacturing, expands on that. "On naturally ventilated houses we like to start at 14' (4.3 m) and move to 16' (4.9 m) if the conditions allow for it. Some growers request lower heights, and 12' (3.7 m) still works well for nursery, perennials, and annuals being grown on the ground."

For various reasons, however, that 14' (4.3 m) figure isn't universally accepted by growers. The biggest

*Published in *GrowerTalks* magazine, March 2009.

resistance is the old (and now debunked) belief that the taller the house, the more expensive it is to heat. "I still have one or two old-fashioned guys who'll call up and say, 'I want a 10' (3 m) greenhouse—it's cheaper to heat,'" says Gord Van Egmond, "but I explain to them that that's not the case."

Ask any grower who's gone from shorter to taller houses over the years and he'll tell you that the heating cost increase (if any) is negligible. That's because the outside surface of the greenhouse—the part that's in contact with cold air—is only slightly greater on a tall house than on a shorter house, says Bill Vietas, Rough Brothers' commercial division manager. "Your heating bill *will* increase some if you increase the height of the greenhouse, but not as much as most think because the surface area doesn't increase that much the higher you go, especially when you look at a large gutter-connected block."

Consider a 200 × 200' (61 by 61 m) greenhouse with 12' (3.7 m) gutters. It has 9,600 ft.^{2} (891.1 m^2) of sidewall area. Raise that house to 14' (4.3 m) and the sidewall surface area goes to 11,200 ft.^{2} (1,040.5 m^2)—an increase of just 1,600 ft.^{2} (148.6 m^2). Compared to the roof surface area of more than 40,000 ft.^{2} (3,716 m^2), that's a small increase of the total surface area of the greenhouse compared to the gain in interior space. Also offsetting any increases in heating costs is a major gain in the quality and consistency of its growing environment. Says Gary Baze, general manager of Golden Pacific Structures, "Most plant material doesn't react well to sudden changes in the environment. Increasing the volume of air in a greenhouse has the effect of buffering the plants against sudden changes."

Agricultural engineer Peter Ling of The Ohio State University offers a scientific explanation: "From a control engineering point of view, the combination of small but sufficient actuators (heaters/fans) and a larger buffer (the interior greenhouse volume) provides a smaller temperature overshoot/undershoot than that of a large actuator/small buffer combination." In other words, the larger the air mass, the easier it is to hold your greenhouse at a certain temperature. It won't fluctuate above and below your desired set-point, which means you'll save energy and your heating and ventilation equipment won't operate unnecessarily. You can get accurate control in a lower house, but it takes more sophisticated environmental controls.

The Downside to Going Up

To make your house taller, you can't just make your columns taller. Columns and other structural components have to be beefier, to resist wind and snow loads and to meet building codes. And don't forget about all that heavy overhead equipment you're going to put in your tall house.

That, of course, raises your construction costs, but it's a negligible increase compared to the total cost of the structure, says Gord Van Egmond. He says that going from 14' (4.3 m) to 16' (4.9 m) would probably increase your costs by about 5%. "If you have a basic plastic-covered greenhouse running at $3.75 a square foot, you add 5% to that, you're now at $3.93." That's just 18 cents a square foot more for the taller house, which matches Bill Vietas' estimate of 10 to 20 cents more per square foot to add 2' of height to a house.

Also, as with any structure, the quality of the steel is essential. You don't want your investment rusting off at the ground. Allied Tube & Conduit's Dan Kuzniewski says their GatorShield tubing has a unique galvanizing process that helps "give the longest service life in the field." It's a triple-coat process, with hot dip with zinc and two other coatings, including a clear organic top coat that is "friendly for fabrication by the greenhouse manufacturers doing the bends and swedging that they need," he says. "And it's a weldable coating system, too."

Plus, Dan says they offer higher strength steel than your "ordinary, everyday" tube mill, which allows builders to go higher without excessively increasing the overall size of the tubing, thereby allowing maximum light into the house.

When Tall Isn't Tall Enough

One thing about growers: their greenhouse is never big enough . . . and it's never tall enough.

"We're at 14' (4.3 m) and wish it was higher," says Lloyd Traven, Peace Tree Farms, of his almost-new Nexus greenhouse. "It seems like 18-plus feet (5.5 m) is more de rigueur nowadays."

But is 18' (5.5 m) enough?

"When we built our [Van Wingerden Greenhouse Company] MX 1 and 2s, our gutter height was 18' (5.5 m)," says Art Van Wingerden of Metrolina Greenhouses. "If we rebuilt today we would go with probably 20' (6.1 m)."

These two growers illustrate a good point: What seems to be more than plenty today will be barely adequate tomorrow. Consider this thought by Art when you're finalizing the deal for your new greenhouse. "We feel the extra cost is well worth the height you gain. The nice thing is, if you have the height from the start you can add anything you need—curtains, lights, ECHOs, and so forth—later on. Also, I've never seen anyone cut height away from a greenhouse, but I've seen plenty of people add height to a greenhouse after the fact."

Figure 1-9. For extremes in greenhouse height, look no further than the Netherlands. Ovata's new cactus and succulent range boasts a gutter height of 28½' (5.6 m). Photo: Chris Beytes

Open-Roof Greenhouses

Richard Vollebregt

Greenhouses with retractable and hinged roofs have been used commercially since 1990. They were initially used as season-extending structures to protect outdoor-grown crops—such as perennials and woody ornamentals—from late or early frosts, rain, hail, and other inclement weather in regions with relatively mild climates (the Pacific Northwest and southeastern U.S.). Growers from Florida to Canada now use open-roof houses throughout the entire production process, from stock plant production, propagation, and plug production, to growing on of finished plants and even retailing. They're used in every climate—cold with lots of snow, cool with lots of rain, hot and dry, and hot and humid—to grow poinsettias, plugs, cut flowers, perennials, tree seedlings, ornamentals, bulbs, garden mums, and the list goes on and on.

There are two basic styles of open-roof greenhouses: retractable roof and hinged roof. There are two styles of each of these.

Retractable Roofs

Curtain-style retractable-roof greenhouses use a flexible roof covering made from reinforced polyethylene or porous, woven polyethylene. These coverings are suspended from hooks that slide on wires and are opened and closed by a drive motor. (Cravo in Brantford, Ontario, Canada, is the originator of this design.) With this type of suspended roof "curtain," the roof profile can either be flat or A-frame.

Figure 1-10. Retractable-roof greenhouse with a peaked-roof profile.

Rolling-roof greenhouse designs were developed by Rovero Systems, the Netherlands, and by Jaderloon, Irmo, South Carolina, which markets the roll-A-roof in the United States. Both designs use powered drive tubes upon which a single or double layer of polyethylene covering is rolled and unrolled. Roll-up houses are used on an arch-shaped or round roof. If two layers of poly are used, they can be inflated with air when closed to create a double-poly greenhouse.

Both styles of retractable-roof house can be freestanding or gutter-connected.

Figure 1-11. A rolling-roof greenhouse.

Hinged roofs

The hinged style of open-roof greenhouse uses a Venlo design (multiple roof sections spanning one bay) and is covered with a rigid glazing like glass, polycarbonate, or acrylic or covered with double poly. The best covering choice will depend on the crop and location of the greenhouse.

There are two styles of hinged-roof houses. The first is hinged at each gutter, was originated by Van Wingerden Greenhouse Company in the United States, and is often referred to as an MX style, which is their trade name. The second is hinged at the peak and at one of the gutters. It was originated by Defosche in Belgium and is called a Cabrio. In the gutter-hinge style, a rack and pinion or push-pull drive system pushes each roof section from an inclined position to a vertical position, in essence making the entire roof a vent. In the peak-hinge style, the two roof sections fold together accordion-fashion. When the roof is in the fully open position, approximately 80% of the roof area is open.

Figures 1-12, 1-13. Two styles of hinged-roof houses: MX (top) and Deforsche (bottom).

Why Choose an Open-Roof Greenhouse?

Growers cite many benefits to open-roof greenhouses, but the biggest is the improvement to crop quality and production efficiency due to the improved range of environments they provide. A traditional greenhouse offers good climate control during inclement weather, but during warm, sunny weather it can be a struggle to maintain the best temperature and humidity much of the year without expensive, sophisticated environmental controls. With an open-roof greenhouse, when you open the roof, you expose the crops to the same growing environment they'll experience in the consumer's garden. In fact, many growers consider open-roof greenhouses to be the ultimate growing facility, offering the most environmental flexibility possible—from complete climate control to outdoor growing and everything in between. This versatility is vital because what you're growing today may not be what the market wants five years from now.

This type of greenhouse is also gaining popularity with retail garden center owners because it can provide a comfortable outdoor shopping environment during good weather, rain protection on dreary days, and warm indoor shopping in the winter.

Other benefits to open-roof houses include flexibility in size and configuration because there are no limits to the size of the greenhouse due to cooling equipment capacity; lower utility costs since you don't need ventilation or horizontal air flow (HAF) fans; the ability to install insect screen without compromising on cooling or ventilation; more light reaches the crop when the roof is opened; crops receive the full spectrum of solar radiation; plant growth is more compact; condensation dries quickly; rain can be used to naturally irrigate the crop; and insect and disease pressures tend to be less than in a traditional greenhouse.

There are a few drawbacks to open-roof greenhouses. It can take from two to eight minutes to close the roofs (depending on design), which may not be quick enough if a storm comes up quickly. They can also be expensive: a flat-roof retractable house costs a little more per square foot than a freestanding hoop house; the hinged-style roof with glass is the most expensive commercial greenhouse design available, usually costing several dollars per square foot more than a similar Venlo house.

The retractable-style roof should not be operated when there is ice or snow on the roof, as damage to the drive system could result. While traditional greenhouse poly normally lasts three to four years, the reinforced polyethylene retractable roof coverings tend to last eight to twelve years but are more expensive to replace than conventional greenhouse poly.

The roll-up style roof requires regular monitoring of the condition of the poly glazing, which lasts about three years. The roll-up mechanism must also be adjusted carefully to ensure that it's properly aligned.

Choosing a Style

There are many differences between the various retractable and hinged-roof designs. When trying to decide which style of open-roof greenhouse is best for your application, consider the following criteria:

Covering

The roof covering you select most significantly impacts the greenhouse environment, primarily when outside conditions are cold and light levels are low. Most growers tend to choose the same or similar roof covering as they would install if they were building a conventional greenhouse. If they would normally build a glass-covered greenhouse, then they tend to build an open-roof greenhouse with a glass roof. If they would normally build a poly-covered greenhouse, then they tend to build an open-roof or retractable-roof greenhouse that's covered with poly or rigid plastic sheets. A porous woven or knitted polyethylene roof is normally selected for rain-tolerant crops needing protection from excessive cold or heat.

The selection of the roof covering can automatically dictate which style of hinged-roof or retractable-roof greenhouse you can consider. If you want glass, polycarbonate, or acrylic glazing, you require a hinged-roof house. Then you need to decide between a roof hinged at the peak or at the gutter. If you select a flexible roof covering such as polyethylene film or reinforced polyethylene, then you can choose from either the hinged or retractable-roof houses.

Both the hinged-roof and retractable-roof designs can ventilate very effectively because you can create a very large opening in the roof. This means cooling is no longer a problem.

Figure 1-14. Retractable- and open-roof houses allow for maximum ventilation with good-to-excellent weather protection, depending on design.

Light

When the roofs are open or retracted, there are significant differences between a hinged roof and a retractable roof. When a hinged roof is open, the impact on light levels reaching the crop is different depending on the angle of the sun. In the early morning and late afternoon, light levels are low and the sun has a low angle of incidence. When the hinged roof is open, the early morning and late afternoon sun must pass through both of the vertical roof coverings, causing a significant reduction in light levels and infrared radiation. This light loss is occurring precisely at the time of the day when light is already a limiting factor to plant growth.

With a retractable roof, when the roof is retracted during the early morning and late afternoon, the roof covering essentially disappears, resulting in the plants getting up to a 50% increase in light levels compared to leaving the roof closed.

From 11:00 a.m. till 3:00 p.m., light levels are high and many plants need to be shaded. With a retractable-roof greenhouse, the roofs can be closed 85% of the way, using the roof covering to diffuse and reduce incoming light levels. If a retractable shade-curtain system has been installed, the shade system could be closed and the roof left open. Under a hinged roof house, the roofs could be closed part way and/or the shade system can be closed.

Wind

For many plants, wind is beneficial for proper plant conditioning. With a retractable roof, crops can be exposed to as much or as little wind as desired, based on the roof position. When a hinged-roof house is open, the vertical roof sections may act as baffles, which can reduce the wind at the crop level. However, excessive wind can dry out plants and knock them over. With both the retractable- and hinged-roof designs, wind levels should be monitored to ensure that the roof and walls are in the appropriate position.

Although both types of houses are well engineered, there are differences in their susceptibility to wind damage. Check with individual manufacturers to determine the wind tolerance of particular designs.

Ventilation when raining

When it's raining outside for an extended period of time, ventilation is required for humidity control. Most greenhouses that have roofs that open should also have sidewalls that open. These curtains are commonly opened partway for ventilation when it's raining. This has proven sufficient in most cases. However, some retractable-roof and hinged-roof greenhouses allow the roof to open slightly for ventilation when it's raining without allowing rain to enter. At least one open-roof design uses push-pull drives and computer controls to allow you to move each side of the roof into a sawtooth vent configuration, for improved ventilation during inclement weather.

Costs

As with all greenhouses, costs vary widely depending on the manufacturer, greenhouse size, and desired equipment. The larger the house, the lower the square-foot cost. Each of the following figures are based on a 1 acre (0.4 ha) structure (about 44,000 ft.^{2} [4,047 m^2]), materials only (no labor).

According to manufacturers, the typical flat-roofed house, used primarily to protect plants from excessive heat and cold, costs about \$2.00–2.75/ft.^{2} (\$21.50–29.60/m^2). A retractable with a peaked roof, which offers more of a year-round growing environment, costs about \$3.75–4.50/ft.^{2} (\$40.35–38.50/m^2).

The Rovero rolling-roof greenhouse (which, incidentally, the manufacturer says can easily be retrofitted on an existing arch-roof structure), costs approximately \$4.00–5.00/ft.^{2} (\$43.00–53.80/m^2). An open-roof greenhouse house, hinged at the gutter or at the peak, glazed with glass, and equipped with the appropriate computer controls to operate the roof, costs from \$7.00–8.00/ft.^{2} (\$75.00–86.00/m^2).

Open-Minded*

Chris Beytes

What have we learned about open-roof greenhouses in the relatively short time we've been growing in them? Quite a bit, actually—although there's much more to be discovered.

In December 1993, *GrowerTalks* toured its first Cravo retractable-roof greenhouse with Clay Murphy at Plants Inc. in Huntsville, Texas. We were intrigued by the promising new technology, which offered the benefits of outdoor growing with instant weather protection when needed.

Since that time, we've seen scores of retractable- and open-roof houses here and abroad from numerous manufacturers. They've become commonplace among businesses looking for a flexible, energy-efficient growing environment. In fact, growers love them. Says Nexus's Jeff Warschauer, "I don't have any customers, nor have I heard of any, who've said, 'Geez, I wish I had my old greenhouse back, with all the fans and pads and what have you.' I think growers are pretty tickled with the culture end of the greenhouse and the quality of the environment."

Tickled is right—every grower we talked to said their next house will be some form of open-roof. But it can't all be sunshine and rainbows. What have we learned about these greenhouses in the subsequent years?

Open vs. Retractable

First, let's talk terminology. Open-roof and retractable are not interchangeable terms. As the technology has developed, an "open-roof" house has come to be defined as a rigid roof panel that hinges open. It can be glazed with poly film, twin-wall sheeting, or glass. "Retractable" describes a fabric roof that's suspended over the crop, like a curtain. The curtain can be flat, angled, or in a traditional peaked shape.

*Published in *GrowerTalks* magazine, March 2010.

On the surface, it would seem that the two provide the same function: offering you the choice of indoor or outdoor conditions at the flip of a switch. In fact, both styles of house do a few things extremely well: They're energy efficient, requiring no cooling fans; they're great for hardening off crops; they offer natural plant height control through easy DIF applications and high light; and they protect your crops from sudden inclement weather.

But there are differences between them. An open-roof house is designed to function as a traditional greenhouse, except with extremely effective natural ventilation. It doesn't quite provide an exact outdoor environment due to the all the structure that surrounds the crop, which impacts the radiation reaching the crop. But when the roof is closed, it functions exactly as its fixed-roof cousin does.

A retractable-roof house functions best when left open, allowing for full outdoor growing. Then, when conditions are bad—too cold, too hot, too wet, too windy—you (or the computer) can close the roof to protect the crop. They can be used year-round in areas with moderate climates, where there's not too much snow or many days below freezing. In many climates, they're used as season extenders, allowing growers to put crops outside earlier in the year and leave them out later in the year—such as pansies in the spring and mums in the fall. At Mid-American Growers in Illinois, they use their 7 acres (2.8 ha) of Cravo from late February until November.

It's a Moving Object

Whether they offer open-roofs or retractables, manufacturers list two key lessons they've learned since bringing their houses to market: durability and maintenance.

The first-generation open-roof houses were based on existing technology. Van Wingerden Greenhouse Company launched its MXII in 1997 with the goal of getting as much natural ventilation as possible and getting a consistent temperature across the entire growing area whenever the roofs were opened, says general manager Rick Worley. Since the open roof was going to be nothing more than an extra-large vent, they chose aluminum for the rack-and-pinion roof drive, to save weight. Other manufacturers did the same, as aluminum was proven to work with other roof vent systems.

Aluminum might have been fine for standard vents, but the open-roof panels were considerably heavier.

And growers were sometimes making their temperature set points too narrow, which led to lots of movement of the roofs in an attempt to optimize the temperature. The result was excessive wear and tear on racks and pinions. The solution was simple: switch from aluminum to steel for durability and provide more frequent lubrication.

At the same time, growers have had to learn to make regular adjustments to prevent drips and air leaks, and regular inspections and tightening of bolts and set screws. "It'll work if you don't, but it will work a whole lot better if you do," says Rough Brothers' Bill Vietas. "It's a lot of moving parts." Adds Jeff from Nexus, "You get into bigger ranges and there are a thousand racks and pinions, and it only takes one set screw to come loose to cause major havoc."

The retractable-roof story is similar. Cravo's first-generation retractables, which debuted in 1990, were simple flat or angled structures designed for weather protection. The second-generation structure (which is what we saw at Plants Inc.) had a peaked roof and a full truss, allowing for hanging baskets and booms. It looked like a greenhouse. So that's how growers treated it.

"What basically happened was that people bought a retractable roof—which you could call an unconventional house—because the whole roof opens instead of just a vent," says Richard Vollebregt, president of Cravo. "But they were utilizing conventional computer control strategies to control their unconventional house." As a result, the roofs were constantly in motion, opening and closing as air and sunlight changed the inside temperature more than a few degrees. "That whole control strategy was negatively affecting the life of the covering and causing excessive wear and maintenance on the drive system," Richard says. Think of a petunia growing outside, he says. "Do you think it really matters whether the air temperature is 70°F (21°C) or 72°F (22°C)? Of course not."

To solve the problem of excessive opening and closing, Cravo developed a whole new set of computer control strategies and sensors. "In a retractable roof, the philosophy is 180 degrees opposite to a conventional house," he explains. "Instead of opening a vent only when it's too hot [as in a regular house], we want to retract the roof whenever outside conditions are optimal. And we only want to close the roof when outside conditions are too cold or too hot or too wet or too windy."

Reducing the Rolls Royce Cost

The first open-roof houses weren't considered the "Rolls Royce" of greenhouses for nothing: costs could exceed $10 to $12 per ft.² ($107.60–129.12 m²) for a glass-glazed structure with all the bells and whistles. But over time, builders have fine-tuned their structures and found ways to reduce costs while making them more dependable. For instance, X.S. Smith, which has experimented with all natures of retractable and open-roof houses since the early 1990s, settled on double poly for glazing rather than glass. Their first open-roof house, for Norm White in Chesapeake, Virginia, was double poly, says X.S. Smith Executive V.P. Scott Thompson. Norm says he likes double poly for all his houses, both fixed and open-roof.

Another cost is motors. One motor per peak is optimal, allowing you to operate each peak individually. But to reduce costs, some builders offer several drive options. For instance, Rough Brothers will install gear boxes that let you run three to six roofs from one motor, or they can install a push-pull system that operates six bays with two motors—and with this system, one side panel can operate independently of the other, allowing you some unique venting options. Another option is only installing the drive equipment in every third bay, then adding it later on. Rough Brothers' Bill Vietas says that's a good way to cut costs while leaving the option available to open the other bays later.

A Hybrid Solution

Which leads to today's open-roof trend: partially open roofs. One example is Nexus's Dual Atrium design. Picture an open roof but instead of hinging at the gutter, the hinge is located half way up the roof panel. The top half of the roof opens, and the lower half stays stationary. You only have about 50% of the vent area of an open-roof house, but you get "pretty close" to the same ventilation results for considerably less money since here are fewer gutters, fewer moving parts, and less installation labor.

Mike Goyette, operations manager at Pleasant View Gardens in New Hampshire, grows in both kinds of houses, and he likes the modified open-roof better, saying it actually lets in more light because there's less overhead structure to cast shadows. Climate-wise, "I think they're pretty comparable," he says. George Lucas, owner of Lucas Nursery, agrees with Mike about the modified open roof. "We really

like the concept and will continue building the Dual Atrium-type houses in the future," he says.

Van Wingerden offers their own hybrid between their MX open-roof and AF aluminum A-frame house: a double poly house with 12 ft. (3.7 m) peaks, with every third peak being an MX open-roof. Rick Worley says they can build that house for under $5 per ft.² ($53.80/m²). "That seems to be the best bang for the buck for the grower who's working for the box stores and is trying to put some square feet of greenhouse up," he says. The disadvantage is that two of the three peaks don't open, so you do have some heat buildup in those sections.

What have growers learned?

The biggest downside we heard from growers? For retractables, it's the cost of replacing the roof fabric, which lasts from five to ten years or so, depending on use and climate. But they accept that as a regular maintenance item. For open roofs, it's heat buildup in the middle of summer. Norm White says he can't use his houses for about six weeks in July and August because they're 6–8°F (3.3–4.4°C) warmer than the outside air. Dave Wiesbrock of Mid-American (which has 29 acres [11.7 ha] of MX and 7 acres [2.8 ha] of Cravo) said the same thing. "You can still struggle with getting good air movement into them in the heat of the summer versus the retractable," he says.

Still, an open-roof house seems to be the design of choice for growers looking for a year-round greenhouse that offers exceptional natural ventilation. Want outdoor growing with occasional weather protection? Go for a retractable.

Shadehouses

Gary Baze

Providing shade to light-sensitive nursery and greenhouse crops is as important to growers and retailers as providing clean water and fresh air. Shading takes on multiple forms, from the simple application of liquid shade compounds ("whitewash") on poly or glass glazing to sophisticated retractable curtain systems opened and closed by computerized environmental controllers.

While shading represents only a portion of the overall growing process, some growers and retailers employ structures designed specifically for shading. These are typically simple structures, with the primary purpose of suspending shade fabric over plants to protect them from excessive sunlight and/or over retail customers to create a more comfortable shopping environment. These structures are commonly referred to as shadehouses.

Figure 1-15. The primary function of a shadehouse is to protect shade-loving plants from the harsh rays of the sun. This rigid-frame type is the most common shadehouse style.

Applications

Shadehouses are employed worldwide to enhance the quality of products and maintain a level of comfort for individuals. The most common use of shadehouses is to reduce the level of direct sunlight reaching the plant. Reducing sunlight also serves to create a cooler, more comfortable climate.

For commercial growers, the lure of a shadehouse is the relative low material cost involved. Provided the outdoor conditions are conducive to growing, shadehouses offer not only a low-cost alternative for expanding your growing area, but also provide an excellent environment for hardening off the plants prior to sale. Obviously, warmer regions can take advantage of shadehouses for a longer period of the growing season. Foliage growers in Florida, for example, grow in shadehouses year-round.

For retail operations, shadehouses offer a comfortable environment for customers to leisurely make their purchases. Most consumers are comfortable, regardless of the outdoor temperature, provided they are shielded from direct sunlight. Customer comfort can be further enhanced by introducing air circulation fans and/or localized evaporative cooling systems.

The benefits of shading extend even when shading of a crop or environment is not the primary intent. For example, the retractable flat roof structure was initially designed as a frost protection system. However, growers quickly recognized a benefit as the system offered an excellent means to shade their crops as well. In another example, some vegetable growers, especially in areas where moderate weather conditions exist, incorporate structures covered with insect screen (see chapter 9) in place of conventional greenhouse coverings. The intent of this practice is to reduce insect intrusion and to promote natural ventilation within the environment. Insect screen also provides a degree of shading which is, in most instances, considered a benefit.

Fixed roof shadehouses have traditionally incorporated black woven or knitted shade fabrics to produce the required shading. These fabrics have a proven track record, are relatively inexpensive, and fairly long lasting. It is generally accepted that knitted fabrics are slightly more expensive though they do resist the tendency to tear even if damaged. Shade fabrics are available in a variety of shading density, from 30% up to 80%, depending on the application.

A third family of shade fabrics has begun to emerge as a more effective alternative—the aluminum or reflective shade fabrics. Reflective shade fabrics have been employed for years as internal retractable shade systems installed in greenhouses. Recently though, growers and retailers have come to appreciate the increased efficiencies available with these systems as they apply to outdoor environments. Whereas traditional shade fabrics absorb heat, which then can be re-radiated toward the crops, aluminum-based shade fabrics reflect heat-producing rays away from the crop, resulting in substantially cooler temperatures. As an added benefit, this very same reflective technology increases the environment's ability to hold heat, when desired, by radiating the heat escaping from plants and the earth back down toward the crop. Reflective shade fabrics do represent a higher price when compared to traditional woven or knitted fabrics, though the increased efficiencies achieved are considered adequate to offset the difference.

Structural Designs

In general, there are three recognized designs for shadehouses including the cable-frame, rigid-frame, and retractable roof systems.

Cable-frame system

These systems generally employ upright columns

spaced evenly along the length and width of the structure. While the spacing of upright columns varies depending upon manufacturer and regional wind conditions, cable frame systems are typically provided with columns on 20–30' (6.1–9.1 m) spacing. For obvious reasons, the closer the columns, the stronger the system becomes. Virtually any rigid material can be used as an upright column, including wood, galvanized steel tubing, or preformed steel profiles. It is generally accepted that steel columns, with a galvanized finish, will provide the highest return on investment. Due to the extreme vertical and horizontal forces exerted on a shadehouse by wind, it's essential, regardless of the column material, that each column be securely bolted to or set into an adequately sized concrete footing.

Once the columns are securely in place, cable is pulled tight from upright to upright, creating a crisscrossed patchwork over the entire area. Cable tightening systems are employed to pull the cable taut between uprights with the goal of eliminating any sag in the cable. Due to extreme tensions created, all exterior upright columns typically employ some form of a diagonal cable brace referred to as a "dead man" to prevent the bending of exterior columns.

Figure 1-16. A cable-frame shadehouse.

Shade cloth then is suspended between the cables using commercial shade cloth clamps, hog rings, S hooks, bungee cords, or nylon ties along the edges. To insure the fastening system employed won't rip through the fabric, the shade cloth is prepared with a reinforced strip sewn around the perimeter with grommets strategically spaced. Fasteners then secure the edge of the fabric to each run of cable. In most cases, regardless of the type of fabric, shade material

applied to cable frame structures are secured only at the perimeter of the fabric. In some isolated cases, where extreme winds prevail, growers may choose to install a restraining system, either a strap or a second cable, over the top of the shade fabric. This added step prevents excess wind from "whipping" the fabric up and down on the structure.

Rigid-frame system

These systems incorporate rigid framing instead of cables. Due to the spanning limitations of steel or wood, upright columns have to be spaced much closer together, in most cases from 12–18' (3.7–5.5 m). Due to the added rigidity of the framework, many rigid-frame systems employ diagonal "knee braces," which then eliminate the need for cabled dead man assemblies. Rigid-frame systems are generally favored by retail operators due to the aesthetics of their design, the flexibility of the package, and their ability to meet specified building codes. Fabrics can be secured to the rigid frame either with the same methods as for the cable-frame system or sandwiched between the rigid cross members and aluminum or wood lathe, using screws to secure it in place.

Some manufactures offer rigid-frame systems with a "certified" wind loading. This is especially important to retail centers, as more and more building departments are requiring "certified engineering" for any structure open to the public. Also, rigid-frame systems offer additional strength that allows the suspension of product, such as hanging baskets, from the structure itself. Both growers and retailers benefit from this feature.

Retractable systems

Outside retractable flat-roof systems have become a proven staple in our industry. While initially employed as an effective means of frost protection, retractable systems offer the added benefit of shading products and individuals.

Retractable flat-roof houses incorporate the traditional concept of a fixed shade structure, with upright columns and dead man bracing, though with a very distinctive difference: These systems employ a mechanism which opens and closes the fabric on demand. Typically, the drive mechanism consists of a drive motor, a drive shaft, and a series of drive cables and pulleys which allow the shade fabric to travel from one set of columns to another. Due to the unique nature

Figure 1-17. Although not a shadehouse, per se, this retractable system does shade the greenhouses and plants below and can be retracted during periods of less light.

of this system, shade fabrics require an added degree of security to maintain their position over the crops. Shade fabrics are provided with added reinforcement tape or wire running the length of the fabric at a given spacing. Custom hooks are inserted into the fabric, along the reinforced strips or wire, which then is connected to slide cables allowing the fabric to freely move back and forth.

This system's ability to cover the environment when necessary and then open it at key times of the day offers a huge advantage over traditional fixed roof shadehouses:

- It regulates shade on intermittent cloud covered days.
- It increases air circulation around plants–increased circulation reduces standing water, which can otherwise promote disease and insects. In addition, increased fresh air circulation improves plant quality.
- It reduces crop production time due to more efficient cooling, reduces watering requirements, and promotes hardening off of plants.
- Systems incorporating reflective-style shade fabrics offer increased frost protection capabilities even when compared to most closed weave fabrics.
- Reflective-style fabrics are used to hold and extend cooler morning temperatures when applied to cool-weather crops.

Shadehouse Limitations

Wind and snow generally represent the greatest threats to shadehouses. Even retractable flat-roof shade structures can, if not properly maintained or controlled,

accumulate damaging snow and ice. It's always recommended that the upright columns be set into adequately sized concrete footings with tension dead man cables provided to maintain the integrity of the structure. While snow can easily bring a shadehouse down, winds can produce devastating vertical lift, easily damaging the fabric or even the structure. Because of this, it is strongly recommended that shade fabrics of fixed roof structures be removed prior to heavy precipitation forming or extreme winds. Retractable flat-roof shade structures should employ environmental computer controls capable of monitor winds, rain, and snow and automatically open the structures prior to damage.

The Headhouse

Jeff Warschauer

The term *headhouse* is recognized universally in horticulture as a building used for many functions, including material handling, storage, potting, transplanting, shipping, physical plant location (heating, electrical, and irrigation systems), offices, staff facilities, retail sales areas, and a host of other uses. Today we find ourselves building steel buildings for many uses and so we can call these buildings utility structures.

The first question growers ask is, "How big a headhouse do I need?" Most industry consultants and greenhouse operators offer this advice: As a general rule you need at least 10% of your total greenhouse growing area for your headhouse area. For example, if you have 100,000 ft.² (9,290 m²) of greenhouse, you need roughly 10,000 ft.² (929 m²) of headhouse.

However, while you may know your needs today, what will be your future needs? If you plan on adding space for shipping, storage, automated equipment, offices, lockers, a break area, and restrooms, then you may need more space. Developing a ten-year master plan of greenhouse expansion will give you some insight into just how much space you need now as well as a few years down the road.

It is also wise to have your headhouse builder offer a drawing detailing all space requirements for the different functions you're planning—few growers have ever had too much headhouse space.

Don't forget the importance of selecting the best location for the headhouse. What seems to be the best plan today may be the worst plan five years from now due to greenhouse and outside growing area expansions. Important issues such as parking, utility expansions, truck turnouts, water retention, and utility access may limit your options.

Frame, Walls, and More

Headhouses start with a single common denominator: the frame. The most common frame materials are wood, steel, and aluminum. In most cases wood is less expensive than metal, but metal can typically handle longer spans and heavier loads. Metal structures typically offer a broader range of pre-engineered packages in custom shapes and sizes.

Figure 1-18. The headhouse is where just about everything happens to the crop except the growing.

Growers today often use a greenhouse structure as their headhouse. By covering part of a steel headhouse roof area with a greenhouse covering such as opal polycarbonate, you can gain some of the benefits of a greenhouse for such uses as holding plants for shipping for longer periods without effecting quality. Hanging baskets and hanging basket systems can help justify the cost of this added growing space by hanging baskets overhead and shipping below.

Using greenhouse frames for your utility structure can save time and money on construction. Also, greenhouse structures often face less stringent building code requirements than steel warehouse buildings. However, there are some limitations. Most greenhouse manufacturers deal with single-story engineering. If you're considering having a second floor in your headhouse, then you might consider using a steel building manufacturer that specializes in this type of construction (although a second floor for storage can be added with freestanding frames attached to the floor instead

of affixed to the structure's frame). Many greenhouse manufacturers do not have the trade people on staff to provide the concrete, electrical, plumbing, drywall, and permit acquisitions when required. Be sure to verify that your greenhouse manufacturer can provide the level of services that you require both in design, manufacturing, and installation.

Space

One specification usually requested is wide spans with no columns in the middle of the floor plan—or at least as few as possible. Using column eliminators, better known as beams, allows you to eliminate columns as required to open up interior space. If you're seeking a wide span structure, it's not uncommon for steel buildings to be 40–100' (12–30 m) wide. With greenhouse frames, your structure is typically limited to about 63' (18 m). After that it has to be either a custom design or you'll need to have two gutter-connected buildings, such as two 42' (13 m) wide buildings, for 84' (26 m) total. However, pre-manufactured buildings are usually freestanding structures, whereas greenhouses used for headhouses can be either freestanding or gutter-connected to the greenhouse to create an overall larger facility.

Doors

Regardless of what type building you choose, you have many door, door covering, and hardware choices, such as overhead, sliding, swing, and pedestrian doors, with manual or electric openers, and even entire side- or end walls that fully open, allowing people and equipment to pass through. Be sure that the structure's sides and ends are tall enough to accommodate your door needs. Many building codes may require you to have more doors than you may have planned. Codes may also require certain hardware for special issues, such as handicap accessibility and emergency use. Make sure you verify with your building supplier that all doors and framing material, as well as installation, are included.

Covering

Your choice should be based on the building's use as well as durability and cost of materials and installation. For example, if the building is used as a retail hard goods area, you'll want a covering to block out the sun, thus reducing temperature as well as condensation and drips. In most cases you'll have several choices. If you desire a solid insulated roof covering, you may go with a batt-type reinforced insulation that's installed prior to the corrugated metal outer cover. A great option when using the corrugated outside metal roof with underside insulation is adding a light-colored corrugated metal underliner. This underliner covers the steel roof purlins and insulation, giving a finished look to your utility buildings ceiling.

Another popular but more expensive alternative is insulated steel or aluminum one-piece roof panels such as a standing seam roof panels. These panels offer a finished metal or aluminum surface inside as well as outside, and the metal underside allows for pressure cleaning. Very few screws are used on the exterior of this type of panel, which greatly reduces the risk of leaks. Unlike the corrugated sandwich panel outlined above, you will see the roof purlins from the underside of the one piece bonded panel or standing seam panels.

Side- and end wall coverings can range from insulated metal panels to non-insulated wood, masonry, metal, polycarbonate, or glass combinations. Installation costs vary accordingly. When installing a masonry facade, you often have to add a foundation wall. This can be more costly than a metal or polycarbonate sidewall, which only requires building your structure using caisson piers and burying the coverings into grade.

An important option to consider on the inside walls when using batt-type insulation is adding another layer of corrugated steel skin to prevent equipment, crates, boxes, and the like from tearing the batts. It also makes for a clean, durable finish that can be washed down as needed.

Insulation Options

Today's revised energy codes are changing the ways utility buildings are being insulated.

New federal and state laws require certain buildings to meet higher R-values, in some cases R-36 and higher. In many cases the requirements are based on the building type and use.

Electrical service

You should discuss your headhouse electrical service not only with your structure provider but also with your electrician. Again, try to consider your equipment needs now as well as ten years from now. Keep in mind that sometimes it pays to spend more at the start because you can save much more in the long run. The type of power you require now as well as in the future is key, such as single-phase versus three-phase power.

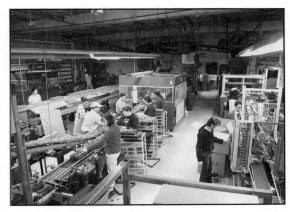

Figure 1-19. A widespan headhouse gives you maximum working area and flexibility.

Plumbing and runoff

As most headhouse buildings are very large, removing the water from the roof area via the gutters and then transferring this water to a remote area requires proper planning. The building engineers need to be involved in what will be needed to carry the water from the gutters to the specified area. For instance, the quantity of downspouts should not be overlooked. Other issues include floor drains, restrooms, boiler room runoff, boiler needs, irrigation, and fertigation water requirements.

Cooling and heating

Uncomfortable employees are unproductive employees. Cooling can range from natural to mechanical fans and coolers. Heating can be through simple unit heaters (inexpensive and quick to heat or reheat a room, but not very efficient); overhead radiant heat (a standard in steel utility buildings and quick to reheat the space if a door is opened); or radiant heat, which is hot-water running in pipes in the slab (quiet and energy efficient, but more costly up front and slow to reheat the space). Consider the efficiency of using hot-water heat in the floor combined with unit heaters overhead for supplemental heat on the colder days when the slab heat can't produce enough heat. In a three- or four-season climate zone, slab heat alone won't offer enough of your required heat. This combination offers excellent efficiency while keeping your costs down, and the unit heaters offer that fast extra heat recovery when needed.

Lighting

In most cases you'll need some type of mechanical lighting. This will be based on your needs as well as building code requirements. A great source for lighting is the use of sidelights. This can be accomplished by adding a strip of semi-clear plastic, such as opal polycarbonate, under your gutter for about 24" (61 cm) around all or part of your structure. Roof skylights are also an option. Just remember that the more semi-clear cover you add, the more solar heat you'll gain inside the structure.

Cost

The basic steel building single floor with a corrugated metal insulated roof, sides and ends may range from $9.50–15.50/ft.^{2} ($102.22–166.78/m^2) for materials and labor to install just the building, covering, and one or two doors. This typically wouldn't include the concrete or labor for concrete work, electrical, plumbing, and windows, nor the costs associated in obtaining permits. If required, fire protection (sprinklers) would be another very expensive cost to consider—from $5.00–8.00/ft.^{2} ($53.80–86.08/m^2)! Using a firewall in your design may be less expensive than a sprinkler system while still satisfying some building codes in your area. Building codes vary from town to town—be sure to check yours.

Here are a few options that affect pricing:

- insulated sandwich panels on the roof and side-, end-, and knee walls rather than using single-layer corrugated metal with batt insulation
- inside walls covered with corrugated metal under liner to protect the batt insulation
- different structure sizes as well as very tall sidewall heights
- custom doors
- side or roof skylights for natural lighting
- cooling equipment or vents
- beams to eliminate columns and provide more open floor area
- building in areas of the country that receive heavy snow or excessive winds, which will require more steel in the design
- custom painting of the frame, coverings, or flashing
- heating equipment
- a freestanding building or connecting the building to an existing greenhouse structure.

Most communities have warehouse and storage building dealers, and in many cases these dealers are general contractors. They can assist you with the overall project planning, along with the construction of your headhouse and organizing the necessary tradespeople, such as electricians, plumbers, and concrete workers. Your greenhouse manufacturer also can arrange headhouse construction and certain design services, but they typically don't offer overall project management.

2

Greenhouse Glazing

Figure 2-1. A glazing's primary purpose is to allow light into the greenhouse while allowing the grower to manipulate the environment inside the greenhouse.

Glazing: It's What Makes the Greenhouse

Gene A. Giacomelli

The greenhouse comes "alive" only after its glazing, or cover, is applied. Air temperature, humidity, carbon dioxide level, soil temperature, and light define the greenhouse and plant environment. It must be in balance with the solar radiation entering and the heat leaving through the glazing. The grower then modifies the greenhouse environment to the desired needs of the plants through the use of environmental control systems (heating, ventilation, and cooling) in response to the outdoor environment.

The glazing directly influences the amount (intensity) and the type (diffuse/direct and partial or full spectrum of the sun) of solar energy that reaches the plants inside the greenhouse. The solar energy affects plant growth through plant physiological responses, such as water movement through the plant (for transpiration) and capture of solar energy (for photosynthesis). Solar energy also affects leaf temperature, which is indirectly controlled by the plant through leaf evaporative cooling (evapotranspiration). The plants give off water vapor, which increases the moisture content of the air (humidity) in the greenhouse. This moisture in the air can be removed by ventilation, which exchanges inside air with outside air. Or it may condense on cool surfaces of the greenhouse structure, primarily the glazing.

No glazing material is perfect. Each influences the climate within the greenhouse in unique ways, and the greenhouse climate determines the final appearance and/or productivity of the crops.

Plastic versus Glass

As mentioned in chapter 1, plastics have revolutionized the greenhouse industry in many ways, including plastic pots and flats for plant production and sale, irrigation systems for water and nutrient delivery, and glazings for greenhouse covers. However, the simplified, less costly procedure (compared to glass) for enclosing the greenhouse structure with plastic film or rigid-plastic panels is the most dramatic change. Many new greenhouses, as well as all temporary structures, are covered with plastics.

Total greenhouse area for firms focusing on floriculture crops (cut flowers, potted plants, foliage, annual bedding plants, perennials, and cut greens) in the United States was 10,254 acres (4,150 ha) in 2009, according to the 2009 Census of Horticultural Specialties. This is down approximately 9.1% from the 11,281 acres (4,565 ha) recorded in the 1998 Census of Horticultural Specialties 11 years earlier for greenhouse space used for floriculture production. In 2009, about two-thirds of the space (68.3%) was single or multi-layer poly film, 17.8% was rigid plastic, and 13.9% was glass. These percentages have changed little over the last decade.

Selecting a Glazing Material

If you purchase your glazing material from a reputable manufacturer, you can be assured that the fundamental material properties of strength, consistency, durability, manufacturing quality control, and safety will be present. With those factors out of the way, your main considerations should be:

1. How much energy (light) does it let into the greenhouse, and how much energy (heat) will go out?
2. What are the purchase, installation, and maintenance costs?
3. How well can you manage the environment that's created by the glazing to produce a quality, salable product for profit?

The physical properties of the material directly influence the answers to Questions 1 and 2. Question 2 can be answered by glazing manufacturers or your greenhouse builder. Question 3 is generally more difficult to answer. However, it's related to other factors, such as the experience of the grower, the crop produced, the local outside environment, and the environmental control systems you have in the greenhouse.

To begin to answer Question 1, consider the following general choices available in glazings:

- Is the glazing made of single- or double-layer construction?
- Is the glazing made of rigid plastic or flexible, thin film?
- Is the glazing material glass or a form of plastic?
- What special-purpose additives, if any, are included?
- How do these choices in glazings influence the plant environment?

Energy Coming In

Energy from the sun is transmitted through the transparent greenhouse covering, where it can then power the photosynthetic process of converting carbon dioxide in the air and water in the plant to produce a larger green plant, which generates oxygen. The capability of the covering to transmit light in wavelengths useful to plants, of which only a portion is visible to the human eye, is extremely important. The wavelengths within the group from 400–700 nm (primarily the visible portion of solar radiation) directly influence growth and development in green plants. The importance is so great that this waveband has been defined as photosynthetically active radiation (PAR). The energy intensity within this waveband has been shown to be directly proportional to the activity of specific plant processes. However, it's generally and more simply considered proportional to overall plant growth. In other words, the more intense the PAR and the longer it is present (day length), the faster the plant growth rate . . . up to a point, of course.

Other non-visible solar radiation wavebands include the ultraviolet (UV), far-red (FR), and infrared (IR) wavebands. They, too, influence plant growth, although much more subtly, and the extent of their influence isn't completely understood or even known.

How important is a claim of 1, 2, or even 5% greater transmission for glazing A than for glazing B? Generally, it's insignificant. In practice, the slightly

Figures 2-2, 2-3. It's easy to see the difference between direct (left) and diffuse (right) light.

improved transmission of material A will be more than offset by the shading caused by the greenhouse structure and the other systems located overhead in the greenhouse. Nearly all greenhouse structures affect the light transmitted to the plant canopy to a greater degree than comparable covering materials of similar transmission (within 1–5% of each other). However, when the greenhouse structure has been designed for optimal light transmission and minimal shading, such as high-tech structures used in low-light areas such as in northern Europe, then growers can take advantage of even small improvements in light transmission.

Other factors affect transmission of PAR into the greenhouse structure. They include the location of greenhouse (especially at latitudes more than 25° from the equator, which means anywhere in the United States); orientation of the glazing surface to the sun, whether it's a freestanding or gutter-connected structure, season of the year, and number of glazing layers.

Direct versus diffuse light

Transmission of light is actually the sum of direct and diffused components. Transmitted radiation received directly from the sun, without prior reflection, is called direct radiation. It's bright and strong and reaches you (or a sensor or the plant leaf) from one direction—the sun.

Diffuse radiation results from the scattering of direct radiation within the atmosphere (by clouds and dust) or by the diffusing nature of the greenhouse cover itself. Diffuse radiation is the sun's rays reaching your eyes (or the plant leaf) from many directions. Think of a day with a clear, deep blue sky that would have primarily direct radiation. Turning away from the sun easily shades your eyes from the high-intensity light. Now think of a diffuse, but brightly lit, day, caused by high, thin clouds. Even if you turn away from the sun, the light may still bother your eyes and make you want to squint.

The greenhouse glazing transmits both direct and diffuse radiation, but the glazing may also alter the proportions of each because of its physical properties. The diffuse component will always increase while the direct component will be reduced. This is particularly true for most plastic films, but all double-layered glazings will also increase the diffuse component of the light.

Technically, the plant can't distinguish the difference between direct and diffuse light. Each type will cause photosynthesis equally if provided at the same intensity. Diffuse light is direct light that has taken an indirect path to reach the plant. Look at the sharp shadow patterns of the overhead structures created on the floor within a glass-covered greenhouse, compared

Figure 2-4. In low-light regions such as northern Europe, greenhouse manufacturers strive to reduce the amount of structure in their greenhouses to maximize light transmission.

with the blurred-edged shadows within a poly-covered greenhouse. The glass allows more direct light to reach the crop below. However, if there were no diffuse light, only the upper portions of the upper leaves would be brightly lit by the sun. It's the diffuse light reflecting within the greenhouse that provides energy to the lower tiers of plant leaves.

Double-layer glazing, whether glass or plastic, will provide more diffuse light to the plants than single-layer glazing. Two layers will also reduce the intensity at the crop more than a single layer. Plastic glazing will generally provide more diffuse light than glass because of its translucent nature.

Age

Light transmission for plastic films or panels (of equal numbers of layers) will decrease over time due to aging (yellowing) and to the accumulation of dust, dirt, and air pollutants. Transmission losses may be as much as 10% or more during the three- or four-year life of flexible plastic films. Rigid-plastic and glass glazing (which can have a lifespan of twenty years or more) require a stable, washable material (either mechanically or by natural rainfall) to help maintain maximum light transmission. Shorter lived, "disposable" plastic films resolve the cleaning requirement but need more frequent replacement than glass or rigid plastic panels.

Additives

Some films and rigid panels incorporate additives that cause them to modify very specific wavelengths of sunlight that have been demonstrated to change the plant growth response, specifically the height, of many types of flowering plants, without the need for chemical growth regulators. The amount of the red light compared with far-red light that the plant receives will increase (less red, more far-red) or decrease (more red, less far-red) the final plant height. This concept of specific color light management opens many new opportunities for manipulating plant growth with greenhouse coverings.

The structure beneath

Finally, a glazing that is lighter in weight will require supporting structures with fewer and smaller support members, thereby minimizing the shading and light transmission reduction caused by the greenhouse structure itself. Such a structure may also be less expensive to build. Other structural factors, such as the maximum spacing between glazing support bars and attachments, the size and strength of the supports, the maximum distance from the gutter to the ridge, and the type of attachments, will be affected by the choice of glazing based on its cost and light transmission.

Energy Going Out

Solar energy can be transmitted, reflected, or absorbed by the greenhouse covering. The transmitted portion of the visible (PAR) light is needed for plant growth, but only a small fraction (1–5%) is actually utilized by the plant. The unused PAR (and the remainder of the solar radiation other than PAR) is absorbed by the plant and the greenhouse internal components (i.e., soil, concrete, and benches) and the greenhouse structure. The absorbed energy warms the components, and they emit the energy as infrared (IR) heat, warming the greenhouse air. This "greenhouse heating effect" is the result of radiation transmission into a closed space and the prevention of some of the heat from leaving through the cover of that space. It's a welcome effect in the winter but not so welcome during summer's heat.

Insulating value

The insulating ability of glazings is primarily dependent on whether it's applied as a single or double layer. This is an important consideration when selecting a glazing if supplemental heating is required. If the cover is constructed of two layers (air-inflated double poly or twin-wall polycarbonate), it can insulate against heat loss better than can a single layer (single-layer poly, corrugated plastic, or glass). During the cool season, double-layer glazing will require less solar energy in the day and fossil-fuel energy at night to maintain the inside air temperature.

However, greenhouse heating costs can be further reduced if the glazing has an additive that acts as an infrared heat barrier (low transmission of infrared radiation). Glass has traditionally been an excellent barrier to infrared transmission, but the plastic film covers may not be. The IR barrier improves the "greenhouse heating effect" by trapping the IR radiation so that it can be absorbed within the greenhouse for warming the air instead of passing through the glazing to the outdoor environment.

The energy efficiency of a glazing material is more dependent upon whether the glazing is a single or double layer and whether the glazing is a continuous surface or is constructed of numerous individual panels (which would potentially have more air leaks) than whether the glazing has the IR barrier. The insulating properties of the dead air space between two-layer or twin-wall glazings will generally reduce energy loss 35–40% compared with single-layer covers, regardless of the type of material used.

Condensation

Reducing air leaks by sealing the glazing material tightly can lower heating costs. However, such a "tight" greenhouse contributes to high humidity conditions inside the greenhouse. Condensation of water vapor onto the cool surface of the covering material represents another method for heat loss from the greenhouse. The energy released from the water vapor as it changes to liquid is immediately lost to the glazing—and then to the outside. This represents an undesirable situation for the crop, as excessive moisture on the glazing will cause dripping and can damage the quality of the crop and increase the risk and spread of disease. Glazing manufacturers have incorporated condensation inhibitors that help prevent droplet formation and have somewhat reduced this problem. A sloped roof (rise to run of 1:2) will encourage moisture to flow toward the gutter and collect without dripping, compared with a roof with a shallow slope. A double-layer glazing will have a warmer interior-layer surface temperature because of the air-gap insulation between the layers, and thus less condensation. Condensation during the daylight hours will also reduce solar energy transmission.

Need More Information?

Your knowledge of the fundamentals of greenhouse glazings can be greatly enhanced with information provided by research and extension publications as well as industry design and application experiences. To obtain a greater depth of understanding, refer to the sources listed below. It's especially important to include up-to-date reports in your personal research in addition to fundamental information because of the rapidly changing materials, products, and greenhouse systems within the marketplace.

For a fundamental, research-based background on the subject of greenhouse glazings relating to light transmission and to nighttime heat losses, see "Energy Conservation for Commercial Greenhouses" NRAES-3. For general information on planning, constructing, and controlling a commercial greenhouse, see "Greenhouse Engineering" NRAES-33. Both can be obtained by writing to NRAES, Cooperative Extension, 152 Riley-Robb Hall, Ithaca, New York 14853-5701; calling (607) 255-7654; e-mailing nraes@cornell.edu; or visiting www.nraes.org.

The National Greenhouse Manufacturers Association (NGMA) is a professional trade organization for manufacturers and suppliers of greenhouses and

Table 2-1. Heat Loss from Various Glazings*	
MATERIAL	U (BTU PER HOUR PER FT.2/°F) = (1/R)
Glass	1.1
Single poly	1.1
Double poly	0.7
Double poly w/energy curtain	0.3–0.5
Twin-wall acrylic	0.6
Twin-wall polycarbonate	0.6

*Adapted from *Horticultural Engineering*, a publication of Rutgers University Bioresource Engineering and Rutgers Cooperative Extension, New Brunswick, New Jersey.

greenhouse components. NGMA has produced standards for greenhouse design that incorporate the experience and knowledge of manufacturers in the industry. Contact NGMA, 20 West Dry Creek Circle, Suite 100, Littleton, Colorado 80120; fax (303) 798-1315; or visit www.ngma.com.

References

2009 Census of Horticultural Specialties, USDA-NASS.

Polyethylene Film

Paul Jacobson

No other technology has had more of an impact on the commercial greenhouse industry than the introduction of wide-sheet, UV-stabilized polyethylene film as a greenhouse covering. Prior to the initial development of films, growers were forced to contend with the relatively high construction and installation costs, heat loss, leakage, and maintenance/replacement headaches of small glass panes. The introduction of polyethylene film after World War II as an inexpensive, lightweight greenhouse glazing had a huge impact on what had been a sleepy cottage industry.

As a result, commercial greenhouses rapidly multiplied in size and number, satisfying the increased suburban demand for bedding plants in the decades following World War II. Today, most professionals in the greenhouse coverings business would estimate that polyethylene film (commonly referred to in the business as poly film or double poly, when applied as two layers) covers 99% of world's commercial greenhouses.

Why Poly?

The reason most growers choose poly film is economics. Poly film is substantially less expensive to purchase than other glazing products, which also require more hours of labor and more accessories to install. For example, a double poly costs roughly $0.36/ft.²

Figure 2-5. Because of its relative low cost and convenience, poly is the most popular greenhouse glazing material worldwide.

Table 2-2. Greenhouse Coverings Compared*

The following comparison has been constructed in very general and broad terms. While quality, price, and performance can vary widely from manufacturer to manufacturer, the figures shown are to be considered "average" for each covering category. Consequently, cost and performance will likely increase or decrease as you add or remove features. For more detailed specifications regarding individual coverings, request technical specification sheets and installation guides from the manufacturers.

	Single-layer poly film	Double-layer poly film	Corrugated fiberglass	Corrugated poly-carbonate	Multi-wall poly-carbonate	Multi-wall acrylic	Double-strength glass	4-mm tempered glass
Average cost per ft.²	0.06–0.09	0.12–0.18	0.65–1.05	0.85–1.30	1.15–2.20	2.20–3.20	0.45–0.55	0.75–0.85
(per m²)	(0.75–1.00)	(1.25–2.00)	(7.00–11.25)	(9.25–14.00)	(12.25–23.50)	(23.50–34.50)	(5.00–6.00)	(8.00–9.00)
Cost for installation materials per ft.²	0.15–0.25	0.12–0.18	0.25–0.35	0.25–0.35	0.65–0.95	0.65–0.95	0.65–0.95	0.75–1.05
(per m²)	(1.50–2.75)	(1.25–2.00)	(2.75–3.75)	(2.75–3.75)	(7.00–10.25)	(7.00–10.25)	(7.00–10.25)	8.00–11.25)
Light transmission	91%	83%	87%	90%	76–80%	80–85%	90%	89%
Hail resistance	Poor	Poor	Fair	Very high	High	Fair	Poor	Fair
Wind resistance	Poor	Good	Good	Very good	Very good	Very good	Fair	Good
Flammability	High	High	High	Low	Low	High	Non-flammable	Non-flammable
UV Protection	Additive	Additive	Laminated	Co-extruded	Co-extruded	Co-extruded or lacquered	None or lacquered	None or lacquered
Typical warranty (years)[1]	4	4	0–20	10	10	10	None	None
Typical productive life	1–5	2–5	5–15	25–30	20–25	20–25	20–25	20–25
Clarity/appearance	Good	Poor	Poor	Excellent	Good	Very good	Excellent	Excellent

*Courtesy of SPS Corporation.

[1] Warranties can be quite misleading. Some are limited warranties that place conditions on installation that are nearly impossible to meet. Others have long warranties but are heavily prorated almost immediately after purchase. Look beyond the number of years in a warranty to find out what "value" the warranty will actually have for you, just in case some sort of manufacturer's defect should be found.

($3.75/m²) for the plastic and the installation materials, compared to roughly $1.50/ft.² ($113/m²) for glass and its installation materials.

However, every grower who grows under poly must accept this basic truth: The choice of poly film as a greenhouse covering is a tradeoff between low initial cost versus limited life. This means that at best, a poly film roof will have to be replaced after four years. Glass can last twenty to twenty-five years or more if properly maintained. A grower seeking more than four years of warranted life from his glazing must make a huge leap in the initial cost of material and labor. Moreover, this wide gap in cost also represents the risk assumed by the grower with regard to loss or failure of the roof due to hail, powerful storms, and snow and ice buildup. (See table 2-2 for a full comparison of glazing material costs and features.)

How Poly Is Made

Poly film is created when polyethylene resin pellets are melted together in a giant cylinder and are pushed, or extruded, under enormous pressure through a hollow, ring-shaped die many feet in diameter and lying horizontally at floor level. A film bubble (called a tube) emerges and is blown up to 50' (15 m) or more into a tower, which allows it to cool. As the tube reaches the top of the tower it encounters numerous rollers at different angles that compress the tube and fold it tightly until the tube is folded flat and narrow. At this point, it descends the tower. If the order calls for a sheet of poly, the tube is slit as it's rolled onto a cardboard core. This way, a 25' (8 m) tube becomes a 50' (15 m) sheet. Wide tubes are folded down until they fit a narrow core in order to reduce damage by shipping and handling. An advantage of these tubes of poly is that they allow the grower apply two layers of film to the greenhouse at one time.

Covering the Greenhouse

Double-poly installations, where two thin layers of poly film are transformed into a dependable roof, are the most common application of greenhouse poly film.

To cover a greenhouse, a work crew places a pipe through the paper core of a roll of poly film, to serve as an axle. At one end of the structure the roll is hoisted into the air and several members of the crew unroll the poly like a giant roll of paper towels, carefully dragging it down the length of the greenhouse. As this is done, the crew gently unfolds the width of the film down the top of the structure until it is completely open to its original width. Once the entire greenhouse is covered, the process is repeated for the second layer of film. (Depending on the width and length of the structure, you may also use a poly tube, which lets you apply both layers of film at the same time.)

The layers are then pulled taught and placed into fastening devices, called poly locks, that run the entire perimeter of the structure. When the entire perimeter has been secured, an airtight seal exists between the two layers of film. A squirrel-cage blower inserted into the inside layer of the film inflates the roof. This creates an energy-saving dead air space and keeps the film taut and smooth. Thus, the wind will be inclined to slide over the poly-film roof instead of "flagging" the poly and pulling it loose.

Figure 2-6. There are various types of poly lock, but all are designed to securely hold the poly in place while being easy to install and remove.

Value-Added Films

Over time, product offerings for poly film have evolved into several varieties and thicknesses and with various additives to suit the needs and budgets of most growers. The industry first segregates its films by the amount of UV inhibitors they contain. This is because the intense ultraviolet (UV) radiation of the sun is detrimental to plastic. If the poly is not produced with an additive to retard the sun's effects, the film lasts for only a period of months. UV-inhibiting additives currently extend the life of poly film up to four years. However, these inhibitors are expensive. For this reason, films have come to be categorized by the amount of warranted UV life they offer, e.g., overwintering and one-, three-, or four-year films.

Anti-condensate film

Anti-condensate film has a surfactant applied to one side that helps condensation spread out and slide off the film. Because of the temperature and humidity extremes between a greenhouse and the elements outside, the laws of physics dictate that condensation will form on the inside of greenhouse film. This condensation can be damaging in several ways:

Figure 2-7. Corrugated fiberglass is a relatively low-cost choice for a rigid-plastic glazing. Its biggest drawbacks compared to twin-wall acrylic and polycarbonate glazing is its lack of energy efficiency and its tendency to become yellow and brittle.

- Water droplets can form on the inside layer and reduce the quality of sunlight reaching the crop by reflecting and refracting it away.
- As the droplets grow larger, they will travel to the lowest point on the greenhouse covering and drip onto the crop, which may destroy the plants underneath.
- Drips can bother workers and customers in retail greenhouses.

The surfactant breaks up the surface tension of the water droplets, allowing the moisture in the air to condense on the film in a solid sheet. This "sheet" of moisture won't impede the light, and as it continues to condense, it will tend to slide down the side of the poly film away from plants and people.

This surfactant treatment isn't permanent and migrates out each time condensation forms—the more condensation, the faster it migrates. At best, most anti-condensate poly film loses this feature completely in eighteen months. Care must be taken ensure that this side of the film faces inside the greenhouse. Thus, all anti-condensate film is printed so that the treated side can be easily identified. If the untreated side is wrongly installed facing into the greenhouse, this feature will not work. Some growers check their anti-condensate with a simple coffee-cup test. When anti-condensate poly is held over a steaming hot cup of coffee, the steam will condense but appear clear. If there is no anti-condensate, the steam will create an immediate opaque fog.

IR film

Also referred to as thermal film, IR film features an additive that captures the infrared radiation emitted by the objects inside the greenhouse. As sunlight strikes an object on the earth, it's reflected in the form of radiation. Thus, your hand will feel warm in the sun even if the air temperature is cold. IR film traps the radiation that's reflected off the plants and objects in the greenhouse during the day, holding it in the greenhouse. As outside temperatures cool at night, the heat load of the greenhouse is dramatically reduced and much less energy is needed for heating. Heat savings vary widely by climate but have been reported up to 25%.

Colored film

Pigments are applied to the poly film in an effort to manipulate the quality of the light reaching plants underneath. Nearly every color of film has been tested, with varying degrees of success. Even when a film has shown some positive effects on plant growth or flowering, the high cost and large minimum requirements to produce a special film (10–20 tons) make it costly to develop and market a new, unproven product. White has been the most commercially successful of the colors tried. White reflects a major portion of the sun's energy, maintaining a cooler environment inside the greenhouse. The trade-off is that plants needing full sun tend to go dormant under white film, which is a benefit for overwintering and retail applications. Other colors have failed either because they did not produce the desired effects on the crop, they didn't stand up to UV degradation, or their manufacturing constraints did not fit the market's ability to use the product.

Nursery film

This term is applied to a broad range of low-cost films used primarily to overwinter nursery crops or protect crops from winter frost in warm climates, such as Florida. They have little or no UV resistance because they don't need it. After four to six months of use, they will have served their purpose and are disposed of. Nursery film is almost exclusively used in single-layer applications where the risk of a roof failure is relatively low.

The Future of Film

Polyethylene film will continue to dominate the market for greenhouse coverings due to its convenience and low cost. Growers will continue to look for improvements in film, but generally speaking, only those that offer a direct, immediate economic benefit to growers will be commercially successful. Recent trends indicate that these improvements will offer increased strength with decreased thickness as well as increases in UV resistance and longevity. Colored film trials will continue, but will probably be limited to market niches that can accept the large, single-production runs necessary to produce them.

Rigid-Plastic Glazing

Tami Churchill

For years, glass was a grower's only choice for greenhouse glazing. Then along came plastics—both flexible and rigid. The first commercially used rigid-plastic greenhouse covering was fiberglass, which was for many years the only alternative to glass. However, growers today have three choices in rigid-plastic coverings: fiberglass, acrylic, and polycarbonate. They also have three choices in the configuration of the sheet: flat, corrugated, and multiwall.

Fiberglass

Fiberglass panels had been the grower's choice for many years in both residential and commercial greenhouse coverings. It's a popular choice for home-built structures since it is available at large DIY stores, is relatively inexpensive, and can be fastened down with rubber-gasket aluminum nails. When fiberglass is new it is fairly strong and not brittle. The glass fiber content creates a prismatic diffusion of light, helping spread light through the entire growing area. The diffused light helps eliminate the glare and hot spots found with regular glass panels.

Fiberglass is available in flat and corrugated configurations. Corrugated panels are commonly used for greenhouse roofs, as its corrugated shape lends strength and rigidity to the panels. Flat panels are usually used for sidewalls, windows, and vents. Most fiberglass panels are manufactured from a general-purpose polyester resin embedded with chopped strand fiberglass matte. Chemicals can be added to make the panels fire retardant, and the sheets can be modified with acrylic for additional clarity. Exposure to UV rays will make fiberglass yellow and brittle over time, so Tedlar film can be laminated to the panel surface to enhance weather performance. Fiberglass panels offer a wide range of light transmission, ranging from 87% down to 55%, depending on the color of the sheet. The most common colors are clear, white, and green.

Commonly identified by weight, fiberglass panels range from 4–12 oz. (113–340 g). The weight corresponds to the thickness of the panel, with the most commonly used panels in the greenhouse industry being 4 oz. (113 g) and 5 oz. (142 g).

You can expect to get eight to ten years of life from your fiberglass if you clean the panels and periodically apply a refinishing coat. In general, fiberglass manufacturers do not offer a warranty against yellowing or offer any condensation control feature that is commonly available on other rigid coverings. Of the three rigid plastics, fiberglass is the least expensive material, has the shortest life span, and has an SPI classification of 7, which as of mid-2010 is not being collected as material for recycling.

Acrylic

The first solid acrylic sheets were produced in 1936 and played a large role in World War II as bullet-resistant glazing for warplanes. Long-term clarity is one of acrylic's most well known characteristics, something no other plastics glazing could match until the "high performance polycarbonate" arrived in the U.S. from Europe in 2008. Acrylic sheets are offered in a double-skinned configuration in both 8 mm (0.3") and 16 mm (0.6") thicknesses. The airspace between the walls acts as an insulation barrier. Acrylic offers high clarity and an excellent light transmission of up to 86%. It's relatively light, weighing less than half as much as glass but twice as much as polycarbonate. High impact acrylic is the most uncompromising and advanced line of acrylic sheets in the market place today. Regular acrylic is seven

Figure 2-8. Like acrylic, polycarbonate is more expensive than standard glass, but offers two hundred times greater impact resistance.

times stronger than ordinary glass, but polycarbonate is ten times stronger than acrylic.

With its double skin, also referred to as twin wall structure, acrylic offers excellent thermal insulation values because of the thicker wall; whereas glass and fiberglass sheets can't match that value since they are a single layer. Of the rigid plastics designed for the greenhouse industry, acrylic is the most expensive, but it offers consistently high light transmission and clarity over the long term. The ribbed twin wall structure offers some diffusion properties, which helps cut down on hot spots in the greenhouse. Manufacturers of acrylic sheet for the greenhouse industry offer the condensation control feature. The product life of acrylic is estimated to be thirty years if no breakage or fires occur. As of 2010, acrylic is recycled for making consumer goods. Acrylic sheeting materials come with a fire precaution notice that the sheets are made of molding compounds and are classified as a "combustible thermoplastic." In other words, the fire performance of acrylic is very poor compared to fire-retardant fiberglass and polycarbonate.

Polycarbonate

Polycarbonate was developed in 1953 and initially was used for electronics and electrical applications. The extruded polycarbonate sheeting for the greenhouse industry is available in both multiwall and corrugated configurations. The beneficial characteristics of polycarbonate make it the material of choice for many greenhouse and building projects. Polycarbonate is virtually unbreakable and offers high insulation values. In addition, it provides high light transmission of up to 90%—the same as glass. It's incredibly strong, with two hundred times greater impact resistance than glass, twenty times greater impact resistance than fiberglass, and ten times stronger than acrylic, yet its weight is just one-eighth of glass. Unlike glass and acrylic, polycarbonate is highly flexible and can be cold formed into many bending radii.

High performance "coated" polycarbonate will not yellow or become brittle, but regular "co-extruded" polycarbonate tends to degrade over time. Sheets intended for use on open-roof greenhouses are available

Figure 2-9. Greenhouses aren't commonly referred to as "glasshouses" for no reason; glass has long been the glazing material of choice.

with UV protection on both sides of the panel. This protection can either be co-extruded into the sheet or coated onto the sheet. Both multiwall and corrugated panels are available in a smooth finish or with a light diffusing feature. Recently, manufactures have designed a polycarbonate product both in corrugated and 8 mm multiwall that offers up to 85% light transmission while giving 100% light diffusion. This latest innovation in light scattering polycarbonate greenhouse glazing offers higher crop yields—about 7.8% over the traditional clear sheets. Most polycarbonate manufacturers offer condensation control and a ten-year warranty against yellowing and damage caused by hail. High performance polycarbonate offers the best warranty in the industry. The warranty should offer no more than 2% light transmission loss over ten years and less than a two delta change in the original yellowing index (YI).

In general, polycarbonate is more expensive than fiberglass but less expensive than acrylic. With proper care, high performance polycarbonate can be expected to last about twenty to twenty five years.

Pros and Cons

Compared with acrylic and polycarbonate, fiberglass is the least expensive but is more difficult to fabricate

on the job site and has the shortest life span. Double-skinned acrylic sheets are also difficult to bend and fabricate in the field compared to polycarbonate, which is the most user- and environmentally friendly glazing of the three rigid-plastics.

For high transparency, acrylic and polycarbonate are excellent throughout their product life; however, acrylic and high performance polycarbonate hold up better against UV radiation exposure compared to fiberglass. Fiberglass becomes cloudy and loses light transmission from UV exposure in a relatively short period of time.

Virtually unbreakable, polycarbonate is stronger than acrylic and fiberglass. Polycarbonate offers the best fire performance as it is considered a "self extin-guishing" thermoplastic, whereas acrylic is considered a "combustible thermoplastic" and burns very much like hardwood. Both acrylic and fiberglass have a high burn rates, whereas polycarbonate will not support the flame so it is safer for employees and will lower your insurance premiums substantially.

Growers are starting to understand the importance of diffused light. Polycarbonate is now available with 100% light-diffusing properties while still maintaining 79% light transmission in the 8 mm twin-wall sheets. Neither acrylic nor fiberglass can compare to the performance of light-diffusing polycarbonate. A published study about growing under diffused light vs. clear light, showed increased production of 7.8% under diffused light.

Another important concern now and for many years to come is "green products." Polycarbonate and acrylic are considered a "green product," as they can be recycled and offer numerous LEED credits based on the specific application. Fiberglas may offer one to two LEED credits and is currently not recyclable.

Cost-wise, for the greenhouse covering only (no installation materials included), expect to pay roughly $0.65–1.05/ft.² ($7.00–11.25/m²) for fiberglass, $1.50–2.80/ft.² ($16.14–30.13/m²) for high performance polycarbonate, and $3.20–4.50/ft.² ($34.43–$48.42/m²) for acrylic. (See table 2-2 for a full comparison of glazing material costs and features.)

Overall, polycarbonate is the greenhouse covering with the most to offer the grower in regards to increased crop yields under diffused lighting, no yellowing due to the high performance UV protection, excellent insulation values, high fire performance rating, and durability.

Glass Glazing

Arch Vermeer

Glass greenhouses have a long history. In the eighteenth and nineteenth centuries, almost every castle and monastery had a small, freestanding greenhouse or conservatory for overwintering plants that couldn't survive the cold. Glass was used to cover the greenhouses because no other transparent materials were available.

In the twentieth century, the greenhouse was repurposed to a structure in which the growers actively controlled the climate to produce flowers, plants, and vegetables for commercial purposes. Low-cost, high-quality plastics have become an alternative to glass over the past thirty years. However, the profitability of a greenhouse isn't determined just by capital costs, but also by production output and crop quality.

Like the other glazing materials, glass has its advantages and disadvantages. Advantages include:

- extremely long life,
- better humidity control in moderate climates,
- high solar gain during daytime hours, and
- high light transmission.

Disadvantages include:

- possibility of breaking during extreme weather conditions,
- low humidity problems during the winter (in inland climates),
- potential crop damage due to high light intensity during the summer,
- higher initial cost,
- higher energy loss, and
- requiring energy curtains for cold-weather energy management.

Glass can be used on any style of greenhouse, but is commonly found on Venlo and widespan houses, which were developed with glass glazing in mind. Even curved-roof greenhouses can be glazed with glass because large sheets of glass will actually bend to fit the curve. (Glass measurements are often given in metric units, as the greenhouse designs—especially for Venlo houses—originated in Holland, where glass is the most common glazing material.)

Venlo houses range from 21–42' (6.4–12.8 m) wide per bay, with glass panes usually about 3' (0.9 m) wide and 6' (1.8 m) long. The glass is installed using aluminum H-bars to hold it in place. The roof structure usually is all aluminum.

Figure 2-10. Here is a typical Venlo-style house glazed with glass.

Widespan houses have bay widths ranging from 26' (7.9 m) to more than 65' (19.8 m). Glass size is generally about the same as Venlo houses. Glass is seated on aluminum glazing bars that have rubber caps that hold the glass in place. The roof structure generally is constructed of steel trusses with aluminum glazing bars.

Table 2-3. Heating Costs without and with Energy Curtain	
GLASS GREENHOUSE WITHOUT ENERGY CURTAIN:	**GLASS GREENHOUSE WITH ENERGY CURTAIN:**
Total heating cost/year: $94,266.15	Total heating cost/year: $77,769.57
Heating cost per ft.^{2}/year: $1.59 ($17/m^2/year)	Heating cost per ft.^{2}/year: $1.31 ($14/m^2/year)
PLASTIC GREENHOUSE WITHOUT ENERGY CURTAIN:	**PLASTIC GREENHOUSE WITH ENERGY CURTAIN:**
Total heating cost/year: $73,286.83	Total heating cost/year: $60.461.64
Heating cost per ft.^{2}/year: $1.24 ($13/m^2/year)	Heating cost per ft.^{2}/year: $1.02 ($11/m^2/year)

Figure 2-11. A curved-glass greenhouse takes advantage of glass's natural flexibility and strength.

Curved-glass houses have bay widths of 18–32' (5.5–9.75 m). Glass size is generally 6' (1.8 m) wide by 10' (3 m) long, depending on bay width. The glass is seated in glazing bars with caps and rubber seals. Generally, the roof structure is made of steel and aluminum.

Construction and Operation Costs

A glass-covered greenhouse is more expensive than a poly-covered greenhouse because glass as a glazing product costs more than polyethylene and the support and fastening systems required for glass are more costly. The overall cost of building a glass structure will also be substantially higher due to the increased material content of the structure, the requirement of greater precision in the assembly, and the extra time to complete. For example, a Venlo greenhouse is about twice as expensive as a poly-covered greenhouse; a curved glass greenhouse is about two-and-a-half times more expensive; and a widespan greenhouse is about two-and-a-half to three times more expensive. (See table 2-2 for a full comparison of glazing material costs and features.) Under some circumstances, special glass—such as tempered or safety glass—is required by code. This is especially common for retail businesses where the public has access to the greenhouse. This type of glass further increases the cost of a glass greenhouse.

The operating costs of a glass greenhouse are also higher than for double-poly or twin-wall polycarbonate greenhouses. Because glass offers little insulating value, it costs more to heat a glass greenhouse. However, there are a number of factors that can level out the differences in operating costs, such as the benefits of increased light in the winter and the use of heat-retaining energy curtains.

Here is an annual heating cost comparison of four 18,000 ft.^{2} (5,500 m^2) greenhouses two glazed with glass and two glazed with plastic. Similar glazing and energy curtains are also compared with a glass and a plastic house. The climate ranges from an average low of 21°F (6°C) in January and February to an average high of 70°F (21°C) in July.

As you can see, plastic is 22% more efficient in this example, but adding the energy curtain to each house cuts the heating costs an additional 20%.

The Glass Growing Environment

The environment of a glass greenhouse is substantially different than that of a double-poly or rigid-plastic greenhouse. In general, you can expect the glass house environment to be less humid and brighter, particularly during the winter heating season. During the warmer months with higher light levels and high solar gain, you'll find that cooling a glass greenhouse is more difficult, and more attention should be given to venting and cooling systems. Also, during the months of the year when there is abundant light, most crops respond well to the diffused-light conditions of a poly-clad greenhouse. If glass is to be considered, a shading system for control of the summer light levels is a must.

How Do You Decide?

There's no simple answer to the question of which is better—plastic or glass. Following are some things for you to consider when you're making your decision.

- What do you plan to grow? This should always be your first question when considering the type of glazing you should use. Many crops do better in a poly greenhouse environment, regardless of the growing area or time of year. Others require maximum light that only a glass greenhouse offers, especially if you're in a low-light region.
- Where do you plan to build? In many cold areas it can be very bright with few overcast days, so a light-diffusing but energy-efficient glazing, such as rigid-plastic sheets, might be desirable. In areas with more moderate temperatures, you may find more overcast and dark days, and you might want to choose glass for its light-transmission qualities.
- How much do you want to spend? Regardless of any other consideration, money may be the factor that determines what you're able to do. Most growers would agree that if money were no object, a glass greenhouse is likely to be your best choice since you can always add subsystems to get the desired environment.
- What are you most comfortable with? A grower with all her experience in a glass house environment may find the adjustment to a poly environment too difficult to make.
- What's your style? If you like to pay attention to the smallest details, the glass house environment might be the one for you because control of that environment requires more attention and many small adjustments. The poly house environment can be more forgiving, with fewer factors impacting the environmental conditions at any given time.

A new spin on the old question is the recent availability of open-roof greenhouses with roofs that open completely to take advantage of outdoor conditions. These greenhouses are available with the same glaz-ing options of traditional greenhouses. But because of their relatively high construction costs, growers generally choose glass for these all-purpose structures.

Greenhouse Glazing 101*

Your greenhouse covering—or glazing—is the one thing that stands between your plants and the dangers of your climate, as well as the essential light needed to produce a perfect crop. Whether you're just setting out to pick the right glazing for your facility or if you're looking at replacing or maintaining what you already own—here are some tips from the experts on how to select the right material—be it glass, poly film, or a rigid plastic glazing—and how to keep it clean in the years to come.

Selecting a Glazing Material

If you purchase your glazing material from a reputable manufacturer, you can be assured that the fundamental material properties of strength, consistency, durability, manufacturing quality control, and safety will be present. With those factors out of the way, your main considerations should be:

How much energy (light) does the glazing let into the greenhouse, and how much energy (heat) will go out?

What are the purchase, installation and maintenance costs?

How well can you manage the environment that's created by the glazing to produce a quality, saleable product for profit?

The physical properties of the material directly influence the answers to the first two questions. Question 2 can be answered by glazing manufacturers or your greenhouse builder. Question 3 is generally more difficult to answer. However, it's related to other factors, such as the experience of the grower, the crop produced, the local outside environment, and the environmental control systems you have in the greenhouse.

To begin to answer question 1, consider the following general choices available in glazings:

- Is the glazing made of single- or double-layer construction?
- Is the glazing made of rigid plastic or flexible, thin film?
- Is the glazing material glass or a form of plastic?
- What special-purpose additives, if any, are included?
- How do these choices in glazings influence the plant environment?

---

* Published in *GrowerTalks* magazine, June 2009. Information provided by the National Greenhouse Manufacturers Association.

Tricks to Keeping Plastic Glazing Clean

Cleaning glass glazing is straightforward. But cleaning your polyethylene or polycarbonate glazing is another challenge.

National Greenhouse Manufacturers Association (NGMA) member Nick Calabro of Klerks Hyplast Inc. notes that there are many factors that can influence the process of keeping your glazing clean, from the type of additives you may be using to your location.

Greenhouse polyethylene film isn't inherently smooth and allows contaminants to adhere to outside surfaces. Manufacturing techniques incorporate anti-dust additives into polyethylene to create smoother surfaces, which reduce the occurrence of dirt accumulation. The addition of anti-dust additives also leads to higher light transmission and a smooth outside layer that facilitates cleaning. Nevertheless, airborne particulates such as road dirt, pesticides, carbon-based fuel emissions, soilless media particles, and algae can eventually contribute to film surface dirt buildup. Follow the tips below to prevent dirt buildup.

Polycarbonate sheets are also vulnerable to road dirt, pesticides, carbon-based fuel emissions, soilless media particles, and algae. To minimize scratching and clean greenhouse glazing, mild soap or detergent and lukewarm water may be used with a clean sponge or soft cloth. Glazing should always be rinsed well with clean water. Abrasive tools, alkaline cleaners, benzene, gasoline, acetone, or carbon tetrachloride should *never* be used to clean glazing. Cleaners that are known to be compatible with polycarbonate include: Formula 409 (Clorox Co.); Top Job (Proctor & Gamble); VM & P grade Naphtha Joy (Proctor & Gamble); Windex with Ammonia D (Drackett Products); and Palmolive Liquid (Colgate Palmolive).

Above all, the NGMA recommends that you contact your supplier directly and follow their directions regarding cleaning instructions. To learn more about the members of NGMA and to find a local supplier near you, visit www.ngma.com.

Three Ways to Reduce Dirt Buildup

Here are a few ways you can reduce and eliminate greenhouse film dirt buildup on polyethylene.

1. Use an outside air source for double-layer air inflation installations

Inflation units having an outside air source draw cooler and lower-moisture air that normally has lower levels of airborne contaminants and pesticides. Outside air intake units used in combination with mesh filters can reduce the intake of outside road dirt and insects. Road paving, grass buffer zones and wind breaks also can reduce airborne contaminates from entering the outside air flow.

2. Clear greenhouse film surfaces

You can physically clean exposed outside and inside film surfaces with non-reactive cleaning mixtures and non-abrasive soft brushes. Quaternary ammonium chloride salts (Green-Shield, Physan 20, and Triathlon) are commonly used by growers and are quite stable. They work well when used according to label instructions. Sodium carbonate peroxyhydrate (GreenClean Granular Algaecide, TerraCyte) algaecides are granular and activated with water.

3. Avoid pesticide contact

Pesticides containing sulfur and chlorine have a negative influence on the lifetime of a film. Avoided direct pesticide contact with greenhouse film surfaces, keeping in mind that many pesticides will accelerate aging of the film when used in high concentrations.

From the Top Down— Recovering Poly Greenhouses*

Don Grey

Many growers choose polyethylene greenhouse film to cover everything from hoop houses for overwintering to heated and cooled freestanding and gutter-connected houses. Properly covered houses will protect plants through all kinds of conditions. But sooner or later they need to be recovered—or "reskinned"—with new film. Growers and suppliers share their tips and techniques for this routine but critical task. After all, there's more than one way to skin a greenhouse.

Poly Coverings

Today's poly films are better than ever, but they don't last as long as glass or rigid sheeting. So, poly needs to be changed on a regular schedule depending on its

---

* Published in *GrowerTalks* magazine, March 1998.

thickness and rating, and where and how it's being used. Poly typically comes in one- to three-year ratings (ratings reflect durability against weather and UV degradation). It comes in white, clear, and colored and single sheets or two sheets melded into a tube as well as different thicknesses.

Manufacturers fold the poly in several styles—center, gusseted, or double-gusseted, for example—so make sure you buy it folded to your specifications. How it's folded determines how you put it on your house.

A single layer of one-year poly may be suitable for mild climates, whereas a three-year film installed in a double layer typically works well for greenhouses in more demanding weather conditions. The air inflation between the two layers provides excellent insulation, strength, and durability.

"Plastic requires more maintenance than glass, but it still results in a tremendous heat savings compared to glass," says Jim Gapinski of Heartland Growers in Westfield, Indiana. Heartland grows potted and bedding plants in nearly three hundred greenhouse bays. "Make sure you buy your poly from a reputable dealer," Jim recommends. "Have your best people put it on. It's there for three years, so make sure it's done right, because you want that poly to last."

Inspection First

To help your new poly last, first look for problems with the old roof. Before you reskin your houses, inspect the existing poly for wear points, especially premature wearing. This could indicate problems with loose or defective poly locks, which can cause poly to rub against roof supports and shorten its life. Look for areas that are torn or punctured and have been repaired with poly repair tape. Also look for sharp metal shards, nails, or wood slivers, and file or sand them smooth. Remove old lath boards and nails.

Off with the Old

After inspecting the existing poly cover, it's off with the old and on with the new. It's tempting just to unfasten the old poly and let it drop to the ground, but careful removal can help keep the film clean for recycling.

Tanasacres Nursery Inc., Hillsboro, Oregon, a potted and bedding plant grower, folds the plastic in half or thirds, starting from the endwalls. For longer houses (most are 28 x 100' [9 x 30 m]), workers cut the poly into two or three sections for easier folding. At least 75–80% of its houses are covered in one-year poly, so they're usually uncovered in June, when bedding plants don't need supplemental heat, and reskinned in September in time for poinsettia production. The film is recycled, so cleanliness and neatness are important.

Keys to removing poly are calm, dry days. You don't want poly flapping or blowing around as it's coming off. Likewise, it's very difficult to pull wet poly, so wait until rain and dew are gone.

Here's an interesting twist. While most growers remove old poly first and then reskin with new, one Northwest grower simply lays new poly atop the old and then pulls the old layer down through the greenhouse. Because the old poly film is still durable and stretched taut, workers can walk right over it, if necessary, and pull the new poly into proper position. The old layer is then unclipped from the poly locks, folded, and fed through the bows into the empty house.

On with the New

The first rule in covering greenhouses is the most obvious and practical: calm, still days are essential. Even the slightest breeze can cause problems. You don't want the film flapping around or blowing away. Ron Schmidt, a production manager at Woodburn Nursery & Azaleas Inc., Woodburn, Oregon, relies on a commercial agricultural weather forecast to pinpoint still days. "Even with a mild breeze, you can't do much," he says. "The biggest obstacle is the wind." When conditions are favorable, work crews reskin as many houses as possible.

Getting the poly up on top or over the house is probably the next biggest challenge. For freestanding houses, it's common to pull the poly from one side of the house to the other, but this isn't recommended. It's best to keep the poly off the ground to keep it clean and avoid snagging or tearing the film. Instead, hoist the poly to roof level, set it on the ridge, and unfold the sides. Tanasacres Nursery, for example, has a device it uses for its freestanding houses to lift the poly to roof level. It has metal poles on each side that fasten to a tractor's scoop to hold a poly roll. Once hoisted, the poly is unrolled over the top, and then down the side- and endwalls. A crew of four will cover as many houses as possible, loosely fasten the plastic, and then go back to finish clipping the houses more securely. Endwalls are done first, followed by the sidewalls. The crew can cover a house in about twenty minutes.

Gutter-connected houses are more challenging. At Heartland Growers, Jim uses a forklift and a pallet to lift a poly roll to roof height. A crew of six (two to unroll the poly and four to pull it down the gutters and clip it in place) can cover a bay in about twenty minutes. Heartland uses a three-year poly tube and typically reskins its houses in October.

Ron says Woodburn Nursery built a jig that holds a poly roll (locked so it doesn't slip), which fastens to a 4 × 8' (1.2 × 2.4 m) safety cage. A forklift hoists the cage, jig, and poly to just above roof level. A worker inside the cage feeds the poly off the roll. Four workers on each side of the house's gutters unroll the film and set it in place. The bottom layer is clipped at the corners and center; the top layer is installed next. Then everything is fastened securely. "The bottom layer is pulled tight, and the top is left a little looser," Ron says. "When it's inflated we want a 6" [15 cm] balloon effect."

With a crew of ten, it takes about twenty minutes to skin a house. The nursery typically reskins at least eighty houses each September, usually on a three-year cycle.

Figure 2-12. When pulling poly, be sure to work on a dry, calm day. Cover the entire bay, installing just enough poly lock to prevent the roof from pulling off. Once both layers are up, you can lock it down tightly.

Latching It Down

It's critical to pull the poly to its desired tension and hold it in place. Poly should be pulled just tight enough to eliminate wrinkles and keep water from forming puddles, but not so tight that it stretches. If the poly is stretched too tight during warm weather, it can't contract in the cold and may tear.

Once the new poly is in place, it has to stay there. That's where a good lock is important. On steel greenhouses, most growers use commercial poly locks to secure the film. You'll find at least two basic locks: clips, or springs, and wire inserts. They cost about the

same, are quite secure, and can accommodate several poly layers. Clip-type locks are made from aluminum and are fairly durable, so they can be used year after year. Some locks use a plastic insert to hold the poly.

The clip or spring has a base and top section. It comes in styles for flat and arched roofs. Simply insert the poly film into the base and attach the top. Today's locks won't cut the poly, and they hold it intact, even in strong winds. "For larger gutter-connect greenhouses, I'd use a clip," says Gary Baze, director of Golden Pacific Structures, Redlands, California. "I have more confidence in it. I know from experience that when a good-quality clip goes into a good-quality base, it's there to stay."

Wire locks also perform well. An extruded aluminum frame houses one or two wires that are used to secure the film inside the extrusions. Two wires allow you to anchor a double-poly roof one sheet at a time, a handy benefit. They also work great on flat, straight roofs but don't appear to be as effective on sloped or arched roofs, one supplier notes.

Locks do have a limited life, so inspect them carefully when the house is reskinned. Sometimes a clip just needs a new rubber gasket.

Keep in mind that locks can and do malfunction. One grower sends workers out to walk the gutters in windy weather and inspect the locks just to make sure they will hold. "You'll know in winter if the clips pop out of the house and it deflates," he says.

Some growers use wood lath strips on their greenhouses or hoop houses to secure poly. Lath doesn't work as well as poly locks. Although cheaper up front, in the end the strips are more time consuming to attach. If you do use lath, make sure you fold the poly to the outside to prevent water penetration, which over the course of a season can rot the lath. Also, use form or two-headed nails, which are easier to remove.

Inflation

Double-poly houses need proper inflation to achieve full insulation and strength. Air space of 6–8" (15–20 cm) between layers is a suggested optimum. A space of 2–3" (5–8 cm) may not be enough in many areas, but 2' (61 cm) is excessive. Uniformity between layers from one end of the house to the next is important.

Guard against overinflation. Again, poly stretched too taut during summer can't contract in the cold and is more likely to condensate during winter. Use a manometer, an inexpensive tool that measures air pressure—to gauge the amount of air pressure between the two poly layers. Insert the manometer's rubber tip between the two layers so that it's pressurized and look for a reading between 0.2" (0.5 cm) and 0.4" (1 cm) on the scale. Check with poly manufacturers for their specifications.

Use blowers to keep the insulating air level between the poly layers inflated and constant. Blowers (often called squirrel-cage fans) are small and relatively inexpensive. It's best to use air pumped in from the outside, because air drawn from inside the greenhouse is moist, heated, and often contains chemicals, which can cause condensation, channel heat from the inside, and degrade the poly. Thus, a blower with an intake and exhaust manifold is necessary. Use fans big enough to inflate the amount of covered square feet (meters); a variable-speed motor or an adjustable baffle over the intake will let you vary the blower's output.

Before installing new poly, check the blower motors to verify that they work and are adjusted properly. To be safe, check them monthly. Because they are on continuous duty, you may want to replace motors when you change the poly. Then, after you install the poly, make sure the blower fan is hooked up, cut a hole in the bottom poly layer, and attach it to the fan's brackets. You'll want a tight seal around the fan's base to prevent pressurized air from escaping.

Maximizing Poly Life

Some growers have been known to paint or coat the greenhouse's tubing to prevent poly abrasion, says Gary Baze. Although he doesn't know growers who paint the tops of arches, it's true that poly degrades much quicker where it touches the metal, particularly in areas with high sunlight levels, he says.

Instead of painting the tubes, Woodburn Nursery installs a house's structural purlins on top of the tubes rather than underneath. The poly sits atop the purlins instead of directly on the tubing and lessens abrasion. It's this attention to detail that leaves nothing to chance for such the routine, but critical, task of covering and protecting your crops.

3

Curtain Systems

Figure 3-1. Because it pays for itself so quickly, an energy curtain is almost standard equipment in new greenhouse construction.

Curtains? In a Greenhouse?

Chris Beytes

Energy efficiency is an indispensable part of running a profitable greenhouse business. The days when heating costs could more than be made up by the profit from your crops are long gone. Today, growers need to account for every penny they spend, and heating fuel is a major expense that can make or break a business.

Growers first experienced that during the energy crises of 1973 and 1979, when fuel shortages caused energy prices to rise significantly. This led to the development of the first energy conservation curtain systems. They felt it again during the winter of 2000–2001, when a natural gas supply shortage, combined with a cold winter and increased demand for gas from utility companies, caused natural gas prices to soar. Some growers saw their monthly fuel bill increase five- to tenfold. It was so bad that some businesses, most notably in California, had to close their doors—they couldn't absorb the tremendous expense of heating their greenhouses. Energy curtains helped keep the problem from being even worse than it was.

Simply put, an energy curtain is a fabric or plastic barrier used to help hold warm air inside the green- house while reducing the volume of air that needs to be heated. Experts say that an energy curtain can cut energy costs between 30% and 60%. During the natu- ral gas crisis, one small Midwest grower we know saw his typical monthly fuel bill go from about $11,000 to more than $70,000. Much of his facility, being quite old, wasn't equipped with energy curtains. With them, he could have potentially reduced his fuel bill to $40,000 or $50,000—still significant, to be sure—but enough of a savings to possibly pay for a curtain system.

In addition to retaining heat, energy curtains are also used for shade during sunny periods, helping keep the crop and greenhouse cool. In this way, they can save energy and cut utility costs during the summer. Another type of curtains, blackout curtains, are used for controlling photoperiod (see the section on page 52).

As with all structures and equipment, the cost of a curtain system depends greatly on its design, configura- tion, and size. For argument's sake, you can figure that a basic curtain system for a 1 acre (0.4 ha) greenhouse will cost $1.00–1.25/ft.^{2} ($10.75–13.50/m^2) for standard material, and $1.50–1.75/ft.^{2} ($16.00–18.75/m^2) for fire-resistant material. This encompasses only materials; figure roughly the same amount for installation labor. A few rules of thumb: narrower bays or shorter distances between trusses mean a higher per-square-foot price, as will a greenhouse that's smaller than an acre.

However, even at $2.00–$2.50/ft.^{2} ($21.50–27.00/ m^2) installed, an energy curtain is an investment that will pay for itself in just a few seasons. That's why you find an energy curtain in almost every new greenhouse you visit.

In the following sections, you'll learn the details about the different styles of curtain systems, and their uses and benefits.

Types of Curtain Systems*

Adapted from the National Greenhouse Manufacturers Association Curtain Standards

Edited by Kurt Parbst

Greenhouse curtain systems are also called shade curtains, screens, energy curtains, and even blankets. Regardless of what they're called, curtain systems consist of movable panels of fabric, plastic, or metallic film used to cover and uncover the space enclosed in a greenhouse. Curtains may cover an area as small as a single bench or more than an acre. Small systems are often moved by hand; large systems are motor driven.

Internal curtain systems mount to the green- house structure below the rigid or film covering of the house. They're used for heat retention, shade (and the cooling effect of shade), and day length or "photoperiod" control.

Along with curtain systems inside the greenhouse, advancements in drive system and shadecloth tech- nology have made moveable exterior curtain systems practical. Exterior systems are used in two ways. In some cases, the curtain replaces the greenhouse cover- ing (basically creating a retractable-roof greenhouse, as described in chapter 1). In others, the system is installed above a standard greenhouse structure. Typi- cal applications of the first type of system are to pro- vide a hardening-off area or to add seasonal produc- tion space in jurisdictions where zoning restrictions make it difficult to build a traditional structure. The second type of outdoor system provides shade for light intensity control and blocks the solar radiation before it enters the greenhouse, giving an improved cooling effect. These external shade systems are usually located in hot climates, such as Florida.

The History of Curtains

Early research conducted in England indicates that there was interest in finding ways to insulate greenhouses as early as the mid-1950s. The result of installing a fixed polyethylene sheet in a glasshouse was a 40% reduction in heating requirements, with an accompanying 14% reduction in light transmission. But because greenhouse

---

* This document was prepared by NGMA members and associates to familiarize growers with curtain system technology. It does not publish standards nor does it endorse any company or any brand or type of curtain system.

Figure 3-2. An energy curtain offers shade in the summer and heat retention in the winter.

heating fuels were relatively inexpensive, researchers and manufacturers had little incentive to pursue the technology. That is, until the energy crisis in the early 1970s.

At the beginning of 1973, oil sold for $2.50 a barrel. By the end of 1974, OPEC actions had driven the price to $11.25, and energy costs of all kinds followed the sharp rise in oil prices. Heating costs for greenhouses in cold climates reached nearly $1.00/ft.^{2} ($10.76/m^2) per month. The world had changed, and growers had a dramatic incentive to search for ways to cut energy costs. One approach they tried was internal curtain systems for heat retention.

The relentless rise in energy prices continued through 1980, when oil prices peaked at $37.00 per barrel. The acceptance of curtain systems for heat retention in greenhouses paralleled this trend. As the number of installed curtain systems increased, growers identified other benefits of these systems. It became apparent that they had value for daytime shade and cooling, and even damping the noise of fans and heaters. In markets where shortages caused public utilities to put growers on natural gas allotments and restrictions, the energy savings provided by curtains was critical—they sometimes allowed a business to expand because the energy savings made it possible to build additional greenhouse space without needing more gas.

By 1998, just over 34% of growers polled reported having curtain systems. As of 2011, virtually all new greenhouses are constructed with at least one curtain for energy savings, and most older greenhouses have had energy curtains retrofitted. Some growers are installing two or even three curtain systems for various purposes, proving that the technology has become an integral part of greenhouse environmental control.

Uses of Curtains

Heat retention

Any interior curtain system can be used for heat retention at night, when heating demand is greatest. The percentage of shade doesn't matter under these conditions, and blackout curtains can serve this purpose, even when day length control isn't a consideration. The amount of heat retained and fuel saved varies according to the type of material in the curtain. Experiments indicate savings of as much as 50–60% of fuel costs in greenhouses with heat-retention curtains versus similar houses without curtains. Growers who've installed curtain systems commonly report annual heating fuel savings of 30% or more.

Curtain systems save energy in three ways. First, they trap an insulating layer of air between the cur-

Figures 3-3, 3-4. Here are typical examples of a gutter-to-gutter system (left) and a truss-to-truss system (right).

tain and the greenhouse roof. Second, they reduce the volume of greenhouse air that must be heated. Third, high-tech curtain fabrics with aluminum strips woven into them reflect heat energy back into the greenhouse rather than letting it escape through the roof.

One drawback to curtain systems is that they trap cold air between the fabric and the roof. When you open the curtain in the morning, this cold air falls into the warm space below, potentially stressing or damaging the crop. To avoid this, it's important to open the curtain gradually to allow this cold air to mix with the warm air below. Alternatively, if the crop can tolerate the shade, the curtain can be left closed until sunlight warms the air above the system.

Shade and cooling

Curtain systems are widely used to reduce indoor light intensity and help control internal greenhouse temperatures during the day. Because they're moveable, they can be closed partially or fully when needed and opened fully on cloudy days. This ability significantly increases the amount of time when near-ideal light levels are available for the crop. Curtain systems also eliminate the recurring cost of materials and labor to apply seasonal shading paint (whitewash) or stationary, suspended shadecloth.

Traditional shadecloth is black woven fabric. Most automated curtain systems now use lightweight, high-tech fabrics made of alternating strips of clear and aluminized polyester. The aluminized strips reflect light back out through the roof of the greenhouse. This reduces the cooling load under the shade significantly. The U.S. Department of Agriculture's Florist and Nursery Crops Laboratory in Maryland reports that greenhouses with aluminized shade systems can be kept about 10°F (5.5°C) cooler than unshaded houses during the summer.

Curtain Configurations

The fabric panels in a curtain system can be driven from gutter to gutter across the width of the greenhouse or from truss to truss down its length. In a gutter-to-gutter system, each panel of curtain material is essentially the size of the floor of one gutter-connected house. In a truss-to-truss system, the panels are wide enough to span the distance from one truss to the next and are as long as the combined width of the total number of houses covered.

In both configurations, each panel of curtain material has a stationary edge and a moving or "leading" edge. The drive system moves the leading edge back and forth to uncover and cover the curtain,

---

Fire Prevention

When choosing any curtain material, you must address the issue of fire. The NGMA recommends the use of flame-resistant materials throughout all retail, educational, and research greenhouses. For all other applications, it recommends that flame-resistant curtain material be alternated with standard (non-flame-resistant) material. Every second, third, or fourth curtain panel should be flame-resistant if flame-resistant material isn't used throughout, since the resistant materials serve as firebreaks. It also recommends that flame-resistant materials are used over heaters, generators, and electrical panels as well as anywhere sparks or open flame may be present.

while the stationary edge holds each curtain panel in place.

Gutter-to-gutter systems

In a gutter-to-gutter curtain system, the curtain panels are pulled flat across the width of the greenhouse at gutter height. This configuration minimizes the volume of greenhouse air below the curtain that must be heated. These systems require less installation labor than a typical truss-to-truss system because the installers work at the lowest possible height, the stationary and lead edges of each panel are straight and their total length is typically less than in a truss-to-truss system, and there's a single panel of fabric per house instead of multiple panels as in a truss-to-truss system.

Gutter-to-gutter curtain systems aren't suitable for every greenhouse. If unit heaters or circulation fans are mounted above gutter height, the curtain will block them from heating or circulating the air under the system, where the crop is. The bottom chords of the trusses can't be used for hanging baskets because the baskets would obstruct the curtain. Though the volume of greenhouse space that is heated is minimized in this configuration, the amount of cold air above the system is maximized. This makes it harder to mix and reheat the air above the system when it uncovers in the morning. Retrofitting a gutter-to-gutter system can require that electrical conduits, gas lines, and heating pipes be moved, since these items are often run under the gutters. When the curtain is closed for shade and/or cooling, the space above a gutter-to-gutter system becomes very hot and this trapped hot air reduces the cooling effect of the shade. The "attic" space above the curtain can be ventilated with a louver and exhaust fan in opposite gable ends of each house to reduce this effect. Because the curtain panels are as wide as the greenhouse (typically 24–42' [7.3–12.8 m]), when the curtain is uncovered, the curtain material forms a large bundle under each gutter. This bundle can be a source of unwanted shade.

Truss-to-truss systems

In a truss-to-truss curtain system, the panels of curtain material move across the distance between one truss and the next. This distance (typically 10–12' [3–3.7 m]) leads to more compact bundles of fabric when the system is uncovered than are possible with gutter-to-gutter systems. These systems can

be configured in three ways: flat at gutter height, slope-flat-slope, and slope-slope.

Flat at gutter height

As with the gutter-to-gutter system, this configuration minimizes the volume of greenhouse space to be heated and is relatively easy to install. It has the same restrictions on equipment in the gables and prevents the grower from suspending hanging baskets from the bottom chord of the truss.

Slope-flat-slope

This is where the profile of the curtain system follows each slope of the roof part way up the truss, with a flat section joining the two, sloped segments. This configuration allows the curtain system to be installed over equipment mounted above gutter height, such as unit heaters. The bottom chords of the trusses remain available for hanging baskets. This configuration leaves clearance for roof vents and provides a chimney effect when used for shade/cooling if a 6–12" (15–30 cm) gap is left instead of fully closing the system.

Slope-slope

This is where the profile of the system parallels a line drawn from the gutter to the peak of the truss. This configuration minimizes the amount of cold air trapped above the curtain and maximizes clearance from equipment mounted above gutter height. The bottom chords of the trusses remain available for hanging baskets.

The slope-flat-slope and slope-slope configurations have some drawbacks. They require more work to install because they are higher off the floor. They require more leading edge and stationary edge material than a flat system that covers the same amount of growing area. And they leave more greenhouse volume to heat than a flat system.

Drive Mechanisms

Drive mechanisms use an electric motor and gearbox to extend and retract (close and open) the curtain. Three types of drive mechanism are commonly used: push-pull, cable/drum, and chain-and-cable.

Push-pull drive

This system is used for truss-to-truss configurations. It uses rotating pinion gears to drive toothed racks long enough to span the distance between two adjacent trusses. These racks attach to rigid metal tubes that run the length of the greenhouse (minus one truss-to-truss spacing, to allow the tube space to move back and forth). In each bay a second tube is fastened at right angles to the drive tubes. This second tube carries the lead edge of the curtain material back and forth across the bay. The motor and gearbox for a push-pull drive are usually mounted near the center of a greenhouse. They can also be mounted in any bay except the first and last, because the rack drive mechanism needs one truss-to-truss bay spacing for freedom to travel.

Figure 3-5. Keeping the curtain system close to the glazing doesn't reduce the air volume that needs to be heated, but it does allow the maximum overhead space for equipment, such as irrigation booms or hanging basket systems.

Cable/drum drive

A cable/drum drive system can move a curtain from gutter to gutter or truss to truss. In these systems, the cable is galvanized or stainless steel wire rope (also called aircraft cable). Lengths of wire rope carry the lead edge of the curtain material. A coil of cable wraps around a motor-driven drum or tube. As the motor rotates the drum, one end of the coil unwraps, and the other end of the coil re-wraps on the drum. A cable/drum drive typically mounts in the plane of movement of the curtain system at one gable end (truss-to-truss) or one sidewall (gutter-to-gutter) of the greenhouse. By using pulleys to route the cables downward, the drive motor and gearbox can be mounted at any convenient height on a side or end wall.

Chain-and-cable drive

A chain-and-cable drive system can move a curtain from gutter to gutter or truss to truss. In this system, lengths of roller chain (bicycle chain) are spliced into loops of wire rope that span the length or width of the greenhouse. The motor and gearbox drive a sprocket that engages the chain and drives the loop of cable back and forth. Lengths of rigid tubing attached to the cable at right angles to its direction of travel carry the lead edge of the panels of curtain material. A chain-and-cable drive system typically mounts on the side- or endwall of a greenhouse and uses pulleys and idler sprockets to transfer the motion of the drive into the plane of motion of the curtain system.

Figures 3-6, 3-7. Shown here are two common drive methods: cable/drum (left) and push-pull (right).

Support Systems

The fabric curtains are supported on wires or nylon monofilament lines parallel to the direction of movement of the curtain. These lines are uniformly spaced across the greenhouse at distances of 18–48" (0.5–1.2 m) on center, depending on the design of the system. Two support systems are commonly used: lay-flat and suspended.

Lay-flat

In a lay-flat system, the curtain panels lie on top of the support lines. Curtain panels can lie on top of the support lines only if monofilament or smooth stainless-steel wires are used. This approach reduces installation labor, as the curtain panels need only be draped over the wires. The friction of the panels against the smooth wires doesn't appear to cause premature wear on the panels. In houses with roof vents, lay-flat panels should be trapped from above by additional stainless-steel or monofilament lines to prevent the curtain panels from billowing up as air circulates in the house.

Suspended

Curtain panels can also be suspended from the support lines with plastic hooks. Fewer support lines are required, but the hooks must be installed in the curtain panels and then attached to the lines. Typically, reinforcing strips are sewn into the curtain panels where the hooks attach so the hooks don't tear through the curtain material. Manufacturers of textiles for greenhouse curtain systems now offer fabrics with reinforcing strips woven into the cloth.

Hybrid suspension systems for slope-flat-slope configurations slide the curtain panels on the sloped and flat portions of the system but suspend them at the transition points from sloped to flat sections. These transition points can abrade the curtain panels, so suspending the panels at these points transfers the stress from the curtain material to the plastic suspension hook.

Curtain Materials

Shade and heat retention

Covering materials for shade and heat retention include knitted white polyester, non-woven bonded white polyester fiber, and composite fabrics manufactured specifically for use in greenhouse curtain systems.

The white polyester fabrics offer excellent durability. Some systems are still using the original fabric panels after more than fifteen years.

White polyester has largely been superseded by composite fabrics made of alternating strips of clear and aluminized polyester or acrylic held together with a finely woven mesh of threads. These panels outperform white polyester because their aluminized strips reflect infrared light (heat) out of the greenhouse during the day while holding it in at night. These fabrics can have a service life of ten years or more.

Figure 3-8. Modern composite fabrics retain heat, reflect infrared energy, and provide shade.

Available variations on composite fabrics include fabrics with chemical stabilization against breakdown by UV light; flame-resistant fabrics to meet building code requirements; fabrics where the clear strips are omitted, leaving gaps for air circulation (these are used principally for shading, though they have some value for heat retention by reflecting infrared light); fabrics with colored aluminized strips for esthetic purposes; and blackout (photoperiod) control fabrics.

Photoperiod control

Blackout materials include polyethylene film, knitted polyester, and composite fabrics where all the strips are either aluminized or opaque. Most blackout materials attempt to reduce heat buildup when the curtain system is closed for day length control in summer. For instance, "black/white poly" is a polyethylene film that is co-extruded with a white top layer for light (and heat) reflection and a black bottom layer for opacity.

Knitted polyester is available with a powdered aluminum reflective coating bonded to one surface. Composite fabrics are typically offered as a two-layer system, with a white or aluminized top layer to reflect light. Two layers are used because the looseness of the weave of these materials can't always provide adequate darkening with a single layer.

Figure 3-9. Sidewall curtains are most often used to cover vents or cover walls as part of a black cloth system for photoperiod control. In such a situation, some growers will even paint one or more walls to eliminate the need for a photoperiod curtain.

Polyethylene film is by far the least expensive blackout material, but it's impermeable to water and water vapor. If the greenhouse leaks when it rains, water can build up in pockets on top of the film, and the weight can damage the support system of the curtain. Today, polyethylene is primarily used for temporary blackout purposes over individual benches and pulled by hand.

Better are polyester knits and composite fabrics, which are porous and allow water and water vapor to pass through. This reduces the chance of water-weight related damage to the system. Knit and composite products also offer a longer service life than poly film.

Light-emission prevention

In low-light regions (the northern United States, Canada, and Northern Europe), at times when crops could use more light than the natural sun provides (winter), or on highly intensive crops (greenhouse vegetables, for instance), growers often use supplemental lighting both during the day and at night. However, light emissions from a greenhouse at night can elicit nuisance complaints from neighbors or create other unintended consequences, such as the disruption of nocturnal wildlife. For these reasons, specialty curtains have been developed to prevent light from escaping the greenhouse. These materials are similar to blackout curtains, with the exception that they may have features that allow excess heat generated from the lamps to escape.

Sidewall Curtain Systems

Sidewall curtain systems are used to form interior partitions, to cover walls in blackout systems, to shade south-facing walls, and to cover and uncover sidewall vent openings in place of a glazed vent or louvers.

Three common drive systems are used to raise and lower sidewall curtains. In one system, the curtain material is wrapped around a tube and the wall is raised and lowered by rolling and unrolling the mate-

Figure 3-10. An exterior curtain system is used for shading an entire greenhouse while allowing excellent airflow for natural ventilation. These are most commonly encountered in warm climates, such as Florida.

rial from the tube. The tube can be driven with a hand crank or with an electric motor and gearbox. A second approach uses a system of ropes and pulleys attached to the top edge of the sidewall curtain to drop the curtain open or lift it closed. Lastly, some systems use a tube to roll and unroll the material, rotating the tube by cradling it in rope loops that run through pulleys back to a hand crank or to a block that travels up and down a motorized screw.

Commonly used sidewall curtain materials include plastic films reinforced with fiber mesh, polyester knit fabric, and strengthened versions of the composite fabrics made for greenhouse use.

Exterior Curtains

Three types of exterior curtain systems are available. A motor-and-gear-driven shade system can be mounted above the greenhouse roof to reduce the amount of heat and light that enters the structure. A standard black shadecloth or aluminized mesh can be stretched over the greenhouse roof and left in place for the duration of the high-light season. Or a curtain system can serve as the greenhouse roof (a retractable-roof green-

house), uncovering for maximum light and ventilation and covering for weather protection.

Maintenance, Longevity, Replacement

Modern curtain materials should be made to resist dust accumulation. Curtains are generally rinsed with fresh water if they become overly polluted with dust. Transparent plastic films will become opaque over time and lose light transmission on the order of 1% per year. These will need periodic replacement.

Curtains used within operations that require disinfection between crops can be treated with hydrogen peroxide solutions. Hydrogen peroxide is non-carcinogenic and doesn't rapidly degrade plastics as other disinfectants can.

Recently, the practice of using hydrogen peroxide/peracetic acid solutions deployed with foggers has been used to solve the difficulties of disinfecting the top side of a curtain. The curtain is parked in a partially uncovered position during fogging. It's not believed that an annual treatment will invite unacceptable levels of corrosion to the metal components of the greenhouse. Hydrogen peroxide can also be effective against algae buildup. Algae are best treated with prevention. Algae can only grow in wet conditions. Parking the curtain in the covered position for a few minutes during the peak of the day is usually sufficient to dry out the curtain.

Greenhouse curtains are typically warranted against UV degradation and excess shrinkage for five years. The typical replacement interval is about eight years, although some installations are stretched to as many as fifteen years. Once the yarns start failing, creating gaping holes in the curtain, the energy savings value is lost. Likewise, an installation that is poorly sealed on the perimeter is missing its full potential.

Photoperiod Control

P. Allen Hammer

Many of the plants we grow in greenhouses respond to day length, or "photoperiod." Photoperiod can control vegetative growth or reproductive growth (flowering) and dormancy or breaking dormancy. It's important for growers to understand photoperiod because it's a powerful greenhouse tool and a requirement for many of the crops commonly produced.

What Is Photoperiod?

Photoperiod refers to the length of the day period (light) and the night period (dark). Our 24-hour day is divided into light and dark periods that vary depending on the time of year and longitude. This day length varies from the shortest day/longest night that occurs on December 21 and the longest day/shortest night that occurs on June 21. Equal day/night periods occur twice a year—March 21 and September 21.

The night length, or dark period, is the important part of the 24-hour day for photoperiod control. When applying photoperiod treatments, plants respond to the length of the dark period, not the length of the light period. During the dark period, a chemical conversion occurs in the plant. This may be viewed as a chemical conversion clock. If this clock requires 11.5 hours of dark, the most effective way to disrupt the clock is to apply light during the middle of the dark period. That's the reason growers most often run their photoperiod lights between 10:00 p.m. and 2:00 a.m.

Figure 3-11. Many growers use simple strings of lights, linked to a 24-hour timer, to provide photoperiod control.

We classify photoperiodic plants by their "critical day length." For example, the critical day length of the poinsettia is 12.5 hours. That means the poinsettia will flower when it received continuous darkness for at least 11.5 hours (24 hours minus 12.5 hours equals 11.5 hours) each day until flowering. It also means that the poinsettia will only grow vegetatively when the night length is less than 11.5 hours.

The Mechanics of Photoperiod Control

Long days/short nights are artificially provided during naturally short days of the year by lighting the crop in the middle of the night. A minimum of 10 f.c. (108 lux) is generally supplied, using incandescent lamps. One-hundred watt incandescent bulbs spaced 6' (2 m) apart, 4' (1.2 m) above the plant canopy, or 60-watt incandescent bulbs spaced 4' (1.2 m) apart, 2–3' (0.6–0.9 m) above the plant canopy, is recommended. The fixtures should have reflectors attached above each bulb to increase lighting efficiency (aluminum pie plates work well for this). Incandescent lamps are used because they provide a lot of light from the red portion of the spectrum, which is the most effective wavelength for photoperiod control. Also, they're inexpensive to install. Growers are beginning

Figure 3-12. Black cloth systems are used primarily by growers who produce weekly potted crops, such as mums and kalanchoes, year round.

to use compact fluorescent lamps (CFLs) in the place of incandescent lamps to save energy. It is important that the light intensity reaching the canopy is at least 10 f.c. (108 lux) from warm white or daylight lamps. It is also very important to avoid breaking these lamps in the greenhouse to avoid mercury contamination, which can affect plant growth. LED lamps are presently being tested for greenhouse lighting and photoperiod control. Although presently expensive, LED lamps hold great potential in greenhouse production.

Short days/long nights are artificially provided during the naturally long days of the year by covering the crop with blackout material. The material can be suspended by hand over simple pipe frames built on each bench or be part of an automatic curtain system controlled by a time clock. This automated system is vastly favored since the grower doesn't have to manually apply and remove the black cloth every day.

Black cloth is usually applied from 7:00 p.m. until 7:00 a.m. to avoid heat buildup under the curtain, which can cause delayed flowering and plant damage. It is extremely important that the blackout fabric has no openings or tears because even a small opening can provide enough light to prevent photoperiod control over that portion of the crop. Blackout material is also used to block the effects of artificial light pollution. For example, poinsettias won't flower properly when exposed to streetlights or even vehicle lights on a busy highway.

4

Benches, Floors, and Baskets

Greenhouse Benches

Sara Grosser

Employees who work in a greenhouse where plants are grown on the ground often wonder, "Why don't we grow on benches? My back hurts!" This is one of the reasons growers select benches—worker convenience. Yet there are a multitude of horticultural benefits to growing on benches.

Bench Benefits

Crop health

Every grower faces the challenge of producing a uniform crop without the presence of pests or diseases when that crop leaves the greenhouse. These pests and diseases come into the growing area when conditions are less than ideal, particularly when air circulation is poor, weeds are present, and excessive moisture remains. Growing on benches diminishes the presence of these conditions. The challenge of producing a pest- and disease-free crop now is less intimidating.

Airflow

Benches provide a microclimate for plant material, as plants are elevated from the ground with air circulating around each container. With increased air circulation, there's less risk of excessive moisture on the foliage and in the soil, reducing the opportunity for insects and diseases to thrive.

Weeds

Although greenhouse managers strive to maintain a weed-free environment, weeds often times do succeed. Benches elevate plants above this nuisance, decreasing the infestation of insects and diseases that weeds can host. Benches also make it easier to keep the growing area free of weeds. They prevent the intermingling of weeds with ornamentals, increasing the quality of plant material since there's no longer competition for the light, water, and nutrients required for a healthy crop.

Water

Finally, the level surface benches provide prevent wet areas often encountered when growing on the ground. Wet areas not only result in a non-uniform crop, but also attract pests to the excessive moisture.

Construction Materials

Regardless of style, benches can be constructed of a variety of materials, from metal to wood to plastic to concrete. The material chosen depends greatly on budget, crop grown, aesthetics, and durability.

Metal

Commercially produced benches are almost exclusively constructed of metal. The most common design is galvanized steel tubing legs and bench supports with bench tops constructed of aluminum or steel side rails surrounding an expanded metal surface. These benches are ideal in both production and retail situations, as they're the most durable benching material available. Increasing the quantity of crossbars and legs as needed can easily accommodate any weight capacity. Advantages of this construction include longevity, ease of construction, low maintenance, light weight, high durability, good air circulation, corrosion resistance, passage of water and soil through the bench top, pleasing appearance, versatility in placement and arrangement, and ease of movement (depending on length). Disadvantages include high initial material and installation labor costs. Commercial metal benches usually cost about $3/ft.^{2} ($32.25/m^2).

Wood

Wooden benches are also commercially produced, most commonly for retail applications where the natural look of the wood blends in attractively with the plants. The legs, sides, and tops of these benches are constructed of rot-resistant woods, such as pressure-treated lumber, locust, western red cedar, redwood, or cypress. Advantages of this construction include pleasing appearance, custom design, versatility in placement and arrangement, and ease of movement. Disadvantages include high cost; increased maintenance; absorption of undesired stains from soils, fertilizers, and chemicals; and shorter life span. Cost of these commercial wooden retail benches is $7.00/ft.^{2} ($75.32/m^2).

A simpler variation of the wood bench is almost always built by the grower, using legs made of either pressure-treated lumber or concrete blocks; a rim made of pressure-treated lumber; and wooden lath, welded wire, or expanded metal attached for the growing surface. Advantages of this construction include low cost, versatility in placement and arrangement, and ease of movement (depending on length). Disadvantages include decreased durability; increased maintenance; lack of esthetics; shorter life span; and absorption of undesired stains from soils, fertilizers, and chemicals. Built by the grower, these benches usually cost anywhere from $0.75–1.50/ft.^{2} ($8.00–16.25/m^2).

Plastic

The least expensive commercially produced bench is constructed of plastic. Plastic benches are available with all components including legs, supports, and bench tops constructed of plastic as well as bench tops only constructed of plastic. Advantages include low cost, ease of assembly, light weight, and low maintenance. Disadvantages include lack of durability and short life span.

Concrete

In the early days of greenhouses, some benches, primarily for cut flower production, were made completely of concrete cast in place. Today, benches constructed of concrete are most commonly hybrids, with legs of concrete block and tops constructed of wood or commercial plastic bench tops. Advantages include low cost, versatility in placement and arrangement, and ease of movement (depending on bench length). Disadvantages include decreased durability, esthetics, and lifespan.

Ebb-and-flood

Another type of plastic construction, used only for bench tops, is ebb-and-flood trays, or subirrigation benches. These benches are constructed using the same bench legs and supports as commercial metal benches, with minor modifications to accommodate bench tops constructed of watertight, molded plastic trays. These trays are flooded with plain water or a liquid fertilizer solution. The liquid remains in the tray for a set period of time, allowing plants to take up the moisture through the pots' drain holes via capillary action. The liquid is then drained from the bench and is either collected for reuse or drained to the local sewage system. Some growers have noted a 50% decrease in water and fertilizer use employing an ebb-and-flood system (see chapter 5 for more on ebb-and-flood irrigation). Advantages of this type of bench include reduction in irrigation labor costs, decrease in water and fertilizer cost, reduction in disease potential (because the foliage remains dry), and increased uniformity of crop. Disadvantages include the need for retention tanks and pumps if water is to be recirculated. The ebb-and-flood bench system is also less than ideal when plants with dissimilar water requirements are grouped together. Ebb-and-flood benches cost approximately $5.50 ft.^{2} ($59.18/m^2), excluding tanks and plumbing for water supply and drainage.

Bench Styles

There are several ways to classify greenhouse benches, with slight variations and combinations of each. In terms of the type of bench support and placement of the bench top, benches can either be stationary or rolling. Stationary benches have tops that remain fixed upon the bench legs, while rolling benches have tops that roll from side to side.

As for the construction of the bench top, benches can either be open or ebb-and-flood. "Open" is a broad term, as some materials used in this construction achieve drainage better than others do. Ebb-and-flood bench tops are constructed of a watertight, closed tray. Both open and ebb-and-flood benches can be either stationary or rolling.

A third variation among benches is the method used for setting the legs, which can either be set permanently in concrete or set on top of the ground. When set in concrete, bench placement is permanent, while if set on the ground, benches can be moved as needed. As you may imagine, there are endless variations of benches.

Stationary benches

Bench layout and design

Two basic designs exist for the arrangement of benches in the greenhouse: longitudinal and peninsular.

Figure 4-1. The most common bench layout is longitudinal, with all the benches running parallel to each other.

Figure 4-2. Peninsula benches are an old system that may not be the most efficient for space use, but it does provide easy access to plants, such as in this propagation greenhouse.

Longitudinal design, also known as linear or straight design, results in the arrangement of benches in a linear fashion, with all benches and aisles running the same direction. Advantages of this layout include simple performance of routine tasks such as watering; lower cost, as there are fewer, larger benches; and simplification of the greenhouse layout. Disadvantages include decreased maneuverability with fewer aisles and decreased ability to separate crops onto individual benches.

Peninsular design utilizes a large main aisle with benches running perpendicular to the main aisle, with smaller aisles between these benches. Advantages include segregation of crops, ease of maneuverability around the greenhouse, and pleasing display in retail setting. Disadvantages include increased cost due to the higher quantity of smaller benches and inefficient use of space due to amount of area devoted to aisles.

Growers agree: Your growing area is where you make your money. The size of the benches and width of the aisles greatly affect the amount of available growing area you have. Larger benches and narrow aisles will maximize growing area, while wide aisles and smaller benches will decrease growing area.

Bench size

Regardless of the layout and construction materials you choose, you should follow certain guidelines to ensure maximum production space paired with convenience and comfort. Benches constructed approximately 30" (76 cm) tall by 6' (1.8 m) wide are ideal when they're accessible from either side. Should a bench be accessible from only one side, its maximum width should be 36" (91 cm). If your benches are going to be taller

than 30" (76 cm), observe a maximum height of 36" (91 cm) so they're accessible to workers or customers in wheelchairs.

Benches may also be tiered, provided there's sufficient growing space between the tiers. There are two main concerns in this application: the potential of overwatering plants on the lower tier as the upper tier drains and the shade cast by the upper tier adversely affecting the plants on the lower tier.

Rolling Benches

Available primarily as commercially constructed metal in either open or ebb-and-flood varieties, rolling benches are built in the same fashion as stationary benches, except with a top that can roll several feet from side to side. Rolling benches optimize the growing area by eliminating most of the greenhouse aisles. Benches are arranged in a longitudinal or peninsular design with one "floating aisle." Bench tops are placed on roller tubes, allowing them to be rolled side to side either by hand or with a hand crank inserted in one of the two roller tubes. The movement of these bench tops changes the location of the aisle. Rolling benches can increase the growing area to up to 90% of the available greenhouse space.

Rolling benches require a few special considerations. When loading rolling benches, it's vital to load each bench uniformly across the bench so that one side is not overloaded, causing the bench to tip. Anti-tip devices, commonly in the form of a chain bolted to both the bench leg and select bench top crosspieces, help prevent such occurrences.

Figure 4-3. Rolling benches make excellent use of space by eliminating most of the aisles in the greenhouse.

Because there's only one aisle in each greenhouse (in the case of freestanding greenhouses) or each bay (in the case of gutter-connected greenhouses), rolling benches are not practical for retail applications or where workers need constant access to the crop. However, more and more growers are finding the added space use outweighs these inconveniences and labor concerns.

The main advantage of rolling benches is the increased growing area. Disadvantages include slightly higher initial cost than stationary benches, the inconvenience of only having one aisle available at a time, and the tipping potential.

Container benches

Container benches, also termed pallet benches or Dutch trays, offer complete handling of plant material from planting to shipping. The intensity of a particular business's production and automation will dictate the relative necessity and usefulness of a container bench system. Growers who are germinating plugs

may sow seeds in plug trays and automatically load them onto container benches, roll the containers into the germination chamber, then out to the greenhouse for growing on, and finally on to shipping, all in a four-week period, without ever touching a single tray. If the same grower is also producing finished plants, these plugs can be transplanted into growing containers, taken to the greenhouse for finishing, and then rolled on to the shipping area, again without the labor of spacing plants or loading, pushing, and unloading carts. Combine these operations, and a season's worth of plants can be moved with little effort.

Constructed of steel and/or aluminum, a container bench support system is created as a series of legs set in concrete with a pair of rails welded to them that serve as tracks. Some sections of the track are equipped with rollers that the benches ride upon. These rollers can be motorized or manual to carry containers into the greenhouse. At the end of each run of leg structures, another series of rollers is present to permit perpendicular movement of containers into each greenhouse

Figure 4-4. Container benches, or Dutch trays, combine a bench system and a transport system in one.

bay. A pneumatic lift raises and lowers the perpendicular rollers to allow the container to be moved sideways. This network of tracks, often called "rollerbahn" (like the German autobahn), is what allows the benches to flow through the greenhouse range. The containers are constructed of aluminum, with bench surfaces made of expanded metal or plastic ebb-and-flood trays.

Bench tops can be virtually any size, ensuring efficient use of space in any size greenhouse. Common sizes are from 12–20' (3.6–6.1 m) long and 5–6' (1.5–1.8 m) wide.

The most sophisticated greenhouses in the world make use of this type of system. Controlled almost completely by computer, robotic cranes can carry containers in and out of the greenhouse twenty-four hours a day. Special overhead cranes can retrieve any bench from the thousands in the greenhouse. Containers can be spaced very closely together, with a minimum of aisles for maximum production space because the crops can be brought to the workers in the production barn for sorting,

pinching, or spacing, rather than the workers going into the greenhouse.

Advantages of this system include flexibility, efficient crop movement, labor savings, and the ability to segregate crops. Disadvantages include the need to move multiple containers to access one in the center of the row, careful planning of material handling, increased installation and material cost, and requirement for compressed air to operate the pneumatic lifts and specialized equipment, such as pot spacing robots, to make the best use of the system.

Ebb-and-Flood and Trough Benches

Bruce Zierk

Ebb-and-flood benches first appeared some sixty years ago. Growers tried several methods. Concrete that was formed and poured in place was one of the most common. A few examples of these old benches can still

Figure 4-5. Ebb-and-flood benches allow for easy, efficient irrigation.

be found in greenhouses in North America. Probably because of the expense and labor of installing these early subirrigation benches and a lack of the sophisticated pumping and control systems currently available, the early ebb-and-flood benches fell out of common use.

Modern ebb-and-flood benches came into popular use in Europe in the early 1980s. Due to the very high cost of labor there, growers started searching for ways to automate every possible part of the production process. Ebb-and-flood benches (and other forms of subirrigation, such as flood floors) are now used in virtually every greenhouse in Europe, practically eliminating all labor involved in watering.

The first North American installations of these modern ebb-and-flood benches occurred around 1982 to 1984. While subirrigation watering systems are by no means standard almost thirty years later, there are at least eight hundred greenhouses in North America with ebb-and-flood benches. These range from small greenhouses with a few ebb-and-flood benches to bench installations measured in acres.

Ebb-and-flood benches typically consist of a sturdy bench frame that can be easily and precisely leveled, and a waterproof liner to hold the plants and contain the irrigation water during watering cycles. The liner or bench top is typically thermal vacuum-formed polystyrene, though a few installations use other materials, such as aluminum sheets or flexible plastic or rubber sheeting. Because of the design of benches with rigid aluminum liners and the extremes of temperature in much of North America, there were problems with expansion and contraction, causing the aluminum liners to bow up in areas, becoming unlevel, and unable to water the plants evenly. Some designs also had problems keeping the aluminum liners sealed, resulting in frequent leaking. The typical design of the benches with the polystyrene tray inserts solves these problems. While polystyrene does expand and contract with changes in the ambient temperature (as much as 2" (5 cm) in 100' (31 m) of bench), the typical ebb-and-flood bench has the trays sitting on top of the bench framework, floating freely, with an appropriate allowance for expansion at the ends.

Early on, there was concern about the service life of the polystyrene trays, as well as concern about disposal/recycling. We now know that the typical installation using the polystyrene trays lasts sixteen to twenty years and much longer if the trays are protected from exposure to light (UV rays). Also, there are many avenues open now for the recycling of the polystyrene along with most other agricultural plastics.

Why Ebb-and-Flood Benches?

The primary reason for installing ebb-and-flood benches is the tremendous savings in labor costs. When fully automated, one person can water 0.5–1.0 acre (0.2–0.4 ha) in twenty to thirty minutes. This is the time it takes to check the crops on each bench, decide which ones need water, and set the irrigation controller. Many growers have studied the costs associated with installing ebb-and-flood benches and calculate payback taking anywhere from two to six years, with most reporting three to four years as the actual repayment of their investment. This is for growers who replaced existing benches with ebb-and-flood benches. If you are installing the benches as part of new construction and not replacing existing benches, the difference in cost is minimal and the payback period much shorter.

In addition to the tremendous reduction in labor and labor costs, there are many advantages to using ebb-and-flood benches. Most growers report much lower use of fungicides for disease prevention. This is partly due to the fact that the plant foliage is always dry. Since the area below the benches and walkways are always dry as well, humidity is much easier to control. Dry foliage and lower humidity help prevent diseases.

Some growers worry that an ebb-and-flood system can spread disease organisms from one pot to the next via the irrigation water. However, research at several universities in the early 1990s showed that most diseases (especially soil-borne diseases) are extremely difficult, if not impossible, to spread with a properly run ebb-and-flood system. The main reason for this seems to be that the irrigation water enters the pots or flats in a one-way fashion—it moves into the pot through capillary action but doesn't move back out of the pot. Since there's no leaching or runoff from containers, diseases don't spread, even from infected plants to healthy neighboring plants.

Figure 4-6. Because the plants are watered from below, foliage stays dry—helping prevent disease, and often improving plant quality.

Since only the water actually taken up by the plants is used and the remainder is recycled, the use of water is greatly reduced compared to most other methods of watering. In addition, experts recommend using only half of the fertilizer concentration you'd use with an overhead or drip-irrigation system. The combined savings in water and fertilizer can be considerable.

Watering is much more uniform than with other methods, especially compared to hand watering in small pots. Most growers report that many crops finish 8–10% faster on ebb-and-flood benches compared to hand- or drip-irrigation methods. The reason for this response isn't clear, but is probably related to the even and thorough watering and lower stress on the crop.

Another advantage compared to other automated irrigation systems is the ease of growing different crops on the same benches. For example, if you grow a year-round crop of 6" (15 cm) pots that are always spaced 12 x 12" (30 x 30 cm), a drip-irrigation system will

Figure 4-7. Ebb-and-flood troughs are most often seen in the northeastern United States and Canada and are most often used on pot crops, such as the *Exacum* pictured here.

work fine. But if you follow that crop with 4" (10 cm) pots spaced pot tight, you're stuck with hand watering the second crop because you won't have enough emitters for each 4" (10 cm) pot. With ebb-and-flood benches, any size container placed on the bench is automatically watered.

Ebb-and-flood benches are also becoming very popular in retail areas. They present a very neat appearance and eliminate puddles, mud, and hoses. In addition, watering can easily be done while customers are present.

What Does It Cost?

In 2010, costs for typical production ebb-and-flood benches run about $6.00–6.75/ft.^{2} ($64.56–72.63/ m^2). Add $0.60–1.20/ft.^{2} ($6.46–12.91/m^2) for plumbing and controls. This is for 6' or 6.5' (1.8–2 m) wide production benches. The price for narrower or very short benches is more, as is their cost for plumbing and controls, due to extra control zones and valves needed for smaller benches as well as more benches. This is about $1.50–1.90/ft.^{2} ($16.14–20.44/m^2) more than the typical installed cost for flood floors. Compared to a quality, commercial expanded metal

or wire mesh bench equipped with a drip-irrigation system, the cost is roughly the same.

If you already have sturdy benches that can be made level (such as typical expanded metal benches), you can retrofit them by placing the polystyrene trays directly on top of the existing bench. This conversion costs about $3.00–3.45 per ft.^{2} ($32.28–37.12/m^2), not including plumbing and controls, and is a popular way to convert to ebb-and-flood irrigation.

Trough Benches

Trough benches are another form of automated subirrigation with similarities to ebb-and-flood benches. In a typical system, there is a sturdy bench framework supporting a series of troughs running lengthwise across the bench. The troughs are usually made of aluminum, typically roll formed on the job site in one continuous run. Other materials, such as polystyrene plastic, are sometimes used.

Unlike an ebb-and-flood system, which is perfectly level, trough systems are usually sloped slightly from one end to the other. When the crop needs water, it is introduced at the high end of each trough and slowly runs to the lower end, where the excess is collected and returned to a holding tank for reuse. The plants take up water and nutrients by capillary action, the same as with other methods of subirrigation.

Trough benches are relatively easy to install and are usually cheaper than ebb-and-flood benches. They're very efficient for irrigating crops and easily automated, providing the some of the advantages of ebb-and-flood benches, such as labor, water, and fertilizer savings. The troughs typically have some space between them, allowing good airflow through the crop, especially if there's heat under the bench.

The main disadvantage to trough systems is their relative lack of flexibility. Once the trough system is installed, it's fixed for one particular container size and/or plant spacing. This makes troughs an excellent choice when there is continuous production of plants in the same or similar container size grown on the same spacing (for example, year round 6" [15 cm] pot mum production), so they're most often found in potted crop production. Troughs would be a poor choice where different crops, pot sizes, or spacing is required. The trough systems also usually won't work for flats or trays.

Growing on the Ground

Ratus Fischer

If you asked greenhouse growers a few decades ago why they grow on the ground, they may have replied. "Well, I guess because it's there." Or maybe, "I wish we could afford benches, but we can't yet."

These days, the decision to grow on the ground isn't quite that simple. Growing on the ground can be the least expensive way for a new business to get started or an old business to stay in business. Or it can be as high-tech as any technology found in the greenhouse industry.

Pros and Cons

Growing on the ground usually requires less investment than comparably equipped bench systems. Floors provide great flexibility in crop spacing, and space utilization tends to be better than with bench growing systems. On the downside of growing on the ground are the challenges of maintaining cleanliness and keeping pathogens away. If the floor doesn't have a hard surface, movement of carts and other means of transport are limited.

The microclimate near the ground is different from higher up. Generally, there's less air circulation near the ground, which may lead to excess humidity in the leaf canopy. Evaporation from the ground may add to this effect. On the other hand, edge effects (where plants at the outside of a block of plants dry out more quickly than those near the middle) may be smaller than on benches. Heated floors completely change this picture and offer a great deal of control over the microclimate around the foliage.

Performing work on plants growing on the floor is strenuous. Plants that require much manual work are better grown on benches. Moving and transport of pots and trays on floors requires workers to bend down, unless tools such as pot forks or automated equipment are used. On the other hand, carts can usually be brought right to where the crop is, making it easy to move large numbers of plants quickly.

Types of Growing Floors

Natural soil

Traditionally, growing in greenhouses often meant not only growing *on* the ground, but also *in* the ground. This practice has all but disappeared in commercial growing, except for small-scale cut flower and vegetable production. Growing in containers on natural soil isn't common anymore, except for nursery crops in cool houses. Muddy conditions due to irrigation, roots growing into the soil, and the challenge of controlling weeds make this practice hard to manage unless the soil is naturally very well draining.

Sand and gravel floors

These offer good drainage, which eliminates the mud problem. But with the easy availability of groundcloth, this practice is mostly relegated to hobby growers.

Groundcloth

Covering a well-draining soil or bed of sand or fine gravel with woven groundcloth has become the low-cost greenhouse floor of choice. It's also widely applied in outdoor growing. Quick and inexpensive installation makes these growing floors practical for temporary and permanent setups. With good drainage under the cloth, the floor stays reasonably clean, although algae may build up in moist areas. Cart tracks and footprints

Figure 4-8. Concrete, with or without flood capabilities, makes for a clean, solid growing surface.

may lead to puddles. Depending on the quality of the subfloor and the cloth, these floors can last for many years. Cost of the cloth is just $0.05–0.10 ft.² ($0.54–1.08/m²). Grading, proper drainage, and installation of the cloth will probably cost more than the cloth itself.

Porous concrete

These became state-of-the-art during the 1980s. They consist of fine gravel mixed with a small amount of concrete, which leaves the floor porous. Porous floors offer a solid surface and promise good drainage. What has made the trend short-lived has been dirt accumulation in the pores of the floors, which limits drainage, leads to growth of algae, and harbors pathogens and unwanted chemicals. Increased environmental awareness and regulation now question the wisdom of water leaching uncontrolled into the ground. This is true for any unsealed floor, of course. But why spend the money on a porous floor if for

little more money you can install a runoff-containing concrete floor?

Concrete

Concrete greenhouse floors have been around for a long time, but in the 1990s they became the predominant way of growing on the ground. Reasons for this include the trend to large-scale, highly automated production; the need for higher standards of sanitation; and the shrinking percentage of the cost of the floor compared to the cost of a fully equipped greenhouse. Most concrete floors are sloped for proper drainage, with inground piping allowing for containment or recirculation of excess water. Good concrete floors will cost around $1.60–2.00/ft.² ($17.22–21.52/m²) for material and installation. Don't forget to include the cost of proper drainage.

Floor "Accessories"

Radiant heat

Also called floor heat, radiant heat adds new dimensions to growing on the ground. Not only is heat to the crop provided in an energy-saving way, but floor heat also allows you to control root and foliage temperatures independently. This opens new options to promote growth and control diseases. Radiant heat is mostly installed in concrete floors. Cost for high-quality heat tubing, heaters, and installation run about $0.80/ft.² ($8.61/m²). This doesn't include the hot water source, transport lines, and valves. Radiant heat can be applied to other types of growing floors, such as beneath groundcloth. Lower expectations in terms of longevity allow some savings compared to an installation in concrete.

Flood floors

Flood floors, also referred to as ebb-and-flood floors, have become the floor-growing system of choice over the past two decades. They combine a heated concrete floor with a recirculating irrigation system. Section by section, minimally sloped concrete floors are filled with 1–2" (2.5–5 cm) of water and drained again. The plants wick up the irrigation water. Short flooding times of less than ten minutes minimize the risk of disease transfer.

The water enters and leaves the floor through in-ground piping that's connected to a tank and water recirculation system. No water or fertilizer is wasted. Cost for a complete flood floor system is around $7.00–8.00/ft.² ($75.32–86.08/m²) for a turnkey installation. This includes concrete floor, floor heat, water supply, and recirculation system, plus fully automated controls.

Some growers use rubber liners instead of concrete to grow on and contain the floodwater. Puddles and the resulting growth of algae usually make these systems a temporary solution at best.

Which Crops Perform Best on the Ground?

There are few general answers, but some trends. A large number of bedding plants are grown on floors, often in large batches, and barely touched except for placing the flats on the floor and shipping. Most foliage and perennial crops have traditionally been grown on the ground. Increased availability of automated equipment for handling and spacing pots and shuttle trays on the floor will keep it that way.

I'm often asked if it's better to grow on floors or on benches. The answer is always to ask more questions:

Do the plants need work during the growing period, such as pinching or disbudding? Are there many small batches of plants that need to be selectively picked? Do you mainly produce plugs? Do retail customers enter the area? Can you justify the cost of a moving bench system because you want seamless automation from seed to shipping? If one or more answers are yes, you may want to consider a bench system.

Do you grow seasonal and holiday crops in small or large batches? Is fast handling of the crops and flexibility crucial? Are you on a budget? Is high maintenance eating away your profits? If some of these answers are yes, you may well be on the way to growing on the ground.

Growing Overhead

Jake Van Wingerden and Chris Lundgren

Growing overhead, whether hanging baskets or regular pots, has many advantages. The first and most obvious is that you're using free space. You're already paying to heat and cool that space, so why not use it? Most growers use this "free" space to grow hanging baskets, but this isn't always the case. We've seen 6" (15 cm) pots of poinsettias and trays of African violet plugs grown overhead as well.

The second reason to grow overhead is the great growing climate that exists up in the air. Heat is more evenly distributed the higher you go, so there are rarely cold spots in the overhead space. Air circulation is also at its best, so preventing the plants from getting diseases, such as root rot or botrytis, is made easier.

Drawbacks to growing overhead include the chance of compromising the quality of the crop grown on the benches or ground below. Sometimes this risk eliminates the option of growing overhead, as is the case for plug or propagation growers who don't want to risk contaminating, damaging, or shading their high-value crop. In most cases, growers can find an acceptable balance of the right plant material to hang without adversely affecting the crops that grow on the ground or benches.

Another drawback is that it can be difficult to access the plants hanging in the air when the floor or bench area is full of product. Unless the plants are hung over or near an aisle, they can be difficult to get to. Plus, it is necessary to install irrigation for each overhead plant, or water them by hand, which can also be problematic. Overhead products also have a tendency to drip on the crops below.

Figure 4-9. Growers today need to take advantage of every bit of greenhouse space to be profitable.

Most baskets or other product that can be hung overhead will grow to become a much larger, healthier plant that's worth a lot more money. Most hanging baskets get a higher sticker price as the demand for premium varieties and specialty baskets has increased. In our fast-paced society where instant gratification is a must, a self-contained plant that hangs on the porch has more appeal than a flat of plants the homeowner needs to plant in the ground.

Containers and Crops

Because most crops can be grown overhead, the real decision what type of container to put your crops in. Plastic hanging baskets are the most popular, with typical sizes ranging from 6–16" (15–41 cm). By using custom wire hangers, any size pot or flat can be grown in the air with good success. Molded fiber baskets as well as wire baskets lined with moss or coco fiber are increasingly more popular with consumers, though they can present issues to the commercial grower. These issues include shipping/handling, keeping the

plant's media moist, and keeping the plant looking good once it is at the store or final point of sale due to the amount of care that they typically need. Most of these issues have been addressed by the manufacturers that make these products, so a little research goes a long way to make sure the right product is being used at the commercial level.

What to grow overhead can be determined by what the shade and light requirements are of the plants on the ground. A high-light crop of petunia flats on the ground shouldn't have a crop of large fern or fuchsia baskets hung over it. Those big, bushy baskets should be hung over low-light crops, such as impatiens. Hang the smaller, more compact varieties, such as New Guinea impatiens, over high-light crops. It is also possible to vary the density of the baskets grown overhead to match the light requirements of the crop below. Instead of hanging the baskets on 24" (60 cm) centers, try hanging them on 36" (90 cm) centers to allow more light to get through.

How to Grow Overhead

Growing overhead can be accomplished in several ways. The least expensive way is to lay ¾" (2 cm) pipe on the trusses or attached to posts, running the length of the greenhouse. It is easy to hang baskets from these pipes by using wire hangers. If possible, these pipes should be located over or near an aisle to facilitate loading and unloading of the lines.

As mentioned above, there are two ways to water the baskets: by hand or with drip tubes. Walking with a hose and a long watering wand to water each basket by hand is very labor intensive and imprecise. The more efficient way to water is to install a drip tube to each basket. This tube is usually constructed of ½" or ¾" (1.5 or 2 cm) PVC or polypropylene with emitters or drip orifices evenly spaced along the line. The baskets or pots are hung underneath these emitters to allow the water to "drip" into the plants' media. Irrigation can be turned on and off by using a hand valve or by use of an electronic solenoid controlled by a timer or computer.

While drip irrigation is a cost-effective way to water plants, it does have its drawbacks. If an emitter gets clogged with particulate, the plant hanging below it doesn't get water and could die. If the water is left on too long, the basket drips all the excess water out onto the crop below it, causing damage. When shipping baskets, any hanging plant removed from the line will have an emitter that will drip water on the crops below unless it is plugged.

Automated Systems

There are automated hanging basket systems that will eliminate most of the issues that go along with other conventional styles of growing overhead. The first automated system on the market was the ECHO Hanging Basket System (Cherry Creek Systems, Colorado Springs, Colorado).

Imagine a very small chairlift at a ski resort, but instead of little chairs, imagine hanging plants. An ECHO has one continuous loop of cable with hooks attached to it. So, just as a ski lift travels up and down the mountain, the ECHO carries the back and forth in the greenhouse, from the main aisle to the back of the house and back again. This allows for growing over areas that would otherwise be inaccessible.

Figure 4-10. The ECHO System automates the overhead hanging basket line, bringing plants to the main aisle. Watering is automated as well.

Watering is done automatically. The system can be programmed to bring each plant past a watering station. As each basket trips a trigger switch, it activates a solenoid valve and each plant gets a precise amount of water, all programmed by the user. The watering station can be placed anywhere along the system, eliminating any splash or drip from hitting the crop below. This also allows precise applications of chemicals such as insecticides or growth regulators, as well as getting fertilizers where they're needed without unnecessary waste.

The ECHO is considerably more expensive than a drip system (about $6.00–8.00 per basket depending on options/upgrades), but the savings on labor alone will generally pay back the system in less than two years. Utilization of inaccessible overhead space can shorten the payback time even further. Since you are already incurring heating and other overhead costs with the ground crop, any increase in production per square foot will greatly increase your profits.

5

Irrigation

The Science and Art of Watering

P. Allen Hammer

Watering greenhouse plants is one of the most difficult jobs growers face because watering has both a science and an art component. The *science* component is the easy part because the scientific principles can be taught and learned. The *art* of watering is extremely difficult to teach.

The Science: What Happens in the Container?

An understanding of the science of watering begins with an understanding of the relationship between the root medium and the water we apply to it. The water characteristics of a root medium in a container are very different from the water characteristics of soil in a field. Concepts such as "container capacity" and "perched water table" are very important in understanding the science of watering container plants. Perched water table means that the container has "free water" at the bottom of the container right after watering, when drainage has occurred. This means the water characteristic of the root medium in a container is similar to the container sitting in water. It's the same as if the water table of a field was within the root zone of the plants growing in that field. Very few field soils with such a water table would grow plants because the soil would be too saturated and would have very poor aeration. One of the reasons we add large particles to root media is to improve aeration, to account for the perched water table.

It's also important to understand container capacity. Container capacity means that when a container is properly watered and drainage occurs, the container is fully saturated. At this point the container's root medium holds all the water it can hold. Applying additional water will only result in more water draining out.

Figure 5-1. Irrigation is both a science and an art.

A good root medium has both water- and air-filled pores at container capacity. We often label poorly drained root media as those that contain few air-filled pores at container capacity. The science of root media is most often a balance between air-filled pores and water-filled pores. We would like a root medium to hold enough water so it doesn't have to be watered every hour, yet it must have adequate air for good root growth even when watered to container capacity.

The Art: When and How to Water?

The art of watering is determining when plants need to be watered and then applying water properly. Plants should be watered just before wilting or water stress occurs. The scientific tools available to make such a determination are expensive and aren't practical in

Figure 5-2. Even hand watering can be made easier and more accurate with the right tools.

normal greenhouse production. Therefore, the grower must make such a determination with skill and experience—the art of watering.

Outstanding growers tell me they can simply look at a crop and determine its water needs. Plants do tend to take on a dull appearance just before wilting. Growers also lift pots, and with experience and attention to detail they can accurately estimate their water content. The real art is applying water just before crop wilting, taking into consideration the particular crop, the greenhouse, and the weather.

Watering properly requires that each pot reach container capacity at each watering. This often means the containers should be watered twice (double watered) to ensure drainage of every container at each watering. With automated watering, applying water for a minute, waiting a few minutes and then applying enough water to reach container capacity provides much improved water distribution within the container. There's a very important principle in greenhouse watering: Overwatering occurs when plants are watered too frequently, not when too much water has been applied at a single watering. Remember, once container capacity is reached, excess water drains from the container. This same principle applies for both top-watered and subirrigated plants.

When watering by hand, growers should also avoid spot watering different containers of a uniform group of plants, even when some uneven drying occurs—unless they're watering the perimeters of benches because of the edge-drying effect (when plants on the outside of the bench dry more quickly than those in the middle of the bench because of increased airflow and/or light). Why not spot water? Because it increases the complexity of watering and decreases the uniformly of crop growth. Crop growth is more uniform when plants are watered uniformity, making sure each container reaches container capacity at each watering. This is why a properly designed automated overhead, drip, or subirrigation system almost always produces a more uniform crop compared with a hand-watered crop.

Figure 5-3. Overhead sprinklers, usually used outdoors but occasionally inside greenhouses as well, are the simplest form of automatic irrigation.

The Importance of Automation

Watering is one of the most important jobs in the greenhouse—and one of the most labor intensive. That's why the automation of watering should be your first automation project in the greenhouse. Of all the possible tasks to automate in the greenhouse, watering will always have the highest return on investment, often paying for itself with a single crop.

Greenhouse watering is a tough job. It must be done properly each and every time. Growers have to make watering decisions many times daily during each crop's production period, and each decision can significantly affect crop health and finished plant quality. Watering decisions can make or break a crop. That's why outstanding growers understand both the science and the art of watering. They're able to base watering decisions on both the scientific complexity of the plant as well as the constantly fluctuating greenhouse environment.

The Top Three Ways to Water: Hand, Overhead, and Drip Irrigation

Kurt Dramm

There's an old saying: "The person on the end of the hose is the most important person in the greenhouse." Without question, this task is one of the most basic to the growth of plants. It's also one of the most difficult to master. Proper irrigation technique is an art more than a science. Most growers trust their most experienced personnel with this job or do it themselves.

With that said, many tools exist that will help make the job of watering easier. From hand tools that help growers water evenly and with varying degrees of volume and coarseness, to automatic misting and overhead watering systems, the choices of irrigation equipment are extensive. Systems can be crude, such as the turret-type impact sprinklers commonly watering suburban lawns, or very precise, such as pressure-compensated drip systems that control the exact amount of water each pot receives.

Hand Watering

Even the most sophisticated greenhouses still occasionally depend on a human with a hose to water crops. Various wands equipped with special nozzles have been designed to provide a specific flow with a specific pattern and a specific coarseness. The most common nozzle used in the horticultural industry today for hand watering is the Dramm #400 Water Breaker. Invented in 1942 by John Dramm Sr., the #400 was originally available only in a machined aluminum housing. Today it is also available in ABS plastic, giving the grower a choice of weight versus durability. Water Breakers deliver large quantities of water without damage to plants or washing away the soil. Several specialized Water Breakers have been developed for watering of plugs and nursery containers.

Overhead Irrigation Systems

Nearly all growers use some sort of automatic irrigation system to save labor. Overhead sprinklers are the simplest and least expensive automatic system to install. They use multiple sprinkler heads placed throughout the greenhouse that can be turned on and off by hand, by a timer, or by a computer controller. Overhead irrigation systems are plumbed with the nozzles threaded into a PVC or galvanized pipe that's hung over the crop, or on pipe risers that stick up from the ground or through the bench. They can also be hung from individual tubes below hanging baskets without a rigid pipe. Depending on the output and coarseness of the droplets, overhead irrigation can be used for misting (for propagation) or irrigation. Boom irrigation (see page 73) is a more sophisticated method of overhead irrigation.

Drip Irrigation

Drip systems, sometimes called spaghetti tubes, utilize a supply line that delivers water to individual tubes that run to the individual plants. Each tube has some sort of weight or stake, called an emitter, to keep the line in the pot.

Figure 5-4. Drip irrigation puts a precise amount of water directly in each pot.

Traditional systems control the flow rate to each pot by the diameter of the tubing. These systems are widely used and inexpensive, and the grower can install them.

More recent advances have led to pressure-compensated systems that employ flow-controlled emitters between the supply line and the leader tube to the pot. The advantage of the pressure-compensated systems over unregulated systems is that they provide an accurate flow rate at a wide range of pressures, ensuring that each pot gets the same amount of water. Most pressure-compensated systems also employ a check valve that closes when the line is turned off, keeping the line full and ready to go. Unregulated systems without check valves drain into the lowest pots on the line each time the system is turned off, often flooding some plants while leaving others dry. After draining, each line on an unregulated system must be refilled, meaning that plants closest to the head of the line often get more water than those at the end of the line. Because of their low cost and numerous benefits, drip tubes are often one of the first laborsaving tools growers install. Their cost is minimal at $0.25–0.50/ft.^{2} ($2.70–5.38/m^2).

Another type of drip system utilizes "drip tape," which is like a hose that has built-in emitters spaced at regular intervals. The tape is laid out across the tops of the pots and positioned so that each pot has an emitter. Drip tape is most often used for field-grown crops, such as fall garden mums. It can also be attached to pipes overhead in a greenhouse to water hanging baskets suspended below it. Its benefits include low cost, quick instal-

Figure 5-5. Booms offer the benefits of overhead irrigation with considerably more precision and less waste.

lation, and the ability to easily roll it up and store it when not in use. One drawback is that the emitters can't be turned off if there are no plants under them.

Regardless of the type of drip system you choose, make sure you install a good filter in your water-line, as small particles can clog the emitters. You won't know an emitter is clogged until the plant not receiving water wilts.

Boom Irrigation

Doug Winterbottom

Boom irrigation is a method of overhead irrigation that combines two elements: a spray bar with an even spray pattern and the movement of that spray bar over a crop at a uniform height and speed. Boom irrigation is considered the most accurate

and flexible form of overhead irrigation in the greenhouse industry.

Propagators Were First

Commercial plug growers and young plant propagators were the first to use booms. These pioneers in boom irrigation first built their own boom systems, then purchased the early boom models that came on the market in the 1980s. The benefits of these early boom systems far outweighed their high cost ($6,000 and up) and unreliability.

A commercial propagator or plug producer has to think about the needs of a very small plant in a very small cell. Traditional overhead misting or sprinkler systems can easily be off by +/-60% in delivery of irrigation to that small plant. A boom can be accurate to +/-5%. A good analogy would be a surgeon operating with a butcher knife when a scalpel would do a much more accurate job.

Because growers aren't going to let some plants live and some die, an inaccurate irrigation system

Figure 5-6. The Plug Connection in Vista, California, successfully uses homemade booms to water their plug crops.

usually results in overwatering. They'll run the irrigation system long enough to deliver enough irrigation for all plants to live. This means that some plants are probably getting more irrigation than they need. This can create a whole host of problems, including non-uniform plant development, disease, delayed rooting, poor root development, and wasted water. If the grower compensates by reducing the irrigation, then some plants will become stressed due to lack of irrigation.

Booms overcame another big problem inherent in fixed overhead systems: inflexibility. Many plug growers and propagators have several different crops in a bay, each with different irrigation requirements. Standard overhead irrigation systems put out a fixed amount of water over an entire bench. Booms can be programmed to provide various amounts of water as they travel, allowing the grower to lay out the crops in any format.

Bedding Plants Were Next

Bedding plant growers started purchasing booms in quantity during the 1990s. They, too, were faced with a young plant in a fairly small growing cell. By this

time, the price of a typical boom system had come down to about $4,000. Growers found ways to install booms at the lowest possible cost per square foot. A boom system for a 21' (6.4 m) wide bay is almost the same price as a boom system for a 42' (12.8 m) wide bay because the only difference is that the spray bars are longer. The cost per square foot is almost half, because a 42' (12.8 m) boom has double the coverage area.

Booms can also be reliably run in 400–600' (122–183 m) long greenhouses. A boom system for a 600' greenhouse is just 50% more expensive than a boom for a 300' (91 m) greenhouse. This means that you get the second 300' (91 m) for half the cost of the first 300' (91 m). With proper planning, a grower can purchase booms for as little as $0.35–0.40/ft.^{2} ($3.77–4.30/m^2) for a basic system.

Some boom designs allow for moving one boom from bay to bay. This again helps to reduce the cost per square foot for boom irrigation since one boom can water several bays or several greenhouses. The drawback is the labor of moving it from place to place. But it's a good way for a small grower to make use of modern irrigation technology.

Figure 5-7. An automatic boom does exactly what the operator has programmed it to do. No human need be present.

Today, boom prices continue to decline, with individual booms costing $1,800 to $6,000 or more—but averaging about $3,500. Reliability has continued to improve over the past ten years, with several current systems offering relatively low maintenance. Boom capabilities have continued to increase. Many larger growers who were unimpressed with the value delivered by earlier booms have had second thoughts. Also, there have been many small- to medium-sized growers with a variety of applications—including in-house propagation, plug production, bedding plants and small potted crops—who now see booms as invaluable.

How Simple or Sophisticated Can You Get?

Level 1: Manual booms

Manual booms are defined as machines that require an operator to be present when they're watering. One example is the push boom. There are many examples of growers who've built their own booms. In most of these cases the boom consists of a frame on wheels, spray bars, and a hose trailing behind on the floor. The watering person literally pushes the boom from one end of the bay to the other, turning a ball valve on whenever he or she wants to water. These growers are to be admired because they recognized the benefits of booms but can't justify or afford the cost of a commercially available boom.

The pros of a manual boom are low cost and simplicity of design. The cons are uneven watering because it is dependent on the pace at which the grower is pushing the boom and high labor costs because an individual has to attend the boom when it's watering (although labor is no higher than for hand watering). Also, the longer the greenhouse bays, the less attractive this method is.

Tired of pushing their booms by hand, a few growers have attached reversible motors to their push booms. However, these booms still need an operator present in order to stop the motor and start the boom in the reverse direction.

Level 2: Automatic booms

Automatic booms do not need the operator to be present when the boom is running. These booms do exactly what they're programmed to do.

The simplest of the automatic booms treats the bay as a single zone or crop. Typically, a basic boom will water from one end of the greenhouse to the other, possibly skipping areas that the grower doesn't want to water (usually using small magnets mounted on the rail upon which the boom travels). The grower can program the boom to make a certain number of watering passes or have the boom make a single pass at intervals, such as every fifteen or thirty minutes.

Smart booms can treat the bay as multiple zones. The grower can define a series of crops in the bay and program the boom to make a number of passes at predetermined speeds over each crop or a single pass at timed intervals over each crop.

The greatest benefit of automatic booms is the valuable labor savings. The booms also deliver even irrigation at a preset speed over the crop due to their motorized control. The disadvantages are their relatively high initial cost and the regular maintenance they require. These booms incorporate multiple solenoid valves, a variable-speed DC motor, various sensors, a microprocessor controller, a hose and power cord handling system, rollers, hose hangers, and more subsystems that can fail and render them inoperable. The quality of the service provided by your boom manufacturer and their reputation for equipment reliability are key to your success with any automatic boom.

Level 3: Environmentally sensitive booms

These sophisticated automatic booms can change their watering program to adapt to changes in the greenhouse environment. This high level of control is especially important in Stages 1 and 2 of plug production and propagation.

Momentary contact

Many environmental control computers have built-in irrigation software that can open a valve or trigger a momentary contact when the irrigation software calls for watering a crop. Most current basic booms can be controlled this way. The environmental computer remotely triggers the boom to start. Since basic booms treat the bay as one zone, the bay needs to be filled with a single crop.

Boom spooler, GO-1 System

The most recent advances in boom control involve the creation of network clusters of up to sixteen booms each. These systems allow you to create various zones within each bay and control the watering of each crop uniquely, based upon changes in the environment. This approach combines the most accurate overhead delivery system (booms), flexible zoning, and control of irrigation of individual crops via the environment.

Boom Designs

Single-rail

As the name implies, single-rail booms run on a single rail centered in the bay. They're low cost and are an excellent irrigation solution for bays from 21–28' (6.4–8.5m) wide and up to 200' (61 m) long. Because these machines are lightweight and are balanced on a single rail, they're not very fast—about 60' (18 m) per minute—which is a disadvantage in light misting applications. Also, they can't support watering over more than one row of crops, which usually extends the full width of the bay. Single-rail booms cost from $1,800–3,000 each.

Double-rail

Double-rail booms run on two rails mounted about 3' (1 m) apart in the center of the bay. These booms account for probably 75% of all booms sold in the United States. They are ideal for bays from 21–42' (6.4–12.8 m) wide and up to 300' (91 m) long for propagation or plug watering, and up to 600' (183 m) long for other basic watering applications. These booms can cruise at 100–120' (31–37 m) per minute. The frame designs available can support watering of one to ten rows of crops in a bay. Cost ranges from $2,500–4,500.

Gantry

Gantry booms look like large horizontal trusses on wheels supported on rails mounted to the posts on each side of the bay. These booms are heavy duty with a life expectancy greater than the greenhouse. Gantry booms are ideal for bays from 21–45' (6.4–13.7 m) wide and up to 300' (91 m) long for propagation or plug watering, and up to 600' (183 m) long for other basic watering applications. These booms cruise at 100–120' (31–37 m) per minute. Installation is more difficult than for double-rail booms.

Figure 5-8. A gantry boom is designed for heavy-duty use in wide-span greenhouses.

Besides their heavy-duty watering capabilities, there are other possible advantages to gantry booms. Platforms have been mounted on the tops of these booms for maintenance people to work on the greenhouse or to hanging baskets above the crop. Lights have been attached to these booms for photoperiod manipulation. Also, some growers have experimented with gantry booms for moving container benches in and out of the greenhouse bays. Cost ranges from $3,500–6,000 or more.

Ground runner

Ground runner booms have a design similar to double-rail booms, but instead of running on rails suspended above the crop, these booms run on two rails mounted on the ground. These booms are primarily used outdoors. There are many installations of these booms in California, mainly at vegetable young plant nurseries. Cost ranges from $4,500–8,000. (An interesting fact about ground runner booms, according to *GrowerTalks* magazine, is that they were being tested in greenhouses as long ago as the early 1960s.)

Boom Options

Multiple sets of spray bars

Water, mist, and chemical application spray bars can be outfitted on your favorite boom. These bars can be programmed to work at various times over various crops in a bay.

Fixed or portable injectors

Chemical injectors can be plumbed into your boom's irrigation manifold to apply chemicals when needed. Portable frames have been designed that include quick disconnects, reservoirs, and injectors and can be moved from boom to boom for spot application of growth regulator or pest control chemicals.

End sweep assembly

This is an assembly at the end of the bay that allows the trolleys, hose, and power cord to move out of the way so that the boom can touch the wall at both ends of the greenhouse, allowing for maximum irrigation coverage.

Subirrigation

By Ratus Fischer and Thad Humphrey

Subirrigation comes in many styles: benches, troughs, and floors. It has many names: ebb-and-flood, ebb-and-flow, flood floors, flood benches, and gutter or trough irrigation. Regardless of the system style or name, subirrigation is based on the principle of watering from the bottom up, using capillary action of the soil to wick up water into the container.

Watering with a subirrigation system is different from watering overhead. The delivery systems look different, and the physics of water movement in the potting media is different, with considerable impact on growing practices and results. Table 5-1 compares some characteristics of subirrigation versus overhead watering.

How Does Subirrigation Work?

There are two basic styles of subirrigation systems: flooding and flowing. In a flooded system (such as trays or flood floors), plants sit on benches or concrete floors that can contain a fixed body of water that has been pumped from a storage tank. After the desired water depth is reached, typically 0.5–2.0" (13–50 mm), water is immediately drained. While one section drains, another one fills. Using this technique, large areas can be watered in a short period of time (such as several acres per hour).

In a flowing system (such as troughs or flow floors), plants sit on troughs or concrete floors that are positively sloped to continuously and uniformly displace a thin stream of water from a high point to a low point. When the desired watering is achieved, flow is stopped and watering of another section begins. Similar to flood floors, large areas can be watered in a short period of time.

Figure 5-9. Concrete flood floors are gaining in popularity because they serve as bench, heat, and irrigation system all in one.

It's generally accepted that plants (whether in pots or flats) may intake up to 90% of their water-holding capacity within the first two minutes of flooding. Consequently, an average fill and drain time of six to ten minutes per zone easily allows each container to reach full capacity, resulting in uniform watering of the crop.

Table 5-1. Subirrigation versus Overhead Irrigation

	SUBIRRIGATION	OVERHEAD IRRIGATION
WATER DISTRIBUTION	To bottom of container	To top of potting media
WATER UPTAKE	By capillary action	By seeping down
AMOUNT OF WATER UPTAKE/WATERING	Less	More
SUBSTRATE PORES	Only smaller pores filled with water	Temporarily all pores filled, risk of oxygen starvation
WATER MOVEMENT	Up only	Down first, up after watering
LEACHING	None, may lead to salt accumulation when overfertilizing	Excess water leaches. Wasteful, but can be used to manage salt content
DISEASE TRANSFER THROUGH WATERING	Possible, but rare	Through splashing

Irrigation cycle time is important because quick fill and drain times can prevent oversoaking. It's important to drain the excess irrigation water during plant uptake to minimize the potential for pathogen infiltration and distribution. Also, faster irrigation cycles within each zone allow greater control of the timing when nutrient uptake occurs.

Water storage

Irrigation water is most effectively stored in closed containers such as reservoirs or tanks. This provides a means to better control water quality as it protects water from outside contaminants in addition to minimizing loss of water due to evaporation. Filling a group of benches or a floor requires that large amounts of water be supplied in a short time, typically 50–1,500 gal. (189–5,678 L) per minute. Most plants can intake 5–25% of the water that's pumped to the floor or bench. The remaining water drains back into the storage tanks to be filtered and recycled to another zone. Most subirrigation systems are designed with two to four tanks, each containing different fertilizer solutions that can be selected according to the crops' needs.

Tanks can be installed above or below grade. Below-grade tanks usually have a higher installation cost but have several advantages. Irrigation water can return to the tanks by gravity so an energy savings is recognized because no power is required to transfer the water. If the power fails, crops won't oversoak since the floors or benches are still able to drain. The unoccupied space above the tanks can be utilized. Larger below-grade tanks are usually made on site of cast-in-place concrete, while smaller ones may be precast concrete or plastic.

Above-grade tanks have a relatively lower installed cost and can also be used where high groundwater or rocks prevent digging. In colder climates, above-grade tanks need to be protected from the elements and are best located in a heated or insulated area to limit heat loss and to prevent freezing. Larger tanks are commonly assembled from corrugated steel panels and lined with plastic. Liners have to be handled with care when cleaning sediment from the tanks. Molded plastic tanks up to 15,000 gal. (56,781 L) are also practical but may be less cost competitive with corrugated steel tanks at larger diameters.

Figure 5-10. Subirrigation systems may require above-grade storage tanks to hold the system's irrigation water.

Recycling water

Water is fully recirculated in a subirrigation system as irrigated areas are designed for containment. The water is filtered each time it returns to the tank or at the end of a multizone irrigation cycle. Special gravity filters (such as cascade filters, roll-media filters, and drum filters) can handle large volumes of water and peat fiber, which has a tendency to clog up most other types of filters. This type of coarse filtration (as small as 7 microns depending on the style of filter) has proven to be sufficient to keep the vast majority of greenhouse crops free from disease in addition to help successfully manage the water quality.

Additional water sanitation may be required for propagation, highly disease-susceptible crops, and specialized research facilities (see the section on sanitation on page 95). The high water flow rates of subirrigation systems make fine filtration, UV, ozone, heat pasteurization, and other water treatment systems rather costly. An economical option is to batch treat the water at reduced flow rates at the end of a multi-zone irrigation cycle. This may not eliminate the possibility of contamination since sanitation will not occur during the irrigation of each individual zone, but it does prevent accumulation of pathogens in the system. Chlorination, copper ionization, adding hydrogen peroxide, and other modern technologies are the more common treatment options. These can be affordable and can help control algae growth. However, they require careful monitoring to be effective and safe.

Other aspects of water quality still need to be researched. For example, some growers report that aerating the water in the holding tanks has improved their crop quality noticeably.

Replenishing water

Because subirrigation systems are recirculating, returning water to the storage tanks decreases as plants take up water. As a result, stored water should be replenished. Tank capacity should be able to contain and manage a full irrigation cycle.

There are two basic approaches to manage nutrient concentration and pH of irrigation water: supply a fixed fertilizer mix solution to each tank or maintain a fixed fertilizer concentration (which is measured by the water's electrical conductivity or EC) and pH within each tank.

Supplying a fixed fertilizer mix may be appropriate for systems with short watering times, as the return water may be nearly unchanged from its initial mix concentration and risk of dilution is minimal. It's appropriate to use computer-controlled systems to deliver different recipes on demand where multiple recipe tanks exist.

For systems with longer watering times, the return irrigation water may significantly change from its original concentration. To avoid dilution, additional fertilizer mix must be added to the solution in order to maintain a constant nutrient concentration. This can be achieved by monitoring EC and pH levels within each tank and injecting a variable mix (as needed) to balance the concentration. Where concrete storage tanks are used, extra care in monitoring pH levels is necessary due to the presence of lime in concrete.

Heat

Except in very warm climates, floor heat is essential for floor irrigation, and under-bench heat is beneficial for bench and trough systems. It allows the growing surface to dry quickly after irrigation and provides a dry microclimate in the foliage. Plus, separate control over root and foliage temperatures provides important tools to control and enhance the growth of the crops.

Automation

Automation of subirrigation systems is an opportunity for the grower to improve control of their subirrigation system while increasing system efficiency and reducing the amount of labor required for monitoring. Simple control schemes may use preset timers and level control switches to turn irrigation systems on and off, allow phasing of irrigation cycles, help replenish irrigation water, and warn of system overflows.

More complex control schemes can accommodate remote control of the entire irrigation system from a centralized location. System components may include a computer, local control panels, variable flow control to each irrigation zone (to accommodate a variety of crops), weather stations (to adjust irrigation cycling as a function of exterior climate), water quality monitoring, and automated fertilizer dosing, to name a few.

Automated systems have the ability to proactively adjust subirrigation system requirements in addition to reactively use system feedback to fine tune system set points. Now that greenhouses can have fully automated climate control systems, it makes sense to take advantage of this and integrate subirrigation systems into this control scheme.

Benches, Troughs, or Floors?

The question isn't which system is better, but which one best fits the operation's needs along with the grower's preferences and budget.

Flood benches

These come in three basic shapes: fixed benches, rolling benches, and container benches (or mobile trays).

Fixed benches

These consist of a wood or metal frame that supports a plastic or aluminum pan with walls up to 2" (50 mm) tall. Pans are typically flooded to a depth of 0.5–1.0" (13–25 mm). The bottom of the pan is usually grooved to promote drainage and reduce algae growth. Bench width is typically 6' (1.8 m) or less for easy handling of the crop. Lengths of up to 100' (31 m) are common. Fixed benches are filled and drained by pipes or hoses that connect to main feed and drainpipes. These pipes run under the benches, overhead, or under the floor where they don't interfere with traffic. Depending on the number and size of the benches, one or several benches are filled or drained at a time. Control valves (electrically operated solenoid valves or air-operated) switch between fill and drain mode.

Rolling benches

Rolling benches (or moving aisle benches) are similar to fixed benches, except they are able to laterally move a fixed distance to accommodate temporary access. Because they can move, they do not require a dedicated access aisle for each individual bench, which increases the available growing space. Consequently, rolling benches require flexible plumbing connections to each bench.

Container benches or mobile trays

This system uses smaller containers (or trays), usually 5–6' (1.5–1.8 m) wide and 12–20' (3.7–6.1 m) long, which reside on a system of conveyance tracks. They can be rolled throughout the greenhouse and can serve as a growing and transport system all in one. Since these containers don't stay in a fixed location, fill and drain piping cannot be connected to them. Containers are filled from the top by network of distribution piping rigidly connected to the greenhouse structure. Containers drain into a system of fixed gutters that are rigidly attached to the conveyance track structure. Because of the usually large number of rolling benches in a system, they're typically filled and drained in larger groups.

Trough or gutter systems

These come in similar configurations as benches. Instead of a flat bottom tray, the plants sit in mildly sloped narrow gutters. The irrigation water discharges at the upper end of the gutter and drains to the lower end, with a thin stream of water moving across the bottom of the pots along the way. Growers cite the vertical airflow between the gutters and a reduced risk of oversoaking as advantages. Although these systems limit the sizes of containers that can be grown, usually they are optimized for potted crops.

Flood floors

Flood floors are gaining popularity worldwide. Plants are grown on concrete floors, which are typically flooded to a depth of 0.5–2.0" (13–50 mm). Flexible rubber water barriers contain the water, allowing free movement of people and carts in across the floors in any direction. The watering sections usually correspond with the greenhouse bays—typically 1,000–6,000 ft.² (93–557 m²). Smaller sections allow more flexibility with crop spacing and location, while larger sections allow faster watering of large areas but also require larger tanks, pumps, and piping.

The floors are pitched from the edge to the center at approximately 0.5% slope. This is just enough to allow puddle-fee drainage while minimizing water depth profile. Depending on the width of the bay, a single V or W shape is customary. Multiple smaller

Vs will make a flatter floor, which is especially desirable for small pots and for bedding flats. A flatter floor mean less water depth is needed to give all plants a full watering and helps prevent potential oversoaking of plants at the lowest floor elevation. Also, distribution piping can be smaller. Studies have been performed at the Connecticut Agricultural Experiment Station (Hamden, Connecticut) confirming the effectiveness of a multi-V floor in contrast to a single V floor.

At the bottom of each V, a PVC pipe runs immediately under the floor to feed and drain the floor. Typically, holes are drilled through the concrete into the pipe to allow for filling and draining. It's critical that the subsurface piping be encased in concrete and anchored to the floor slab in addition to maintaining a positive seal between the pipe and floor to prevent leakage under the slab.

Figure 5-11. Flood floors allow growers to irrigation thousands or even tens of thousands of plants at one time.

Each floor is connected to the storage tank system with a main fill and a main drain line. For larger commercial greenhouses, pipe sizes typically range from 4–15" (10–38 cm), allowing flow rates ranging from 300–1,500 gal. (1,136–5,678 L) per minute.

Pouring a good concrete flood floor requires skilled installers with precision equipment (typically used in installing "super-flat" floors) and an attention to detail. The surface of the floor should be a very smooth ("hard") finish for fast drying, free of cracks and resistant to corrosion from fertilizers. Once the concrete is poured, the transmission and distribution pipes become inaccessible, so proper engineering and installation of the system's plumbing is essential if the system is to perform as expected.

Flow floors

Flow floors are a relatively new subirrigation alternative to traditional flood floors. They have the same growing area advantages to flood floor systems; however, the primary difference is the transport of water across the floor in contrast to the more traditional fill and drain approach.

Plants are placed on a precision sloped concrete floor and are irrigated by a constant thin stream of evenly distributed water that travels from the high end of the floor to the low end of the floor (typically widthwise across the bay). Water uptake occurs by capillary action until the irrigation water is shut off. The remaining water is recycled during the process. Flow floors can handle large- and small-scale growing.

Similar to a traditional flood floor, flow-floor irrigation cycle time ranges between six to ten minutes to ensure the plants are watered sufficiently. Flow floors require constant pump run time to irrigate, in contrast to a traditional flood floor, which only requires the pump to run during the fill cycle. The remaining irrigation water returns to the storage reservoirs and is available for reuse before the irrigation cycle is complete. Flow floors tend to have a lower installed cost than flood floors, as water is recycled back to each floor during each irrigation cycle. This reduces the required storage tank volume, eliminates the need for drainage valves at each floor, and may reduce subsurface distribution piping.

Which Subirrigation System Is Most Appropriate?

Flood bench and gutter/trough systems

- Practical where plants need to be at working height.
- Small irrigation units adapt to small batches of varied crops.
- With benches and troughs, plants are typically transported by hand (unless a monorail or conveyor system is installed).
- Container benches are a fast and flexible transport system.
- Maintenance can be higher, as more equipment and hardware is used.
- Life expectancy before major renovation needs is approximately ten to fifteen years.

Flood floors

- Appropriate for large and small-scale growing. Various size containers with similar watering needs can be grown on the same floor section.
- Well suited for crops that don't require intensive hand work (such as disbudding) during the growing period.
- Best use of greenhouse space, with maximum flexibility to adapt to a wide variety of crops.
- Handling plants on floor is cumbersome, but easy access allows for fast crop movement. Plant handling equipment such as gantries, forklift attachments for spacing and transport, and conveyor carts are often used.
- Combines a bench system, an irrigation system, and a heating system all in one.
- Maintenance is low.
- System life expectancy can be more than twenty years.

Growing on Subirrigation Systems

In spite of relatively high initial investment costs, subirrigation systems are attractive to growers because they work well for practically all potted crops and for most bedding plants. Watering is highly uniform; labor for watering is minimal; and flood floors (and benches, to a slightly lesser degree) allow great flexibility in crop spacing, choice of containers, and efficient use of space. (Gutter or trough systems can have additional limitations and require work to adjust gutter spacing.) Foliage doesn't get wet, so you have fewer problems with the spread of foliar diseases, thereby reducing fungicide use. Pots of different sizes can be grown in the same watering zone since capillary uptake naturally regulates the uptake. Water recirculation saves fertilizer and water costs. Plus, full recirculation of the irrigation water means zero runoff, and growers are under increasing regulatory pressures to reduce or completely eliminate irrigation water discharge.

However, subirrigation systems have their own peculiarities to consider. With traditional flood floors and bench systems (but not with troughs, flow floors or multi V flood floors), each irrigation cycle is a full watering, so partial watering to hold back the crop doesn't work. But due to the even watering in the first place, crops can be allowed to dry out more between irrigation cycles before the first plants suffer damage. Many, if not most, growers combine subirrigation with an overhead system (such as booms or overhead sprinklers) for maximum flexibility. Potting mixes have to promote good capillary action while maintaining air volume. Standard peatlite mixes with a wide range of pore sizes work well, while a high bark content in a mix can restrict water uptake.

The Future

In the Netherlands at the time of writing, reportedly up to 80% of crops are grown on subirrigation. In North America, subirrigation systems are fast becoming the predominant mode of irrigation. The initially high investment in subirrigation systems is recovered through labor savings, improved crop quality, and increased flexibility to adjust to fast-changing markets. Plus, with environmental concerns and regulations becoming a key issue for growers' long-term planning, zero runoff is insurance that will keep growers in business.

Drip Line or Flood Zone?

Jennifer Duffield White

Irrigation choices can leave growers seesawing with indecision. Flood tables, drip irrigation, or the practiced human hand? Schaefer's Greenhouses Inc., Montgomery, Illinois, has drip irrigation in about half their production space and flood tables in the other half. Mike Schaefer admits that while he likes both systems a lot, if he had to choose one over the other, he'd pick the ebb-and-flood. However, he points out that the labor savings really makes drip irrigation worthwhile. "In this day and age, with labor costs being what they are, I'd really take a good hard look at it," he says.

Capillary Mats: Another Way to Subirrigate *Bruce Zierk*

Capillary mat watering systems have been around for many years as a method of subirrigating small pots. Though not widely seen today, they were especially popular in the 1970s and early 1980s, and some growers still make use of them.

A capillary mat system consists of the mat itself, which is typically a non-woven, thick, cloth-like material, and some method of manually or automatically delivering water to the mat to saturate it. The mat is placed on a growing bench (or less commonly on the ground), usually with a waterproof material, such as polyethylene sheeting, beneath it. The pots sit on top of the mat, making contact with the wet mat and taking up water as needed through the capillary action of the media in the pots.

Capillary mat systems are fairly economical to install, especially on existing

Figure 5-12. Green Master Inc., Apopka, Florida, still makes extensive use of capillary mats. Here, owner Filip Edstrom shows the capillary fabric under his African violet crop.

benches, but have fallen out of favor due to some disadvantages. They remain wet all the time, or at least for a long time. This can result in considerable growth of algae on the mat surface. Unless the mats are thrown out after each crop, they must be cleaned and disinfected before placing another crop on the mat. This problem can be somewhat alleviated by placing a sheet of micro-perforated black polyethylene on top of the mat. Some manufacturers offer the mat material with the micro-perforated poly attached, sometimes even with convenient markings printed on the poly to make even spacing of pots easy. Another problem with mats is that since they're wet for considerable lengths of time, there's more of a problem with disease spread than with other methods of subirrigation, where disease spread is virtually nonexistent.

Capillary mat systems are still used very successfully today by some growers, especially for niche crops such as African violets, or when growing large numbers of very small potted plants.

Figure 5-13. At Schaefer's Greenhouses, they make good use of drip and flood irrigation.

Drip Time

At Schaefer's Greenhouses, they grow and retail high-quality pot plants along with standard bedding flats. Hand-watering tens of thousands of plants each day becomes a daunting and sometimes unprofitable task, and drip irrigation usually pays for itself in labor savings. It's a simple system and can be equated to hand watering, except you do it all at once. You can even follow the same fertilizer regimes as you would with hand watering.

With drip irrigation, Mike says they have to keep an eye out for the occasional emitter that falls out of the pot. In addition, the outside rows on the end of the bench (the last emitters in the zone) tend to plug up from time to time and they occasionally need to touch up the end of the benches with a hose. Mike recommends walking the aisles every morning if you have drip irrigation (a good practice no matter what) to look for out-of-place leader tubes or problem spots.

Overall, the main drawback with drip irrigation at Schaefer's is that they aren't set up to recycle the water, as they do with their ebb-and-flood system. Depending on the growing media, the water can sometimes run right through the pot, causing them to run the system longer than normal and wasting water. However, compared to hand watering, it's still vastly more economical.

Flood Zone

At Schaefer's, flood tables are the preferred choice for the large quantities of 4.5" (11 cm) material destined for their retail garden center. Mike raves about the ebb-and-flood benches and notes they haven't run

into any disease problems. While plants seem to dry out a bit quicker, it only take about seven minutes to thoroughly wet them again.

The computer-controlled system simplifies the hectic life of a grower, as it monitors EC levels and automatically adjusts fertilizer formulations for each bench. However, Mike cautions that growers must still pay attention to the EC levels, as you don't tend to need as much fertilizer with this method of watering.

Remember to clean your tanks out two to three times a year, or after every crop cycle, he says. Sanitize the benches and maintain good cultural practices to avoid disease problems.

Which Plant Where?

While you might think anything in a pot is suitable for drip irrigation, keep in mind that spacing will dictate the number of leader tubes you need. Drip irrigation works great with poinsettias that sit five or six across a bench. But with geraniums in 4.5" (11 cm) pots spaced close together, you'll probably find the high number of leaders needed for one bench to be counterproductive.

While they've successfully grown nearly every crop in every size pot on their flood benches, including bedding flats, Schaefer's reserves the benches mainly for 4, 6, and 6.5" (10, 15, and 16.5 cm) potted plants. Three-quarters of their geranium crop grow on ebb-and-flood benches; the other quarter receives hand watering. This includes their smaller poinsettias, bedding plants and 4.5" (11 cm) mums. The 6.5" (16.5 cm) mums and other large pot plants are grown with drip irrigation.

Again, when you're considering your irrigation choices, think about your labor costs, the size and types of crops you produce, and what you want your automatic watering system to accomplish. Remember you don't necessarily have to choose one system over the other. Most growers use several—including the ever-essential hose.

Mist Systems for Propagation

Bryce Anderson

Mist systems are an important part of any greenhouse operation, as they play a vital role in the production of both seed and vegetative plant material. Their fundamental purpose is to deliver an intermittent source of water in low volumes to plant material being vegetatively propagated or to seeds being germinated. Mist systems, when compared with irrigation systems, typically deliver a smaller particle of water for shorter intervals of time. Depending on how a mist system is used and the type of crop it's being used on, the crop's production period can either be accelerated or slowed.

There are many types of mist systems available, including traditional inline, upright mist nozzles; inverted mist nozzles with leak prevention devices; irrigation booms with mist heads; and water- or air-driven fogging nozzles. Mist systems can be operated manually or automatically.

Nozzle Spacing

The most common mist systems used in greenhouses consists of a series of mist nozzles inserted into a water-supply pipe suspended over the propagation area, whether a bench or section of ground. A common misting diameter for nozzles is 6' (1.8 m) wide, which can be delivered in a circle, half circle, or oval spray pattern. Nozzle spacing is dependent on the size of the area you intend to cover, considering width as well as length. The objective is to achieve an ideal overlapping spray pattern of the mist nozzles to reach optimum uniformity and distribution of the water being delivered. When determining the proper spacing of the nozzles, it's important to follow each manufacturer's installation instructions.

Nozzles installed upright in a series are typically placed 6–12" (15–30 cm) above the crop. You will need to consider which crops you'll be producing and the types of containers they'll be started in to determine a height that will accommodate all possible scenarios. Plant material or containers that obstruct the misting pattern can greatly influence the uniformity and distribution of the mist. It may be to your advantage to make your system height adjustable if you'll be misting crops with a variety of heights. However, if these crops will be mixed with one another throughout the production schedule, it's best to settle on a height that will accommodate all of them.

Figure 5-14. Mist nozzles are used to put out a fine mist for a short duration to keep cuttings or seeds moist during propagation.

Attaching the Nozzles

There are multiple ways to attach mist nozzles to the supply pipe, and water pressure will influence which method you choose. Many nozzles have a male threaded end that can be directly screwed into the supply pipe. It's fairly easy to drill and tap the holes yourself. This is most desirable under high-pressure situations—50 psi and up. Another option uses a rubber grommet that's inserted into a predrilled hole in the supply pipe. When the nozzle is screwed into the grommet, the grommet expands and holds the nozzle in place. There are also threaded adapters available that can be installed into threaded holes or grommets. The threaded adapters are used when the mist nozzle being used has a compression fitting. These two options should only be used when water pressure is 45 psi or less to avoid blowing the grommet out of the pipe.

Inverted Nozzles

Another option for a fixed mist system uses inverted mist nozzles. These have the same considerations as upright nozzles as far as spacing is concerned, with the primary difference being they're mounted facing downward. With an inverted mist system, nozzle height above the crop is usually 3–4' (0.9–1.2 m), which provides a height that will accommodate most crops being produced without any major adjustments needing to be made.

The nozzles can be directly inserted into the supply pipe using the same methods as the upright method. Some manufacturers also offer a hanging assembly to serve as a secondary water delivery tool. The hanging assemblies are available in varying lengths and will allow you to place your water supply pipe as far above the mist area as you wish to avoid any unwanted obstruction. The hanging assembly is inserted into the water supply pipe at the same spacing recommended for the mist nozzles and the nozzles attach to the end of the hanging assembly.

Mist nozzles for any stationary application are available with and without a leak-prevention device. A leak-prevention device serves as a shut-off for the nozzle when the mist is turned off to prevent water from draining from the pipe and dripping onto the plant material below. It's advantageous to select a nozzle with a leak-prevention device for any inverted mist system. For upright mist systems, a pressure-relief valve can be used to drain water from the water supply pipe after the mist cycle has been terminated. Pressure-relief valves operate on water pressure alone and are located at the end of the water supply pipe. To work properly, the water supply pipe is usually sloped to one end and the pressure-relief valve is located on the low end. When the mist cycle begins and water pressure increases, the valve closes, allowing water to be forced through the mist nozzles. When the mist cycle ends and water pressure drops, the valve opens, allowing any water remaining in the water supply pipe to be drained away. This prevents the water from dribbling out of the nozzles onto the crop below. A pressure-relief valve can be used on an inverted mist system; however, any water remaining in the hanging assembly won't be carried away and will dribble onto the plant material below.

Costs and Options

Mist systems are relatively inexpensive to install. Piping can be the greatest contributing factor to their cost based on the type of pipe you select. Polyethylene tubing is the least expensive but should only be used for inverted systems that utilize a hanging assembly and should always have proper support to prevent sagging. Schedule 40 or schedule 80 PVC and galvanized pipe are options for all mist systems and would cost more, respectively. Taking these factors into consideration, costs could range from $0.25–0.75/ft.^{2} ($2.69–8.07/m^2).

Regardless of which mist system you choose,

there are several requirements and options that all mist systems have. Since the orifice of a mist nozzle is very small, most manufacturers require water to be filtered by a 140–200 mesh screen prior to the mist system to prevent clogging. Filters range in price from $15–300, depending on the volume of water they need to accommodate. Some nozzles have a recommended operating pressure and may require a pressure regulator. Pressure regulators range from $5–50, depending on the style and size your operation requires.

Controlling the Mist

Operation of your mist system is the single greatest consideration. There are many options for operation. The least expensive, as well as the least efficient, would be using a manual ball valve to turn the system on when mist is desired. This requires constant monitoring and allows little room for error. Forgetting to turn on the mist one time could be the end of your crop.

The most practical method is to use a low-voltage solenoid valve wired to a time clock that will automatically turn the mist on and off. Solenoid valves are inexpensive, costing $15 and up, and are available in a variety of sizes to match the size of your system's piping. Time clocks vary greatly in price. A simple lamp timer may be used to turn the mist on or off at predetermined times but allows the least flexibility in mist cycle time and duration.

There are controls available that are specifically for mist systems that range from $200–$500 and can accommodate one or more mist zones. These controls usually have a twenty-four-hour time clock and allow the flexibility of choosing the amount of time between mist cycles in minutes as well as hours. They also allow mist cycle times from a few seconds to several minutes. Some have a built-in sun sensor that automatically turns the mist off at night, if mist is undesirable.

Most computer environmental controls are capable of managing mist systems and inputs for mist cycle occurrences and duration are limitless. Unless you are currently using one, computer environmental controls can run into the thousands of dollars by the time they're installed and offer the most expensive alternative to mist control.

Figure 5-15. Mist controllers range from simple time clocks to sophisticated computer controls.

Booms and Fog

Traveling booms with mist nozzles can be useful for misting large areas. Programming and stop/start magnets can be used to control the mist cycles in the same manner that stationary boom irrigation is performed.

For crops requiring an ultra-fine mist, fog nozzles may be used. Fog nozzles provide the smallest water particle size available. Fog nozzles usually have a smaller fogging diameter than mist nozzles and require much higher water pressure, usually 800–1,000 psi, generated by a high-pressure pump, to obtain their very small particle size. Fog nozzles may be water-pressure driven, which is the common type used in greenhouse bench or floor systems, or air driven, the type used in seed germination rooms where high humidity is desired and an air source is easily added. Fog systems can be controlled using the same timers as mist systems or by using a humidistat. A humidistat can be a simple wall-mount type that triggers a solenoid valve to open a water or air source when a drop in humidity occurs or a humidity sensor integrated into a computer environmental control system that has multiple set points.

Hydroponics

John DeVries

Growing hydroponically allows for environmentally sustainable production of plants, fruits, and flowers. Many of the technological advances available to a grower are rooted in the adaptability of the hydroponic growing method.

Hydroponic plant culture is one in which nutrients are supplied to the plant through the irrigation water. The growing substrate is soilless (mostly inorganic), which takes us out of the ground and allows for many different growing systems to be considered for use. Hydroponics is all about water, with the soilless growing media used to support the plant root system physically and provide for a favorable buffer of solution around the root system.

In horticulture, hydroponic systems are used in greenhouses to produce cut flowers or vegetables which are harvested from long-lasting stock plants such as roses, gerbera daisies, and fruit-producing tomatoes. The same growing concepts are used to grow fast spring annual crops and many potted crops.

Types of Systems

A hydroponic system can be one of two types: open or closed. An open system is one in which the nutrient solution (water and fertilizer) is applied to the plants, with any runoff, or leachate, from the plant container going to waste. A closed system recaptures this leachate and stores it for reuse. A closed system must be constantly monitored (manually or by computer control) to make sure it stays within the desired nutrient parameters. Disease must be monitored in a closed system, as the reused solution from an unhealthy plant can infect other plants within the system. Different types of water disinfection units are available to manage the risk of a disease outbreak. Hydroponics started as an open system and then, with the help of technology, moved to a more sustainable closed system. More and more focus is put on how we use our raw water resource, so the closed system presents many opportunities to use water most effectively.

Growing Media

Hydroponic culture allows commercial growers to more effectively steer the plant in the direction they find most desirable: toward the development of plant structure/leaves, or toward flower and/or fruit production. Part of this steering is made possible by choosing a growing medium that has favorable characteristics. Physical and chemical properties are considered here. Physical characteristics include its water-holding capacity and porosity. Chemical characteristics include its ability to store and release nutrients and any soluble nutrients that may be

Figure 5-16. Hydroponic tomato production in a Dutch greenhouse.

naturally present in the medium. Many different types of growing media are used in hydroponics. Perlite, sawdust, peat moss, rock wool, and coconut fibers are common. Since all of them are viable choices, a grower's decision usually depends on what's locally available and which one offers the most industry support.

The size of container is also important. When the plant has a root system developed into a media that has a very large volume, it can be difficult to control the moisture content within the media. If this large volume of media becomes too wet, it will be difficult to dry it out before having a negative effect on the plant. Conversely, when a low volume of media is used, it can be difficult to maintain a constant level of moisture content; it can easily dry out and cause plant damage.

Through the selection of the growing media, a grower has the power to choose the nutrient make up that is delivered to the plant as well as determining how the growing media will "respond" to nutrient and water applications.

How Hydroponics Works

The hydroponic system is used to control the supply of water and nutrients to the crop throughout the entire growing season. A sample of the raw irrigation water must be tested to determine its suitability for the crop to be grown. The water's suitability is determined by whether its minor and major nutrients are within certain parameters. With this test it's also determined what the water will require to bring its pH (acidity/alkalinity) into an acceptable range. With the above test complete and given that the water is suitable, the grower will make a schedule of chemical fertilizers that will be mixed with the irrigation water to produce the nutrient solution that the plant requires.

This fertilizer is dissolved in water into concentrated stock tanks. A fertilizer-injecting unit then injects the solution into the greenhouse irrigation system. The irrigation system applies a controlled amount of this solution to the soilless growing media. This can be done very accurately to each and every plant.

The type of irrigation system to be used is dependent on a few factors, including accuracy, plant container system, the crop or crops being grown, and cost effectiveness. The most common types of irrigation systems for hydroponics are ebb-and-flood and drip emitters.

A certain amount of extra nutrient solution is required to be given to the plants. This means that more solution is given compared to what the plant needs for evaporation and plant processes. This over-watering allows the grower to keep balanced nutrient and pH levels in the root zone. For this reason a collection system is usually employed to recapture the extra solution that drains from the plant container (a closed system). A common collection system is a seamless metal trough that runs the length of the plant row and drains into a main collection pipe. This pipe then drains into collection tanks to await treatment and reuse. The drainage solution doesn't usually come back from the plants with the same composition as when it was pumped to them, so before it is reapplied, it is usually mixed with fresh water and adjusted back to the desired solution the grower has in mind. Computer controls are typically used to manage the system.

Why Use Hydroponics?

When compared to traditional soil-based culture, hydroponics has its greatest advantages in higher productivity and more efficient use of water and fertilizer. A hydroponic growing system offers a sterile growing medium for the crop to start in. This reduces the risk of soil-borne diseases, which can greatly reduce a crop's productivity or wipe it out altogether. A hydroponic system has the advantage of capturing and reusing all of the nutrient solution that drains off of the crop. Some municipalities now require that greenhouses not allow any waste nutrient solution to be released outside of the greenhouse. A closed system is the only way of achieving this.

Local urban production is now possible. Arable land is not necessary when you can grow in a container which in turn can be incorporated in the greenhouse structure. In fact, "land" may not be necessary as we see the beginning of rooftop growing structures. With hydroponics, the plants can be grown in a way that enables a more efficient and enjoyable labor component. Stooping to the ground level is a thing of the past when all your plants are grown at a height you choose. Because of advances in the greenhouse climate and use of natural bugs to control pests, "fresh," "quality," and "pesticide free" are all labels made possible for crops in large part to hydroponics.

Fertigation Equipment

Al Zylstra

Fertigation is the common term for the application of liquid fertilizer through the irrigation system. Concentrated water-soluble fertilizer is mixed into the water using a wide variety of fertilizer injection or dosing equipment. It's the standard method of fertilizer application throughout the industry and is commonly used as a sole source of nutrient application.

Why Liquid Fertilizers?

The characteristics of liquid fertilizers are generally more easily understood and are more predictable than granulated fertilizers and are less affected by other environment factors. Liquid fertilizers allow you to maintain more precise and flexible control of application timing and quantities than do slow-release fertilizers mixed in the growing media or soil. Fertigation can also be used to supplement media that's been enhanced with slow-release fertilizers.

There are a wide variety of injectors and mixing units available for applying liquid fertilizer to your crops, from simple portable units that connect to a garden hose to sophisticated computer-controlled mixing stations, supplying multiple feeds to an entire facility. At the highest end, computer-controlled injection stations can continuously monitor the irrigation water, including its pH, EC (electroconductivity, which is a measure of fertilizer levels), and temperature and will inject acid, fertilizer, micronutrients, and heat the water, as needed.

System Design

There's no simple key to selecting the unit appropriate for your facility or application. However, there are three important concepts that will help in the design of an effective fertigation system.

Design the system, don't just select an injector

By its very nature, fertigation is an integrated system, not simply a piece of equipment or an injector. The

Figure 5-17. Pictured here is a sophisticated and complex irrigation injection system at Plantpeddler, Cresco, Iowa.

injector itself is not a fertigation system any more than the engine under the hood is a car. The performance of an effective system is dependent on the cohesive integration of everything from the water source to the irrigation emitters at the crop. This includes the injection pumps, but equally critical is the proper sizing and positioning of pumps, valves, piping, sensors, controls, and tanks as well as the proper selection of the control system that manages it all.

Start at the plant and work backward

Since the system is simply a means to feed the plants, we should begin with the type, amount, and frequency of feed the plants need. Many growers choose to use a single constant feed, generally at a lower dose, for their entire greenhouse facility, which works fine if done correctly. Many growers are replacing this practice with more selective feeding systems that are based on the specific requirements of each group of crops. Today's automated and often computerized fertilizer mixing systems make it much easier to feed each crop or group of crops with individually formulated feed regimens to meet individual crop requirements. So, instead of picking an injector style and then trying to make it do what you need, look at your crops and their individual requirements, then work backward to determine the performance requirements of the sys-

tem as a whole. The type of injector to use will become apparent in the process.

How does that work? Starting with the plant, the particular crop culture determines the type of water-distribution device needed. Mist, overhead sprinklers, drip tubes, traveling boom, flood floor, benches or troughs, or hand watering? Each type of device has different pressure and volume requirements and tolerances to water turbidity and, consequently, places different demands on the system used to inject fertilizer and chemicals.

Next, the volume and pressure requirements at the emitter determine the valve and pipe sizing of each branch. All irrigation devices operate best within a specific range of water pressures. While drip or dribble emitters operate only at low pressures and require that the pressure be reduced; devices such as boom irrigators, mist emitters, and precision sprinkler heads may require minimum pressures of 30–60 psi for proper flow characteristics and distribution patterns. The pressure drop of the fertilizer injector, piping, and valves must be taken into consideration to assure the appropriate pressure to the emitters.

You will next need to decide how you want to feed. Will you feed with the same fertilizer at every irrigation or will you change feeds or use clear water at some irrigations? How will the system be controlled? How many different feed solutions are required in your facility? How frequently will you change the feed solution? Do you need to inject acid to adjust the crop pH? If so, do you need the same pH for all crops or will that vary? What type of acid will you use? All types of injectors don't handle all types of acid.

Finally, decide how you want to control the system. Controls range from turning a knob on an injector unit, manually opening the valve on each bench, and testing the water with a kit to a fully computerized system that does everything including heating the water to the optimum temperature for the root zone. A good control system will manage your system based on the volume and pressure capacity of the water source (well or city water) and can dramatically reduce the sizing of the fertigation system and your overall water demand. Some growers report reduction of overall water use by as much as 70% through the use of computer controls. Today's computer controls are reasonably priced and, given the savings on water use and installation of other components, may be a good choice for most growers, regardless of size.

All of these requirements combined into a common system or systems will yield the specification for your fertilizer injection and mixing system.

Work with a professional

Equipment manufacturers and vendors know system design, so take advantage of their knowledge and experience by getting their help when you're ready to design a fertigation system.

Injector Types

There are a wide variety of injector units that can be assembled to meet virtually any fertigation requirement. Ranging from simple hose-end venturi units costing less than $20 to sophisticated, multiple feed centralized systems, any injector system will inject and mix fertilizer to varying degrees of accuracy. You need to evaluate the components in view of the design and cost of the entire system. Examples abound where poor performance and the need for more units and the higher cost of related piping and valves to accommodate higher flows negate the lower cost of simple units and controls. Conversely, some growers have installed expensive, sophisticated systems where a simple, inexpensive dosing unit would have done the job nicely.

Bypass pressure tank

This provides simple and cheap inline dosing. The fertilizer solution is contained in a bag or bladder inside a pressure tank. A control valve mounted on the water main or bypass creates a pressure differential that forces the stock solution through a mixing valve and into the water flow. These systems allow only limited flexibility by adjusting the mixing valve to change the flow of solution. This system requires frequent refilling of the stock solution and tends to become less accurate as the solution is depleted and with changes in water pressure. It's good for a single small crop but isn't a viable, long-term solution.

Venturi proportioner

Best known by the trade name Hoz-On, the venturi proportioner is perhaps the simplest device available for injecting liquid fertilizer. The venturi concept is broadly used in devices as simple as a home gardener applicator to the most sophisticated computer-controlled injector units. A tube is installed on a bypass on the water main or in the line itself, and the resulting pressure differential siphon solution from the tank and into the water stream. This assures a proportional stream of solution into the water and relies only on water turbulence or a downstream pressure tank for adequate mixing. These devices are inexpensive and reliable. However, in their basic form they lack flexibility. Proper filtering of the fertilizer stock solution is important to prevent clogging of the venturi's small inlet. The accuracy of a venturi is quite pressure sensitive, so it's important to provide constant pressure in the line with a regulator to assure a consistent injection ratio. A venturi also creates a significant pressure drop that must be compensated for in the initial line pressure. The pressure drop can also be overcome by installing the venturi in a small bypass line, diverting some flow off of the water main and using a lower injection ratio or higher concentrate in the stock solution to compensate for the partial flow.

The use of venturi injectors has become popular in recent years in many high-speed computer-controlled injection systems because of their simple reliability and low cost. In this application, multiple venturis are installed on a bypass line to inject multiple stock solutions or staged to accommodate higher turndown ratios. In these systems, small direct-acting valves are installed on the siphon tube to allow the computer to control the feed rate into each venturi.

Volumetric flow-through injectors

Available from Dosatron, Dosamatic, and Smith, to name three, these units are the ubiquitous workhorses of the horticulture industry and are a cost-effective solution for many applications. Simple in design, the water enters one side of the unit, forcing up a piston. This action draws in the stock solution from a stock tank under the unit and into the chamber of water. The force of the water then pushes the piston back down, expelling the mixture of water and fertilizer out the other side always in proportion to water flow. Units are available in a range of capacities, from 10–200 gal. (38–757 L) per minute. The feed ratio can be adjusted manually.

Each unit will proportion through a range of flows, up to its maximum rating, with reasonable accuracy. These units are relatively inexpensive, making them good for small facilities and startup operations. Many large operations also use them for touch-up watering or special crop requirements. Their best application is where only a single stock solution is used and the flow range is relatively narrow. They can be mounted on

a cart to make a handy portable unit or mounted on watering booms to serve up a special solution for each boom. These units are limited in their ability to handle high flow ranges and can't be directly controlled by a computer. It's possible, however, to utilize them in a computer-controlled system by placing them in a parallel manifold connected to computer-selectable valves.

High-pressure, positive-displacement pumps

This category includes the broadest selection of pumps, which can be configured to handle a wider range of flows and are more easily controlled by a computer than other devices are. The water doesn't run through the pumps; instead, the pumps are remotely located and inject the solution through a tube and fitting into the pipe. They're capable of injecting solution into a high-pressure line, generally up to 120 psi. Positive displacement pumps can be powered electrically, pneumatically, or hydraulically (water). These pumps also require a water flow meter in the line, which is connected to a controller to adjust injection rates according to flow. The flow meter can create a substantial pressure drop that must be accounted for in the initial pressure of the system. Accuracy and capability to handle higher turndown ratios (see "Understanding Turndown Ratio" on page 93) vary depending on the type of injector selected, the number of pumps, the method of control, and the type and configuration of flow meter.

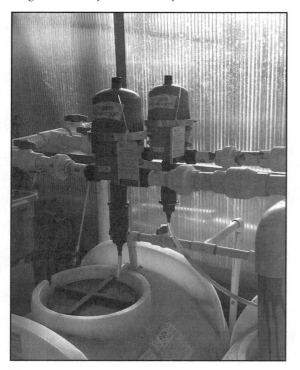

Figure 5-18. Flow-through injectors offer low-cost, accurate chemical injection. They can be installed in place or attached to a cart or hand truck for portable use.

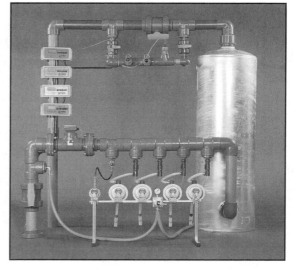

Figure 5-19. Water-powered pumps have been around for years and are widely used. You can easily expand their capability by adding pump heads.

Water-powered pumps

Manufactured by companies such as Bartel and Andersen, these are common and are generally controlled only volumetrically through the flow meter control. Adjusting the ratio requires a manual adjustment on the pump head, although the use of computer-controlled direct-acting valves can automate this.

Electric pumps

These are also commonly used and are controlled volumetrically through water meter control. Ratios can be adjusted by hand or directly via a controller. Pump units are available in multiple sizes to match various flows, so they work well where separate feeds are desired for individual greenhouse areas. There are a wide variety of pump styles available, the most common being reciprocating piston and diaphragm style.

Understanding Turndown Ratio   *Al Zylstra*

Water flow turndown ratio is the ratio between the highest flow rate and the lowest flow rate passing through the fertilizer injection system.

Any injection system can be easily configured to achieve a high level of accuracy at a fixed constant flow rate. Accuracy becomes increasingly difficult to achieve when the flow rates vary, and the more they vary the more difficult it becomes. This has become more of an issue in recent years as operations have become larger, causing maximum flows to increase while the minimum flow is nearly always the same ... one person with a hose in his hand. Dealing with this requires an understanding of how fertilizer injection systems deal with varying flows. It's much more complex than how fast an injector can pulse fertilizer into the line. Even injector units that claim to meet high turndown ratios can't do that if the supporting systems aren't designed correctly.

If the highest flow rate when the maximum number of valves are operating is 100 gal. (379 L) per minute and the lowest flow rate is a person on a hose at 5 gal. (19 L) per minute, the ratio is calculated as 100 divided by 5 (379 divided by 19), or 20, which yields a turn-down ratio of 20:1. Achieving accurate fertilizer injection and mixing at all flow rates is critical, and the higher the turn down ratio is, the more difficult it becomes to achieve an acceptable level of accuracy. This is particularly true with traveling irrigation booms and hand watering where inconsistent fertilizer injection means one pot or group of pots may be watered with a different concentration than the next.

Turndown ratios can often be as high as 30:1, 40:1, 50:1, or even more, particularly where outdoor field irrigation is combined with greenhouse watering on a single system. To meet these high ratios, a system must begin with a good-quality turbine water meter (not a paddle wheel type) that's sized to measure the flows accurately over the complete flow range. A meter that measures accurately at 100–200 gpm probably won't be so accurate at 5–10 gpm in the same system. Still, even the most accurate flow meter must be installed in the proper place and in the correctly sized section of pipe to achieve accurate resolution of flow. Placed too close to an elbow or other constriction, the back pressure may affect the accuracy of the meter; and in a pipe section that's too large, it will reduce accuracy; and in a pipe that's too small, it may restrict the range, create too much pressure loss, or both. And finally, it must be connected to the correct transducer to translate the correct resolution. If the transducer can't resolve the reading to less than 10 gpm, it can't possibly give accurate readings from a meter at 5 gpm.

Injectors must also be able to accurately deliver nutrients over the full range of flow. At a turndown ratio of only 10:1 (50 gpm/5 gpm), 200 parts of accurate linear resolution are required to provide an absolute accuracy of +/-5% reading at the low flow rate. Higher turn down ratios require proportionally more resolution. This level of resolution is impossible to achieve using conventional controls, such as variable-speed drive motors coupled to positive displacement pumps, particularly when working against variable line pressures. More sophisticated control methods, generally only available from computerized controls, are required, along with a sufficient blending tank to absorb and smooth out the bumps. Additionally, external mixing forces (e.g., aerator, water jet, or paddle wheel) may be required at lower flow rates simply because there is insufficient energy contained in slow-moving water to do the job. At higher flow rates, there's sufficient turbulence to complete the mixing.

Fixed-flow injection systems with low turndown ratios are much easier to design and operate with reasonable accuracy. These systems must be controllable only over a very narrow range, allowing sufficient accuracy with lower resolution and generally less costly meters, injectors and controls. Irrigation systems designed to operate only one valve or set of valves at a time are good candidates for this type of system. If the flow rates change later, you may need to reengineer and reconfigure the system to match the new flows.

Peristaltic pumps, long used in the medical and research industry for their simplicity and reliability, are also finding their way into new fertigation injector applications. One way electric pumps set themselves apart is by adapting easily to computer control. The pump's pulsing frequency, and in some cases the amount injected per pulse (stroke), can be automatically adjusted, allowing the computer to change feed ratios on the fly. This makes electronic pumps ideal for centralized systems where multiple feeds and feed ratios are desired from a single system.

While a centralized computer-controlled system can work quite well for automatically changing feed solutions, an important detail to remember is what you'll do with the previous feed already in the lines after you make the change. This can become a somewhat complex problem, particularly when it is necessary to avoid applying a particular feed to certain crops. It can be handled by either feeding out the remaining feed or purging the lines manually or automatically.

Dilute tank systems

Dilute tank systems are an increasingly popular alternative to inline injection. Fertilizer is dosed or injected into an atmospheric (open) tank and pre-mixed with the water rather than injected in concentrated form directly into the stream of water. The water is then re-pressurized with a pump for delivery out to the irrigation devices. This same pump can also serve for agitation (mixing) of the tank. This system allows the use of simple, low cost, and even relatively inaccurate low-pressure dosing pumps while still achieving excellent accuracy and smooth control. One of the most significant benefits of a dilute tank system is the ability to achieve excellent turndown ratios, particularly when large tanks are used. Because the fertilizer is pre-mixed with the water, it doesn't matter if it is served up with an eyedropper or a fire hose—the mixture is always accurate.

In simplistic terms, dilute tank systems come in two basic types—the defining difference being the size of the tank. Systems with large tanks are slow, lazy systems that have plenty of time to add and mix the correct fertilizer dilute ratio. The tanks are typically sized to hold fifteen to thirty minutes of irrigation water (for example, a 100 gpm flow rate requires a 1,500–3,000 gal. [5,678–11,356 L] tank). A large tank enables the use of simple, inexpensive, low-capacity dosing pumps. The primary disadvantages of these systems are that the tanks require a relatively large floor space, and if you want to change feeds it requires either an additional tank for each feed or draining and refilling the large tank. Still, for many operations it's the epitome of simplicity and safety.

High-speed dilute tank systems are also available. These units use a very small blending tank, with a typical holding capacity of only thirty seconds to perhaps two minutes of irrigation water capacity. These units mix the fertilizer solution on the fly in the small tank and rely on the turbulence of rapidly exchanging water to provide adequate mixing. This in turn limits the accuracy in applications with high turndown ratios. Because the water passes through the tank very quickly, it requires more expensive, more precise high-speed pumps and injection valves to achieve reasonable accuracy. Like their larger cousins, the pump re-pressurizes the water out to the greenhouse. The primary advantages of these systems are the ability to change feed solutions quickly and their relatively small space requirements. While they tend to be more expensive, they are typically pre-mounted on a rack and delivered ready to connect and use, while the large-tank systems are built on site.

When it comes to prices of injection equipment, you need to think in terms of a system. Granted, for simple injection jobs, a flow-through injector and the necessary plumbing will cost you as little as $500–2,500. A more sophisticated system, with two injector heads for nutrients and one for acid, can cost $5,000, plus controls. A large grower with complex fertigation requirement may spend $30,000–50,000 on a fertigation system.

Fertigation Room Design

Begin the design of your fertigation system by setting aside a designated area for the greenhouse "crop kitchen." This area will house the mechanical systems and preparation facilities that comprise the actual fertilizer and chemical handling, injection, and mixing functions. Ever-increasing safety regulations are another reason for having a dedicated fertigation room. Ideally, this area should be enclosed with a locking door, be well ventilated, and be in an area not typically occupied by people. This will provide safe storage for labeled chemicals and caustic fertilizers and acids. The room shouldn't be exposed to natural sunlight because even indirect sunlight will encourage algae growth in tanks and on wet floors. It's also hard on plastic or PVC components and piping commonly found in most systems. Exposing sensors and pipes to heat, from the sun or any other source, will have a negative effect on sensor accuracy and reliability as well as injector performance.

A hot water source with a hose attachment should be available for mixing fertilizers and for cleanup tasks, and a large sink should be installed for rinsing chemicals from skin as well as other mixing and lab functions. An eye wash station at the sink is a good idea, too.

A curbed area or pan, with a drain, should surround the injection and mixing equipment and the area used for filling and mixing tanks. This provides for catching overflow, cleaning water, and spillage of chemicals or treated water. The drain should empty into an isolated sump rather than the regular or storm sewer, where it can evaporate or be sprinkled onto a field or landscaping. While law may not require it now, it probably will in the future, and taking care of this now will most likely make any inspector happier than seeing haphazard attention to runoff and environment safety.

Install a small workstation in the fertigation room where you can keep a log of fertilizer applications and stock mixes, a list of safety requirements, and the required regulation compliance forms. This, too, will make any inspector happy. While you're at it, put a pH and EC test kit here and use them regularly to check the accuracy of your feed solutions and injector unit output.

Other Design Considerations

Stock tanks
Use a stock tank that will hold several days' worth of stock solution. This reduces labor and assures a more consistent mix. If you plan to switch solutions throughout a week, use a separate tank with a simple manual valve system to switch tanks. Use warm water, at 140–160°F (60–71°C), to dissolve soluble fertilizer material and assure better suspension. Make sure that your drain or foot valve is installed at a point 2–3" (5–7.5 cm) up from the bottom of the stock tank to prevent pulling precipitates and other sediment into the injector units. Tanks should be kept in the fertigation room and kept free of debris.

Filters
Adequate filtration is always a critical consideration with any irrigation application. Filtration is recommended downstream of the injectors to remove fertil-izer precipitate and other sediment deposits that can clog irrigation devices. In many injection systems the water has little or no contact with the injector pump itself, and a simple strainer before the injection units may be adequate. However, flow-through injectors and other water-powered injectors will benefit from filtration upstream of the injector to extend the life of the injector, where elevated turbidity can damage seals, valves, and other moving parts.

Water hammer
Excessive pressure and the pulsing action created when a valve suddenly closes or opens cause water hammer. This nasty phenomenon can damage piping, valves, and the injector unit. There is sufficient energy to separate pipes, damage the piston mechanism in an injector, or bypass a solenoid valve. Proper engineering, including correct pipe sizing and layout, and choosing the appropriate valves based on flows and pressure, generally reduce or prevent water hammer problems. However, appropriately placed check valves and water hammer arrestors can be added, if needed.

Backflow protection
This is required by most municipal water systems, but it's a good idea even if it isn't required. You may have a backflow preventer installed at the main service into your facility, but you should install another one directly upstream of any inline injector and downstream of any pump or T fitting just before the injector. A vacuum breaker or relief valve allows air to enter when there is no pressure in the line, thus preventing back pressure and siphoning. These simple devices prevent treated water from flowing or siphoning back into and contaminating a fresh water system.

Water Recycling and Sanitation

Al Zylstra

Day to day, season to season, there is no more critical input than water to supply hydration and nutrients to the plant. Now we also know that supplying water of the highest quality and purity is also critical to plant health and producing the most saleable and profitable plants. It's logical then to treat this vital resource with the level of importance it deserves as a critical resource and contributor to profitability.

Figure 5-20. Greenhouse growers are putting more and more emphasis on water conservation and water quality.

The horticulture industry in North America and elsewhere has long paid little attention to water-related issues, focusing instead on improvements in structures, equipment, and other inputs that reduce production costs or boost output. Water, in most locations, has been easily accessible, lightly regulated, and inexpensive. Disposal of excess irrigation water was not generally a concern, and margins were sufficient to cover a little shrink or some extra chemical applications resulting from poor water quality and inadequate water management, irrigation practices, or both. Often, water conservation action is taken only if forced by government agencies or grants are available to fund it.

This is changing—very quickly in some areas, and coming soon in others. Most producers can ill-afford the loss of an extra percent or two of shrink for any reason or to waste the fertilizer contained in the irrigation runoff stream. And water, while still abundant in most areas, is getting less accessible. Quality is reducing as aquifer levels reduce and salt intrudes. It's becoming more expensive. There are more demands competing against a static supply—the regulations regarding use, runoff, and pollution are becoming more restrictive. And growers cannot afford to waste profit margin dollars on excess applications of just about everything.

Figure 5-21. A goal of all growers is to minimize water runoff and waste. These otherwise efficient drip tubes are wasting water.

Also, there is the consideration of environmental responsibility and sustainability. The horticulture industry is the leader in crop production efficiency, and some view us as "the original green industry," as most believe we should be. Isn't it a logical extension then that we should lead in water use efficiency and related reduction of pollution from runoff? That is why more growers are taking action on this front and reviewing their options and plans as relate to improving water conservation and water quality.

Should You (Can You) Recycle Your Water?

Deciding to install a water recycling system is not a foregone conclusion, as one may believe in this age of environmental awareness and pressure to recycle virtually everything that is consumed. Sometimes it's not necessary or appropriate to recycle greenhouse and nursery water. Below are six key steps in the process of evaluating the value of recycling your irrigation runoff.

First, reduce water use

Before you consider more elaborate conservation methods such as recycling your runoff, take the simpler steps to make sure you will be dealing with the least amount of runoff possible. This may sound trivial, but the importance should not be overlooked. Growers, educators, researchers, and extension agents continue to report that most growers overirrigate. There are many excellent tools available to effectively reduce irrigation applications, and thereby runoff. If a crop is irrigated just a little more frequently than necessary, with just a little greater flow than necessary, and for just a little longer than necessary, the result is that all parts of the water management system that serves a given area must be larger than necessary as well. Bigger pumps, pipes, valves, filters, disinfection systems, tanks, etc. are all required to accommodate the higher peak flow rates and greater daily water volume. Furthermore, the cost of many of the components increases exponentially with size, so reducing flows pays off very quickly when you are expanding or modifying your water management system.

Reducing irrigation water use by 40–70% is achievable by employing high-efficiency irrigation systems, automated computer controls, and current best management practices (BMP). The difference in water use and infrastructure required is often amazing.

Learn local regulations

Don't begin capturing your runoff until you have identified what you will need to do with it and what regulations you will need to abide by. It may not be practical or affordable. What are the regulations that impact your facility? Web sites will help identify the regulations that apply to your locale. Begin with the USDA Natural Resources Conservation Service's site at www.nrcs.usda.gov, which will lead you to programs for each of the states in the United States. Environment Canada's site at www.ec.gc.ca will lead to both national and provincial programs.

In some locations, capturing your irrigation runoff may be unwise unless you are also ready to immediately install a recycling system. A grand plan to capture rain water runoff could be met with the realization that the government owns the rainwater and you're not allowed to capture it for your exclusive use (true in some western states!). Be sure to check local regulations and restrictions that are specific to local streams, lakes, rivers, and aquifers. The reward for researching the regulations is that it will also lead you to any funding that may be available.

Be careful of point source discharge issues

If you capture and retain your irrigation runoff, you need to have a plan to treat it and reuse it. It may not be until sometime in the future, but at some point it will need to be reused, either because you recognize the value of reusing water you've already invested in or because a government agency or local organization will compel you to do so.

Do not assume that you can "dump" the water you store onto the ground after you capture it. There are places and water conditions where it is technically against the rules to pump water directly from a well onto the ground from which it came.

Learn what's in your runoff water

Is it just fertilizer leachate? What about the residue from PGRs, pesticides, and fungicides, as well as accumulated pathogens and algae? If it goes on the crop, you have to assume at least a trace of it will make it into the runoff water, where it may cause problems if not dealt with properly.

The presence of these constituents in your runoff water should not dissuade you from recycling it, but it is important to determine the levels (ideally seasonally, to track how they may change) and identify what may be required to remove them. PGRs in your lawn irrigation may be kind of nice, but your neighbor might not appreciate it on his bean crop.

Total soluble salts and individual elements such as iron and manganese may require special attention when recycling water, even if they were not an issue before recycling. Any element that is not taken up by the plant or lost to evaporation or media absorption is returned and concentrated. An elevated but tolerable level of salts will become excessive after just two or three irrigation and reuse cycles. Depending on the crop and other factors, an EC level in excess of 0.5 to 0.7 millimhos/cc may result in excessive soluble salts in the recycled water. In this situation it may be necessary to employ a reverse osmosis system to remove or reduce soluble salts in the original water source.

Identify how you will use the captured water

Decide where and how you will use the recycled water before you design the system to capture the runoff. Capturing it in a basin or pond without an adequate demand for its use will result in excessive overflow, which is generally classified as a point source discharge. A point source discharge of water containing anything that may be considered a pollutant, such as nitrates or residues from PGRs and pesticides, is considered pollution, whether it overflows the pond, leaches into the ground under the pond, or is piped over the side. Regulators dislike point source discharge because it bypasses natural methods of dilution and ground filtration and concentrates pollutants, making them potentially more harmful.

The most common reuse of irrigation runoff, at least initially after a system is commissioned, is irrigation of local landscape. There is an important cautionary note when applying recycled water to landscape. This has, on occasion, resulted in a concentration of one or more waterborne pathogens and the consequent outbreak of disease on the greenhouse or nursery. This, of course, will also threaten your crops with more disease pressure. For this reason, some level of additional filtration and disinfection should be considered even for the application of recycled water to exterior landscape. A similar use, with similar cautions, is to sell or allow the use of this water for irrigation of adjacent land, such as a neighboring field crop or golf course. When doing this, always provide full disclosure of what may be in the water, be sure to always retain the rights to the water, and always obtain a release from liability for any crop damage that may result from using your runoff water.

Finally, the ultimate benefit of recycling your irrigation runoff water is achieved when it is applied to irrigate your own crops. This requires close attention again to the contents of that water, the crops that will be irrigated, and the treatment requirements that result. Water treatment technology has advanced to the point that affordable systems are now available to adequately treat nearly any kind of runoff and apply the treated water to irrigate any crop.

Using untreated recycled water to irrigate a short-term crop, such as bedding plants sold at retail, is a common practice often accomplished without problems. This is common with flood irrigation systems that employ proper BMP to limit flood duration to less than ten or twelve minutes. However, it's not a good plan to irrigate long-term crops with untreated recycled water because pathogens and other water quality issues will have a cumulative impact over the months that the crop is in place. It's also strongly advised to avoid using untreated irrigation runoff to irrigate crops that are shipped to other growers, such as seedlings, plugs, liners, and mother plants used for cuttings. With these crops, full treatment, including disinfection, is a must, is affordable, and will enhance the marketability of those plants.

Any crop can be successfully irrigated with recycled water if careful consideration is given to providing the most appropriate method of treatment. This is true even for particularly sensitive crops such as gerberas and critical crops such as seedlings, plugs, and vegetative liners.

Find the funds

You may not need to shoulder the cost all on your own. There are tax incentives, preferential term loans, grants, and free research testing and design resources available to help defray costs and complete the planning necessary to improve your water conservation and management systems.

Check them out well in advance of starting any design process so you will know what's available and how to access it. Projects that at first may not appear to be economically viable may turn out to be quite advantageous when outside incentives and resources are factored in. Also, timing is often critical in some incentive programs. Some growers have undertaken the design of a system and initiated installation only to find that significant funding was available for the asking . . . but only if it was requested and/or approved in advance of the purchase or installation.

A final reminder on incentives: Don't overlook resources associated with a local waterway or conservation districts at the county or municipal level.

Make sure it pays

It may seem odd to put this item last, but the return on investment will largely depend on the information from the first five steps in the process. There are four key potential economic benefits to recycling water. If none of these apply, then it is highly unlikely that you will achieve a worthy objective from recycling your water. It may even be a negative. If one or more do apply, however, recycling your water can pay off very quickly, sometimes in as little as two years.

• Reduce dependence on a limited or costly water source
• Re-use fertilizer captured from runoff and reduce fertilizer costs
• Reduce water pollution and possible fines or regulatory costs
• Sustainability credits from retailers and market value added to your product

Capturing Your Runoff

Of course, to recycle your irrigation runoff water, it must first be captured and stored. Capturing the water is something that's entirely site-related and depends on the type of irrigation, the area covered, topography of outdoor growing areas, type of floors in the greenhouse, and other issues. This is best taken up with a local specialist or your greenhouse manufacturer, although your water system design specialist should be able to offer helpful suggestions based on experience at other facilities. It may be as simple as digging shallow trenches in the ground of an outdoor nursery, or as complex as tile drains or concrete floors in the greenhouse. The water can be routed directly to a common pond or cistern, or to a series of smaller sumps distributed around the property where needed when considering larger facilities or topography.

How much runoff can you expect to capture? Whether the irrigation runoff is a trickle or a gusher will depend on your irrigation system and practices. With some overhead sprinkler systems you may recover as much as 75% of the total water volume applied, minus ground absorption and evaporation. A propagation mist system or a highly efficient drip system with good BMP could result in a recovery of as little as 10-15% of the volume applied, less ground absorption and evaporation. Going back to the first point above, the volume of irrigation water applied is important, and this is the first place where reducing the use pays off.

The next step in handling runoff water is generally storage. Again, this is an issue that will be site specific, depending on the storage volume required, temperatures, topography, local regulations and codes, aesthetics, and budget. Aboveground storage tanks are a good option in temperate areas (no concern of freezing the water). Installing the tank(s) indoors is an option, where storage volumes are relatively small (under 500,000 gal. [1.89 million L], for example), and where codes allow aboveground storage tanks. Storage tanks are readily available in volumes from a few thousand gallons to a million gallons or more. Smaller tanks of 250,000 gal. (946,000 L) or less can be relatively inexpensive ($0.15–0.25 per gal. [$0.04–0.07 per L]) using corrugated steel and an inside tank liner. Larger tanks of bolted or welded steel are more expensive and can be custom engineered for certain water quality considerations or code requirements. Inground cisterns are also an option but can become very expensive for larger sizes, particularly if there are soil concerns or code requirements. Finally, digging a pond is a cost-effective solution if you have the space and the need to store a large volume. Ponds can be lined or unlined and must be designed and engineered by local professionals.

Figure 5-22. Typical water storage facility.

The volume of water storage is a key consideration in determining the design of many water treatment systems. As discussed previously, flow rate and daily volume of water to be treated are significant factors in determining the sizing of a treatment system as well as the operating cost of that system. Water storage allows peak flow rates throughout the day to be averaged into a smaller flow rate over a longer period. In the best design, the storage capacity would be sized to handle twenty-four hours of net runoff, and the treatment system would be sized to treat that runoff over a twenty-four-hour period.

Suppose a facility uses 200,000 gal. (757,082 L) per day of water on a maximum irrigation day, with a maximum peak flow rate of 500 gal. (1,893 L) per minute. If the storage is adequate for twenty-four hours, the treatment system could be sized to treat as little as 138 gal. (522 L) per minute instead of the 500. That 72% reduction of system size could pay for a lot of water storage.

Treating Recycled Water

There are four water treatment essentials to consider for water reuse.

Plant Health

Research and experience have proven beyond doubt that high-quality water helps build healthier root systems in plants, which in turn improves the plants nutrient uptake ability and utilization, increases its immunity to disease, makes it less inviting to pests, and improves overall plant quality and size. Healthy plants generally respond more predictably to inputs, making crop management simpler with the net effect of reducing shrink and cost per unit produced.

We now know that plants, like animals, grow and produce better when they receive the best water. Poultry, swine, and dairy farmers have understood for many years that high-quality water contributes substantially to improved animal health and improved feed conversion rates. They closely track the relationship of feed input to market weight and grade. Getting paid by the pound and grade obviously helps focus attention on this.

However, in horticulture we experience this in the vegetable and cut flower markets and, to a degree, in the potted plant market. But the retailing trend of pay-by-scan and increased pressure to provide merchandising for retailers mean that plant quality (or grade, if you will) matter a great deal. From the consumer's selection of a particular plant, to the accepted price point, to how long that plant will last on the shelf and whether or not the retailer will need to mark it down or dump it, are all impacted by the health and resulting quality of that plant. It doesn't necessarily cost more to produce a healthy plant for that retail special, but it sure gets put into the shopping cart faster, and that's where it counts to the bottom line at the end of the season.

Continuous monitoring of the fertilizer input and the plant's response is important to provide the best control of the feed input. Affordable computer control systems can continuously monitor and present graphical and tabular historical data of actual EC and pH of your irrigation water and provide critical input for controlling fertilizer input and irrigation timing and quantity.

Filtration

Filtration of runoff water typically requires two or more levels of filtration, depending on the level of treatment employed. Due to high contaminant loads, a single filtration system will generally not provide sufficient filtration or will clog or back-flush too frequently. There are three levels of filtration to consider for the recycling of runoff water.

Debris removal

There should always be a level of coarse filtration provided at the point(s) where runoff flows into the detention basin or pond. This is the place to filter out the big stuff, e.g. leaves, twigs, peat moss, perlite, etc. These filters can be as simple as a cascade screen filter, bag filter, or an inline screen at the end of the pipe

that is cleaned out daily. There are also filter options that are more labor efficient and provide a finer level of filtration, such as roll media filters or rotating drum filters. Whatever you chose, it is best at this point to filter down to 100–150 mesh or a 150–100 micron particle size. You may also consider a combination of coarse filtration and a settling basin.

Pre-irrigation

If there is no further disinfection treatment desired, this may be the final filtration level required, but if there is disinfection treatment, this will serve as post-treatment filtration. It's as straightforward as filtering out the maximum particle that can easily pass through irrigation emitters, and it can be accomplished with a single filtration stage or a main filter and secondary inline filters for drip emitters and mist nozzles. For post treatment, this may require removal of solids that have precipitated out of solution during the disinfection process. The target here is typically to bring it down to 300–400 mesh or 50–35 micron particle size or better. Sand filters, disc filters, bag filters, and rolling media filters can all be used effectively.

Figure 5-23. Debris removal is only the first stage of filtration, removing only the "big stuff" from the irrigation water.

Pre-treatment

This is the finest and most demanding level of filtration. Organic material in the water is a major factor affecting the efficacy of any form of disinfection; therefore it is a major factor in the cost of disinfection. Mechanically removing as much of the organic load as possible before disinfection will help keep the costs as low as possible. It's expensive to use up disinfecting capacity on contaminant loads that can otherwise be easily removed through mechanical means. The target filtration level prior to disinfection will require 800 mesh or better to filter down to a 15–5 micron particle size. The typical filter options are limited at this point. This fine of filtration typically requires a custom-sized deep media filter with specialized filtration media.

Filtration is not disinfection

It's true that some pathogens can be filtered out with filtration levels down to 5 microns or better, but filtration itself is rarely ever adequate for protection from pathogens. First, filtration never removes all pathogens, and second, the pathogens that are filtered out are not destroyed—they are simply concentrated. Once concentrated in the filter media, rapid pressure changes or unusual loading can cause the filter media to channel, releasing these concentrated pathogens into the distribution system and defeating the filter.

What happens to these concentrated contaminants and their organic food source, which is also captured in the filter? They are removed by backwashing the filters. So where is the backwash water being discharged? Back to the water source it came from? If so, a rather serious problem has been created: the continual contamination of the water source. If the concentrated pathogens are released onto the ground or into another surface water source, this could be maintaining a resident population of these potential pathogens on your property or that of other growers in the area.

Disinfection

Water recycling and disinfection should always be considered together, but they can also be considered independent of each other. Many growers have been recycling irrigation water successfully for years without disinfecting it, primarily using ebb-and-flood irrigation systems. Conversely, particularly in recent years, growers have begun treating their well water

supply and even municipal water to achieve benefits and generally improved water quality.

The most common reasons for treating irrigation water, recycled or not, are the elimination and control of biofilm, control of algae, and destruction of waterborne plant pathogens such as *Pythium, Phytophthora,* and others.

A word that has entered the industry nomenclature over the past decade or so is "biofilm." Destruction of waterborne plant pathogens is what most growers think of when regarding water disinfection, and it is very important. However, experts have come to a much better understanding of how those pathogens are spread throughout a facility, and biofilm is a major source of problems. Biofilm results when fertilizers and organic matter form a fine film of nutrient source—a biomass—on the inside of pipes, filters, valves, and emitters. The residue of bacteria then stick to that biomass and form a disease-laden slime we know as biofilm. This biofilm consumes oxygen, lowers pH, and stores then releases bacteria, molds, fungi, algae, and other pathogens into the water on the way to the plants. It's present in the irrigation pipes and emitters of every greenhouse and nursery operation, unless the irrigation system is properly treated. Biofilm is one of the most common, very possibly the most common, methods of spreading pathogens there is, and it is increasingly linked to root diseases such as *Pythium.*

Figure 5-24. Biofilm is present in the irrigation pipes and emitters of every greenhouse and nursery operation, unless the water is properly treated.

Figure 5-25. Ozone treatment system.

Eliminating existing biofilm and keeping it away are more difficult than just neutralizing the pathogens in the water. In the words of one grower, "Cleaning up the water without eliminating the biofilm is about the same as putting clean food on a dirty plate." In fact, growers frequently struggle with pathogens mysteriously showing up on their plants after having taken steps to disinfect their water. Biofilm is the reason. It does, in fact, exist in every pipe with water in it that's not being continuously and effectively treated. It exists in municipal water supplies and lines, well water lines, and irrigation mains and laterals. Even if lines are cleaned through some temporary method, such as chemical shocking, the biofilm begins to reform nearly instantly and within a few days it's back and spreading molds and fungus and algae. The reason is relatively simple: Not all disinfection methods will eliminate biofilm on a continuous basis, and many that can are expensive to use continuously for that purpose.

Ultraviolet (UV) light treatment, for example, if properly used, can destroy the pathogens in the water as it passes through the UV light tube; however, there is no residual established in the water and so it's incapable of destroying biofilm. The result is that immediately upon leaving the UV system, water flows back into biofilm-lined pipes and is repopulated with the same pathogens and algae spores that were just eliminated. Heat pasteurization, slow sand filters and biofilter systems, and copper ionization have the same limitations. It's also true of many popular chemical disinfection methods. Chlorine liquid or gas, for example, has been tested by municipal water supply systems at concentrations ten times greater than the toxicity level for plants and found to be ineffective against biofilm.

There are a handful of disinfection methods and chemicals that will both disinfect irrigation water and eliminate biofilm. Ozone, chlorine dioxide, hydrogen peroxide, peroxyacetic acid, sodium hypochlorite, and others will kill biofilm and keep it away if used continuously. However, some of these are banned in some countries. Then, there's the question of cost. In general, it's a question of capital cost versus operating costs. Chlorine dioxide, hydrogen peroxide, peroxyacetic acid, and combinations of these require relatively low capital costs to purchase and install but can rack up pretty sizeable monthly consumable bills. Ozone, on the other hand, has a relatively small operating cost but comes with a sizeable capital investment cost.

In addition to disinfecting the water and eliminating biofilm, there are other benefits of some types of treatment. For example, dissolved oxygen (DO) is the primary byproduct of ozone after it has oxidized the pathogens or is depleted. In fact, since ozone is more than twelve times more soluble in water than pure oxygen, ozone injection is the best possible method of enhancing the dissolved oxygen level of your irrigation water, making it possible to achieve 20-30 ppm of DO.

The use of ozone is one of the most promising developments of the past few years. Ozone is the most powerful oxidizer available for water disinfection, and it has been around, literally, forever. That fresh, crispy smell after a thunderstorm? Ozone. Until the past few years, ozone was not used extensively in the horticulture industry as a water disinfectant. There was little knowledge of how to size and design the systems to be cost effective. That has changed, and there are well-established knowledge and capabilities available now to design and size systems. The cost has also come down, making ozone disinfection a quite affordable technology. Among the most significant benefits of ozone treatment is its extraordinary disinfection capability and low operating costs.

Good oxidizers, such as ozone and chlorine, also cause elements such as iron and manganese to precipitate. This can be a negative and require reinjection of these microelements after treatment, which is pretty affordable to do. However, if high iron levels cause problems with leaf staining and emitter clogging, you could use ozone or chlorine to force these to precipitate and then filter them out after.

In as much that it is common practice to inject liquid fertilizers into irrigation water, (known as fertigation), it is vital to be aware of how each disinfection or treatment method will affect or be affected by nitrates and microelements. For example, chlorine products become fully neutralized within seconds of coming into contact with nitrates. Consequently, if chlorine is injected into the irrigation lines after the fertilizer is injected, it will be of little to no value. If the chlorine is injected prior to the nitrates, it is critical to design the system to allow the required chlorine contact time, up to twenty minutes, before nitrates are injected.

Pasteurization has been utilized effectively for many years as a very good method of disinfection. The upside is that it is reliable and effective. The downside is that it can be very energy intensive to operate. While still used, pasteurization is falling out of favor as more cost-effective methods are now available and much easier to install and operate.

Copper ionization is effective at destroying a limited type of organism, is relatively inexpensive to purchase and operate, and is easy to install. However, the efficacy of copper ionization is limited and very difficult to measure.

Constructed wetlands, slow sand filtration, and biofiltration are all definitely effective at some level of disinfection, are environmentally friendly, are very low cost to operate, and may provide some level of beneficial water treatment. However, installation is more involved and can be expensive and even require special permitting. Additionally, the efficacy of the systems is widely variable and very dependent on the type and quality of installation. This technology continues to present promise and is evolving.

For More Information

There are many disinfection methods available, and the subject is far too complex to adequately address all of the details in this section. To gain more knowledge and access a significant volume of research and educational material, it is suggested that the reader be directed to an extraordinary resource for education, research and information. The Water Education Alliance for Horticulture is a university- and industry-supported program led by the Dr. Paul Fisher and the University of Florida IFAS Extension that educates growers on water quality and treatment. Their website, www.WaterEducationAlliance.org, provides many informative sources, research results, and educational workshops. This includes detailed comparisons and evaluations of various water disinfection methods.

Figure 5-26. Design of a modern, effective, efficient water treatment system requires professional resources and advice.

Nutrient Replenishment

The last tour stop for the water before it is reapplied as irrigation is to top off the nutrition value. This will focus on a few key points specific to recycled water. See the section on fertigation equipment (page 89) for more detail specific to nutrient injection equipment.

Irrigation runoff will generally contain nutrients originally injected into the water or from the leachate from time-release fertilizers. However, the nutrient value in this runoff water will typically be depleted. Additionally, the NPK and micronutrient balance may have been altered from the original blend. Unless the water will only be used for landscape irrigation or as an occasional source, it will be necessary to replenish and rebalance the nutrient levels before reuse for crop irrigation.

The first step in this process is testing to identify the nutrient values of the captured runoff. In most operations, changes will typically be only seasonal with changes in crop mix and feed. For outside irrigation it will also change with weather events, such as significant rain or drought events or periods of excessive heat. Manual testing will usually suffice due to the relatively slow or infrequent changes and can be done on a weekly basis, sometimes every few weeks. Automated monitoring of nutrient levels is not yet practical in most situations because it can be very expensive, unreliable, or simply not available. For example, a continuous nitrate sensor alone can run between $5,000 and $15,000, and calibration can be somewhat challenging.

Once the water is tested and you know what stock solution needs to be re-injected, the injection process can be relatively simple using any of the common injection methods and systems available. There are systems available that can accomplish this automatically by monitoring the EC level of the runoff water and injecting based on EC and flow rate. Or, the simple and reliable method of fixed injection ratio and volumetric injection can be used.

Finally, the specific injection location of the nutrients is often as important as what is being injected, depending on the type of disinfection system that is used, if any. Oxidizers in general can cause precipitation of some microelements, which may then need to be replaced. Chlorine products are rendered ineffective in the presence of nitrates, so all disinfection needs to be completed prior to injection of fertilizers if chlorine in any form is used.

The Design Process

After doing the due diligence to determine what you should/can and can't/shouldn't do and who might help pay for it, it's time to get on with developing the concept of what to do. Whether a complete new system is required, or an existing system simply needs to be upgraded, here are a few basic steps that are important to follow:

Work with a professional

Water is a very complex resource. How plants utilize water is even more complex. The water management systems that treat and handle that water are dramatically affected by the makeup of the water. Further, the plants that are irrigated with that water will be dramatically affected by the final quality of that water. Too little knowledge here can quickly land your plants, and your bottom line, in trouble. Even if you understand your water pretty well, get a professional involved.

Take a holistic system approach

As the source of a grower's most critical input, the water management system deserves significant attention and resource to assure that it is as good as it can be. Even if only a single process or component will be added to a system, it's very important that the entire system design and operating dynamic be reviewed by a qualified water management professional and designed or modified as necessary. Only in this way can there be certainty that all of components are operating as a system and that this system is operating at peak performance and efficiency.

Filtration, fertilizer injection, irrigation type, emitter size, even plant container size—these are all topics that should be addressed throughout the water treatment system discussion. Where is fertilizer injected in the system? How about the acid? These are just two examples of questions that can be critical when designing a treatment system or even inserting just one additional component (such as finer filtration) into an existing system. Assume that everything affects everything else, because it usually does in water treatment.

Know your water

If you don't have a good water analysis, the knowledge to interpret that analysis, and the engineering ability to design a solution based on it, you are only guessing at the solution. Always begin the process with a water analysis. Water is a complex resource, and there is far more than must be known than meets the eye, even aided with a microscope. Filtration and disinfection solutions, even pumping and valve design, are affected by the chemistry and characteristics of the water. Realize that it may take multiple analyses, taken from more than one location, at several different sampling occasions, to get the complete picture of your water quality and content.

Understand the effect on the plant

What is required and desired by the plants that you grow in the environment in which you grow them? How high can the salts be? At what levels will certain chemicals you may be considering for disinfection become toxic to your plants? Ideally, the method of treatment should have a double benefit of also improving the health of the plant.

In summary, all of the above topics could be chapters, if not books, unto themselves. Supplying the highest quality water to your plants is critical to producing the most saleable and profitable plants. The most important thing is to ask a lot of questions and involve others that deal with water in our industry for a living.

The importance of water in the greenhouse industry and in our world is undeniable. Considered by some to be the most pressing issue of the coming years, it makes a lot of sense to be prepared. Take action and at least do a thorough review of your options and plans as it relates to improving your water conservation and water quality.

6

The Greenhouse Environment

Greenhouse Ventilation

Ted Short and Peter Ling

Greenhouses need ventilation year round to maintain ideal temperature, humidity, and carbon dioxide levels for optimal plant growth and quality. A greenhouse's ventilation requirements depend on climate conditions both inside and outside the greenhouse. Its required rate of ventilation will vary significantly with time of day, season, and crop.

Natural ventilation, forced ventilation, or a combination of both is used to reduce the high temperatures that result from daily solar radiation heat loads inside the greenhouse. Natural ventilation uses wind pressure differences and air buoyancy effects, while forced ventilation uses mechanical fans to move the air.

A greenhouse in any part of the United States on a clear, sunny summer day will have a noontime solar radiation input of 300–350 BTUs per hour/ft.^{2} of floor area. This solar energy input causes the greenhouse air temperature to rise rapidly and increases the humidity by evaporating water through plant transpiration. Ventilation becomes essential for controlling the temperature and for removing the humid air to keep the plant transpiration process active.

Regardless of whether you vent naturally, by forced air, or both, some form of controlled shading, as described in chapter 3, is an integral part of any good ventilation system. The shade material can be located either externally or internally. To be effective, the shading material must reduce the solar heat load that would normally reach the plant leaves if no shading were used.

Natural Ventilation

Naturally ventilated greenhouses rely primarily on wind pressure to force air in one side of the greenhouse, past the crop, and out through the opposite sidewall or through the roof vents. Wind can also create a vacuum pressure along the roof and sides to "suck" air out that has entered at some other location. A secondary, much smaller effect is that of buoyancy (the effect of hot and/or humid air rising), which becomes most important on hot, still days.

In all cases, it's essential for efficient natural ventilation that there is at least one effective inlet directing air into the plants and multiple outlets removing warm air above and beyond the plants. For gutter-connected greenhouses, a combination of windward side vents and continuous leeward roof vents will result in the most effective ventilation design. Even for retractable or open-roof designs, an open windward sidewall is very important for the area under the open roof to achieve good midsummer cooling.

Everyone knows that hot air rises because it's less dense than cool air. Most people, however, are surprised to learn that moist air also rises because moist air is less dense than dry air. The reason for the confusion has been that water as a liquid is dense; water as a vapor, however, is less dense than the surrounding air and rises until it forms clouds in the atmosphere. That's why it's essential that hot, moist air in a naturally ventilated greenhouse have a smooth path up and out. The slightest entrapment will stall the natural ventilation process on a calm day.

Wind and aerodynamic vents, with a little help from buoyancy in the internal air, are the primary natural-ventilation system drivers. The ultimate test of a natural ventilation system design is the response to a "no wind" period. All growers can recall hot days when it felt like there was no wind. However, such moments were recorded hourly for five years at precision weather stations in Ohio, and it was found that all of the actual "no wind" cases occurred at temperatures below 75°F (24°C). Above 75°F (24°C), there was always measurable wind above 1 mph (1.6 km/h), with the average being approximately 5 mph (8 km/h). Growers responses to effective naturally ventilated greenhouse are almost always positive. All doors can be open on warm and hot days, allowing easy access for employees moving plants as well as browsing customers in retail houses. Inside, the greenhouse is very quiet except for the occasional noise of wind at the vents. While the greenhouse may sometimes be 5°F (3°C) warmer than outside during a midsummer day, the greenhouse will still be more comfortable than outside due to the 50% or more shading from direct solar

Figure 6-1. Retractable roof, ridge-vent, and gutter-vent are three major designs available commercially.

radiation. On the flip side, plants may dry unevenly due to non-uniform air movement in inadequately designed greenhouses. Various designs of naturally vented greenhouse are available commercially.

Fan Ventilation

Fan ventilation systems in greenhouses can provide consistent airflow to plants while producing enough air velocity at the inlet to operate evaporative cooling pads, which cool the incoming air through evaporation. As the air flows through the plants in the greenhouse, it absorbs heat and increases in both temperature and humidity before exiting the greenhouse through the fans. Cooling effectiveness of the airflow reduces as it travels across a greenhouse, resulting in a temperature gradient between the air inlet and exhaust. Increasing the airflow rate or limiting the length of the greenhouse can control the rate of temperature and humidity rise. An air exchange rate of one greenhouse volume per minute is a common design value that will result in a temperature rise of 10°F (6°C) or less. The distance between the air inlet and fan outlet should be 150' (46 m) or less to be most effective.

Ventilation fans are typically propeller type and must have a properly sized air inlet at the opposite end of the greenhouse for efficient cooling. While a few large-diameter fans would be more energy efficient than many small fans, a number of small fans are usually used, spaced no more that 25' (8 m) apart, to provide uniform airflow for temperature uniformity. Plus, if one fan is out of operation, the others will maintain ventilation. For best efficiency, exhaust fans ideally are located on a leeward sidewall and inlet vents are on the opposite, windward sidewall of the greenhouse. This way the prevailing wind helps push air into the greenhouse, increasing fan efficiency. When fans must face into the prevailing winds for practical reasons, airflow capacities and motor horsepower ratings need to be increased by 10–15%.

By using numerous fans in conjunction with an evaporative cooling pad system, fans and water can be operated in stages as the temperature increases. To provide uniform airflow, staged fans should be separated, for example, so that only one out of three comes on initially. The second and third stages of fans are switched on as the temperature rises and are shut off in reverse sequence as the temperature falls. Two-speed fans may also be used effectively in some situations. Once all the fans are running, the cooling pad pump can be turned on as an additional cooling stage.

Fan capacities are rated based on the static air pressures that they must pump against. Pressure values of 0.125" (0.3 cm) of water (column) are normally used for fan selection and the volume of air to be moved (or exchanged) is calculated as the number of volumetric air changes per minute (usually 1.0–1.5/min.). For example, if the greenhouse is 30' wide by 150' long by 10' high (9 × 46 × 3 m), its volume is 45,000 ft.^{3} (1,274 m^3). The fan capacity required for one air change per minutes is 45,000 cubic feet per minute (cfm). This ventilation rate can then be achieved with two 48" (120 cm) diameter fans with 1-hp motors pumping against a static air pressure of 0.125" (0.3 cm) of water.

For greenhouses taller than 10' (3 m) at the gutters, fans capacities are usually sized for 8–10 cfm/ ft.^{2} (0.00378–0.0047 m^3/second/m^2) of floor area for summer ventilation and 3–4 cfm/ft.^{2} (0.0014–0.0019 m^3/second/m^2) of floor area for winter ventilation. The 8–10 cfm/ft.^{2} (0.00378–0.0047 m^3/second/m^2)

value assumes that the ventilation height is no more than 10' (3 m) high, even though the greenhouse may be twice that height. Primary reasons behind this are (1) heat gain of a greenhouse from solar radiation is mostly determined by its footprint, not height, and (2) air above the ventilation height is essentially assumed to be stagnant and not part of the ventilation air. Air velocities across most greenhouse plants should never be more than 3.3'/sec. (1 m/sec.) or 2.5 mph (4 km/h).

Fans will be most energy efficient if the motors are sized properly and have an efficient design. If three-phase electric power is available in the greenhouse, three-phase motors should be used because they're cheaper and require less maintenance than single-phase motors. Fans mounted in "bell-mouthed" housings will give slightly increased air delivery at no extra power input compared with fans mounted in flat "diaphragm" housings. Regular maintenance to keep fan blades clean, bearings lubricated, and fan belt properly

Figure 6-2. Most greenhouses, except perhaps those in the coolest climates, use some fans to help remove warm air.

tensioned are key to energy efficient fan operation. Dust accumulation on fan blades, housings, and shutters can reduce air movement.

The total air inlet opening in the wall should be approximately 1.5 ft.^{2} per 1,000 cfm (0.14m^2 per 0.47 m^3/sec.) of fan capacity. For multistage cooling, it is important to control air inlet opening to maintain air velocity in a greenhouse: larger inlet opening is needed for higher airflow rate, for example. To prevent air exchange when the fans are off, outlets of exhaust fans should be fitted with shutters that open easily when the fan starts. The air inlet should also have shutters or a vent cover that's motorized and wired into the fan control system.

A greenhouse with fan-powered exhaust ventilation will always have a slight vacuum inside the building when the fans are running. Openings in the exterior of a poorly maintained greenhouse will leak air and may result in insufficient airflow through the plants and cooling pad. Leaks usually occur around doors and sidewall vents in addition to the edges of sidewall glazing material. Greenhouses in good repair will have the most efficient ventilation system unless doors and side vents are left open unnecessarily. Airflow shortcuts between opened side vents or doors to exhaust fans can dramatically reduce airflow through plant canopies, thus reducing cooling capacity.

Winter Cooling and Dehumidification

To control temperature and humidity during the winter, one may need to bring a small amount of cool, dry air into the greenhouse. Air distribution systems should introduce cold air high into the greenhouse so it can mix with warm air before it gets close to the plants.

Leeward roof vents that are high on the roof can be used effectively to let cool and dry outside air in and warm and moist inside air out for moisture purging. This works best for growers in mild winter climates, where they rarely have to worry about the vents freezing shut. If the vents are totally or partially frozen shut, the opening mechanisms and vents themselves can be severely damaged when the opening mechanisms are activated.

Powered shutters and jet fans that circulate air into the upper level of the greenhouse through perforated poly tubing or with the help of horizontal airflow fans are effective systems for dehumidification. These systems are especially common in cold climates. A humidistat should be used to open the motorized shutters at the jet fan, delay a few minutes to allow good mixing with greenhouse air, then turn on low-speed exhaust fans of the same air capacity.

Humidity control is most difficult during the fall and spring seasons, when the outside temperature and humidity is similar to those inside the greenhouse. In this damp, cloudy weather, overheating the greenhouse air for a short time and then ventilating the greenhouse can control high humidity. Heating the air will increase its moisture-holding capacity and lower its relative humidity.

Figure 6-3. Powered shutters and jet fans are often used for winter dehumidification as well as distributing warm air from unit heaters.

Horizontal Airflow Systems

Recirculation fans are important for internal air movement and are essential for uniform temperature, humidity, and carbon dioxide distribution. They can greatly minimize water condensation on plants where many disease organisms thrive, especially during winter growing seasons. Overhead horizontal airflow (HAF) fans are the most common recirculation fans in greenhouses. Vertical airflow fans and bottom air flow systems have been used to promote vertical airflow through dense plant canopies.

One key HAF fan feature is fan shrouding. Many inexpensive fans are unshrouded. If only short crops such as bedding plants and plugs are being grown, the unshrouded fans can work quite well. When the greenhouse is filled with tall, dense plants or a mix of plant materials including hanging baskets, only shrouded fans will provide the desired horizontal airflow within the plant canopies.

Figure 6-4. Unshrouded HAF fans can work quite well on short crops such as bedding plants and plugs.

A shroud can be as simple as a sheet metal ring, or cylinder, around the fan blades. The closer the shroud is to the blade tips, the more effective and efficient the fan is at moving air along the axis of the fan. If the velocity across the tops of the plants near the shrouded fan is too great, you can reduce the fan speed or angle it slightly upward.

The airflow capacities of unshrouded fans are actually the same as shrouded. The undesirable characteristic of an unshrouded fan, however, is to push most of the air directly off the blade tips. This can damage plants growing directly under (or above) each fan if the fan is located 2–3' (0.6–0.9 m) from the crop. The air velocity across the plant canopy in any location should

be no greater than 3.3'/sec. (1 m/sec.) or 2.5 mph (4 km/h) to prevent desiccation (drying) damage.

A well-designed HAF fan system consists of fans moving air the length of each greenhouse. Fans are often spaced 50–80' (15–24 m) apart down one bay and aligned with similar fans pushing air the opposite direction down an adjacent bay. Fan diameter can range from 12–36" (30–90 cm), with the larger fans working best on deep canopy cut-flower crops and trellised vegetables.

Whether shrouded or unshrouded, the fans should be designed to move about 2 cfm per square foot of floor area. For example, if a greenhouse is 30' wide by 150' long (9 x 46 m), the total design airflow should be 9,000 cfm. (Note: to convert cfm to the metric equivalent, 1 cfm equals 0.00047195 cubic meters per second.)

Fans should be spaced down the centerline of each greenhouse that's 30' (9 m) wide or less and separated by no more than thirty times the diameter of the fan blade. For instance, if the fan is 2' (60 cm) in diameter, the fans should be lined up and no more than 60' (18 m) apart. The last fan (looking in the direction of airflow) should be no more than 60' (18 m) from the endwall.

The inlet side of the first fan (looking in the direction of the airflow) should be about eight fan diameters from the end of the greenhouse wall. For instance, if each fan is 2' (0.7 m) in diameter, the first fan should be no more than 16' (5 m) from the endwall. A fan has to work harder against larger static pressure and often results in less air capacity when it is placed too close to an obstruction such as a wall.

Depending on the climate uniformity in a greenhouse, the recirculation fan systems maybe be turned off to conserve energy when the summer ventilation system (natural or fan) is running. The recirculation fan system will generally have neither a negative or positive effect on high-capacity natural and fan ventilation systems. Its greatest value will always be in winter when the greenhouse is tightly closed or when a small amount of cold outside air is brought in for CO_2 replenishment and dehumidification.

Greenhouse Cooling

RedBook *Staff*

Nearly all serious United States and Canadian production facilities that are growing year-round potted plants and major cut flower crops are equipped with fan-and-pad cooling. The only exception might be cool-summer areas, such as the Pacific Northwest. A pot chrysanthemum crop without cooling, even in the Midwest or eastern United States, is a good bet for major losses from heat stall in summer. Farther south and in the Southwest, cooling is an absolute must. Surprisingly, there are major greenhouse ranges even in Florida with fan-and-pad cooling. In spite of Florida's relatively high humidity, there is enough cooling effect from fan and pads to make the technique economical.

Though most production of potted plants and cut flowers in North America is fan-and-pad cooled, growers are considering natural ventilation anywhere it's a viable option. The rapid rise of electricity costs, plus the advent of open-roof greenhouse systems for natural ventilation, has caused growers in some areas to reconsider rows of giant fans and pads as a cooling system.

Evaporative Cooling

Drawing air through a water-saturated pad evaporates the water and cools the incoming greenhouse air. The air released to the outside has absorbed 8,100 BTU of heat energy for each gallon evaporated.

The original evaporative cooling systems used woven "Aspen" pads that were about 2" (5 cm) thick. Modern "pads" are made of corrugated cellulose material that has been treated to keep it from rotting and are 1' (30 cm) wide, 4–6' (120–180 cm) tall, and 4–6" (10–15 cm) thick. They sit in an aluminum or plastic trough. A "wet wall"—consisting of pads, a water distribution system to wet the pads, a water pump, and a sump—is erected continuously along one wall of the greenhouse. The pads must be kept wet to facilitate the evaporative cooling process. On the opposite wall, fans that are properly sized for the greenhouse size and location are placed to provide smooth airflow across the greenhouse.

Size your pads to provide the most efficient, economical system possible. Cellulose pads 4" (10 cm) thick operate best at an air speed of 250' (76 m) per minute through the pad. For 6" (15 cm) cellulose pads, use 400' (122 m) per minute.

Figure 6-5. Cooling pads use the cooling effect of evaporating water to reduce the temperature of the air being drawn into the greenhouse.

How Cool?

The amount of cooling achievable by evaporative cooling varies with the dryness of the air the differential between the wet bulb and dry bulb temperatures. This differential varies not only with location and season but also during each day. Although the dry bulb could vary as much as 25°F (14°C) in one day, the wet bulb varies only approximately a third as much. Therefore, cooling can be accomplished even in high-humidity areas in the middle of the day, when it's really needed.

A well-designed evaporative cooling system should be able to reduce the dry bulb temperature inside the wet wall to approximately 85% of the difference between the outside dry bulb and wet bulb temperature. Expect a temperature rise of about 7°F (4°C) from the pad to the exhaust fans.

Don't cheat on the size of the intake air openings—the larger the better. A smaller size than called for creates static resistance, which greatly reduces the efficiency of the fans and causes increased electricity usage. Use continuous vents whenever possible.

The calculations are simple—the problem is that the need varies by locality. Some areas have consistently high (90%) humidity on summer days (Dallas, for example). Others, such as Chicago, will experience 90% humidity for many days in summer but not all. Generally, fan-and-pad systems work best in dry climates. Systems must be "oversized" in high-humidity areas such as Texas and Florida.

To give a rough idea of the equipment needed for cooling an acre (4,046 m²) of conventional gutter-connected greenhouses, here's the way it's figured: Length of house x width x 8 cfm per ft.² of greenhouse space (adjusted for elevation, light intensity, etc.). This gives the cubic feet per minute required for air movement.

To figure the pad area required, divide the total cfm by 250 for 4" (10 cm) pads and by 400 if using 6" (15 cm) pads. Then divide this total by the number of linear feet of wall the pad vent will cover. This last number will tell you how tall the system will have to be. In humid climates, oversize the fans and pads by 20%.

A caution on pad installations: Pads cause resistance to airflow, so be sure that all air passes through the pads; all other openings (with less resistance) need to be closed. Even an open fan-jet shutter will greatly reduce pad efficiency.

Sample Calculations

Here is one example: Fourteen bays, each 21' wide by 144' long (6.4 x 44 m), have a total area of 42,336 ft.² (3,942 m²). With an 8' (2.4 m) gutter height, this greenhouse section—for proper fan-and-pad cooling—requires moving 338,688 cfm. After determining cfm requirements, select the fans. Then, based on their total cfm performance, size the pads to match the fans. For example, to select fans, we must move 338,688 cfm. A fan drawing air through a 4" (10 cm) pad will move air at 250'/min. and can move 21,090 cfm per fan (according to the fan manufacturer's specifications). So we divide 338,688 cfm by the 21,090 cfm capacity of each fan. Answer: We need 17 fans. (Note: to convert cfm to the metric equivalent, 1 cfm equals 0.00047195 cubic meters per second.)

Assuming the use of a pad that will move 250 cfm/ft.² of pad area, we divide the 338,688 cfm by 250 and will need 1,355 ft.² (126 m²) of pad area. Again, 4" (10 cm) thick paper pad flows air at 250 cfm and a 6" (15 cm) thick pad at 400 cfm. Assuming the pads are mounted in the gable wall, we have 294' (89.6 m) available to mount the system (14 bays x 21' [6.4 m]). The square feet required divided by the available linear feet of mounting space means the pads will have to be at least 4.61' (1.4 m) tall to do the job. Always figure pads up to the next even foot (or meter), not down. In this example, then 5' (2 m) tall pads should be used.

Pads are used as one of the final steps or stages in greenhouse cooling. The first stage is to open sidewall and/or roof vents. The next stage or two is to turn on one or several fans. Once all the fans are running, the pad pump is turned on, beginning the evaporative cooling process. An additional level of cooling would come from partially or fully closing the shade curtain system.

Fan Maintenance

For fans to work at peak efficiency with minimal electricity usage, certain maintenance guidelines should be followed. Keep all the belts tight to eliminate slipping. Slipping would not only reduce the air output of the fans but also increase the motor's electrical use (automatic belt tighteners are available). Be sure that all air leaks in the greenhouse are kept plugged in order to get top efficiency from your pads. Air leaks in the house can increase temperatures in the greenhouse 4–10°F (2–6°C) because air is going through the leaks rather than the pads. Be sure the pads are kept completely wet, without any dry spots. Control algae with chemical algaecides or household bleach, but be sure the bleach won't be toxic to the crop you are growing. During winter months, check for air intrusion through fan shutters or inlet shutters to reduce heat loss. All these simple steps will help keep your greenhouse cooler in the summer and warmer in winter.

Fog (Mist) Cooling and Humidifying

Using high pressure for cooling and humidifying greenhouses for ornamental, vegetable, nursery stock, and cut flower production is steadily increasing due to its ability to provide even temperature reductions and levels of humidity. Fog offers these advantages in arid climates as well as the humid climate typically found in the southern United States.

The principles of cooling with fog and with pads are primarily the same. The difference is how efficiently the water is used for cooling. In pad cooling, water saturates a pad, concentrating all the cooling potential in one location in the greenhouse, achieving 85% efficiency. Fog systems distribute the water in a vaporized form evenly throughout the greenhouse, through selected placement of the atomization lines. Because of the flash evaporation characteristics of fog, 100% efficiency is achieved.

From air inlet to exhaust fans, temperature differentials with fog cooling can be as low as 1°F (0.6°C). In a typical fan-and-pad installation, temperature differentials can be 7–10°F (4–6°C) from air inlet to exhaust fans. A fog system can be installed in any house configuration, such as with natural or mechanical ventilation, and lends itself to houses where insect screens are used to protect air inlets.

Because fog systems operate with very high pressure pumps (in excess of 1,000 psi) and extremely fine fog nozzle openings, it's very important to keep the system properly maintained. Fog systems are designed for each grower, taking into consideration ambient weather conditions, greenhouse configurations, ventilation methods, crops to be grown, and desired temperature reductions or humidity levels. Once temperature objectives are known, for example, a psychometric chart is used to define the amount of water required to meet the cooling objective. Simple division of the nozzle flow rate into the required gallons (liters) per minute will tell how many nozzles need to be in the greenhouse.

Greenhouse Heating

Jim Rearden

Most laypeople have no idea that greenhouses need heating. "Don't they just get warm on their own?"

they ask. Nothing could be further from the truth. It's been estimated that the commercial greenhouse industry in the United States spends as much as $250 million annually on heating fuel. Further, greenhouses are probably the most unique structures to design heating systems for. They have very poor thermal resistance to heat loss, and their contents are typically quite sensitive to any variations in heating delivery. The occupants of our buildings can't just get up and move away from a cold spot on their own . . . most likely, they'll just wilt and die.

Unless you're blessed with a greenhouse location that provides perfect temperatures year-round, you'll need a heating system to optimize production of your plants. That's because most of the crops we grow evolved in temperate, subtropical, or tropical environments. For most plants, growing successfully is about trying to create an environment akin to the region of the world where they originated. That's much more involved than filling a plastic or glass structure with hot air. It involves consideration of media temperature, humidity levels, foliage temperature, and controls integration.

The good news is that greenhouse heating technology has kept pace with the changes in the industry. As fuel prices increase, more fuel-efficient systems become available. As breeders and cultural experts find out how things such as media temperature and DIF (the difference between day and night temperatures) affect plant physiology, manufacturers introduce more systems to help growers stay in these production guidelines. And, as our greenhouses become more mechanized, manufacturers and growers create adaptations to provide the flexibility needed to accommodate the new equipment.

Figure 6-6. Even in the mildest climates, good heating is essential for good crop growth.

For proper heating design, you must first take into account all the "external" variables: fuel type, availability, and cost; mechanization and automation systems in the facility; and environmental requirements or local code compliance issues. Then you have to balance those against the most important needs of all—the cultural requirements of the plant—for peak production and profitability.

Much has been learned in the last twenty-five years about the climate of the greenhouse. It used to be a common approach to simply warm the air (all the air) in the greenhouse and call it good. Now we have a sophisticated understanding of the roles that media and plant temperature play in the way plants grow. The process of planning heating systems now includes considerations of temperature needs in a more layered or "stratified" way.

Not long ago, "zones" of heating typically lined up with entire greenhouse bays. Now it's not uncommon to see heating systems zoned horizontally as well as vertically. For instance, many growers are now growing on heated flood floors. They typically will control the temperature of the plants on the floor separately from the plants hanging above. Further, there may be yet another horizontal level of control at the gutter or roof level for snow and ice removal or dehumidification.

As an industry, we now have the tools to create just about any type of environment needed for optimal control of the temperature of plant products. The modern greenhouse operator has more heating options than ever.

Heat Loss: The Reason for Heating

As mentioned above, greenhouses lose heat quickly. They're covered with materials that need to transmit light, and this usually means thin plastic or glass. These materials aren't much of an insulating barrier to heat loss. It's common for northern greenhouses to lose as much as 100 BTUH or more per square foot at low temperatures . . . but we're getting ahead of ourselves. First, let's cover some basic heating terms.

BTU

A British thermal unit is the amount of heat energy it takes to warm 1 lb. (0.454 kg) of water 1°F (0.556°C).

BTUH

The quantity of British thermal units transferred in one hour. This is the number that's most commonly used when discussing and specifying heating systems in the United States. Most heaters and boilers carry a "BTUH capacity" rating.

Delta T

Usually signified using the symbol ΔT, delta T is the difference between two temperatures—in this case, the difference between inside and outside.

U value

The inverse of the commonly understood "R" (insulation) value, where U=1/R. It's the measurement of the ability of a material to transfer heat, stated in BTUs/ft.^{2} per degree delta T per hour. The higher the number, the more heat that can be transmitted through a material. In other words, the lower the U value of your glazing system, the easier it is to heat your greenhouse.

Heat loss occurs when the inside temperature of the greenhouse exceeds the outside air temperature. Glazing systems have varying resistance ratings to this outward movement of heat energy. All of the common glazing systems on the market carry a U value rating. A U factor provides a means of calculating heat loss. For example, let's say you have a greenhouse sidewall that is 12' (3.6 m) tall by 100' (30 m) long, which is 1,200 ft.^{2} (108 m^2), is made of double inflated polyethylene (a U value of 0.7), it's 0°F (-18°C) outside, and you're maintaining 70°F (21°C) inside (a 70°F delta T [39°C]). To figure the heat loss of this wall you would simply multiply the area by the U by the delta T:

$$1,200 \text{ (area in ft.}^2) \times 0.7 \text{ (U)} \times 70 \text{ } (\Delta T)$$
$$= 58,800 \text{ BTUH}$$

Note: This simplified version of a heat-loss formula is just for illustration and doesn't account for important wind or air infiltration factors. If you'd like in-depth information on greenhouse heat loss, contact the National Greenhouse Manufacturers Association (www.ngma.com). They publish an excellent pamphlet on this subject titled "NGMA Heat Loss Standards."

How Heat Transfer Works

There are three basic ways that heat moves from one place to another inside the greenhouse: conduction, convection, and radiation. Note that all three of these are at play simultaneously and to varying degrees in all greenhouses. Properly harnessing the effect of each one will hugely affect your heating success.

Conduction

Conductive heat transfer occurs when plants are actually touching the heating system. This is the kind of heat transfer that enables benchtop and warm-floor heating systems. Heating energy is conducted from the growing surface directly into the container, the growing media, and, subsequently, the plant.

Convection

Convection uses the forces of air circulation to transfer heat. The two basic precepts of convection are: cold air displaces warm air and warm air rises. In greenhouses, convective heat transfer is what's occurring when you see the "mirage" around a heating pipe. When convectively heated air passes by plant material, heat is transferred to the plant. In most convective heating system designs, even heat transfer is facilitated by use of fans to "stir" the heating energy around.

Radiation

Radiation uses electromagnetic infrared waves to transfer heat energy. Anyone who has warmed their hands in front of a wood stove or felt the warmth from a sidewalk or brick wall once the sun has gone down has experienced radiant heat transfer. In both cases, the air may not be warm at all, but the heating energy is felt just the same. In greenhouses, radiation heat transfer occurs when plants are warmed in the proximity of heating pipes (which may be simultaneously convecting). It's the primary means of heat transfer of infrared-style heating systems.

Choosing a Heating System

There are myriad choices for the modern grower to create the optimum greenhouse environment. Whether the heating needs to be delivered above the plants or below, around the perimeter, or to melt snow and ice, systems are available offering a balance of value and performance that will be right for your situation.

There are several industry firms that offer in-depth heating advice. Take the time to talk to them and find someone who you feel comfortable with guiding you through the many choices available. It's a good idea to work with designers, suppliers, and contractors that are familiar with the industry because there are many unique aspects to greenhouses that these people will know beforehand. The last thing you want to do is have someone learn (at your expense) that it's not a good idea to put pipes in a place that will cast big shadows on your production areas or that residential furnaces won't stand up to the wet, caustic greenhouse environment.

Beware of oversimplified heating solutions that don't take into account the dynamic environment that greenhouses represent. Greenhouses tend to lose heat quickly, but because they're really glorified solar collectors, they tend gain heat quite readily, too. The benchmarks that many greenhouse-heating systems are now being judged by are responsiveness and flexibility in a fast-changing environment. Further, in your quest for the ideal heating system, remember that your plants exist simultaneously in two very different environments: rooting media and the surrounding air. Will the system that serves you best need to address them distinctly and separately? Make decisions in this area based on the best culture for what you intend to grow.

Types of Heating Systems

There are so many choices in heating systems. In many cases, the most effective solution is found by using a combination of systems in the same greenhouse. The current "crop" of heating options breaks down into five choices: unit heaters, hot water systems, steam heat, infrared heat, and electrical resistance systems.

Unit heaters

In the United States, unit heaters enjoy a market dominance of approximately 60% of all heating equipment dollars spent on greenhouses. The United States is unique in this regard compared with the rest of the world, which depends more on hot water heat. Still, unit heaters provide a lot of "bang for the buck" and should remain a popular choice for heating long into the future.

Unit heaters come in several styles, but they all share the same description and function: self-contained devices for generating hot air and distributing it using an internal fan system. Typically, unit heaters are mounted near the endwalls of the greenhouse and deliver their heating energy toward the middle of the structure. Most of the market is served with gas-fired units that are mounted up high. In the northeast United States, where fuel oil is predominant, you'll see larger oil-fired units with multidirectional ducts set on concrete blocks at greenhouse endwalls. Besides gas-fired and oil-fired units, unit heaters are also available in electric, hot water, and steam styles.

Most of the developments in unit heaters have been in the gas-fired arena. In the last few years, growers have been installing "high-efficiency" units that save fuel compared with older units. The newer units have induced draft fans in their exhaust pipes that reduce or eliminate standby losses from the heated greenhouse. Further, many of the products being offered today boast enhancements that use outside air for combustion air rather than greenhouse air. This feature augments efficiency gains as well as increases heat exchanger life.

Combustion technology has improved as well. There are now unit heaters that offer efficiency ratings in the mid-90% range. They do this by adding a "secondary" heat exchanger that cools and condenses the exhaust from the combustion process. The scavenged heat is then put into the greenhouse rather than going up the stack while the condensate from the exhaust drains through a small pipe to the outside.

Unit heaters are located in very harsh environments, and many of the products on the market weren't originally engineered for this. Many growers have suffered through troublesome unit heater issues that range from corrosion vulnerability to heat exchanger failure and crop problems resulting from leaking flue gas contamination. Manufacturers have responded with more robust heat exchanger designs to reduce these problems.

"Direct-fired" unit heaters have no heat exchanger at all. They mix the products of combustion into the heated air directly. While the payoff is elevated efficiency and CO_2 augmentation, it's important to be cautious when using these units for a couple of reasons. Because water is a byproduct of the combustion process, unvented unit heaters can create humidity problems in tight greenhouses. Most of the units on

the market are designed with a catalytic system that ensures that noxious combustion products are cleaned up before delivering the heated air and exhaust mix to the growing area. However, many flowering crops exhibit high sensitivity to products of combustion. So the buzzword here is "caution." Most direct-fired unit heaters utilize ducted-in fresh, oxygen-rich outside air for combustion, diluting possible contaminants. This also helps to optimize the combustion process.

Hot water systems

These are the most common systems seen in modern greenhouses the world over. Water offers unparalleled flexibility in terms of heating capacity and manageability. Hot water can carry tremendous amounts of energy over great distances, and once there it can be directed to transfer its heating energy in a multitude of ways. From the utility of a central boiler system, the greenhouse operator can use this wonderful fluid to heat floors, heat under benches, heat on top of benches, heat around the perimeter, preheat irrigation water, or melt snow and ice. It can even be pumped through a hot water-style unit heater.

Water is a great medium for transporting and delivering heating energy. For instance, did you know that per volume, water can carry 3,500 times the energy that air can carry? To put this into perspective, picture 1 ft.³ (0.3 m³) of water—about 7.4 gal. (33 L). Now, picture a 20 x 20' (6 x 6 m) room—about 3,200 ft.³ (91 m³) of air—and less capable of carrying the potential energy of our sample of water!

Figure 6-7. Unit heaters dominate 60% of the market in the United States.

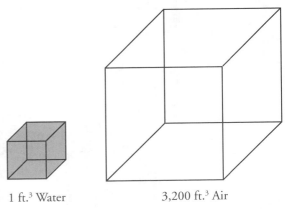

1 ft.³ Water   3,200 ft.³ Air

Heating Energy Comparison
(per volume)

Figure 6-8. Water can carry 3,500 times the energy that air can carry.

The reason hot water is the heating medium of choice for so many growers is because of its inherent ability to be *managed*. Hot water can transport tremendous heating energy over great distances with very little loss of efficiency. Once at its destination, it can be routed to myriad heating projects: floor heating, bench heating, top heating, perimeter heating, snow and ice removal . . . the list goes on.

The most common hot water systems are bare pipes located under growing benches and up high in the trusses—a system that's been used for more than a century. Before unit heaters became commonplace, bare round hot water piping was one of the most prevalent ways greenhouses were heated. The modern twists on these systems are embodied in the way the heating pipes look and are made. Most of the modern systems use thin-wall steel tubing welded together rather than thick cast iron pipes threaded together. The thinner wall increases responsiveness by reducing thermal lag. Basically, less mass means a quicker system.

Further development can be seen in the growing application of piping systems with enhanced surface area designs, the newer generation of "finned heating pipes." Adding surface area to a round pipe enhances the heat-emitting capability of the pipe and, since the surface area of the pipe is enhanced, the water passages can be made smaller, thereby reducing system water volume and increasing responsiveness.

Many of the finned heating pipes being offered are made of aluminum, so they don't need painting or other maintenance. This is a big advantage over the mild steel piping systems, which require regular painting. Further, fewer pipes are typically required to do the same heating job. This reduces shadows, cuts down on excess installation costs and eliminates excess water volume in a system.

Another heat delivery system that utilizes hot water is the warm-floor slab heating system. These systems are typically comprised of evenly spaced thermoplastic tubes (usually 0.5" [2 cm] tubing spaced 9" [23 cm] apart),

Figure 6-9. Hot water, pumped through pipes running through the greenhouse, is the most common form of greenhouse heating worldwide. These are finned aluminum heating pipes.

which are cast into the concrete floor of the greenhouses. The tubes are connected to a manifold set to provide supply and return connections for hot water flow. Floor heating systems like this are becoming more popular as more growers turn to flood-floor irrigation systems to solve their irrigation, runoff, and labor dilemmas. These systems can provide 30–40 BTUH/ft.^{2} of heat transfer.

Floor heat is proving to be an ideal means of heating for service buildings and headhouses as well because it makes a pleasant environment for workers who praise the attributes of warm feet and the quiet of not having noisy unit heater fans running. Using very flexible and durable synthetic rubber tubing, many growers are finding that they can efficiently heat gravel, soil, or sand floors with hot water—some are even heating with tubing exposed. The latest innovation in this field is the tubing being woven directly into weed-mat type fabric for easier installation.

The final example of heat delivery using a hot water source are the benchtop systems that use small, pencil-size tubes, usually spaced about 2" (5 cm) apart. Pots, flats, or trays sit directly on the tubes. These "microclimate" systems use hot water circulating through these little tubes to transfer heat into the growing media. There are also now preassembled fabric mats offered for benchtop heating. Usually, these systems are controlled based on media temperature. Many growers use them in their propagation and/or germination areas.

Steam heat

The steam heating system is disappearing from the landscape of the North American greenhouse. These stalwart systems require substantial maintenance and suffer from poor efficiency and high installation costs. There is, however, renewed interest in steam boilers to generate steam for pasteurization of soil media because the fumigant methyl bromide is being slowly regulated out of use. However, the only new steam systems going in these days are expansions of existing systems, most dating back thirty years or more.

Infrared heat

Infrared energy from the sun travels 93 million miles to the earth in just over eight minutes. This energy is absorbed by the earth and converted to heat. That's why the temperature down here is warmer than in the upper atmosphere, even though the upper atmosphere is closer to the sun. This, in essence, is how infrared heating systems work in greenhouses.

Figure 6-10. Infrared heat warms the greenhouse by giving off infrared radiation that's absorbed by the objects in the greenhouse and then given off as useable heat.

These systems are only available as gas fired (LP or natural) and are installed in or near the peak of the greenhouse; they run the length of the house. A burner combusts the fuel, and as it's routed down the length of the heater through a metal heating tube it heats the tube to a point where it becomes red hot. This heat energy is then reflected down into the greenhouse production space and collected by plant material and all the other objects it encounters.

Infrared systems are almost as easy to install as unit heaters and offer the potential benefits of an environment with warm, dry leaves. Because they focus their heating delivery by heating objects, not air, they offer energy savings over straight air heating systems.

Electrical resistance systems

For spot-heating applications such as germination or propagation tables, electrical resistance heating offers a clean, silent solution that can provide good soil temperatures for strong, early plant development. Other heating appliances such as boilers and air heaters are available in electrical versions, but because the delivered cost of electricity is typically three to six times the price per BTU of other fuels, electrical heat is very rare in our industry. But for the smaller job (usually less than 100 ft.^{2} [9 m^2]), they offer ease of installation and convenience.

Boilers: The Heart of Every Hot Water System

There are several variations in boiler styles, and the debates that manufacturers have about which one gives the peak efficiencies will continue for years. However, there are some solid facts you need to know. The three most common styles of boilers seen in greenhouses are the fire-tube style, the water-tube style, and the cast-iron "sectional" style. The names are descriptive enough to denote the differences.

Figure 6-11. The boiler is the heart of every hot water heating system.

Fire-tube boilers

These resemble water tanks and have many tubes through which the flames from burning fuel are routed. Outside of the tubes is the boiler water, which alternately gathers heat at the boiler and disperses it in the greenhouse while being pumped in a closed-loop circle around the system.

Water-tube boilers

The water-tube boilers are just the opposite. Water is pumped through the tubes while heating energy from burning fuel is transferred through the tube walls. The hot water is then sent to the greenhouse.

Most of the technological development in boilers has been the area of water-tube boilers, driven by the demand for higher efficiency for residential heating. In the last five years, many new boiler products have been introduced that offer up to 99% efficiency. They

achieve this by extracting the heat out of the exhaust, bringing the flue temperatures down so low that condensation is formed and, in many cases, PVC piping can be used for the chimney.

Cast-iron sectional boilers

This is the oldest design. These boilers are made by casting "sections" of cast iron. Each section has water passages on the inside and a "fire-side," where the products of combustion create and transfer their heat. Quantities of these sections can be bolted together to fit a grower's specific needs.

The biggest issue to be aware of in the realm of boilers isn't the brand, the color, or the country of origin. It is how much fuel you have to put in on an annual basis versus what you get out in terms of useful heat. This is known as the "annual efficiency" and is really the bottom line in the boiler decision process. However, there's no standard or government-enforced benchmarking system for units over 300,000 BTU, so you have to be a bit of an investigator yourself. Don't be misled by judging a piece of equipment by the common "combustion efficiency" term exclusively. If a boiler has good combustion efficiency but loses much of its energy through the jacket or up the chimney during stand-by periods, your seasonal efficiency probably won't be very good.

Demand-type boilers

A growing trend is toward demand-type boilers that operate only when there is a call for heat in the greenhouse. These units heat water as it flows by, since they have no appreciable on-board water volume. Also called low-mass boilers, they're typically constructed using copper or stainless steel heat exchangers and are offered in limited capacity sizes. For this reason, they're often installed in groups, or modules. This approach makes sense for many growers because the level of safety and redundancy goes up with multiple boilers. Also, this type of system can be set up to grow as your facility expands. Most of the newer demand-type boilers only operate with gas fuels, such as natural gas and propane.

Biomass systems

Some growers dream of "getting off the grid" and becoming self-sufficient in terms of their fuel resources. If burning wood chips or other biomass is going to be contemplated, there are a few considerations that should be researched and understood before jumping in with both feet:

1. Is your fuel really "free" or "cheap"? Will the price remain steady over a reasonable period of time? Will other businesses looking to biomass create competition and drive up costs? This happened recently when several growers installed corn burners only to watch the cost per bushel rise dramatically.

2. Biomass systems require three times the maintenance (or more) of conventional (gas or oil) systems. Budget for this.

3. Biomass fuel needs to be handled, inspected for quality variances, and sometimes processed before burning. This is a cost that must be accounted for.

4. Biomass fuel needs to be stored. You will need to create a place to store it and protect it from getting moist or damaged in other ways.

5. Emissions laws are tightening up. While you may be able to avoid much scrutiny from air quality regulators if your operation is rural, the recent widespread interest in biomass burning for homes has some regional governments looking into rigid rules for what comes out of a chimney. Adding emission-reducing equipment to your system may be very expensive.

6. Most biomass systems are designed to generate hot water. To make the most of the investment in this equipment, you should plan to install a heat storage tank. A proper heat storage tank is designed to be a vertical vessel that allows for stratification of the water temperatures, with the hottest water in the "layers" near the top. Sizing of this tank is crucial and should be calculated by a qualified, experienced engineer.

7. To take the most advantage of a biomass hot water system, the heating distribution should be optimized to use lower water temperatures than a typical conventionally fueled hot water system. Putting more pipes and tubes in the greenhouse to be able to meet heating loads with lower water temperatures will enhance the operation of a biomass system.

8. There may be incentives available from local, state, or national agencies to offset some of the capital cost involved in the installation.

After looking at this issue with a strong dose of pragmatism, many growers find that the payback picture for biomass is not as rosy as thought at first blush. It's important to "look before you leap," as a biomass system can require an additional department within your company and more equipment and space requirements than expected. However, for some growers, especially those that do not have access to natural gas, biomass systems have been great investments.

Pros and Cons

All of the systems mentioned above are valid heating methods. Each has attributes that give it the qualification to merit consideration for your specific needs. The best way to view all these various options is to see them as "tools" to get a specific job done. Following are a few considerations to add to your analysis.

Unit heaters

Advantages are low cost for lots of BTUs, quick response, and ease of zoning houses. Disadvantages are a lack of focused heating (meaning, lower distribution efficiency), longevity can be poor in the greenhouse environment, unit heaters cast undesirable shadows and can be noisy, and having all the heat output delivered via air movement limits your ability to hang plants near heaters.

Hot water systems

Advantages include flexibility, manageability, and the ability to change heating fuel without changing much of anything inside the greenhouse. Disadvantages include initial cost, complexity, and the special skills needed for proper installations.

Infrared systems

Energy efficiency, dry leaves, and reduction in diseases, such as botrytis, are among the advantages. Disadvantages can be shadowing, proximity-dependent heat transfer, and uneven heat transfer.

Cost Range

Price ranges can be quite misleading in the realm of discussing greenhouse heating equipment. This is because the cost of a system is impacted by the size of the installation, the severity of the weather and temperatures where it will be installed, and the complexity of the system in terms of quantity of zones, level of control desired, and so on. However, for the purpose of discussion, the following rough figures are offered. These costs are in U.S. dollars for a 1 acre (0.4 ha) application, in a northern United States region, with minimal complexity in the design of the system:

Unit heater system (gas fired)	$0.40–0.80/ft.^{2} ($4.25–8.60/m^2)
Hot water system	$1.50–4.00/ft.^{2} ($16.25–43.00/m^2)
Infrared system	$1.00–1.60/ft.^{2} ($10.75–17.25/m^2)

Figure 6-12. Infrared heat warms the greenhouse by giving off infrared radiation that's absorbed by the objects in the greenhouse and then given off as useable heat.

The reason for the existence of all these systems is that they all have a worthy and valid role to play in the grand scheme of heating greenhouses. Finding the appropriate heating method for your facility is a balancing act between your budget, the struggle of comparing initial costs and long-term operational costs, and determining what makes an optimal environment for your plants. Your best edge is to have a good working knowledge of all the options available to you, then challenge your heating supplier to provide the balanced solutions best suited for your needs.

Biomass Heating

Peter Stuyt

The 2008 energy price spike and resulting energy crisis spurred many growers to look for energy sources other than oil and natural gas. Biomass seemed like a logical choice for farmers, and it quickly grew into a serious alternative.

Most Americans probably do not realize that biomass right now is the most widely used fuel in the world. Some 500 million families use wood, crop waste, and dung for everyday cooking and heating. Unfortunately, the open fires or simple clay domes families use to cook are completely inefficient ways of burning wood and waste. The toxic smoke and soot from these fires is considered a major health hazard. Properly designed stoves, priced at $20 to $95, can cut these emissions up to 95%. Fortunately, well-designed technology is readily available, as are biomass fuel products ready to burn. In general, biomass boilers resemble traditional gas boilers in size and shape. They adapt easily to a greenhouse environment, and biofuel prices are competitive.

A number of well-known and respected greenhouse operations already made the step and installed biomass boilers, including Metrolina Greenhouses of Huntersville, North Carolina; Green Circle Growers of Oberlin, Ohio; and Willoway Nurseries of Avon, Ohio. Plainview Growers of Allamuchy, New Jersey, have gone beyond just burning biomass and are on their way to energy independence. Not only do they have a biomass pellet boiler, they are running their own pellet plant, producing switchgrass pellets. And now, with the help of local farmers, they are growing *Miscanthus* and switchgrass, which will make them essentially energy independent. They'll even be able to sell pellets to other biomass users.

What Is Biomass?

For our greenhouse purposes, what do we consider biomass? Almost anything with a carbon value fits the bill. Forestry by-products, agricultural crop waste, and manure are some examples. Others are construction and demolition wood, wood fiber packaging products, municipal yard and food waste . . . essentially most trash and leftovers that are on their way to the landfill. In addition to waste, some farmers are developing and growing crops specifically for their value as a fuel. Miscanthus, switchgrass, hemp, and fast-growing trees such as eucalyptus and poplar are examples of effective products available right now.

Both biomass and fossil fuels are plant-based. The main difference between them is time. Fossil fuels—coal, oil, and gas—go back millions of years, basically storing CO_2 deep underground. Biomass is a recently produced or grown source of CO_2.

Crops absorb and use CO_2 while growing. Crops grown for their fuel value release CO_2 during the combustion process, closing the carbon cycle. Therefore, biomass as a fuel is considered carbon neutral: it results in no net increase of CO_2 levels in the air.

Creating Fuel from Biomass

Turning biomass material into a usable fuel is mostly a logistical challenge. Farmers grow and harvest a fuel crop. Trash collectors and municipalities with trash separation programs produce piles of biomass waste. Both will truck this bulk to processing sites. Dairy, pork, and poultry operations produce large quantities of manure, typically stored on-site in large ponds or lagoons.

At these processing sites, larger pieces of wood and grass bales are chopped down to a size processing equipment can handle. Wood chips must be no larger than 2" (5 cm) to be used as a fuel, but that is fairly simple to produce. Large barns are needed to store chips and protect them from the weather. The drawbacks of chips are quality and moisture variations and uneven burn value. Bulkiness, or low bulk density, is another problem, making handling and freight costly.

Densification offers a solution. Wood chips are further shredded and turned into a powder. Powders of different biomass stocks can be mixed into different blends, or recipes, depending on what kind of biomass is available. This powder mix goes through densification equipment and is turned into logs, bricks, pucks, and pellets. The result is stable, predictable, easy-to-handle product with a precise burn value. Densification also turns low bulk value into a three- to five-times higher bulk density, making handling and freight much more efficient. Manure and other high-moisture waste products can be used in a densification cycle after drying. However, drying is costly and requires energy to heat this waste.

More common is the use of a biodigester, an anaerobic digester working with anaerobic bacteria (anaerobic means bacteria that can live without oxygen). One example of such a system is a covered, manure-filled lagoon in which bacteria turn waste into biogas, primarily methane. Biogas can be used to fire generators, producing heat and power. Leftover sludge of a biodigester can be used as a fertilizer.

Biomass gasification is a process of turning waste into biogas, or syngas, to be used for combustion or in power generators. In producing biogas, biomass is partially burned. This burning process releases syngas, a mixture of carbon monoxide, hydrogen, and methane. The process does need substantial energy input to operate, offsetting some efficiency benefits.

Biomass Boilers

Wood chip–burning boilers

Wood chip–burning boilers have a long history as a heat source and are relatively simple: Chips are fed into the boiler fire box from the top or the front and drop onto a flat or step-grate floor. This floor slowly moves from front to back, moving the chips forward. The boiler uses a small gas burner to start up. Chips

burn while moving forward, heating water inside the boiler body or inside a network of tubes. This water can be used to heat greenhouses directly or is turned into steam. Steam can be used to heat steam radiators that use fans to push heated air inside the greenhouse. Or steam can be used to heat water as the water and steam pass through a heat exchanger sitting next to the boiler.

Figure 6-13. A moving floor system feeds wood and other fuel to a biomass boiler.

As the wood chips travel the grate surface, the wood turns to ash and drops into an auger gutter at the end of the floor. The augur slowly removes ash from the boiler body, dropping the ash into barrels or containers.

Hot air produced by the burning process travels through pipes running the length of the boiler body, right behind the fire box. These pipes are surrounded by water, which heats up as hot air passes by. This air carries with it ash and other small particles that are filtered out by a dry or wet cyclone filter unit.

Getting wood chips to the boiler and maintaining a steady flow of them is the main challenge with these systems. Larger-scale boilers require 15–20 tons (13,600–18,100 kg) of chips a night. All of this wood needs to be delivered and stored in large buildings. To move chips from the front of the building to the back, a moving or walking floor is required.

Since wood chips of various quality and moisture levels produce a substantial quantity of ash, ash removal is the other main problem. Equipment that removes ash must stand up to heat. Because of all this, system maintenance is serious business, and the boiler plant requires round-the-clock monitoring during the heating season.

Fluidized bed boilers

Fluidized bed boilers utilize a sand-filled fire box floor. A sand floor makes it possible to burn a wide variety of fuels, not only biomass products of any quality and moisture levels but also coal, tire chips, and sludge pellets. This gives the operator flexibility in his fuel choices.

The boiler uses a small gas burner to start up, and once the flame is established, a controlled volume of air is blown through the sand layer. The airflow makes for a complete combustion of the injected fuel. Heat produced in the fire chamber in turn heats up water in the boiler body and in a series of tubes running through the sand.

The sand layer at the bottom of the fire box does need regular cleaning since waste products cannot be extracted automatically. These boilers require cyclones to clean flue gases, and have the same maintenance needs as chip boilers.

Feeding the chips into a fluidized bed boiler requires the same buildings, walking floors, and other equipment as a wood chip boiler.

Pellet boilers

Pellet boilers are specifically designed to burn pellets. Pellets resemble cattle feed in shape and size. Pellets are dropped into the fire box, on top of a shaking

Figure 6-14. Storage bins for biomass pellets.

floor. Air is blown through small holes in this floor, producing a complete burn. The shaking floor pushes the burning pellets forward until the remaining ash drops into an auger gutter, extracting the ashes automatically. Based on pellet quality, leftover ash amounts to 3–4% of original bulk. Pellet boilers need cyclone units to clean their flue gasses.

Equipment needed to store and deliver pellets to the boiler is the same as used in cattle feed storage and handling. Large vertical 20–25 ton (18,100–22,700 kg) storage bins are placed next to the boiler house. Auger tubes feed pellets to the fire box. This equipment has been around for a long time, requires little space, and is easy to assemble on site.

Biogas

Biogas extraction from manure or other high-moisture waste requires a large pond lined with a polypropylene or polyester sheet. The pond or lagoon needs to be covered to allow the anaerobic bacteria to be effective.

Bacteria break down the available waste in the lagoon, turning it into a usable biogas. Biogas is primarily methane, similar to natural gas but of a lower quality.

Depending on the location of the lagoon, equipment is sized and installed to transport manure from the cattle barns. Biogas extraction equipment is added to the lagoon, in addition to gas-storage and gas-upgrading equipment. Before the biogas can be used, it needs to be drained of moisture, cleaned of different unusable chemicals, and pressurized.

Biogas is mostly used at the site where it has been produced, which is the only way to make this energy efficient. If freight is required, biogas quickly looses its economic viability and energy efficiency value.

To use this gas, power generators are needed. To use the resulting dry manure matter, farmland is needed around the lagoon location. Greenhouse operations located close to dairy farms are perfectly positioned to use excess heat and power produced by the generators. Outfitted with quality flue gas cleaning equipment, CO_2, produced in the burning process and an important ingredient for plant growth, can also be used inside a greenhouse. However, neither biogas nor syngas (below) are commonly used today at greenhouse operations.

Syngas

Syngas, which is biogas produced using gasification, has been around for a long time, with the technology going back 180 years. Syngas results from incomplete combustion of biomass. This is a two-step process of first burning, or reducing, biomass to charcoal and then burning or converting the resulting charcoal at the right temperature to syngas.

This conversion takes place in a gasifier, which is an upright barrel-shaped vessel. Elevator belts drop biomass into this vessel from the top, allowing for a layering of the reduction and burning process: (1) drying of fuel; (2) pyrolysis, which drives out tar and CO_2; (3) reduction to charcoal; and (4) combustion, which is facilitated by the introduction of air. Syngas is extracted at this point.

The most important design concern of any gasifier is temperature stratification. The different layers of the reduction process require specific temperature zones to be most effective, rising in temperature from 390°F (200°C) at the top to 2,370°F (1,300°C) at the bottom. These temperature characteristics are biomass specific and require vessels designed based on that information.

Preparing biomass for a gasifier depends on input materials but generally requires the same equipment as needed for wood chip boilers. Extraction, cooling, filtering, and handling equipment will be needed for to extract the water, syngas, tar, CO_2, dust, ash, and slag from the gasifier, all at separate layers. Syngas quality control is important in order to for attached generators to run smoothly. All this obviously requires a high level of equipment maintenance and process control.

Four Levels of Climate Control
Chris Beytes

Today, four basic levels of environmental control system are available: thermostats, step controllers, computer zone controllers, and integrated computer systems. But with so many different systems on the market, there's a lot of confusion among growers who want to upgrade but don't understand the differences between a computer zone controller and an integrated computer system. So to clarify the details for you, here's a primer on environmental control systems and what they can do for you.

Level One: Thermostats

Thermostats have been used since electricity was first brought into the greenhouse, and a row of Dayton single- or two-stage thermostats is still the most common way to control greenhouse heaters, fans, and vents. At $50 or $60 each, they're also the least expensive way to control your environment—at least when used on a small scale—and they're acceptable in temporary structures and small houses with very little climate control equipment. If you have a Quonset house with one heater and one fan, a couple of thermostats are probably all you need.

The drawbacks to thermostats are numerous. Most aren't made to survive the greenhouse environment. They aren't very accurate—plus or minus 2 or 3°F is the typical accuracy out of the box, and they get worse with age. They also don't necessarily match one another: one thermostat's 68°F (20°C) may be

Making Pellets

While the burning of biomass pellets is gaining in popularity, production of pellets has thus far been left to specialists, although at least one grower, Plainview Growers mentioned above, has taken on the challenge. Here is how it's done:

A typical pellet line has several machines, each handling a specific step in the process of making pellets. Depending on the type of input material is used, chipping equipment is needed to bring larger pieces or bales down to a 2" (5 cm) chip size. Measuring input moisture levels is important. If the moisture percentage is too high, chips need to go through a dryer. Input moisture percentage should ideally be at 12%.

The next step is a hammer mill, where chips are hammered into a power. Bucket elevators lift this powder up to a storage bin on top of the pellet mill. As the powder drops into the pellet mill, high-pressure rollers push the powder though holes in a round dye. The heat generated by this process further dries the pellets and gives them their distinct shine. Hot pellets require cooling, which happens in a cooling unit using forced air. After cooling, the pellets are ready to be delivered, stored, and burned.

another's 70°F (21°C). Probably the biggest drawback is that they don't link your systems together—there's nothing to prevent your heaters and fans from running at the same time. That's a real energy waster.

Thankfully, modern computer technology has reached even the lowly thermostat. Today you can buy electronic, digital, "smart" thermostats that, because they're designed for the greenhouse, offer very good accuracy and longevity. Their price may be the biggest drawback: $400 or more, according to one manufacturer.

Figure 6-15. A thermostat is the most basic level of environ-mental control.

Level Two: Stage Controllers

For $900 you can buy a dozen or so regular thermostats or two "smart" thermostats. Or you can enter the twenty-first century with a stage controller.

A stage controller combines the functions of several thermostats into one unit, eliminating many of their drawbacks. Most stage controllers offer two stages of heating and three stages of cooling, with a set point (the desired greenhouse temperature) dividing them. It's called a stage system because it works in stages. As the temperature increases from your set point, the first stage of cooling comes on—opening a vent, for instance. If the temperature continues to rise, some fans will come on. If the temperature increases even more, the rest of the fans will come on or the cooling pad pump will start up.

If the temperature falls below the set point, your first stage of heating kicks in—three of your six unit heaters, for instance. If the temperature drops further, the other three heaters come on.

While this is no different from how your old thermostats work, there's no risk of two systems operating at the same time because of temperature sensor inaccuracy. Additional features may include the ability to set separate day and night set points—for instance, you can

set your greenhouse to be held at 72°F (22°C) during the day but only 65°F (18°C) at night. Some devices can be programmed for DIF—a timer will automatically drop your greenhouse temperature before sunrise and then bring it up at 8:00 A.M., for instance.

These aren't "computers," however, which can be both a pro and a con. The pros are that there's no worry of losing memory if the power fails. (Computer-based systems may have a battery backup to preserve system memory.) Also, manual override is a snap (that's an important feature of any type of system). On the con side, flexibility is limited. For instance, it may come from the factory with a "throttling range" (the spread between maximum heating and maximum cooling of 12°F (6.6°C)—about 2.5°F (1.4°C) between each stage.) You might be able to adjust that to be 20°F (11°C), but each stage would increase. Some machines let you adjust the number of degrees between stages; others can be adjusted at the factory. Another con is in data recording. If you want to know what your day and night temperatures were last week, you're probably out of luck, although some manufacturers offer this in their higher-level stage controllers.

Larger step systems that offer more stages are available, allowing you to link in a heat retention curtain, HAF fans, fog system, or other features. They can also connect with outdoor temperature and light sensors to further increase your flexibility. The price jumps to $2,000 and up for these added features. One other important feature of stage systems is the ability to trigger an alarm in case of a problem.

Figure 6-16. A stage controller is like a sophisticated, multi-stage, highly accurate thermostat.

Level Three: Computer Zone Controllers

One thing you'll note about environmental control systems: As cost increases, so does flexibility. As one manufacturer says, "The further up you go, the more it becomes a tool, not just a control."

For a starting price of around $2,000, you can make a quantum leap in features and enter the world of computer climate control. These systems give you a wider range of stages—up to twenty-four in some cases—and allow you to decide what each stage does and at what temperature. Settings are very precise for each stage, and you can modify settings for day versus night temperature and set several daytime set points. They can be linked to an outside weather station, which warns the system of temperature or light changes. They can also operate lights, fog systems, CO_2 generators, and pretty much any other piece of climate control equipment.

These systems don't require a personal computer (PC) to run; the computer is built in. Being computer-controlled allows them to record data—usually twenty-four hours' worth—and they can also be linked to a PC to expand their memory capability. They're also "smarter" than step systems, which means that they're better at linking all your systems together. By expanding the number of heating and cooling stages, you can save energy costs because you're not running more equipment than necessary to maintain your set point.

They're called zone controllers for a simple reason: Most are designed to operate a single zone. If your gutter-connected greenhouse has several zones in it, or you want to run a series of large freestanding houses, you need to have one zone controller for each zone. But they're quick and easy to install, and using the same kind of unit in each zone makes it easy to train employees to operate them.

Some companies' zone controllers can run more zones—up to four, for instance, from one unit—but you lose flexibility with a lower number of heating and cooling stages and a limited range of equipment you can operate.

Level Four: Integrated Computer Systems

If the word "limitations" isn't in your vocabulary, and if you're ready to invest $8,000–10,000 or more, you're ready for an integrated computer system. Running on a Windows-based PC and remotely accessible through smart phones, iPads, laptops, or other PCs via the Internet, a local area network (LAN), wireless, or 3G, the capability of an integrated system is limited only by your imagination and your wallet. There's virtually no greenhouse system they can't operate, and best of all, they link all your systems together for maximum efficiency, such as operating your irrigation system by monitoring water flow, EC, pH, vapor-pressure deficit, and other data.

The manufacturer provides the greenhouse hardware and software for an integrated system; you provide the PC. In the "old days" of computer controls, the PC often needed to be dedicated to just running the greenhouse control software. That is no longer the case. Today, you can use your PC for both, although some vendors like to limit the use of the PC to avoid non-greenhouse-control software crashes from negatively impacting the critical greenhouse environment. In most cases, this PC also acts as a server to support remote access, some alarm annunciation, and other control system support.

A variable between manufacturers is how they link their sensors to the main computer, offering the choice between centrally wired systems where all input/output (I/O) must be wired back to a single, central location; while others use distributed control or I/O hardware distributed around the greenhouse, greatly reducing the amount of wiring required for sensors and equipment. Most vendors now offer distributed I/O at a minimum, with a continued trend toward distributed control as well. Distributed control and I/O also has the added benefit of improved fault tolerance since you are not putting all your eggs into one basket. The consequences of the failure of one piece tend to be limited.

Lightning protection is worth a mention at this point, as it is complex and requires special engineering to minimize damage. It is important everywhere, but especially in lightning-prone states such as Florida. Fiber optic, wireless, and copper wire connections can all be well protected from all but direct strikes. As a general rule, distributed I/O systems are inherently better protected because the wiring connections are short (long wires are more easily damaged). The network connections that join them all into one system are prone to damage but are relatively few in number, so the extra cost of protection is not unreasonable.

Because they've got serious computer processing power behind them, integrated systems support the running of more complex control strategies and models. Integrated control systems, by definition, integrate disparate control functions into a single management system. A high-quality, precision system can almost *anticipate* the greenhouse climate based on what's happening outside. And they are the most precise and most efficient of all systems. For instance, if you want to, and have the hardware that's up to the task, you can control your greenhouse temperature to tenths of a degree, although this is unnecessary for all but the most critical of research-level growth chambers.

Another neat feature is "pulsing" your equipment to maximize efficiency. With other systems, your heaters run until the environmental control's sensor indicates the greenhouse temperature has reached its set point. But because of the lag time between heat output and the sensor reading it, the greenhouse temperature may overshoot even after the heater has been shut off. Pulsing the equipment means the computer will turn off the heater before the set point is reached and then continue to check the temperature and adjust future pulse times to ensure the average temperature is maintained.

Figure 6-17. When combined with the right heating, cooling, and ventilation equipment, integrated computer systems offer the highest level of greenhouse climate control.

Misunderstandings

Precision and efficiency may be the most misunderstood aspects of environmental control. You can save energy with most environmental control systems. You can also control the greenhouse environment more precisely with most environmental control systems. But there's a tradeoff: The more precision you want, the less efficient you are.

Why? Because trying to keep your greenhouse to exactly 73.4°F (23°C) means your heaters, vents, and fans are going to be cycling on and off constantly with every tiny fluctuation in temperature. If you're a plug grower, this level of control may be necessary. But a bedding plant grower shouldn't care if his greenhouse is 68°F (20°C) or 70°F (21°C).

Conversely, if you want to maximize your energy savings, modern environmental controls will help you do that by running only the heating or cooling systems you need at any given time and by running them as efficiently as possible. The more flexible you are with your greenhouse temperature requirements, the more you can save.

Labor is another cost area that's often misunderstood. If you or your employees have to adjust thermostats and manually open and close vents everyday, then you can save on labor costs by investing in a Level Two, Three, or Four system. But remember, the more sophisticated the system, the more time someone is going to have to spend to get the most out of it. That someone is usually a high-priced grower or yourself, not your greenhouse labor. So if you think that having a year's worth of temperature data will be handy, but you're not willing to put the time into using it, that's probably a feature you don't need.

Who Needs What?

The beauty of these new systems is that there are sizes and features for every grower—you can start small and then expand. Step controllers are inexpensive; zone and integrated computers are expandable. But don't underestimate your needs, or you'll spend more in the long run. Why invest in five $2,000 zone controllers when a $10,000 integrated system will do so much more?

The toughest question you have to ask yourself is, "Where do I want to be in five years?" If you have a clear vision of that, then you can make a good decision on the environmental control level that's best for your business.

The Latest Horizontal Airflow Technology
Kurt Becker

Horizontal airflow, or HAF, is an important tool for managing the greenhouse environment. Proper air circulation not only helps to even out the temperature throughout the greenhouse, but also is responsible for distributing humidity, smokes, aerosols, CO_2, and pesticide sprays. Good air movement can keep the foliage dry, helping to curb disease incidence. There's even data to suggest that proper air movement will speed the growth of plants by increasing transpiration, which makes the plants increase their uptake of water and nutrients.

Initially, the solution for improving air movement in greenhouses was to place or hang a number of fans throughout the greenhouse to circulate the air. All sorts of fans and spacings were used, from home box fans to unguarded spinning blades and a motor. As HAF gained acceptance, several manufacturers began to standardize the HAF fan and offer better fans with lower electrical consumption.

Figure 6-18. A shrouded horizontal airflow fan offers the most precise movement of air in the greenhouse. *Photo courtesy Dramm Corporation.*

It used to be that HAF was thought of in terms of velocity—moving a certain amount of air through the greenhouse, usually expressed in cubic feet per minute (cfm). Previous editions of the *Ball RedBook* cited the figure 2,000 cfm. Other sources called for movement as high as 100' (30 m) per second across the crop! This notion was often hard to calculate and difficult to measure, especially given the varied sizes and shapes of greenhouses used throughout the world. Different optimum numbers were given based on different crops.

Today, momentum is replacing velocity as the major factor in greenhouse HAF. The goal of a momentum-based system is to create a stable mass of air that slowly builds momentum as it travels through the greenhouse. The focus is on stability rather than air speed. Often, HAF fans spinning at high rpm may move the air too fast, causing turbulence and uneven drying through-out a crop. High air speeds can also be responsible for

stratification of the air in a greenhouse. Fast-moving air can become a buffer that prevents venting through buoyancy (the effect of hot and/or humid air rising) in a gutter- or ridge-vented greenhouse.

Current systems utilize more aerodynamic fans than in the past. By shrouding the fan in a housing, more of the air is thrown forward and not out the sides or down onto the crop. This helps to build the stability of the air in a forward direction and reduces obstruction created from contrary air patterns. Additionally, the use of shrouds creates an intake as well as an exhaust, something that unshrouded fans don't have. This intake can help keep the forward momentum going by pulling air in the desired direction. As a result of the increased distances and lower speed requirements of momentum-based systems, they need fewer fans and use less electricity.

Another recent addition to HAF technology is the introduction of speed regulation or lower speed fans. High rpm fans often cause uneven drying in the crop due to the spiraling of air created when the blades turn at high speed. By reducing the speed of the blades, this spiraling effect is reduced, eliminating its uneven effect on the crop.

By using a fan with a specific distance and width of throw, a grower can properly fit his HAF fans to his greenhouse. A proper fit is important to avoid dead spots, conflicts between fans resulting in eddies of swirling air, or static pressure from too much air moving in one direction.

Once you've achieved a stable flow of air with good momentum, you can easily introduce and blend heat, humidity, and CO_2. In a momentum-based system, HAF fans can remain running during venting. This more rapidly equalizes the temperature and humidity changes. Momentum-based systems can even remain running during a ridge- or gutter-venting situation without fear of stratification, since these systems use slower moving fans.

Supplemental Lighting
Todd Sherrard

Supplemental lighting of greenhouse crops has been used in commercial greenhouses for more than thirty years. However, it's a complex issue, involving aspects of both plant physiology and business management. If you're going to add supplemental lighting, its installation and operating costs need to be offset by an increase in revenue as a result of additional plant production and/or plant quality.

Since supplemental lighting was introduced, significant research and development has provided the industry with a great deal of knowledge about its benefits. Although the technology and application is far more scientific than an average person might need to know, the following provides some guidance to the questions most often asked about this subject.

Why Use Supplemental Lights?

The main application of supplemental lighting is to increase plant growth, primarily in regions that experience low light and short daylength duration during the winter or experience seasons of dark, cloudy weather.

Supplemental lights can also be used for photoperiod lighting to manipulate the day/night rhythm of short-day and long-day plants. This allows growers to bring plants in bloom at any time of the year outside of their natural growing seasons. As mentioned in chapter 3, lighting to manipulate the day length doesn't require the high light output of the high-intensity discharge (HID) lights needed to increase plant growth. Incandescent bulbs offer enough light to affect the plant, but they won't impact plant growth. However, if you are growing photoperiod plants in low-light regions, HID lights can give you the benefits of day length control *and* added growth at the same time.

Figure 6-19. Supplemental lighting is primarily used in northern regions where light is at a premium, especially during the winter.

Considerations

There are many different considerations and questions that arise when planning to purchase a lighting system. Considerations should be given to crop requirements, light intensity, light source, electrical consumption, and uniform lighting patterns. Financial consideration, including initial costs and ongoing maintenance costs measured against the ROI (return on investment), must also be factored in to your calculations.

It's important to note that when additional light is added, photosynthesis becomes continuous and other factors, such as CO_2, nutrients, and irrigation cycles, must also be adjusted to maximize benefits. It's therefore advisable to consult with lighting companies with many years of experience and technical expertise backed up by proven research results in the horticultural industry.

There are several different lighting companies with many different kinds and styles of light fixtures. To purchase a light system is a considerable investment, and if it is a quality product it will be around for many years to come. Therefore understanding what you are buying and why is imperative.

Be sure the components inside are UL/CSA approved. High-intensity discharge lighting consists of a ballast with a capacitor. High-pressure sodium lighting has a starter as an additional component. It's important to keep these components at their nominal heat temperature to avoid early failure.

Most growers demand greenhouse builders to design their structures to allow as much natural daylight as possible, so consideration to the size of fixture and the shade it will throw should be given. The most important element to a fixture is the reflector that provides the light distribution. There are many different materials, shapes, and sizes available. The size of the reflector has no relationship to the light output or the uniformity it will provide; only the quality of material used and its design has any bearing. It's not recommended to use a painted or powder-coated reflector. This causes early bulb failure due to high heat and the lumen rays being passed back through the arc tube of the bulb. For the same reasons, it's not recommended to use materials that are very lustrous.

Uniform plant growth can only be obtained with uniform light distribution because plant growth is determined by the amount of light. It would not be unusual to see yields increase by 10% just due to uniform light distribution.

Lights and Layout

High-pressure sodium is the mostly commonly used light source in commercial greenhouses, due to its efficiency and light spectrum. For some crops, metal halide fixtures are used, but mostly for research or for crops that are grown completely indoors with no natural light exposure at all. Incandescent and fluorescent bulbs are still used in greenhouses for photoperiod control and in growth chambers.

A variety of high-intensity discharge wattages are used depending on crop requirements and greenhouses specifications, ranging from 150–1,000 watts. Wattage is selected either for different light intensities or different mounting heights.

It's important to request a lighting layout plan and calculation before purchasing a light system. Due to the many different styles of fixtures and methods used by light manufacturers to perform calculations, a good understanding of what's being presented in these calculations is essential. An improperly designed system may result in added expense with little or no benefits.

Some parameters that will determine your lighting layout are:
- The type of fixture and reflector;
- The distance between the top of the crop canopy and the bottom of the reflector;
- The distance between the fixtures on a row and the distance between the rows of fixtures; and
- The number of greenhouse bays to be lit.

Figure 6-20. Shown here is an example of a typical HID light.

For supplemental lighting purposes, it's important to know how much of the radiant energy supplied by a light source is converted into radiation useful to plant growth and the development of plants. In addition, energy distribution over the color spectrum is an important parameter because energy content varies with wavelength. Photosynthetically active radiation (PAR) light (between 400 and 700 nm), is defined as the quality of light available for photosynthesis. Depending on the application, different units of light measurement are used. They are watts per meter squared, foot-candles, lux, joules, and micromoles (µmols). For the layperson, this gets pretty technical, which is why it's paramount to consult with a lighting expert for proper translation of these measurements and their corresponding conversions.

With properly designed quality lighting systems, more and more growers are realizing the potentials to increase quantity, quality, and profits from their existing greenhouse space. Ongoing research continues to discover optimal light levels and light sources corresponding to plant responses in different geographical areas to maximize a grower's profit.

LED Lights

LEDs, or light-emitting diodes, have been considered for supplemental greenhouse lighting since the mid-2000s because of their small size and energy efficiency compared with standard incandescent lights. As of this printing, LED lights were just entering the real-world testing phase in greenhouses in Europe and North America. At least two manufacturers, Philips and Lemnis Lighting, were actively researching LED in commercial greenhouses, taking them from the laboratory to the greenhouse.

The LEDs that are being installed are in strip form—as a fluorescent bulb—with combinations of red and blue lights based on light "recipes" that have been tested to work with a particular crop. They're being used two main ways: (1) As additional lighting in the center of greenhouse tomatoes or peppers, in conjunction with regular high-pressure sodium; and (2) in multilayer young plant or production facilities where HID lights would be too hot or take up too much space.

LED lights are being explored for greenhouse use for two main reasons: They are more energy efficient than traditional incandescent lights, and the light spectrum can be "tuned" by using different colors of LEDs. According to Dr. Erik Runkle, of Michigan State University, "The consensus in academia seems to be that (with some exceptions) we are five to ten years away before LEDs will be economical in greenhouse crop production. In instances where electricity costs are high and lighting is used for a significant portion of the year, returns on investment may already be in the realm of possibility. Regardless, everyone seems to agree that LEDs are the future of greenhouse lighting." In fact, lighting giant Philips speculates that over 75% of the world's lighting in 2020 will be in the form of LEDs.

Figure 6-21. LED lights at a test greenhouse in the Netherlands.

Carbon Dioxide: Building Block for Plant Growth

Neil Mattson and Nora Catlin

Fifty years ago, carbon dioxide (CO_2) was one of the hottest topics in the greenhouse industry. Everyone was asking what is it? Is it really worth using? How much does it cost? Will I obtain results?

Up until the early 1970s, we were primarily a cut flower industry and the bedding plant industry was in its infancy. Many cut flower growers invested in CO_2, having heard or read about the positive reports on its usage from research stations across America. Once used, growers discovered quicker crop times, stronger and stockier stems, improved quality, and higher yields. However, growers rapidly found that they needed to step up fertility programs, increase growing temperatures, and use supplemental light when they wanted to maximize the CO_2 added to the greenhouse environment.

As the industry shifted away from cut flowers and into potted plants and bedding plants, interest in CO_2 lessened. Currently only a small percentage of U.S. growers, mostly cut flower and greenhouse vegetable growers, continue to invest in CO_2.

What Is CO_2?
Carbon dioxide is a gas that occurs naturally in the atmosphere at approximately 390 parts per million (ppm). CO_2 is colorless, nonflammable, and heavier than air. The gas solidifies under atmospheric pressure at -109.3°F (-78.5°C). Solid CO_2 possesses the interesting property of passing directly into the gaseous state without going through the liquid state at atmospheric pressure.

Photosynthesis and CO_2
Photosynthesis is a biochemical process using the sun's energy to chemically combine CO_2 and water (in the presence of catalysts and chlorophyll) to yield chemical energy in a usable form. The actual products of photosynthesis are carbohydrates (sugars and starches), complex chemical compounds, water, and oxygen.

The rate of photosynthesis increases as CO_2 levels increase; supplementing CO_2 to levels greater than natural, ambient levels will thus increase photosynthesis and plant growth. Enriching CO_2 above ambient levels to 700–1,000 ppm typically has a positive effect on photosynthesis and growth; however, maintaining ambient levels of 340–390 ppm can be considered to be equally, if not more, critical for plant growth. During times of reduced venting, particularly in structures that have few leaks and reduced air exchange rates, CO_2 levels can drop below ambient, limiting plant growth. For example, reducing the CO_2 level in a gerbera crop from approximately 1,300 ppm to approximately 350 ppm will result in approximately the same reduction in photosynthetic rate as reducing the CO_2 level from approximately 350 ppm to approximately 220 ppm.

Over the years, research has shown that adding CO_2 during the daylight hours to the greenhouse atmosphere can give increased yields, increased plant height, increased number of leaves and lateral branches, increased rooting, higher quality, and shorter cropping times. The type and degree of response varies by crop as well as the environmental and cultural parameters the crop was grown under. Most plants show positive effects; however, there are reports of some plants, such as tulips and Easter lilies, that do not show any effects. Deleterious effects have been reported for some plants, particularly when grown under higher levels of CO_2.

When to Use CO_2
If CO_2 is limited at any time during the daylight hours, photosynthesis and, ultimately, plant growth, will be limited. CO_2 can be added to the greenhouse environment during these hours to help overcome this limiting factor. Generally, CO_2 is added from around dawn until around dusk. If artificial lighting is used at night, CO_2 should also be added during this time.

Keep in mind that if vents are open more than 10–15% or if exhaust fans are constantly running, it will be difficult and costly to maintain enhanced CO_2 levels. In these situations, growers should strive to maintain ambient CO_2 levels. One strategy is to supplement CO_2 at a constant level, regardless of light intensity or ventilation. Other strategies include using monitoring equipment to automatically adjust the CO_2 level based on the current CO_2 level, light levels, ventilation, and/or wind speed.

How Much to Add?

The amount of CO_2 that should be added to a greenhouse will vary depending on the crop, stage of growth, light intensity, temperature, and ventilation. In general, research indicates that the optimal CO_2 concentration lies in the range of 700–1,000 ppm. Levels greater than 1,000 ppm can cause growth reduction and leaf injury in some cases, and levels 5,000–10,000 ppm or greater can cause dizziness to humans. In addition, higher levels can also increase CO_2 loss from the greenhouse through leakage.

Sources of CO_2

There are many different sources of CO_2. One source is simply to ventilate: Exchanging greenhouse air with fresh outside air will bring the CO_2 level close to, but not up to, the ambient level. Under cool, cloudy winter conditions where air exchange is not required to cool the greenhouse down during the day, it is often more economical to enrich the greenhouse environment with CO_2 rather than to lose air that has already been heated in the greenhouse by venting. Decomposition of mulches, compressed CO_2 gas, dry ice, liquid CO_2, and combustion of various fuels in CO_2 generators (propane, natural gas, or kerosene) are other sources. Many growers remove CO_2 from flue gases after boiler fuels have been burned using specialized flue gas condensers. It is very important that all unit heaters, boilers, and CO_2 generators burn cleanly so that noxious gases such as ethylene, nitrogen oxide, and sulfur dioxide do not harm plants.

Light, Temperature, and Fertility

Several environmental factors such as temperature, light, and CO_2 interact to affect plant photosynthesis and growth. In a CO_2 enriched greenhouse, plants can take the most advantage of CO_2 with warmer temperatures and high light conditions. If, for example, the ideal CO_2 level for a particular crop is between 800 and 1,000 ppm and one or more of the light, temperature, or fertilizer levels were not up to par, growth would be restricted and the full potential of adding CO_2 would be lost.

While reduced temperature or light decreases the optimal effects of increased CO_2, it should be noted that CO_2 enrichment can be a less expensive method to compensate for low light or low temperature. For lettuce plants with a target daily light integral of 17 moles m^{-2} day^{-1} research has found that CO_2 enrichment during cool/cloudy conditions can reduce the need for supplemental HID light by up to 6 moles m^{-2} day^{-1}, leading to significant savings in electricity. Similarly, adding CO_2 up to 500 ppm and lowering the greenhouse daily temperature by a couple degrees Fahrenheit has been reported to be more cost effective than simply maintaining a higher greenhouse temperature to promote growth.

CO_2 enrichment means that fertilizer programs will have to be stepped up, too. Increased growth requires more fertilizer. Plus, it has been found that increasing CO_2 decreases the amount of water that plants need by 20–40%. Therefore, fertility programs that rely on nutrient delivery via the irrigation water need to increase the fertilizer rate to deliver the same or more nutrients in a lower volume of water. Calcium and boron require active plant transpiration for their uptake; levels of these nutrients, in particular, need to be maintained. Use soil and foliar tests to keep your fertilization program on track.

Cautions

Avoid the mind-set that if "some CO_2 enrichment is good, even more is better." Most research results indicate plants respond favorably to levels up to 1,500 ppm—with most of the growth benefit obtained within the range of 700–1,000 ppm. Exceeding 1,500 ppm can cause human health problems, plant toxicity, and excess costs that are not recouped. The Mine Safety Appliance Company has reported that at concentrations of 8–10% (80,000–100,000 ppm), CO_2 can be fatal to humans. A concentration of 1% (10,000 ppm) may cause headaches and listlessness.

Each CO_2 generator should have approved safety controls. Some of these include a flame-failure safety valve, a solenoid valve that automatically switches the fuel on and off, a gas filter, a fine reading gauge showing true jet pressure, and a thermocouple that will shut off the gas flow if the pilot light isn't functioning.

When purchasing fuels for CO_2 generation, be sure your fuel supplier is aware that it will be used for CO_2. This will help to avoid delivery of batches with abnormally high sulfur content. Sulfur should not exceed 0.02% (by weight) of the fuel source. No. 2 fuel oil is not suitable for CO_2 generation.

Unburned fuels escaping into the greenhouse air may contain ethylene or propylene (from propane). Leakage from the piping system or from a burner operating incorrectly has resulted in flower and fruit abortion, delayed flowering, and slow or distorted growth. Exposure to prolonged ethylene concentrations as low as 0.010 ppm (i.e. 10 parts per billion) and higher concentrations of propylene have been shown to cause these symptoms. Failures from greenhouse burners and furnaces or boilers are usually due to inadequate amounts of oxygen being supplied to the combustion process. Other causes may be dirty nozzles, off-center fires, delayed ignition, oil or gas leaks, and fluctuating fuel pressure. Burners with a high flame temperature can form nitrogen oxides (NO and NO_2), which can also cause plant toxicity. Some growers prefer to use liquid carbon dioxide due to its high purity and not having to worry about off-gasses damaging crops.

Does CO_2 Benefit Bedding Plants?

Certainly! Bedding plants, such as geraniums, petunias, marigolds, tomatoes, lettuce, and numerous other crops, benefit from added CO_2. Expect faster seedling growth, faster finishing times, and improved quality. However, the greatest response and the most benefit from CO_2 are in the young plant stages, not near crop maturity. CO_2 is particularly beneficial immediately following germination until bud set. Propagators can make good use of CO_2, especially during rooting of geraniums and other vegetatively propagated cuttings, as well as in growing plugs to the point of transplanting.

Beware: If you start using CO_2, you can expect all scheduling to change. Plants grow faster in CO_2-enriched environments, and finish times are often reduced by 5 to 10%. Watch your scheduling carefully.

What Does CO_2 Cost?

Several factors affect the cost of CO_2 enrichment including the concentration of CO_2 desired, leakiness of the greenhouse, the number of hours per year that CO_2 enrichment is desired, associated equipment, and the source for generating CO_2.

When the CO_2 is scavenged from the exhaust of hot water boiler flue gas, the fuel for CO_2 is essentially free. However, a flue gas CO_2 condenser, blower, and pipes for CO_2 distribution must be installed, costing many thousands of dollars. Another disadvantage of using flue gas is that CO_2 is only available during hours when the boiler is being used, unless the system is equipped with an insulated hot water tank to store heated water for nighttime use.

When the CO_2 source is from combustion of natural gas or propane in generators, several CO_2 generators must be installed throughout the greenhouse. Investments in CO_2 generators are in the ballpark of $0.12/ft.^{2} ($1.29/m^2) to install. Equipment maintenance is generally minimal. In northern regions, CO_2 burners will normally be used only from October through April, with operational hours during daylight hours, or a total of around 1,000 hours annually. The yearly fuel costs for generating CO_2 are on the order of $0.11/ft.^{2} ($1.18/m^2) for natural gas (assuming $12 per 1,000 cubic feet of natural gas), and $0.18/ft.^{2} ($1.94/m^2) for propane (assuming $2.70 per gallon of propane).

When liquid CO_2 is used, the operation will incur tank rental costs and must pay to install a PVC tubing system (typically 18 mm) to distribute CO_2 throughout the greenhouse. The yearly cost of liquid CO_2 is around $0.10/ft.^{2} ($1.08/m^2) (assuming $200 per ton of liquid CO_2, delivered).

If you consider the increase in production and improved quality as a result of using CO_2, there shouldn't be any question about its economics. However, much depends on your market and whether or not your customers will pay for the improved quality. With decreasing profit margins, any increase in production costs or infrastructure may be too much. Know your market before making the investment in CO_2.

Alternative Energy: Does It *Pay?**

by Jennifer Duffield White

Over the last few years, *GrowerTalks* magazine has reported on retailers and growers who have invested in alternative energy systems. Yet, for every business that has taken the plunge, there are many more who've stood back with a wait-and-see strategy.

* Published in *GrowerTalks* magazine, January 2010.

The real question is, after a year or two in operation, do the owners still have good things to say about alternative energy systems? Some do, and some don't. And as you'll read below, nearly everyone has had to make some tweaks. We caught up with five businesses to see what they have to say about their investments.

Living in the Garden

In July 2008, Living in the Garden, a garden center in Pullman, Washington, installed a grid-tied, 3,060 watt solar photovoltaic system. "It was designed to offset 100% of our business's electrical use," says co-owner Suzanne St. Pierre.

The system includes twelve Sharp 170 watt panels mounted on a Zomeworks passive tracker with a Fronius IG 2000 inverter. With the tracker, the panels passively follow the sun from east to west during the day; they use the sun's heat to move liquid from one side of the array to the other, and gravity does the rest.

The cost of the project totaled $22,500, but Suzanne points out that they also had a lot of incentives and tax breaks, including:

- No state sales tax on equipment or installation.
- One-time 30% federal tax credit ($6,738)
- Depreciation of $4,100 for the first year (five-year property for tax purposes)
- Annual Washington State Production Incentive program ($459)
- Electricity bill they'll no longer incur.

For Washington's production incentive program, Living in the Garden receives $0.15 per kilowatt of solar power produced (good through 2020). However, if you have solar panels and inverters that are manufactured in Washington state, that incentive gets bumped up to $0.54 per kilowatt. Suzanne says a system like theirs, if it'd been manufactured in-state, would be garnering them $1,652 per year until 2020—a total of $18,176.

Suzanne says of her investment, "Part of the decision was emotional. It feels great to say, 'Just like plants, we get our energy from the sun.'" However, it's also been a wise business decision. "Going solar works well for us at retail. It sets us apart from other garden centers and is a strong symbol of our commitment to our community and our environment. With a greenhouse expansion planned, I'm currently researching energy conservation and renewable sources for greenhouse heating," Suzanne says (they currently heat with propane).

Any regrets? None. She reports that they haven't had any maintenance issues or duties, and the panels carry a twenty-five-year warranty. "My only worries

have been slight snow accumulation reducing output on the panels, and some days it is too windy for our passive tracking system to overcome the force of the wind," says Suzanne. "At the end of its first year, the system has outperformed its expected output, so these worries were unfounded."

Thinking about installing solar? Suzanne says these two web sites were valuable resources:

www.findsolar.com. This site will provide you with solar contractors in your area.

www.dsireusa.org. This site is a national clearing-house on all local, state, federal, and utility incentives relating to renewable energy and conservation.

Figure 6-22. Solar panels feed electricity back into the electrical grid at Living in the Garden in Pullman, Washington.

Pleasant View Gardens

In January 2011, nearly one year to the day after a fire destroyed an acre of greenhouse space at its Loudon facility, Pleasant View Gardens fired up a new biomass burner there. "That was one fire I wanted to burn," co-owner Henry Huntington joked. The new boiler joins an existing two-year-old biomass boiler that's located at their Pembroke location.

Pleasant View's new system—a Vyncke biomass boiler manufactured in Belgium—produces green and clean energy with wood harvested within forty-five miles of Loudon. According to Russ Elkins, facility manager for Pleasant View, "The Vyncke system is an evolution in technology. It's about 15% more efficient than the Hurst [their first biomass boiler, installed in 2009] through the design of its boiler." The Vyncke boiler utilizes the chamber where the chips are burned, pumping water through and around the chamber and the grate system. "We gain even more heat this way," said Russ.

With the Vyncke system, there is also zero waste; the system is able to break down, utilize, and burn the tops of harvested trees, including limbs that the Hurst burner is not equipped to process. The wood is harvested responsibly through selective cutting in dense New Hampshire forests. The trunks of trees are used to make furniture, floor planks, and other building supplies, and the tops of trees are transported to Pleasant View's Loudon facility in the form of wood chips. According to Russ, Pleasant View contracts three local cutting companies that range in size from a large New Hampshire operation to the farmer down the road.

As with the Hurst system (which cost $2 million), the Vyncke biomass boiler did not come cheap. But it could not have come at a better time. "With oil prices skyrocketing and an extremely insecure Middle East, the investment of $3 million for this state-of-the-art burner reduces our foreign oil dependency by almost 100%," says Henry. Before installing the Vyncke—and taking into consideration fluctuations in the market—Pleasant View was spending nearly $1.5 million per year on foreign oil to heat 6.5 acres (2.6 ha) in Loudon. In comparison, the wood chips cost approximately $300,000.

"At this rate we expect to see a return on our investment within a few years," said Henry. "And we're employing people from our local economy. The investment is responsible on many levels."

Eagle Creek Growers

In the fall of 2006, Eagle Creek Wholesale, based near Cleveland, Ohio, installed a biomass boiler. In March 2009, they added a wind turbine to their alternative energy system. Like other biomass burner owners, Eagle Creek remains pleased with the investment, even as they've tweaked it.

The heating system is a 350-hp Hurst "vertical underfeed" boiler that can burn nearly any fuel that has about 20% or lower moisture content. They've kept their fuel choice local, but they've had to switch it up a bit. Over the last five heating seasons Eagle Creek has experimented with several different fuel sources ranging from cow manure from their family farm, to horse manure from nearby farms, to wood chips, sawdust, tires and even scrap flooring materials.

"It's been a lot of trial and error to see which fuel source is most cost-effective, with a low moisture content, high BTU value, and runs smoothly through the entire process," says owner Jill Cain."It's also been important to have a local and constant supply. So far it seems to be a blend of sawdust and wood chips."

When we first spoke with Eagle Creek in March 2007, the expected payback was four to five years. As they finished their fifth season with the biomass boiler, it has already paid for itself.

Eagle Creek installed a 55KW wind turbine in March of 2009, with some help in the form of federal and state alternative energy grants from the USDA and the Ohio Department of Development. In 2010, they saved 31% on their yearly electric bills and over 75,000 kw of electricity compared with 2008. They get their best output from the turbine during the windy winter months and early spring, December through April. The lowest electrical production is during the summer months, which was expected.

Figure 6-23. Pleasant View Garden's new Vyncke biomass boiler. Between the two they now operate, the greenhouse expects to cut annual heating fuel costs from $1.5 million to $300,000.

Figure 6-24. The 55 kW wind turbine at Eagle Creek Growers, Bainbridge, Ohio.

The base and electrical groundwork are already in place for a second wind turbine which was scheduled to go online as early as 2011, pending government grants being accepted.

Pork & Plants

Pork & Plants LLC in Altura, Minnesota, was one of the first greenhouses in the United States to look at biomass boilers, and now they are even making their own pellets—a venture that earned it Innovator of the Year from the Agriculture Utilization Research Institute (www.auri.org).

"When you're trying something new, you're a guinea pig, to a degree," Eric Kreidermacher admitted. He calls their first corn burner "a total nightmare." The majority of corn burners were geared for residential use, and the commercial-sized ones were often for operations of 50 acres (20.2 ha) or more. As a grower that also has a pig barn (thus the "pork" in their name) and 65,000 ft.² (6,039 m²) of greenhouse space to heat, there wasn't a lot of information to go on.

They now operate five biomass burners that have been burning pellets. Until recently, they were burning corn and wood pellets that they purchased. But at 600 tons (544,300 kg) of pellets a year and corn prices fluctuating wildly, it was still a costly venture that the Kreidermachers wanted to make more efficient and sustainable. And so they bought their own pellet mill, which began operation in March 2009, with the idea that they would produce their own pellets. Previously, they'd also planted 20 acres (8.1 ha) of native prairie with the plan to pelletize the perennial grasses.

Once again, they find themselves in the position of being a pioneer in this field. Maria Kreidermacher reports that they love operating the pellet mill. "There's no way we'd ever go back," she says. But she also says there's no one else doing the same thing, and so finding information has been difficult. "It's been a lot of trial and error."

Pork & Plants uses "residue" from crops grown on the farm to make the pellets—corn stalks, bean straw, prairie grasses, and so on. They've found that certain materials burn better than wood pellets. Currently, they're heating 100% of their greenhouses with the homemade pellets, and they've started to supply a few local people, as well.

Lohmeyer's Farm

Lohmeyer's Farm in Maryland, part of the Bell Nursery Network, has a 1 acre (0.4 ha) wholesale production greenhouse. High propane bills started to cut into the bottom line so much that they decided to invest in a grain-fired boiler to "save money and to support the farm economy." They bought a Pelco 2520 Boiler in 2006, with plans to use it for 75% of their heat, with the propane heaters providing the rest.

Overall, the boiler integrated easily with existing environmental controls. One mistake owner Charles Lohmeyer says they made was putting extra heat exchangers in their design. "The heat exchanger output needs to be matched to the boiler output or else the boiler water temperature drops and the boiler thinks the fire has gone out and does a safety shutdown," says Charles. They ended up using only four of the eight heat exchangers and two of the four distribution side pumps.

Charles says that the heating system cost them $75,000. At the time, with corn at $2.75 a bushel, they thought they'd be saving $21,000 a year in fuel, giving them a return on investment (ROI) in 3.5 years. The reality of their first year in 2007 was that they paid $4.25 for corn. They burned 6,300 bushels of grain (one-third barley and two-thirds corn) that year, costing $22,000, and they burned $4,000 of propane (at $1.62 per gal.). Rather than replacing 75% of the propane, they actually replaced 90% of the propane with the grain-fed heat. All in all, they saved about $14,000 in heating costs, in a year which Charles said was on the mild side, temperature-wise. They are now looking at a ROI of 5.5 years.

In the winter of 2010–11, they continued to burn barley but reported that grain futures for the next season were very high, with corn at $7.00 a bushel and barley at $4.50 a bushel, while propane prices had leveled off. They make their winter fuel decision at barley harvest time, when they know what the price of the grain is going to be.

The Lohmeyers quickly learned that barley would be cheaper than corn, but it did require a few adjustments and one big additional investment. For starters, barley produces three times as much ash and fly ash. They had to retrofit the boiler with a stovepipe to collect fly ash coming off the cyclone. They shut down the boiler during the day on sunny days, which gives them a perfect opportunity to clean out the clunkers and empty the fly ash bin—a task that takes about thirty seconds.

When the Lohmeyers decided on a grain-fed boiler, they figured they'd have a great supply of fuel, since there were six grain elevators within 30 miles

(48 km) of their operation. "We found that the local elevators were not set up to sell grain on an as-needed basis. They would sell to us only when they were shipping," says Charles, noting that it was a hassle to arrange deliveries. Then, by mid January, all the elevators had run out of barley and the Lohmeyers had to go back to $4.25 corn.

The solution was to invest $20,000 in a 6,000 bushel storage bin. They filled the bin with barley from a local farmer at the reasonable rate of $2.30 per bushel. "Problem solved," says Charles. But it also means they're looking at a "very long investment."

While Charlie can burn propane, corn, or barley, he is keeping an eye on other fuel sources. "We are also looking at using switchgrass if it can be pelletized economically," he says.

7

Mechanization

Introduction

Chris Beytes

Whether it's a home-built one-wheeled cart or a computer-controlled transplanter, every greenhouse business makes use of some form of mechanization. The bigger the facility, the more labor-intensive the tasks being done, and the more efficiency-conscious the owner, the more mechanization the business is likely to employ.

Why automate? The Number 1 reason is labor savings. Labor is the largest single overhead expense for most greenhouses, averaging around 28%. But growers employ mechanization for more than just cutting the number of employees they need. Labor availability is another issue. It can be difficult to find enough workers during busy planting and shipping times. Mechanization can help you get tasks done faster, sooner, better, and easier. Of course, the wrong mechanization or mechanization that's implemented without all the necessary elements can do more harm than good. Behind every greenhouse business you will find a scrap pile of tools and machines that looked good but didn't do what the business needed. Invest in mechanization boldly but wisely.

Media Mixing

Paul Whiting and Jim Fowler

Tremendous gains have been made in media mixing methods during the past several years. Now, with today's microchip-control technology, virtually all forms of mixing can be accomplished by machine.

Why Make Your Own Mix?

The answers are as varied as the many growers and the raw materials they employ and as diverse as the cul-

tural requirements for the "endless" multitude of plant types. But the most meaningful answers are found somewhere between economics and crop survivability. In other words, how can I have ready access to a reliable potting mix or mixes at the best possible price?

The grower's physical location, the simplicity or complexity of the mixes he or she requires, the range of different blends needed, and the cost of readily available raw materials versus the cost and reliability of commercially produced mixes weigh heavily in the growers decision to "mix their own" or to buy a manufactured mix.

Who Makes Their Own Mix?

Actually, the answer to this question closely parallels those noted in the "why" section above. Small growers who require limited volumes of media frequently "mix their own." This is especially common where inexpensive raw materials are available and where the operation can justify the initial cost of a small batch mixer. Note that an equal percentage of small operations tend to purchase commercial mixes because of convenience, time, and labor concerns. Conversely, numerous large growing operations have, during the past thirty years, shifted to at least some in-house media mixing. Typically, these operations provide their own basic crop mixes, while continuing to purchase some special-purpose mixes, such as for plugs. In the final analysis, the decision to produce your own soil mix or to purchase a commercial mix is chiefly based on economics and/or quality.

Growers who want absolute control over their potting media will mix their own. Growers who understand the trade-off between the typical 25–45% materials savings that can be gained by mixing their own medium versus the inherent cost of owning machinery, including operating, labor, and maintenance costs will simply weigh the facts and base their decision on their calculations. Not only the cost savings, but the inherent flexibility to produce any mix formula as needed must be weighed during this decision.

Mixing Methods

Pad or skid mixing

One of the oldest forms of media mixing is called pad or skid mixing. This form of mixing is usually accomplished by layering the raw materials to be mixed on a concrete pad. A front-end loader or a bucket mounted on a tractor is used to turn the material over and over, mixing the raw materials. This method is still widely used, especially at larger nurseries and greenhouses that require only two or three different raw materials. Some of the growers using this type of mixed medium do so because it's not critical to their crops to have an exact recipe. This type of mixing should be used with plants that are somewhat forgiving in the growing process because it's almost impossible to get an accurate, consistent mix from pot to pot and batch to batch. Pad mixing can also be used to make small test batches of mixes to examine how different mixes might affect a plant's growth.

The primary advantage of this mixing method is its low cost, since most growers already own a tractor or loader. No other special equipment is required. This method's primary disadvantage is the lack of consistency in the final product. For example, when using a front-end loader to mix 10 yd.³ (7.6 m³) at a time, with a recipe that calls for 1 lb. (0.5 kg) of lime and 1 lb. (0.5 kg) of fertilizer per yard of material, you can imagine how difficult it would be to evenly distribute the smaller trace elements throughout the mass evenly and consistently when rotating the mass with a 6 ft.³ (0.2 m³) bucket on a tractor.

Batch mixing

This is done by taking several types of raw materials at premeasured volumes and adding them to a hopper or a catch basin. The sizes of batch mixers range anywhere from less than 1 yd.³ (0.8 m³) up to 20 yd.³ (15 m³). There are several types of batch mixers used, including converted cement mixers, "ribbon blenders," and tumbling devices. These methods can be highly accurate when specific recipes are called for. This method puts the consistency of the mix in the grower's hand.

After the materials are placed in the mixer, the materials are tumbled or blended until consistency is achieved. Water is usually incorporated to prevent materials such as peat from breaking down or to correct the moisture content prior to filling the pot or cell pack. Depending on the type of batch mixer, cycle

times for consistent blending will vary. With a ribbon-style mixer, the cycle time for a batch is usually three to five minutes, while some other tumbling devices normally can take up to ten minutes per batch. The volume being mixed can and will affect the cycle time.

Figure 7-1. The advantages of using a typical batch mixer (pictured) include consistency in the final mix and ease of operation.

Advantages include consistency in the final mix and ease of operation. Plus, a batch mixer normally doesn't take up a lot of space. A significant disadvantage is cycle time. This includes the time required to "batch," or meter out, the various mix ingredients, load them into the mixer, blend them, and then unload them from the mixer. The raw materials need to be relatively close to the location of the mixer. This can cause clutter, especially for smaller batch mixers that are located close to production equipment such as potting machines and flat fillers. Also, if the raw material is left in the mixers longer than the necessary cycle times, they have a tendency to break down or lose their fiber content, which can affect air porosity and other growing characteristics.

Continuous mixing

This type of mixer ranges in capacity from 10 yd.³ (8 m³) per hour up to 200 yd.³ (153 m³) per hour. Commercial mix manufacturers use several mixing lines to make as much as 400 yd.³ (306 m³) per hour. This method is accomplished by using material hoppers or feeder bins. These hoppers are used to layer material at set volumes onto a main conveyor belt located below the hoppers. After the raw materials are layered, chemicals, nutrient charges and other trace elements such as lime are also dispensed onto the belt. Then a rotating mixing head or a tumbling tube continuously blends the materials, resulting in an accurately blended finished product.

A great deal of planning is involved in developing and installing custom continuous mixing systems. In addition to space requirements and power considerations, material storage and material flow must be taken in to account. The type, quantity, and number of different raw materials definitely come into play. How are they received? How are they packaged: small bales, large bales, loose bags, or bulk truckloads? How will the bulk materials be safely and efficiently moved to the proper hoppers on the mixing line? Will compressed peat moss or other material need to be fluffed? These are just some of the questions to be answered.

The hoppers themselves must be set up to dispense a certain raw material. For instance, a peat moss hopper needs to be outfitted with lengthwise and crosswise agitators, which keep the material from bridging or tunneling and give a consistent output rate at the feed end. Water bars are normally used to moisten the peat moss at this point. This not only keeps down excessive dust but also helps to improve mix quality when going through the mixing head.

Each hopper and material needs to be listed or itemized when the developing process starts for the system. Since the assorted material being mixed (peat, bark, vermiculite, perlite, and so on) all have different bulk densities, these materials will dispense at different rates, thus causing the need for specific hoppers to run specified material. After deciding what materials are required for the final mix, the correct number of hoppers can be specified.

Figure 7-2. A great deal of planning is involved in developing and installing a continuous mixing line.

Maximum output volumes are usually determined by the width of the mixing conveyor, and these vary from manufacturer to manufacturer. Another item to consider is feed rates from the hoppers. If you're mixing 100 yd.^{3} (76 m^3) per hour and the recipe calls for 80% of one item, depending upon the size of hopper used, load times can increase or decrease. For example, a 10 yd.^{3} (8 m^3) hopper would have to be loaded eight times per hour, or once every seven and a half minutes. The larger the hopper volume, the longer the load time will be. Many of today's growers are opting for the "big bale" systems. Sizes range from 55 ft.^{3} (1.6 m^3), 110 ft.^{3} (3.1 m^3), and up to 135 ft.^{3} (3.8 m^3) compressed bales. Automatic bale shavers are used to fluff the peat moss and can be hooked directly to the peat hopper on mix lines to greatly reduce the labor required to refill these hoppers.

Figure 7-3. Many growers, even small ones, are opting for the "big bale" system of compressed peat moss bales.

Options for this type of system vary from one manufacturer to the next, but most will give you automatic alarm and shut down. This will allow the system to sense when a material is running low in a hopper and shut down the whole system or automatically reload the hopper from supply bins or bale shavers, preventing an incorrect mix. Other options include PLC (programmable logic) controls, auto-watering, and VFD logic (variable frequency drive) variable-speed packages that allow a grower to alter his mix recipes through the use of touch-screen technology. This offers the additional flexibility to supply multiple mixes to multiple production lines on demand at the same time.

Flat and Pot Filling

Paul Whiting and Joe B. Ware

Arguably, one of the most important but least acknowledged advances in greenhouse and nursery material handling has been the introduction of mechanized flat and pot fillers. This tool has paved the way for tremendous increases in product sales. It's not unusual to have a grower acknowledge that his decision to invest in a flat or pot filler was the most significant reason that he was able to expand his business.

For the individuals and companies that have spent years in the development, design, and manufacture of automated filling equipment, it's extremely rewarding to hear growers exclaim, "I can now have a day off with my family!" Business owners report that they can spare the time to manage the scores of other unattended needs of their businesses, such as pursuing bigger sales contracts, because they can deliver their product in high volumes with better control of labor costs.

Filling by Hand

Getting a feel for some of the old ways that flat and pot filling was accomplished isn't difficult. Just visit the typical low-budget, "shoestring," start-up operation. What you'll find is almost universal: flats or pots being filled by hand, one at a time, the same way it was done a hundred years ago. You might find this grower (and helpers) utilizing a bench, maybe with seats of some kind, or perhaps a simple stand-up table operation. Those filling the containers may be using their hands, small shovels, scoops, or other similar tools. In this scene, the primary differences between today and long ago would be the type of container and the lighter soilless mixes we now use.

Manual filling continues to be practiced regularly in small- and medium-sized nursery operations. Many nurseries, especially those producing outdoor-grown stock, such as woody ornamentals, rely on front-end loaders of some type to fill empty containers that have been set out on wagons or trailers. Usually, two workers accomplish the finishing process by dragging a board across the top of the load of overfilled containers to scrape off the excess media.

In the modern greenhouse and field-grown nursery operation, flat and pot filling is a completely different story. The appropriately sized machine or system, with

Figure 7-4. While some growers still fill pots by hand, even the smallest growers find it worthwhile to invest in an automatic flat and pot filler.

well-chosen features and complementary equipment, make it possible for virtually any operation to meet their container-filling needs with minimal labor and expense. Coupled with various container-moving conveyors and other automated tools such as seeders, transplanters, labeling machines, tray washers, and watering tunnels, flat- and pot-filling systems have become the heart of the greenhouse production system. Even a small retail grower can justify the investment in a basic filling machine.

Size and Capacity

What about machine size, space requirements, costs, and expected performance? To the benefit of virtually every growing operation, there's a machine to match both current and expected future production demands. Small flat fillers require as little as 10 x 6' (3 x 2 m) of floor space. Medium-capacity machines may need up to 12 x 10' (4 x 3 m) of space, while high-capacity machines may demand 15 x 15' (5 x 5 m) for ease of operation. Overall heights of these machines range from 4–10' (1–3 m). These general dimensions exclude such production-enhancing accessories as soil mixing and delivery systems, staging of materials, and "take-away" conveyors. Of course, dibbling machines, automated transplanters, watering units, seeding machines, and other equipment often used with a flat or pot filler use up even more square footage, but their production payback is significant.

Generally speaking, flat filler production rates vary from 500 flats per hour up to 3,000 per hour. Pot- and hanging basket–filling rates are similar, depending upon the machine type, size, and special features as well as a multitude of varying container differences. Typical fill-and-drill potting machines (which fill the pot and then "drill" a hole for the plant) perform at variable rates up to 3,000 1 gal. (4 L) pots per hour. Super high-production potting systems are available that are capable of filling, compacting, and drilling up to 6,000 1 gal. (4 L) pots per hour. Again, appropriate complementary items are a must to achieve maximum production rates. This is where automated soil delivery and other mechanized material tools complete the labor-saving picture.

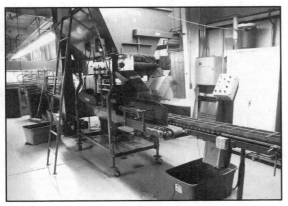

Figure 7-5. A flat filler that costs as little as $8,500 can fill millions of containers during its lifespan.

Cost

If you decide you're tired of filling bedding plant flats by hand and want a small, basic flat filler, expect to pay about $8,500. Even a small machine such as this will fill millions of containers over the years, at minimal maintenance and operation costs. For a midsize but fairly high-production filler that will accommodate flats, pots, patio planters, and hanging baskets, expect to pay $10,000–16,000. A top-of-the-line, high-capacity machine will require an initial investment of $22,000–30,000. These expensive machines offer additional flexibility and capacity and can (along with their lesser siblings) easily be integrated to a PLC-controlled sowing or automatic transplanting line.

Potting machines developed for large nursery stock containers that will fill, compact, and drill range in price from $30,000 all the way up to $125,000. This tremendous price range is due to the wide variety of features and capacities available—from the simplest

machines that fill one pot at a time to large machines with continuous high-speed, nonstop filling and drilling motions. Not only does production speed greatly influence the cost, but also features, such as container size capabilities, soil-holding and delivery capacity, pot dispensing attachments, control logic, and myriad other labor-saving mechanization, do as well.

Seeders

David R. Steiner

Most seeding machines operate on vacuum, picking up seed on an orifice and then exhausting it into a cell of a special seedling tray called a plug tray. Growers use them because they are a much faster and easier seed delivery system than a pair of tweezers and are more accurate and efficient than broadcast sowing (scattering seeds across the top of a media-filled flat). In addition, the finished plug is easier to transplant than seedlings that are not "singulated." Seeders are used by a wide variety of growers, from small greenhouses to the world's largest operations. Small machines sow a tray in one or two minutes, while larger machines can handle twenty or more trays per minute—more than a thousand per hour.

Many growers choose to purchase plugs from specialized plug growers rather than grow their own, thus avoiding the capital costs of the equipment and the challenge of growing plugs. However, producing plugs permits the grower to have the varieties and (hopefully) the quality he wants if a specialty grower can't provide them. For some growers in remote locations, logistics makes getting plugs shipped in difficult, especially in the dead of winter.

Although the seeding machines available today are good quality and usually offer years of trouble-free service, when it comes right down to it, they could be described as a necessary evil—one of the acquisitions you have to make once you decide to grow plugs on even the smallest production scale. The trouble is, there isn't any simpler, easier way to get seed into a plug tray. And without seeds in a plug tray, you're definitely not a plug grower. So you have to invest in a machine, have at least a semi-skilled person to operate it, devote space in the greenhouse for it, or in some environments even build a special seeder room to ensure optimal operation of the machine.

Types of Seeders

There are four types of seeders: manifold, plate, reciprocating, and cylinder/drum. The progression usually equates with price and operational capacity. For small greenhouses, a manifold or plate machine is usually well suited to the production needs. For mega plug production operations, the cost of the cylinder/drum machines, although considerable, is really somewhat incidental in terms of overall production cost. The production capacity of the machine is what's most important: Without such a machine, you simply can't sow seed fast enough to be a player in the world of plug production.

Of course, there are exceptions to the rule. Smaller operations sometimes find it more efficient to purchase faster machines, permitting the grower to spend less time sowing and more time growing. It's difficult to make money sowing seed. Growing is what pays the bills.

Manifold seeders

Operated by hand, these are the most basic of sowing tools. Seed pickup is achieved by vacuum applied to hollow needles. Seed is "sucked" from a seed inventory tray or trough and then sown into a plug tray one row at a time as the vacuum is released. Different orifice sizes, indicated by color-coded needles, permit sowing of different size seeds, from tiny petunias to cucumbers. For different tray configurations, tips sometimes may be blocked off, or a different manifold supplied, making these seeders flexible and inexpensive.

Figure 7-6. Suitable for small growing operations, manifold seeders are flexible and inexpensive.

Their chief advantage is low cost and the capability to sow almost any seed type, be it round or irregular in shape. Prices range from $600–800. They're not fast, and accuracy is dependent on seed type and the operator. Rates of operation can be expected to be one tray every two or three minutes, depending on the tray and seed being sown. Spherical seed such as cabbage or a pelletized seed allow faster rates, maybe even as high as a tray a minute. Manifold seeders are a good fit for small greenhouse operations sowing only a few hundred trays per year and for research greenhouses. In areas where labor costs are low, manifold seeders may even be used for larger-scale operations.

Plate seeders

These machines, again requiring manual operation, sow an entire tray at a time rather than just a row at time. Especially when sowing round or pelletized seeds, they're capable of achieving significant production rates (given an ambitious or motivated operator), in some cases hundreds of trays per hour. However, for odd-shaped seed such as marigold, they can be much more problematic to be used effectively.

Figure 7-7. Plate seeders achieve significant production rates when sowing round or palletized seeds.

Plate seeders require a quantity of seed to be dumped onto the plate, which typically is a shallow pan (resembling a cookie sheet) with a series of holes in it corresponding to the layout of the tray to be sown. Beneath this is a vacuum box that permits each hole in the plate to receive an equal amount of suction. The plate is maneuvered back-and-forth and side-to-side by the operator to distribute seed across it; as a seed passes over one of the holes, it is "captured" by the vacuum.

Once all the holes are filled, the vacuum box/plate is turned over and placed on top of the tray. The operator turns a valve, stopping the vacuum, and the seeds drop from the plate onto the plug tray, often assisted by the operator giving the box a sharp tap to help them on their way. Hybrid versions permit seeds to be distributed on a smaller plate and then transferred through a series of tubes to a plug tray waiting below.

Prices start around $1,000 but can climb to more than $2,000, if a wide variety of seeds and/or trays sizes need to be sown because a different plate is required for each seed and tray size. Rates of operation and accuracy are almost entirely at the discretion of the operator. Advantages are low cost, accuracy, and speed with round or nearly round seed (assuming a good operator). Drawbacks are their slow speed with odd-shaped seed, higher cost if you need more flexibility, and operator-dependent accuracy.

The plate seeder is a good choice for small, entry-level operators or medium-sized vegetable production ranges where labor costs are low.

Reciprocating seeders

This style of seeder represents those used by the most greenhouse operations around the world. From small operations to large-scale facilities, these machines handle a wide range of seeds and trays. Properly adjusted by the operator, they'll sow seed accurately all day long, day after day. While some have hand cranks and are manually operated, most are automatic and will sow seed while the operator fills plug trays or completes other tasks.

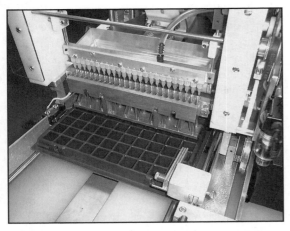

Figure 7-8. Reciprocating needle seeders are the most widely used type of seeders in floriculture, at use in every type and size of operation.

Reciprocating seeders are similar to manifold seeders in that they use hollow needles, rubber tips, or multi-hole manifolds to pick up the seed. A row of seed is picked up by vacuum applied to a manifold with a rubber tip, needle nozzle, or other style orifice. The manifold is moved over the plug tray, and the seed is exhausted from the tips. The tray is automatically indexed forward to the next row, and the process is repeated.

Prices start at $4,000 for a hand-crank model but can escalate to nearly $20,000 for conveyor-belt models equipped with onboard computers called PLCs (programmable logic controllers). Mid-range models with excellent throughput capabilities (100–300 or more trays per hour) cost about $12,000. In an effort to gain even more speed, it may be possible to sow some trays two rows at a time. One manufacturer turns the tray long-ways instead of sideways, thereby sowing twice as many seeds per cycle to achieve higher rates of seeds per hour.

Advantages of reciprocating seeders include their relatively low cost, their accuracy on a wide range of seed, the ability to calibrate them very precisely, and their variable output speeds. As thousands of these machines have been made over the years, there is also pretty good availability of reconditioned machines. Cons include some models' need for air compressors and seed may sometimes bounce out of the plug cells because it may fall a distance after being exhausted from the needles.

As mentioned, they're probably the most widely used type of seeders in floriculture, at use in every type and size of operation worldwide.

Cylinder/drum seeders

These machines represent the fastest and most expensive seeders on the market. But you know the old saying: "You can't get Porsche speed for a Volkswagen price."

These machines typically operate on vacuum, just as the other seeders, but the seed is picked up on rows of orifices or cavities machined into a rotating cylinder or drum (what it's called depends on the manufacturer). As the cylinder turns, the seed is deposited into the plug tray traveling beneath, falling a short distance. The result is exceptional accuracy (assuming the seeds are singulated at pickup), as the seeds don't fall very far and there is little if any displacement due to seed bounce. Some of these machines aren't geared toward very small or very large seeds, nor toward sowing small runs of seed. Others offer more flexibility by incorporating two, three, or four options in the sowing head. Thus the operator needn't make any hardware changes on the machine to switch from sowing a small seed to a large one. A simple "click" changes the cylinder to a different hole size or even tray, so changing to different seed sizes is very quickly done.

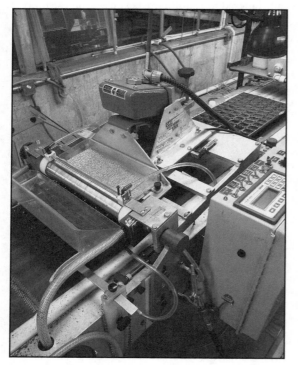

Figure 7-9. Cylinder, or drum, seeders represent the fast-est and most expensive seeders on the market.

Typical throughput is 500–1,200 trays per hour. The limiting factor in most applications is how fast the trays can be taken away from the machine. Remember, 500 trays per hour is one tray every seven seconds! An automated conveyor system is necessary to prevent a bottleneck at the end of the seeding line.

Prices range from $15,000–40,000. The more sophisticated models are designed for inline operation and can be easily integrated with a flat filler to automatically adjust the tray filling speed with the sowing speed. Advantages are tremendous speed combined with great accuracy and the ability to link them by computer to a full sowing line, from tray filler to watering tunnel. However, they're expensive, and some models are not very quick to changeover to different

seed or tray sizes. It is important to consider not just how fast the machine sows seed, but also how fast is it when it is *not* sowing seed. In other words, how long does it take the operator to change seeds or trays? That may be a primary consideration when making small sowing runs. That downtime will greatly affect the throughput at the end of the day. Additional cylinders or drums for different sizes can be expensive, as well. Still, for high-speed, high-volume plug production, a cylinder/drum seeder is indispensable.

Support Equipment

Most seeders may be operated without any additional support equipment, and typically this is the case with the small or mid-range machines. Trays are filled by hand or on some type of tray filler and then transported by hand or cart to the seeding area. However, because of their high speed, the cylinder/drum machines are most efficient when installed as part of a fully automated sowing line, with a tray filler, top dresser, and watering tunnel all linked by conveyor belts. Specialized plug growers often use automatic label applicators to apply bar codes during the sowing process, so they can keep track of the trays as they move through the greenhouse.

Automated Transplanters
Steve Biles, Quinn Denning, and Al Denning

The purpose of an automated transplanter is to automate the tedious, repetitive, and labor-intensive task of extracting plugs from a plug tray and planting them into flats, pots, or baskets that they're grown and sold in. All but one design use some form of grippers, fingers, or other mechanism to extract the plug from the tray and plant it into flats, pots or baskets.

A Little History

One of the earliest transplanter designs was a simple manual unit in which the operator pushed plugs through the bottom of special plug trays. This design was introduced in the early 1970s, at the very beginning of the bedding plant plug revolution. Definitely ahead of its time, it faded away, only to make resurgence in 2001.

Because the early days of plug production produced plug trays with less than 100% germination, plug growers made compensation to the growers by providing extra plugs with each order to ensure growers were getting their full count of plugs. This prompted manufactures to attempt to design a transplanter that would plant 100% into the flats. The above design was used in the Cover Plant Transplanter from France. It extracted the plugs from the plug trays and only placed the viable plugs into a cartridge, which was then transported over the flats and the plants were pushed down through the cartridge into the flat. This process proved to be too costly for the individual grower. The responsibility to provide 100% plants was passed to the plug producers. Many plug producers now use machine grading technology (see page 155) to provide 100% filled plug trays (although the acceptable standard is 280 plugs in a 288 tray and 500 plugs in a 512 tray).

It wasn't until the late 1980s that the first automated transplanters were designed and sold. Most were built in the Netherlands, with prices well over $100,000—affordable to only the very largest growers. In the mid- to late-1990s, smaller, more cost-effective automated units were introduced, with prices as low as $20,000. Still, transplanters were considered an expensive luxury only for large growers who produced more than 100,000 bedding flats per year. Some designs, which were relatively unproven in real-world settings, didn't always save the grower money and in some cases caused great frustration. However, even during the early years, growers realized the potential benefits of automated transplanters, as they helped to increase productivity and improve the quality of the transplanting process.

As the technology progressed and reliability issues were overcome, medium and even small operations began to see the benefits of automating the transplanting tasks. Most growers now realize that having an automated transplanter isn't a luxury but a necessity—small growers ranging from 3–5 acres (1.2–2.0 ha), medium growers with 12–15 acres (4.9–6.1 ha), and large growers of 20 or more acres (8.1 ha).

In the past, there were more than ten different manufacturers of automated transplanters. Today, there are approximately five manufacturers, with many models available, ranging in price from $40,000–85,000. A few are less expensive—$4,000 for a manual model—while some cost over $100,000, depending on features. In general, advances in programmable logic controllers (PLCs), servo-controlled movements, and modern manufacturing processes have added speed, reliability, and versatility to the automated transplanter while reducing its overall cost.

Basic Design Differences

There are two major design differences when it comes to the gripper/finger technology used to pick up the plug: the "finger/pusher pin" design and the "needle" design.

The finger-type design uses four fingers and a planting foot that allows the gripper to make a side shift movement to get under foliage and a pusher pin that is synchronized with the extraction of the plug to insure all types of plugs are extracted, whether they are underdeveloped with no root structure or overdeveloped with lots of foliage and roots that tend to adhere to the side walls of the plug tray. The planting foot

Figures 7-10, 7-11. Today's transplanters range from the simple (left) to the sophisticated, with speed, capacity, and flexibility to fit almost any grower's needs.

is utilized to insure that the plant is pushed off the fingers during planting to insure the plant is placed at a consistent and proper depth. In most cases, pre-dibbling the flat or pot is not necessary. The disadvantages include the need for an ejector system, which requires hardware and time to changeover. The finger-type design allows the operator the advantage of changing out the size of the gripper to fit the size of the plug.

The needle-type design uses a system of four needle-like grippers that extend from a choke tube to insert into the root ball and pick the plug out from the top. The needle design may or may not have an

Figure 7-12. Key to any transplanter is its ability to move the delicate young plant from its plug tray into the final container.

ejector system on the machine. The advantages of this system include operation without an ejector system, which makes for faster changeovers. The disadvantages include possible increased damage to some varieties of plugs and the inability to pick up underdeveloped and overdeveloped plugs. Typically, this design uses a one-size-fits-all non-interchangeable gripper that may only allow the machine to pick up every other plug within the plug tray because of the larger design of the gripper that does not let the grippers to get close enough together for the smaller plug trays' (512 and 288) cell spacing.

How Does It Move?

Actuators, such as pneumatic cylinders (using compressed air) and electric motors, move different parts of the machine, and a PLC or other controller usually tells them what to do. Servomotors can best be thought of as "programmable" or "smart" motors and are used where high speed, smooth operation, and extreme accuracy are necessary.

The PLC can be thought of as the brain of the machine. It generally controls the cycling of the machine by acquiring inputs, such as sensors, push buttons, and operator interface screens, and controlling the outputs, such as valves, motors, solenoids, relays, lights, and any number of other actuators. PLCs are nothing to be afraid of—they're proven technology used in the manufacturing industry all over the world. They allow the programmer to make adjustments to the running of the machine without the rewiring required in the past. They offer the machine builder extreme versatility for comparatively low production costs. Please be aware that when PLCs and servomotors are only the tools that a manufacturer uses to control a machine, the manufacturer's ability to program these components in such a fashion as to give the machine the fluid and accurate movements to move plugs at such high speeds will dictate how good and efficient the machine is at accomplishing the task of automated transplanting.

Machine Design

There are three basic designs for how the planting grippers are spaced over the finished containers. Following are some of the advantages and disadvantages to each of the designs.

The first method is to use some type of belt material to which the gripper assemblies clamp. The user sets the spacing by tightening the gripper to the belt in the appropriate location for that tray. Advantages are precise plant alignment and simple, inexpensive versatility. Disadvantages are slower changeover to different tray types due to adjusting each gripper separately.

The second method is to use a fixed mechanical linkage between each gripper, which will put equal space between each trolley depending on the overall distance spread by the whole group. The advantage is quicker changeover than with the belt design. Disadvantages are more costly design, possibly more maintenance, wear over time, and the inability to precisely place the plant exactly where needed.

The third method is to have a servomotor for each gripper assembly. The controller "knows" where each gripper needs to be depending on which program is selected for the tray being transplanted. Advantages are faster changeover times to different types of flats and containers as well as extreme versatility and precision. Disadvantages are higher machine cost, possibly higher maintenance, and the machine is generally more technically challenging to troubleshoot, possibly requiring a more knowledgeable technical staff.

Impact of Transplanters

What's the payoff time for the machine? There are several factors to consider. Labor savings is the most common consideration. If a machine is fairly priced and you select the right unit for your operation, two to three years is a reasonable amount of time for you to realize labor savings equal to the amount of the original investment. Some larger growers have been able to see payoff in only one year.

There are other areas that have a payback; however, they're more difficult to calculate the savings on. Transplanters can actually do a better, more consistent job transplanting than most humans. Because of that, the finish time can in some cases be shortened by five to seven days.

Another savings that's difficult to calculate is the ability to continue to transplant a second or third crop while most of the work force is involved in shipping out your first crop. Transplanters have helped many growers stay on schedule, allowing them to get those additional crops planted—which, in some cases, is where your profit for the year is. This also allows delivery of promised product at crucial times.

Many growers have noted that the transplanter sets a steady pace for their crew. It keeps everybody moving who is involved in the transplanting process because the machine is going to keep cranking the product out. There's no time to stand around and chat. At the same time, it makes their jobs easier (given an ergonomically efficient system setup with the transplanter).

Transplanting affects your whole operation. For instance, most machines plant best when the plugs are at their optimum size. Because it's easier to stay on schedule when you don't have transplanting and labor bottlenecks, your plugs have a much better chance of being transplanted before they get overgrown in the plug tray. This results in better quality in the end. Germination is very important as well—the fewer missed plug cells, the more efficient your transplanter will be. These things in turn will make the grower better at growing and the manager better at planning and managing.

In the past, the start of the season was a ramping up process, with the initial filling of the greenhouse taking several weeks. This mindset has changed with the addition of automated transplanters. The first generation of transplanters could produce 100–400 flats per hour. The current generation of transplanters can produce 300–1,000+ flats per hour. This gives the grower the ability to put off heating the greenhouses for up to two to three weeks, and the cost of firing up heaters and boilers in January and February can be substantial.

Advantages

- Delay the start of your season; this can reduce your initial labor and heating costs
- Planting time for your initial greenhouse fill is greatly reduced
- More consistent planting
- Reduced loss of plugs
- Quicker grow out, as plant stress can be greatly reduced
- Back-fill time is greatly reduced; when you start shipping, you can send two to three people to operate the transplanter and start back-filling the greenhouse as soon as the space opens up
- Improved reliability
- Improved performance by employees by eliminating a time-consuming and repetitive task
- Large growers can see a reduction in seasonal

employees, and some small growers have eliminated season employees all together

- Reduction in overtime and weekend production.

Disadvantages

- Initial investment cost
- Selecting personnel for maintenance training
- Operator training
- Maintaining inventory of expendable parts
- Yearly maintenance or preventative maintenance provided by supplier

Purchase Considerations

When selecting a machine for your operation, consider the following:

- What is the rate of flats per hour, and how many people are needed?
- Do you want an inline system (directly in line with a flat filler) or the flexibility of a portable unit? Most operations may have already installed a manual line and an automated transplanter can be dropped into an existing line. Most transplanters give the operation the ability to run the automated line as a pass through manual line. But, if an additional manual line is necessary, then keep this in mind.
- How versatile does the transplanter need to be? Don't buy a Cadillac if a Chevy will do. Usually, more bells and whistles require more technically minded people to operate and maintain the equipment. A human is very versatile, but do not expect this type of versatility in a machine. The more versatile a machine becomes, in most cases, the more costly it will be. As a machine becomes more versatile, its ability to do any one thing great decreases. When considering versatility, look at your production schedule. What advantage does a machine capable of doing hanging baskets present if this production is coinciding with flat or pot production? Consider that large containers with few plants take more time and effort to fill, put on hangers and transport than it does to plant. Consider what the most efficient use of the transplanter is.
- Do you have one or two people who will be responsible for the equipment? Will they be sufficiently trained and able to keep things running?
- How will you bring material to and from the transplanter? After purchasing the transplanter, the next thing needed is an efficient way to handle the flow of material after transplanting. Look at the overall picture and develop a workable plan.

- How will a transplanter work in your system? A transplanter is a sizeable investment. It needs to work in your system or you need to be willing to change some or all of your system to work with it. Talk with other growers and equipment companies and formulate a plan to make everything work together. Don't look at any one piece of equipment by itself to solve all of your efficiency problems. If you have an $80,000 transplanter but are filling your flats with a wheelbarrow and shovel, you won't be very efficient.
- Is the transplanter upwards compatible? If you purchase a transplanter of a certain size, can it be easily upgraded in the future and not require you to purchase or trade in for another transplanter.

Plug Trays

Plug trays play a key role in the success of your transplanting machine. Some machines, such as the push-through type, require proprietary trays made by the manufacturer of the machine. They work nicely on that machine but will increase the cost of your plugs. This, of course, is somewhat offset by the low initial cost of the machine. There are also very few plug suppliers authorized to sell plugs for the machine, which could limit availability and increase cost.

Some transplanters have the ability to pull from more than one plug tray at a time, which requires the use of so-called "endless" plug trays. If you get one of these machines and buy plugs in, make sure your tray is compatible.

Changing from one tray to another can require different hardware to be installed on the machine. The CE (common element) marking is supposed to provide a standard for plug trays so that Brand A's CE 512 will be mechanically compatible with Brand B's 512, ideally requiring only minor adjustments. In most cases that's true. However, check with the transplanter manufacturer to be sure. If you bring in plugs from more than one grower, make sure their trays are compatible with your machine or plan on making hardware changes or adjustments, which can take valuable time and reduce the cost effectiveness of the machine.

Ask Around

What's the reputation of the product and company you're considering? As with any major purchase, you should check references. Ask growers who use this equipment questions including: Does it measure up to its advertised capabilities (e.g., rate per hour, ease of use, and reliability)? When it breaks down (all machines eventually have a problem of some sort), what's the tech support like? Are parts readily available? What problems have you experienced and how were they resolved? Is the machine simple enough for you or one of your current staff members to maintain, or did you need to hire additional technical staff? Check a manufacturer's track record for repeat customers. When the need arises, does the grower purchase additional transplanters from the same manufacturer?

Extras

Robert Lando

All of the automation described in this chapter will operate more efficiently when combined and electronically integrated with other automation. For instance, a pot-filling machine won't work nearly as efficiently if you're supplying each empty pot by hand rather than with an automatic pot dispenser. An automatic transplanter produces at maximum capacity and efficiency when linked via conveyor belts to a flat filler, a tagger, and a watering tunnel, creating an entire transplant line. Here are a few of the "extras" that modern, efficient growers can't live without.

Pot and Flat Dispensers

Pot dispensers are made to automatically insert pots (round or square) into shuttle or carry trays. This task, when performed by hand, can be among the most labor-intensive part of a production line. Pot dispensers are available in two versions: size adjustable and dedicated (single or multiple head). A single dedicated head sounds great for an African violet producer or foliage grower who may run one size of pot all day long and only changes to another size occasionally, but because of the wide variety of product sizes, there are relatively few North American growers who could set up to produce one size pot all day long. That's why the average grower might benefit more by having multiple dispensers set up on one belt in his most often used sizes. An example might be a unit set up to run 4" (10 cm), 4.5" (11 cm), and 6" (15 cm) pots. Multiple dedicated heads may still be adjustable so that they can be used for different pot sizes depending on season, but once set up, they are easily selected at the electrical panel and a quick rail adjustment for the shuttle tray finishes the job.

The obvious benefit in having a size-adjustable dispenser is that you can use the dispenser for several different pot sizes, therefore saving the cost of additional heads. The downside is that changing container sizes requires a somewhat time consuming process that needs to be fine-tuned to get the best results.

Production rates for both types are about 1.5 seconds per row. Rows are considered drop steps and can be lengthwise or sideways. An example of a typical 4"(10 cm) configuration is: With fifteen pots per flat in a three-row by five-row shuttle tray, it takes three drops per flat. Therefore, three drops times 1.5 seconds equals 4.5 seconds. Figure an additional second for indexing the next flat into position. Divide 5.5 seconds into 1 hour (3,600 seconds), and you come up with 654 flats per hour.

The cost of an adjustable, single dispenser mounted on a short conveyor belt is about $11,000. A multiple dispenser unit will cost $4,000–5,000 per each additional dispenser, including the extra belt and controls. A photoelectric eye at the output end of the pot dispenser is a must. The photo eye and a built-in timer will pause the pot dispenser whenever the line is full of trays or the rest of the line is stopped.

Figure 7-13. A pot dispenser eliminates of one of the most labor-intensive parts of a production line—pot dispensing by hand.

Watering Tunnel

There are three primary justifications for a watering tunnel. First, it's much easier to keep plants uniformly moistened in the growing area if the first watering is substantial and very even. Second, transplanted plugs and cuttings need to reside in a high-moisture environment while being transported and prior to being set down to the growing area. This minimizes losses due to a displacement during the sometimes-bumpy trip down the aisle on a cart and from drying out, which can occur before someone gets around to watering the freshly planted items. Third, freshly seeded trays require a high-moisture environment in order to ensure high germination as well as the dissipation of the seed coat for pelleted or coated seed.

Almost all of the horticultural machinery manufacturers make watering tunnels. Construction should be of stainless steel or other non-corrosive materials because paint just doesn't last. Ensure that the unit will accommodate your highest and widest containers, including hanging basket hangers if needed. Have the water turned on and off by means of a photoelectric eye or mechanical limit switch to save water. Make sure you get a variable-speed conveyor made of rubber belting or plastic chain. Ensure that you get the correct type of water curtain or spray nozzles for the crop you'll be watering—plugs require a different type of watering than do bedding plant flats. A basic 5' (1.5 m) watering tunnel should cost $3,500–4,500. More elaborate models with elongated drain areas or longer conveyors are also available to keep production areas

neat and dry. Many growers who use watering tunnels in conjunction with seeding machines have chosen subirrigation versions. Subirrigating increases water saturation and is known to dramatically improve germination rates.

Dibbler Conveyor

An automatic dibbler is used to make indentations into the soil prior to planting. It helps workers plant in the correct locations and to as uniform a depth as possible. Usually, a pneumatic cylinder raises and lowers a spike plate once flats have been located beneath. Many dibbler conveyors are made to accept the hand dibble boards that so many growers already have on the shelf. A dibble conveyor costs about $5,000. Growers utilizing larger cell inputs such as 72 and 50 cell sizes may choose turning drills as opposed to fixed pins. The turning drills displace soil to the side like a drill bit so the soil does not become overly compacted, as it does when using large-sized pins.

Figure 7-15. An automatic dibbler ensures that the seed is placed uniformly.

Tagger

An automatic tagger can be used to place tags into flats and shuttle trays. The higher the number of tags per flat being planted, the easier the justification for a tagger. A 3201 flat requires 32 tags per flat, while a jumbo 606 requires 6 tags per flat. Standardizing tags is a huge help. Each tag manufacturer's product differs enough to require additional tag chutes to run more than one type or size. Models differ from a one-arm model that takes several cycles to tag a flat to models that can tag the six packs in a jumbo 606 flat in one cycle. Make sure that the production speed on the highest tag per flat item keeps up with your planting

Figure 7-14. Your watering tunnel should accommodate your highest and widest containers, including hanging basket hangers.

speed. The only downside to an automatic tagger is variety changes. If production runs are too short, the process of changing out tags can actually slow overall production rates.

Figure 7-16. Taggers help growers efficiently place tags into flats and shuttle trays.

Inkjet Labeler

These inkjets (not to be confused with the inkjet printer in your office) utilize high-tech electronics to shoot ink droplets at bedding plant packs traveling at rates of up to 1,150 flats per minute. UPC bar codes, variety information, care instructions, and even logos can be printed almost like magic. The pluses of inkjet labelers begin with their ultimate flexibility. Since the variety information and bar code are printed right on the pack, you don't have to stock massive quantities of plastic tags. You generate the label as you need it and save it to a database. The cost of the ink and solvent is less than one-tenth of regular tags. The minuses are

the black and white–only print and the sophistication of the equipment—you have to go to school to learn how to operate and maintain it. You want the biggest bar code possible, so make sure that you get a unit with two guns on each side in order to get the 0.75" (2 cm) high code. Otherwise, readability can be poor. Bar code verifiers are available to check for good bar codes. Inkjet printers start at $14,000 and go up to $30,000 when equipped with two heads, allowing for both sides of the flat to be labeled.

Figure 7-17. Not to be confused with your office inkjet printer, these inkjets print your bar codes, variety information, care instructions, and logo directly on the packs.

Planting Conveyor

Planting conveyors are utilized to set a pace and improve product handling when planting by hand. Usually a 12" (30 cm) or 16" (41 cm) variable-speed conveyor belt will do. Racks to hold plug trays help, and a counter is nice to have. A 10' (3 m) long planting conveyor for four people, with racks, sells for $3,000. If tagging and hooking baskets is on the agenda, add another 10' (3 m). Dual-level planting lines are utilized for sticking cuttings. On dual-level lines, the upper conveyor supplies filled trays to planters, usually mechanically holding them in front of the planter for easy pick up. After planting, the worker places the planted tray on the lower conveyor for takeaway.

Figure 7-18. A conveyor improves product handling and sets the pace for planting by hand.

Basket Hooker

A fairly recent addition to greenhouse automation is the Hook-On, or "hooker." It is designed to automatically put plastic hooks on hanging baskets. It replaces several people and is loaded by just one person. Some plastic manufacturers package their hooks especially for use on the hooker in order to keep the strands straight and to make it easier to load the machine. Current speeds are just under 1,600 baskets per hour. The machine can accommodate up to 10" (25 cm) baskets with three-stranded plastic hooks. The Hook-On sells for under just under $23,000.

Figure 7-19. The Hook-On replaces several workers by automatically putting plastic hooks on hanging baskets.

Cart Loader

Some growers utilize automatic cart loaders at the end of their transplanting line. A buffer conveyor stages flats according to the number required for each shelf on the cart. Flats are then shuttled onto a conveyor (about the length of the cart) that raises and lowers to the shelf height, and a pusher device shoves the flats onto the shelf. When the cart is fully loaded, the cart loader pulls the next cart into place along with a line of linked carts that follow. The loader can be made for any cart and costs a little over $40,000.

Plug Tray Dispenser

An economical addition to any seeding or cuttings line is a dispenser for plug trays. Most plug tray manufacturers now make trays that are "machine friendly" in order for trays to be fed automatically into a tray filler. Like the pot and flat dispensers, a plug tray dispenser eliminates the need for one person to manually feed trays into the filling machine. Reliable tray dispensers cost under $9,000 and can purchased for single-stack use or with a loading conveyor that will automatically index stacks of trays into the dispenser.

Covering Hopper

Many seed varieties need to be covered with vermiculate or dry seedling mix after the seed is sown. Some seeders have integrated covering hoppers. However, stand-alone covering hoppers are available to add to any seeding line. Units start at $3,500.

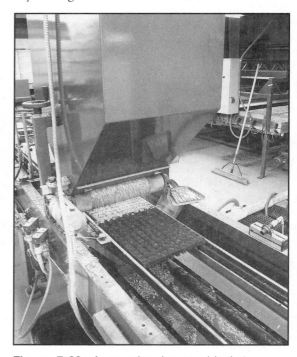

Figure 7-20. A covering hopper blankets sown seeds with vermiculite or dry seedling mix.

Roller Conveyors

Lightweight, modular roller conveyors can be extremely useful and cost effective. They're often used for feeding plug trays and flats to flat fillers and transplanters, as a drain-off area after a watering tunnel, or as a manual planting conveyor after a filler or transplanting machine. Roller spacing and bearing type are both critical. Many of the European-made units will be configured with as many as forty-eight rollers in a 10' (3 m) section. Any less than that and flats and plug trays won't roll well enough for the rollers to be useful. Many of the off-the-shelf "skate" rollers found in industrial supply catalogues won't last in a greenhouse production environment due to the constant water and fertilizer that eventually makes its way into the bearings. The European units may seem expensive, but they will last for ten years or more versus a couple of years with a standard skate roller. Cost is $40–70/ ft. ($132–231/m).

Figure 7-21. Roller conveyors can be used for a myriad of uses, including manual planting and draining off.

Production Counter

A production counter is a simple tool that can really help the production supervisor. By installing a photo eye with a resettable counter on your sowing or transplanting lines, flats or pots are counted as they're produced. This makes it easy to keep track of your production. The cost of a photo eye/counter module is under $200.

Machine Vision in the Greenhouse
Hans Izeboud

Machine vision—the use of video cameras and computers for grading and sorting of plants, flowers, and propagation material—has been in development since the 1990s and now is in common use in certain types of greenhouse ranges. Vision technology can make *objective* decisions about a crop's quality specifications rather than humans making *subjective* decisions. Vision system hardware has become more and more powerful, while software intelligence has also grown rapidly. Companies working in this field have become more experienced in handling the variation of shape, color, and other features that characterize greenhouse products.

There is a long tradition in developing and installing camera systems for grading and handling greenhouse products in the Netherlands, which is where most such systems are being developed and used today. The traditional presence of important seed companies, the relative huge amount of innovative pot plant and flower growers, the large number of monocrop growers, and the presence of highly equipped knowledge institutes such as Wageningen University have all played an important role in this tradition.

While mechanization in the horticultural industry started in the 1960s, the first steps in automation started in the early 1980s. Part of this automation is the introduction and use of sensors and camera systems. There are many different machine vision applications in use in the horticultural sector. One of the oldest applications has been in use for more than two decades, for grading and bundling cut flowers. But machine vision systems are used in many more applications. Vision systems are in use for grading potted plants in several stages, for grading and fixing (patching) plug trays, and for grading and sorting young plants, seed, bulbs, and unrooted cuttings. Machine vision systems, combined with robotics, are also in use for cutting, propagation, grafting, and harvesting.

Vision for Grading Flowers

Cut flowers was one of the first segments to use vision systems for grading individual stems by stem length, stem thickness, stem curve, flower size and color, number of buds, and so forth. The first cameras were used to measure length and thickness of hanging stems of roses. Black-and-white cameras used a back-light for lighting. Later on, color cameras were added for grading the flowers. These systems, from several machinery companies, have been running worldwide for years. There was only one problem: The systems could only handle roses. That's why several machines were developed for other kind of cut flowers, such as chrysanthemum, gerberas, spray roses, *Alstromeria,* statice, and tulips. These systems use several kinds of vision sensors. Most of the systems use a combination of black-and-white and color cameras, but for grading tulips and *Alstromeria* there is a system that uses x-rays for measuring stems, flowers, and buds. The capacity of flower grading systems varies between 6,000 and 14,400 stems per hour.

Today, there is a universal grading and bundling system on the market that can handle all kinds of cut flowers, using a choice from all the available vision sensors (black-and-white, color, and x-ray).

Vision for Plug Patching

Systems for inspecting and fixing plug trays are composed of two parts: the "popper" and the "fixer." The popper has a camera system that detects any empty or substandard cells and then blows the soil of the bad cells with a blast of air. The fixer then "replugs" all the empty cells with good plants.

The determination of good or bad cells is done by a camera and computer and is based on the leaf area of each individual plant within the cell in the tray. Plants with a leaf area below certain criteria are blown out. The criteria can be different for each tray or variety and can be changed easily by the operator.

The advantage of using this machinery is evident. Plug growers are able to offer their customers 100% filled trays. This has an important advantage in the rest of the chain. There are poppers and fixers running worldwide, manufactured by several companies. There are also mobile poppers and fixers available that can be moved to various parts of the greenhouse.

Vision for Germination Tests

In conjunction with the camera systems for the poppers and fixers, these cameras have been introduced in the laboratories of seed companies. These systems are used for determining the germination of the seed and can measure and store information (leaf area, height, color, etc.). Most of the systems are based on data from a color camera, but it will not take a long time before the same tests can be done even more accurately using such things as chlorophyll fluorescence.

Figure 7-23. While the human eye can grade seedlings such as these for germination, a camera and computer can do it more accurately and more consistently.

Vision for Grading Young Plants

The possibilities of using vision systems for seedling opened eyes to another category of young plant growers. It was not enough to grade the seedlings as either good or bad; they wanted to sort them into different

Figure 7-22. A mobile plug popping unit. A video camera resides in the box.

classes. That was the beginning of a whole new type of vision system that could handle this.

Where camera systems for poppers and fixers take a picture of the whole tray, camera systems for grading young plants need to see each individual plant. So transplanters are used to move the individual plants from their tray into a cup. The cups with plant inside are individually transported at high speed past a camera system where, based on the information of top- and side-view images taken by one or more cameras, the grading process takes place. Grading can be done by measuring the plant height, height of the highest leaf adhesion, number of young plant in one cup, volume, leaf area, and so on.

The technology started commercially with the grading of young tomato plants, but today there are vision systems for grading all types of young plants, primarily vegetables and potted plants such as orchids, anthuriums, and bromeliads. The capacity of these grading lines is up to 18,000 plants per hour, depending on the variety.

Vision for Grading Potted Plants

In the past twenty years, many different vision systems have been developed for grading and sorting potted plants, both during growing and just before shipping. There are simple camera systems for grading newly potted plants based on the measurement of leaf area, height, or width, but there are also very complex camera systems for grading crops such as orchids for shipping based on a wide range of different features. This helps the grower pack and ship plants based on flower color, flower count, stem count, size, and other factors, and the plants are all selected and sorted automatically with no human intervention, greatly reducing labor costs.

The simple camera systems use black-and-white or color cameras and are used right after potting and during spacing (which can be done several times). Mostly, camera systems for this kind of job grade the plant into two or three classes.

The plants are picked from concrete floor or aluminum table, transported by conveyor belts to the camera system, and sorted. Automatic pot handling equipment puts like plants together on the tables and sends them back into the greenhouse for growing on. The capacity of these simple camera systems is between 2,000 and 9,000 potted plants per hour, depending on the plant variety and handling constraints.

The advantages of grading plant during the growing phase are evident. Sorting plants brings all plants of the same size together, increasing uniformity of the crop. The grower can then give each plant the appropriate treatment to optimize the plant growth. Larger plants won't crowd out smaller ones on the tables.

In more automated greenhouses, there is another advantage: Information from the camera system about the growing progress of the sorted plants can be used for management and control information. If too many plants are being graded as undersized, the grower can adjust the greenhouse environment, plant nutrition, or other factors. Or the computer can automatically make that adjustment.

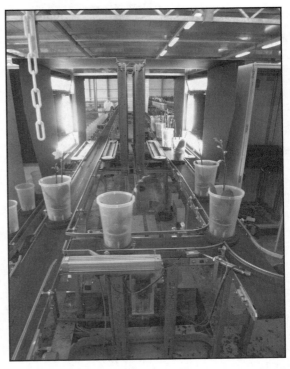

Figure 7-24. Camera system for grading Phalaenopsis orchids during spacing.

Vision for Sorting and Shipping

The camera systems that are used before shipping are more complex than most of the camera systems that are used during growing. Besides the measurements that are important for optimizing the growing process, it is also important to measure the features that determine the ornamental value of the plant. Normally, plants with a higher ornamental value give a higher price for the grower.

For each kind of potted plant, there are different features to measure the ornamental value. The ornamental value of green plants is determined by height, width, volume, symmetry, color of the leaves, structure of the plant, and so forth. By putting plants together with the same set of feature measurements, the grower can guarantee the quality of the plants to his customers. The ornamental value of flowering plants is determined by the same features as green plants plus measurements of the flowers: ripeness, size, and number of buds and flowers; their color; and their dimensions.

Figure 7-25. Camera system for grading flowering potted plants.

There are three different kinds of camera systems for grading flowering potted plants: In simple applications, the camera has to distinguish between plants with flowers and plants without flowers. Plants with flowers go to the shipping area, plants without flowers are sent back into the greenhouse. The medium-complex applications take measurements of the flowers. The camera system recognizes the color or the shape of the flowers and makes an accurate calculation of the number of flowers. This kind of camera system gives growers the extra possibility of grading plants by color and number of flowers.

Finally, there are the very complex applications for a special group of potted plants: orchids. Orchids have become very popular in the Netherlands and the rest of Europe, especially since mechanization and automation was introduced for this crop. Orchid grading systems are also in use in the United States. *Phalaenopsis,* the most commercially popular orchid variety as of this writing, is more and more grown using camera

systems. The most highly automated *Phalaenopsis* growers use camera systems after potting, before spacing (one or more times), after staking of the blooms ("sticking"), and just before shipping.

The simple camera system for orchids is used after potting and during spacing, and it grades young orchid plants into two or more classes based on leaf area. This camera system also determines the direction the leaves are facing and controls a rotation unit to position all the plants in the same direction. This way, plants can receive the same amount of light and there is a reduction of damaged leaves.

The camera systems after sticking and before shipping are the most complex of any used for grading potted plants. These systems are designed to measure every *Phalaenopsis* for the number of branches and side branches, the number of buds and flowers, the height of the plant (following the branch in the sleeve or an absolute height), the size of the biggest bud, the color of the flowers, and size of the flowers. Based on one or more of this features, it's possible to sort the crop into dozens of different grades of plants, allowing the grower to very accurately determine the ornamental value of each plant and to sell a wide range of uniform plant types to his customers. The capacity of these types of camera systems is about 2,000 plants per hour.

Modern orchid growers are becoming highly mechanized and automated. Information from all the processes taking place in the greenhouse is connected to an overall software system. The information from the different camera systems is also sent to this software system and is used for controlling the total growing process. For instance, calculating of the number of buds on an orchid is more difficult when some flowers are already open and some buds are hidden behind flowers. A grower can combine the grading report of a potted plant after sticking (when no flowers are yet open, so the calculation of buds is very accurate) with the grading report of the same plant just before shipping (when the calculation of buds is less accurate because some flowers are open) to have a very accurate bud count for that specific plant. Using and intelligently combining all the available information for controlling the potted plants during growth and before shipping give the grower the best opportunities for optimizing his processes.

Figure 7-26. Orchid grading systems can sort Phalaenopsis into dozens of different color and quality specifications. After sorting, they're held in "buffer" areas. The sales order computer automatically sends the needed number of plants of the proper grade or color to the packing area, where workers box them or put them on shipping racks.

Robotics in Horticulture

While the use of robots is common in many sectors of manufacturing, the use of robotics in horticulture is in its infancy. Besides the use of robots for picking up and placing potted plants from and to concrete floors or aluminum tables, the first intelligent robots are used being used in horticulture for the cutting and propagation of plants, for harvesting roses, for removing leaves of tomato plants, and for picking and sticking cuttings.

Robotic systems for cutting and sticking cuttings in a pot have been operating commercially for the propagation of pot roses since the early 2000s. The idea is simple: Bring a stem of a pot rose in front of a camera, make a 3-D measurement of the stem's position, sent this data to an industrial robot, move the robot to the right position, snip a cutting from the stem, and plant the cutting in a pot. The complexity of this process is caused by the huge variation of shape and density of the products within the different cuttings of the same variety. Between different varieties the variations can be even bigger.

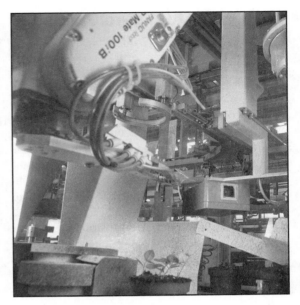

Figure 7-27. A vision-controlled robot for cutting and planting pot roses.

At the time of this writing (2011), there is one camera-controlled robot for harvesting roses in combination with a moving flower production system. The basic idea is simple: Move a row of roses passed a camera system that detects roses that are ready for harvest, send the rose coordinates to the robot, move the robot down along the stem of the rose to the cutting position, cut the flower, and take the flower out of the crop. The complexity of this process is again caused by the huge variation in the crop in combination with the speed needed to make the system commercially feasible.

Another interesting and important development is a robot for automatically removing leaves of tomato plants during their growth in the greenhouse. Also, at the time of this writing there are the very first promising results of a camera-controlled robot for picking and planting of unrooted chrysanthemum cuttings.

One final note about machine vision systems: This technology is only feasible in greenhouses that produce many hundreds of thousands of the same crop, in just one or a few sizes. That is why most of the developments and installations have taken place in the Netherlands, where most growers specialize in one crop. In other regions of the world where growers produce dozens or even hundreds of different varieties and sizes, vision technology and robots would be inefficient and cost prohibitive.

Ten Ways to Figure Payback

Chris Beytes

Twenty years ago, you calculated payback on a new piece of equipment, such as a seeder, conveyor belt, irrigation boom, or transplant line (manual or automatic), simply by figuring how many people it would let you drop from the payroll. Today, most growers know that payroll savings are just one benefit of automation. There is a wide range of other savings that, in many cases, pay for the equipment more quickly than do the labor savings.

In our travels and discussions with growers about greenhouse automation, we've identified at least nine more ways in which a piece of equipment might pay for itself. They fit into five main categories: labor, time, space, quality, and marketing.

Figure 7-28. Reducing labor costs is just one of at least ten ways mechanization and automation can pay for itself.

Labor

Labor availability

We will be the first to admit that this is still the first reason many growers think about buying a piece of equipment, whether simple or sophisticated. That's because it's getting harder and harder to find and keep good labor. If you need twenty people to hand transplant your spring bedding crop versus five to run an automatic transplanter, not having to find, hire, and keep fifteen people is a big money saver. (For some growers, anything that lessens the headaches of being an employer is well worth the price!)

Growers say the big mistake they've made is underestimating how many people they need to run a new machine. They buy a machine thinking it will take two people to run it and it actually takes four, so their payback calculations go out the window.

Your safest bet is to talk to several growers who are using the equipment you're considering and ask what they thought they'd save in labor versus how much they've actually saved.

Ease of labor

The right piece of equipment can help your existing employees do more with less stress and struggle. If you can make their jobs easier, they'll be happier, more productive, more consistent, and maybe have fewer job-related injuries. This could be a custom-built transplant line versus leaning over benches. It could be as simple as hot electric knives for taking cuttings instead of dipping a knife into bleach after every cutting. Comfortable employees who aren't bending, sweating, and stooping are happy, productive employees. And remember: You're often competing for labor against businesses that can offer air-conditioning and a much cleaner workplace.

Productivity

There are plenty of ways to realize increased productivity from mechanization. The most interesting example we've heard came from a manufacturer of manual transplant lines, which are often used for sticking cuttings by hand into trays. These lines can be equipped with automatic counters that keep track of each employee's output on a big "scoreboard" that everyone can see. Well, human nature being what it is, nobody wants to be the slowest worker with the lowest count. So, according to the manufacturer, growers who've installed these scoreboard-equipped sticking/planting lines say that, on average, their employees' output *doubles* compared to sticking the old way.

Time

Faster

Another big reason for automation today: You just can't get a job done in the short window you have to do it. How would you like to hand-sow all the plugs you need for spring? Impossible. Automation allows you to accomplish tasks more quickly. Carts for shipping bedding plants are a great example. Some growers have $5 million worth of carts on hand for the short spring shipping period. They'd rather invest the money elsewhere but it would be impossible to get the job done without them. The bigger your customers and the more product they demand, the more importance you place on this aspect of automation. It almost doesn't matter what it costs if it lets you get the job done.

Sooner

If a customer places an order that they want shipped ten weeks from today, how soon can you confirm that you'll have what they need? And how soon will you know if you have anything extra to sell? The right automation—be it a machine, a computer program, or bar codes—can help you know your availability sooner.

Plugs are a prime example of this: Plug growers who've gone to automatic patching systems can grade and patch their plug trays just a week or two after sowing versus waiting until a week or two before shipping when grading by hand. That two-week difference is a major competitive advantage in the plug game and provides two extra weeks to sell excess inventory.

Space

More space

Some modern systems are designed to let you use more of your production space. Overhead basket systems (such as ECHO) help you get more from your space while making hanging basket production very efficient. Concrete flood floors allow up to 90% space use, compared with bench systems, which are down around 70–85%. However, even simple wood-and-pipe rolling benches can boost space use up near that of flood floors.

Some systems, notably movable benches, can actually decrease your useable space. However, these can offer tremendous labor savings over benches or floors, where plants have to be put out by hand. You have to carefully weigh time and labor advantages against space advantages.

Another way automation can pay back in space use is by helping you gain back empty spaces between plants. A good example is plug patchers. One plug grower explained to us that if he grows 10 acres (4 ha) of 90% useable plugs, 10% of his space—1 acre (0.4 ha)—is wasted, taken up by one bad plug at a time. If he grades and patches the plugs to 100%, he gains back that acre of greenhouse, which he figures is worth $250,000 a year—enough to buy some very nice equipment.

That's one reason European growers are adopting vision-grading systems. If you take all the plants out of a bay, grade out the blooming ones, and consolidate the rest back in the greenhouse, you eliminate holes and gain back useable greenhouse space. Compare that with cherry picking a crop over several weeks, which leaves benches or bays only partially filled.

Turns

Empty greenhouse space is money lost. Many growers aren't concerned about a few days or a week of down time, but we've met growers who try to fill every empty space the very same day to be absolutely sure they're maxing out their facilities during the peak season. Dutch trays, automatic transplanters, and conveyor and monorail systems are great for this.

Marketing: New Markets

Sometimes a machine can get you into a new market, such as plant-and-ship bedding plant flats to help pay for your new transplanter. You might know some smaller growers who'd gladly pay for such a service. We're seeing more pre-finished material being sold from grower to grower. Being able to produce more product could give you enough to get into a new market, such as serving landscapers or fundraisers. The plug industry started when growers started selling their excess plugs to each other when it became easy to grow them by the millions. Any time you can produce more from the same space, you should look for new markets to accommodate that production. Fresh herbs to grocery stores or flats to farmers markets or to local attractions—the possibilities are endless.

Quality

Quality of product

Flat and pot fillers, drip or boom irrigation, automatic seeders, environmental control computers, super efficient sprayers . . . all these things can help you grow a better, more consistent product. Some of the least expensive systems fit this category, such as drip irrigation. But it's a shame when these quality gains get destroyed by poor handling during the packing or shipping process, so don't let that happen.

Quality of life

Here's a personal case study: My first two months in business, I had to be at my greenhouse twice a day, every single day, to pull hot, sticky, black plastic over PVC frames to black cloth my poinsettia crop. That's why I had no qualms about investing in a fully automatic black cloth system that would open and close itself. I could finally stay at home on Sunday.

This is a tough business, and you should make it easy on yourself wherever possible so that you retain the enthusiasm to work hard on the things that will give you a competitive advantage. That means not spraying by hand in the late evening, or opening and closing vents as temperatures rise and fall, or turning the valves on five acres of outdoor irrigation on a Sunday afternoon. Hard, repetitive jobs, especially at night and on weekends, are very discouraging for everybody.

Lean Flow in the Green Industry

Gerson "Gary" Cortés

Lean flow is a business strategy that has been around for decades, dating back to Henry Ford and the Ford Motor Company. Ford and his company were the first really to focus on the "flow." He developed the automotive assembly line that became the basis of every assembly line created in the last ninety years. He understood that getting a product to flow through a factory, from operation to operation, was an efficient method that dramatically reduced the time it took to build a car. Flow is essential to productivity and a major benefit of the lean flow manufacturing process, or simply "lean flow."

Many growers don't understand how lean flow can help them since they don't have a factory and feel that they are not a manufacturing company. But nurseries, greenhouses, and cut-flower operations are indeed factories. These factories buy material (hard goods or input material), convert it by applying labor and overhead to it, and then sell it—just like Henry Ford making his Model T. The biggest challenge of implementing lean flow in this industry is dealing with a living product that has a limited shelf life. This is not a big deal, since other industries also have their challenges and have successfully implemented lean flow.

Figure 7-29. Lean flow has helped growers reduce labor, increase efficiency, and even gain production and growing space, all for a relatively low investment.

The term lean flow is comprised of two essential concepts. For our purposes, "lean" and "flow" are used interchangeably and as a team, even though in reality they are two more or less separate techniques. Lean is the name of the overall production system and speaks to the method's most valuable trait: a focus on the elimination of waste. Flow is the part of lean that focuses on a company's need to have products flowing through the facility and out to the customer in a timely manner. Flow means moving product from process to process continuously, stopping for only a very small amount of time between operations. Flow is essential to speed and productivity, or efficiency.

Ultimately, a company cannot be lean without the proper flow. It also cannot have good flow if it's not lean. Hence, our term *lean flow*.

Breaking the Paradigm

It wasn't until about 2002 that the green industry began seriously looking at lean flow as a business strategy that could help growers improve productivity, increase growing turns, reduce floor space, improve quality, and reduce shrink. The bottom line is that lean flow can help reduce costs, thus improving profitability, market share, and customer satisfaction. When you look at your process, think of it as an assembly line because you are truly assembling a product: your plants. Once you can visualize this, you have made the paradigm shift. This is the first step in your *"lean flow journey."*

The other major hurdle to overcome is that lean flow will change the way you look at every process in your company: in the office, operations, shipping, and the material that you purchase. Because the change is so radical and dramatic, there may be strong resistance from some managers, leads, and employees; the key is to educate and show them that this change is good for them and the livelihood of the company. They may not embrace the change immediately, so consistent reinforcement of the benefits will be required. Change is a hard thing for humans, but change is not bad. It requires us to move out of our comfort zone and away from everything we have done for years and asks us to embark on a new path. Some of the non-believers and staunchest critics usually become the biggest champions of lean flow. Get your people on board and you have won half the battle.

Why Companies Implement Lean Flow

Companies implement lean flow to be more profitable. There are three ways to increase profits: increase prices, reduce product cost, and increase volume. The first choice is usually not an option, especially in the highly-competitive green industry.

As for the next choice: How can you reduce cost? Lean flow focuses on the elimination of waste to reduce costs. Waste is classified as non-value-added activities that do not increase the worth of the product in the customers' eyes. In the green industry, waste usually involves excess or unnecessary, poorly-coordinated, unconsolidated touches, or human work that is suboptimally paced by a belt. Waste increases the cost of the product, not its value, contrary to the grower's objective of reducing cost. By focusing on the elimination of waste, the following benefits are achieved:

- Increased productivity: 15%—30% improvement
- Optimized floor space: 3,000—10,000 ft.² (279–929 m²)
- Increased growing space turns: Double the turns in the same space
- Reduced shrink, up to 50% reduction
- Improved sell-through, as high as 95%
- Improved quality, resulting in fewer credits

Lean Flow in the Green Industry

When implementing lean flow in your facility, you have to ask yourself, "Where is my cost the highest?" In most cases, the greatest costs are in labor. So the focus is to improve productivity, but how can you improve it? The old school says push your employees harder and make them work faster. Lean flow says find

the non-value-added activities and eliminate them. As you observe your operations, have you ever noticed the following?

- You have employees pre-labeling flats or pots or pre-building boxes.
- You pre-fill flats, put them on a cart, and then move them to the greenhouse so they can later be used for sticking.
- You pull orders two days in advance or in some cases a week ahead of when they are going to ship, so you can inspect them, grade them, or do whatever you think is necessary to make them look good.
- A large crew bulk-pulls the day's product to be shipped, while a smaller crew prepares shipping racks laid out by truckload. As all bulk-pull products are brought to shipping near the end of the day, the entire crew hastily offloads bulk products to multiple shipping racks in multiple locations in a short and tight time frame and trucks cannot be loaded until the last bulk pull has been offloaded to shipping racks.

These are classic symptoms of doing work in a batch methodology. With lean flow, the goal is to flow product one piece at a time whenever possible. By producing in batches, costly extra touches are added that may impact the quality of the product, inventory is increased, more space is need to put that inventory, and in the end your productivity is lower.

Lean Flow in the Production Area

The goal of lean flow in the production area is to keep your people sticking, planting, or seeding more minutes and seconds of the day—not to make them do it faster. In many facilities, growers have employees sticking or planting on a belt conveyor because the grower thinks that the conveyor makes the employees work faster. They may work faster on a conveyor, but are they more productive? Also, how is the quality of the work they are doing? Have you ever watched the *I Love Lucy* show where Lucy and Ethel are working in a chocolate factory, packing chocolates on a belt conveyor? The belt speed is too fast; they can't keep up with the speed of the belt conveyor and are not packing the chocolates correctly. This is what your employees look like. When this occurs, the quality of the product is compromised. Spend ten minutes observing your employees on the belt and you will think of Lucy and Ethel.

The other problem with employees working on a paced belt conveyor is that they are less productive—contrary to intuition. You will notice that a portion of your employees are always waiting for product to come to them. The reason this occurs is because it is impossible to balance the work of employees when the product is moving.

With lean flow, we take the belts out and have the employees work on a stationary surface where the product moves only when the employee moves it. The line is set up as a progressive sticking or progressive planting line. Let's say that your employees are sticking cuttings into a 72-cell tray. Instead of having one employee stick the entire tray, have three employees each stick about one-third of the tray (24 cells). Set up the workstations like an assembly line; you will be surprised how more relaxed your people are working and how much more they will produce with much better quality.

There is one more person you need to have on the line, the material handler. The role of this person is to keep the stickers sticking more seconds and minutes of every day by making sure they have cuttings, tags, filled trays, root hormone, etc. The material handler is considered the non-value-added person on the line, yet his coordinated efforts ensure that the value-added people (stickers, planters, seeders) are constantly working, not waiting for material.

The other key to improving the productivity on this line is to make sure that the changeovers are transparent. When you change from one tray size to another, change plant material or change soil, the line should not stop. To put it in perspective: If you have twelve people on the line and you have ten change-overs a day that each take 3 minutes (planters not planting), by the end of the day you have accumulated 360 minutes of idle time. How long does it take to stick a cutting—perhaps 5 seconds? Those 360 minutes equal 4,320 cells, or sixty 72-cell trays. This is how we improve productivity—by eliminating waste, not by making people work faster.

Take this concept of eliminating waste, keep your value-added people working more consistently with fewer interruptions to other processes such as transplanting and sowing, and you will see that you improve productivity. The productivity improvement that you should see is anywhere from 15% to 35%. One grower who implemented progressive sticking got a six-to-one payback in the first season of running the lines. Another grower who was sticking on a belt conveyor and paying the employees piece work converted his line to a progressive sticking line and achieved a 38% productivity improvement.

Earlier, this discussion mentioned a third way to increase your profitability: Increased sales volume. Lean flow offers this opportunity as well, in several ways:

- Lean flow optimal retail inventory level techniques ensure that the right mix and quantity is at the right stores, as well as on your shipping dock, to increase your sell-through and minimize your shrink. One big-box grower's sell-through went from 85% to 95% while reducing shrink by 50%.
- As lean flow minimizes batch work, wasted space becomes available. As a result, growers are often able to recover growing space and increase their volume. One grower recovered 10,000 ft.^{2} (929 m^2) of revenue-generating greenhouse space that he had previously been using to stage a week's worth of product for shipping.
- Many growers and distributors find that they keep and gain customers with high quality and exceptional on-time delivery, in addition to competitive pricing. Because lean flow focuses on quality and customer service, growers and distributors are able to differentiate themselves from their competition and increase their market presence.

Lean Flow in the Shipping and Packing Area

The goal of lean flow in the shipping area is to improve the response time to the customer, productivity, and the product quality. In the shipping area, you set up a "supermarket": a physical location where product is staged, typically a third of a day's to a day's worth. The amount depends on the physical space available and how long the product can stay in the supermarket without affecting the quality. A crew of workers pulls product from the greenhouses, ranges, and fields to the supermarket.

Figure 7-30 shows the product that was pulled being loaded into the supermarket. As one crew is pulling material, another crew is picking product from the supermarket to fulfill customer orders. Figure 7-31 shows the product being picked to a customer order. As mentioned earlier, one of the objectives of lean flow is to "flow" the product, to keep it moving with minimal interruption. With the supermarket you have product flowing into the supermarket and product flowing out at a steady rate.

Figure 7-30. Loading the "supermarket" on the left with plants coming in from the greenhouse on a conveyor belt.

Figure 7-31. Picking orders from the supermarket and loading shipping racks destined for delivery.

By having material in the supermarket first thing in the morning, the order-picking crew can immediately begin fulfilling customer orders. Within the first thirty to forty-five minutes, a truck should be loaded and ready to go. Having the ability to load trucks first thing in the morning allows you to load trucks throughout the day. By the end of the day (nine to ten hours), all the trucks should be loaded and your employees are ready to go home. Currently, during peak weeks, you are probably working countless hours of overtime, yet with a supermarket in place, the peak weeks don't feel like peak weeks.

The grower that set up this supermarket did not have to work any overtime during their peak weeks in spring. This was the first time in the company's history that they did not have to work overtime. Another grower was able to improve productivity 30% the first year and 12% the year after, simply by setting up a supermarket in the shipping area.

The two techniques described above are just two specific applications for growers. There are many other areas in your company that can benefit from lean flow, whether you are a grower, a distributor, wholesaler, or retailer of young plants or finished plants, annuals or perennials. Observe your processes and the work your people are doing and ask yourself, "Is that work adding value to my product?" If it isn't, then you need to try and eliminate it, using proven lean flow techniques and tools.

8

Internal Transport and Logistics

Wagons, Carts, and Monorails
Chris Beytes

The earliest form of internal transport used in a greenhouse was probably a wheelbarrow, since that versatile tool was being used in the garden long before greenhouses existed. The head gardener probably modified the wheelbarrow by crafting a flat deck to better carry wooden seedling trays and clay pots from the potting shed or cold frames to the garden.

Today, one- or two-wheeled carts are still widely used around the greenhouse, although they're usually made of welded steel. In fact, some older greenhouse facilities still use narrow, tall, one-wheeled carts designed more than a hundred years ago to negotiate the 18–24" (46–61 cm) aisles between the old concrete benches. Short of rebuilding the facility with wider aisles, there's no more convenient, cost-effective way of bringing product to and from the benches.

That may be fine for small businesses doing weekly potted plants, but the modern bedding plant business requires high-speed, high-volume shipping during the hectic spring months, which has led to faster ways to move product in and out of the greenhouse. The first way was to simply make the wheelbarrow bigger, add another pair of wheels, and tow it with a small tractor. Soon, growers were adding more levels and more trailers, creating trains of trailers that could move hundreds of flats at once. Pivoting axles created self-tracking trailers able to negotiate tight turns. This method of transport is still widely used both in field nurseries and in greenhouses, although greenhouse businesses usually use electric tow vehicles to prevent problems from exhaust fumes.

Carts

Throughout most of the floriculture industry's history, plants have been shipped to independent garden centers and florists either singly, in trays, or in cartons. Trucks were unloaded by hand, one tray at a time. In the 1970s, when the mass-market garden centers began to market products on a large scale, growers found themselves shipping more product to one store than they used to sell all week. They couldn't load and unload the trucks quickly enough to keep up with demand. That's when a few smart growers developed the shipping cart by either adapting existing carts to handle bedding plants or welding up their own designs. The shipping cart (or rack, as it's also called) allows one person to move thousands of flats or pots easily and quickly, meeting the volume demands of large retail stores. Today, it is almost impossible to serve mass-market customers without investing in

Figures 8-1, 8-2. Sometimes the old way (left) is still the only way (right).

Figure 8-3. Shipping carts come in almost as many config-urations as there are growers.

carts. And as growers began using carts for shipping, they found them to be handy for use within the greenhouse as well, transporting product to and from the production area.

Commercially available carts come in a wide range of sizes, based on the needs of the grower. The idea is to accommodate the most flats or pots possible and to fit the grower's trucks as tightly as possible, eliminating any wasted space. Shelves are adjustable to accommodate various product heights and come with mesh or solid bottoms. Wheels are equipped with brakes, to prevent accidental rolling. At a cost of $200–500 apiece and with large growers having to own thousands of them on which to ship their product in a timely fashion, carts have become an expensive yet indispensable part of the modern greenhouse business.

Monorails

Wagons, trailers, and carts are great for growers who have lots of aisle space. But for older operations with little aisle space or for new greenhouses taking advantage of the space-saving benefits of rolling benches or flood floors, monorails can be a convenient way to move product when trailers or carts can't be brought close to the crop.

Keeping Track

Chris Beytes

Originally designed simply to transport product, carts today are an extension of the store's retail benches. Growers drop off full carts, and the product is either put on the store shelves by store employees or the grower's own merchandisers, or it's left on the cart, which is used as a retail display. In fact, some growers ship their carts with signs taped to them that provide product information and price. Indeed, this is becoming a more common practice, with some chains even requesting or requiring this service.

Naturally, with thousands of racks now being shipped around the country and left at stores, growers often have a hard time finding their own carts and getting them back. Other growers' drivers sometimes pick up another grower's carts, either accidentally or, occasionally, stealing them outright. Store employees sometimes use them for their own purposes in stockrooms. Consumers take them from stores, seeing them as handy garage shelf units. It's a major industry problem. Racks cost from $200–500, and the typical large grower owns anywhere from 2,000 to 10,000, so even a 1% loss each year can be costly.

To combat their losses, growers weld on nameplates and paint them in their own custom colors—including blaze orange—and even add bar codes or RFID (radio frequency identification) chips so they can scan them in and out of their computer system, but the losses still occur. Some growers have even explored the idea of using GPS—global positioning system—which would use satellite technology to track the whereabouts of carts. Others are exploring the idea of a national cart-tracking website or national leasing program.

However, the growers who do the best job tracking their carts say that it doesn't matter what technology you use, it all comes down to maintaining the system—training drivers and customers to unload and return carts on a regular basis throughout the season.

A monorail is simply a shelf unit that's suspended on wheels from an overhead track, made from metal tubing welded to the greenhouse structure using C-shaped connectors. Workers can pull or push one or more of the shelf units down a bench, load them with product, and then push them back out to the main aisle for transport to the shipping area. Sometimes, growers suspend monorail carts from their boom irrigation rails or overhead heating pipes, making double-duty of the existing structure. A few growers have even combined the mobility of a monorail with the motion of a conveyor belt, allowing them to feed pots or flats from the middle of a bay to the side.

The biggest drawback to monorails is that the network of overhead pipes needed to move the monorail cart from place to place can add shading to the structure. Plus, if you have overhead curtains, the monorail system needs to be below them. Also, it might prevent you from adding overhead equipment such as ECHO systems or boom irrigators at a later date.

Figure 8-4. This powered monorail system travels throughout the facility at Andy Mast Greenhouses, Grand Rapids, Michigan.

Conveyors

Will Knowles and Quinn Denning

A very important consideration for all growers is how to move product from the planting area to the greenhouse, within the greenhouse, and from the greenhouse to the shipping area. Given a particular grower's crops and facility layout, conveyors can be a very simple, effective, efficient, and flexible means of moving plants within most greenhouse operations.

Conveyors are available in any width or length needed. They can be installed permanently or set up temporarily. The conveyors are installed inline so that product can be moved from one conveyor segment to the next.

Belts and Rollers

Belted conveyors and roller conveyors each have their purposes for transporting product within the greenhouse operation.

Belted conveyors

The major advantage of a belted conveyor line is motorization; it will keep the product moving. Coupled with speed control and directional (forward and reverse) control, the operator can create a smooth-flowing movement of product that will determine the pace for the workers on the line and also create a predictable product output. Conveyors are often equipped with electric motors, although hydraulics can also drive the belt.

The belt material itself can be rough or smooth; rough if the belt needs to grip the bottom of the product to move it along, smooth if the belt needs to be able to slip underneath a product that's purposely held in place occasionally, such as on a transplant line. Belted conveyors are an integral component in many pieces of automation equipment including tray fillers, transplanters, and seeders and are well suited to moving pots, trays, and boxes.

Depending upon the width, length, and construction materials used, belted conveyors vary widely in price, ranging from $80–350/ft. ($262–1,148/m), depending on the many variables.

Figure 8-5. Conveyor belts can link equipment together into production lines or carry product a long distance into and out of the greenhouse.

Roller conveyors

Like belt conveyors, roller conveyors are available in a variety of widths and lengths. Because of the bumpy ride the rollers create, this conveyor is better suited for products with long, flat bottoms, such as flats or boxes, rather than individual pots. The rollers are available in various diameters depending upon the size and weight of the product being carried.

The materials used for the rollers will vary depending upon the product weight and use of the conveyor. Many new greenhouse roller conveyor manufacturers are using plastic rollers with nylon bearings and an aluminum frame for lightweight use in the greenhouse. There are no problems when this type of conveyor gets wet regularly.

The roller conveyor can be powered to move product automatically but are most often operated manually, with the workers pushing the product down the line. The manual roller conveyors allow the product to

Figure 8-6. Roller conveyors are often employed at the shipping end of the business, where they can accumulate product for packing on racks or in boxes.

stand still on the line until someone pushes it along, or until the next flat or box moves onto the conveyor and bumps it onward.

Often, roller conveyors are used at the end of a production line to accumulate product that the workers will then pick up and place on a cart or trailer. They're often used in shipping areas to hold finished product for packing. Because the roller conveyor can accumulate product, workers don't have to worry about the product falling off the end of the line while they get additional carts into place for loading. Of course, an end switch can be mounted at the end of the belt-type conveyor that will send a signal to the rest of the line to stop.

Just like the belted conveyors, the prices of roller conveyors vary depending upon width, length, and construction materials. The price ranges from $60–150/ft. ($197–492/m).

Specialty Conveyors

Specialty conveyors are available in the greenhouse industry as well. Hanging basket production has been simplified with use of a cable conveyor that's installed overhead (the ECHO System discussed in chapter 4) to carry the hanging baskets around a loop the length of the greenhouse bay. This system can increase the hanging basket production area for the grower, in addition to providing a means of watering the hanging baskets and moving them to a central aisle for crop work or shipping. The manufacturer of the ECHO System, Cherry Creek Systems (Colorado Springs, Colorado), also offers a cable-style conveyor called the ECHOVeyor for flats and shuttle trays that uses steel cable instead of belts or rollers. Benefits include low cost and easy of fitting into older greenhouses.

Another type of conveyor commonly used in the greenhouse is portable modular conveyor. This type of conveyor consists of two different types of sections. The drive section is motorized and is designed to power slave sections, which do not have their own motors. One drive section can power several slave sections, which helps keep the cost per square foot lower while allowing the user to configure the system to fit their ever-changing needs. Power is transferred from section to section by mechanical connection such as gears or shafts. Another benefit of this type of conveyor is that it tears down for compact storage in the off-season. These conveyor beds are usually aluminum, making them lightweight for easy handling. Typically, portable conveyors are set directly on the floor so they can be stepped over or are placed on tripod stands that set up quickly.

Installation Methods

While conveyors are well suited for moving product within the planting and shipping areas or within the greenhouses, the challenge of moving product long distances from the planting area to the greenhouse and from the greenhouse to the shipping area is the fact that they block aisles and pathways. This type of conveyor system must be designed to minimize the impact on all transportation arteries.

One method is to install the conveyor system from the main aisle down the length of the greenhouse, along the rows of greenhouse columns. This conveyor line then serves two greenhouse bays and leaves the width of the greenhouse bay accessible. A second mobile conveyor is installed across the width of the bay to meet the conveyor along the columns. This conveyor is moved up and down the length of the house depending upon where the crops need to be placed or picked up.

The crops are carried to the greenhouse column conveyor via another conveyor, on carts, or on trailers. The product is placed on the column conveyor and travels to where it meets the mobile conveyor. Typically, a worker is positioned to make the 90° product transfer from one conveyor to another, and other workers take product off the mobile conveyor and set it on the ground. This process is reversed for the shipping procedure. Some growers have even experimented with conveyors mounted on irrigation booms, to carry the product from the column conveyor into the bay to the workers.

Another solution to this situation is for some conveyor segments along a line to be hinged on one end and lifted out of the way to open the aisle.

Movable Benches

Edwin Hoenderdos

Movable benches originated in the Netherlands about forty years ago. In the early 1980s, they made their debut in North America. Today, their use has spread worldwide.

Movable benches are also called container benches or Dutch trays and are benches that can move from the production area to the greenhouse on a system of pipe rails. Typical sizes range from 5–6' (1.5–1.8 m) wide by 12–20' (3.6–6 m) long. Within the greenhouse they move between climate zones and, depending on what types of crops are being grown, can be moved to the headhouse for the intermediate spacing of crops (as discussed in the section on machine vision technology systems in chapter 7). At the end of the growing cycle they're moved to the shipping area.

Why Do Growers Use Them?

The purpose of movable benches is twofold, or even threefold. Not only is the bench used for growing but also for transportation, and even for irrigation, if desired.

Transportation

Movable benches roll from the production area to one of the many zones in the greenhouse, such as the propagation zone. One bench can carry many pots or flats, creating substantial labor savings. The size of the bench is dependent on the width of the greenhouse bays, and thus benches are custom designed to fit each grower's greenhouse. By using a movable bench system a grower can easily move his crops between different climate zones. Some growers move the benches in and out of coolers where plants are vernalized (given a period of cold so they'll initiate flowers). Finished product can easily be moved to the shipping area by one employee or through automation, using motorized "transport lines" or robotic cranes. Depending on what's being grown, the crops might have to be spaced once or twice during the growth cycle. With movable benches, this labor-intensive process can be easily automated with the use of pot-placing robots. These robots can pick up the pots from the bench and put them down again at a desired spacing with little or no human labor required. When you have the ability to automatically space, you can increase your production per square foot in the greenhouse quite easily. This allows for a quicker return on investment.

Movable benches can also increase the space utilization of the greenhouse. The greenhouse can be filled rapidly, with each greenhouse bay kept full of product to maximize the return of each square foot of greenhouse space.

Bench

Once the crop is in the greenhouse, the bench functions as the growing area. The bench can be equipped with an expanded metal bottom or an ebb-and-flood bottom, made from either aluminum or plastic. The bench can be moved easily from one climate zone to another, so climate zones can be permanently set in the greenhouse without requiring more climate control equipment in each zone.

Irrigation system

By using benches equipped for ebb-and-flood irrigation, your bench now serves a third purpose, making watering less labor intensive and more accurate. Also, you can achieve substantial savings in irrigation water and fertilizers through the use of ebb-and-flood (see chapter 4).

Figure 8-7. Movable benches may require a large capital investment, but they offer a plant transport system, a bench, and an irrigation system all in one.

Necessary Equipment

A typical moveable bench system is made up of aluminum benches and their support system, which consists of 2" (5 cm) diameter pipe on which the benches roll. These pipes are held about 24–30" (60–75 cm) off the ground on upright pipes either bolted to the concrete floor or set in concrete footings. In the middle or at the sides of the greenhouse there are transport lines that facilitate the lateral movement of the benches between the bench rows. The transport line brings the bench to and from the headhouse. This system of pipe rails is usually called "rollerbahn" (similar to the German term for highway, "autobahn").

The movement of the benches can be manual, automatic, or a combination of the two, depending on budget and needs. Movable bench automation can consist of automatic stacking of empty benches in

the headhouse, automatic transport lines, automatic bench washing for ebb-and-flood benches, and even robot cars that bring benches into or out of the greenhouse without the aid of manual labor.

Figure 8-8. The most sophisticated movable bench systems use robotic cars that can move one or several benches at a time.

Modern Developments

The newest development to tie in with movable benches are camera grading systems, as discussed in chapter 7. Movable benches are what allow growers to move plants in and out of the greenhouse at intervals during the growing process, for spacing and grading. For instance, a crop can be started pot to pot for maximum number of pots per bench, and then spaced a few weeks later before the plants begin to crowd one another. This can be done completely automatically, with little human intervention other than to tell the computer which benches to space. Grading by size can also be done automatically, greatly increasing the uniformity of the finished crop. And when crops are uniform, they finish at the same time, allowing 100% of the plants on a bench to be shipped at the same time, again for maximum production efficiency.

Another aspect of rolling bench automation is the ability to keep track of each bench's location and status in the greenhouse using either bar codes or RFID tags on each bench. This allows the grower to identify where each bench is in the greenhouse, when it was spaced, when it was watered, and how much water it received. This level of automation is generally used only by the largest growers producing high volumes (usually millions of post per year) of the same crop, such as *Phalaenopsis* orchids, bromeliads, or other flowering potted plants. However, other crops now being grown on rolling benches include cut flowers, vegetables, and citrus.

Pros

As with all greenhouse systems, movable benches have their pros and cons. Following are some of the advantages of movable benches.

Labor saving

Movable benches can reduce the amount of labor hours in your business by up to 40%. If you add to that the automation available for potting, sorting, and spacing, labor savings can reach as high as 60%.

Improved working conditions

Movable benches improve labor conditions by creating separate growing and working areas. Also, arrangements can be made to create ergonomic work conditions through proper working heights. In addition, by reducing the amount of labor taking place in the greenhouse, you'll increase the level of hygiene in the greenhouse.

Efficient management

With movable benches, you can have more control on your production and delivery schedules.

Optimal utilization of space

With careful planning, you can keep your greenhouse functioning at its maximum capacity. It's easy to quickly fill empty spaces in the greenhouse. With minimal aisles between tables, space utilization of 90% can be achieved.

Irrigation control

If your movable benches are equipped for irrigation, you'll be able to cut irrigation labor, reduce water and fertilizer use, and capture your runoff.

Cons

Movable bench systems also have their disadvantages. Following are some of the cons of these systems.

Large initial investment

The up-front cost of a movable bench system can be large, especially compared with fixed benches.

Challenging logistics

Because the benches roll in and out of the greenhouse, it's hard to access plants that are sitting on a bench in the middle of other benches. If you need to retrieve a bench, you may have to move many others first.

Shipping area

Certain crops require a large shipping area because you're bringing entire benches into the area. If you have many varieties, then the shipping area needs to be able to accommodate the various benches.

Partially empty benches

In certain situations there will be partially empty benches in the shipping area. These either have to be consolidated and sent back to the greenhouse or have to remain in the shipping area until the next shipping order comes in.

What's the Cost?

The cost of a movable bench system varies widely, depending on numerous factors, including greenhouse size, crops grown, irrigation requirements, level of desired automation, and needs of the grower. Thus, exact numbers can only be calculated after a complete analysis has taken place with the grower and various site visits have occurred. However, here are some ballpark numbers, based on 1 acre (0.4 ha) of greenhouse space:

A basic system with expanded metal in each bench and manual operation of the system is about $5.00/ft.^{2} ($53.80/m^2) for materials. Then you have to add the installation labor, which can vary depending on the way it's done.

A more automated system with automated bench movement as well as ebb-and-flow irrigation could cost $9.00/ft.^{2} ($96.84/m^2).

If you're looking at automation in the headhouse, such as overhead cranes and cleaning machines for the benches, then the total cost can be as high as $11.00/ft.^{2} ($118.36/m^2).

Always remember, though, that these systems can be installed for manual operation, with automated components added later, to help you achieve a good return on your investment.

Forklifts, Cranes, Wagons, and Robots
Chris Beytes

Moving plants into the greenhouse, putting them down on benches or floors, picking them back up again, and transporting them to the shipping area requires more labor and time than just about any other steps in the plant production process. That's why growers and equipment manufacturers are constantly seeking better, more efficient ways to move product.

The advent of flood floors has accelerated the race to develop plant movement automation because they give us a large, flat, hard surface on which to operate the new equipment.

Forklifts

Possibly the simplest yet most challenging form of "automated" internal transport is the forklift. Growers have experimented with vehicle-mounted forks for years, but Visser International Trade & Engineering, Gravendeel, the Netherlands, was the first company to commercialize the technology, which utilizes special forks mounted on a forklift that is equipped with an automatic gear box that will move the vehicle at a predetermined pace to pick up or set down pots on a set spacing. The system allows one worker to move up to several hundred pots at one time quickly and efficiently.

The challenge of the system is that you have to change or adjust the forks to handle different pot sizes. Also, the system is only as accurate as the operator. One wrong move and you've dumped a load of plants. Also, fork systems work best on a smooth, flat surface with plenty of room to maneuver. There are also forklifts designed for outdoor use in nurseries on rougher terrain.

Some nurseries in the Netherlands use them in much the same fashion as growers use moving benches, bringing plants to a centralized grading area several times during the production process. The fork places the pots on a wide conveyor belt that takes them to a narrow belt for transport through a vision grader. After grading, plants return to another wide belt where the forklift picks them up again for transport back into the greenhouse.

Costs for such a system range from $50,000–100,000 or more, depending on the additional equipment you need to make the system work efficiently.

Seacliff Greenhouses, Leamington, Ontario, Canada, designed another form of truck. It's a small electric cart equipped with a 5 x 15' (1.5 m x 4.6 m) conveyor belt on the back that can be tipped up or down to place plants down on the floor and pick them back up. With it, one person can move more than 1,000 flats per hour into Seacliff's greenhouses, easily keeping up with their transplant lines. The drawback is that it requires wide main greenhouse aisles so the truck can maneuver.

Figure 8-9. This Visser Space-o-Mat allows one worker to move and space thousands of pots per hour.

Cranes

As mentioned in the section on moveable benches, there are overhead cranes available that will allow you to retrieve a bench from the middle of a sea of benches. Some European growers take advantage of this technology, although most have designed their product logistics so they don't have to.

One North American grower has taken this overhead crane technology to the next level. At Metrolina Greenhouses, Huntersville, North Carolina, they worked with Dutch equipment designer FW Systems to develop a gantry-style crane that moves large aluminum racks filled with product. The racks sit on the flood floor of the greenhouse, which was specially designed to accommodate the weight of the crane. Also, the bays of the open-roof greenhouse are some 1,300' (396 m) long—a quarter of a mile!—to take advantage of the speed and efficiency of the crane system. In addition, a spray rig can be suspended from the bottom of the crane, allowing the operator to spray an acre of greenhouse (one bay) in just a few minutes. Cost for such a system falls under the heading of "If you have to ask. . . ." The investment in the greenhouse, crane, headhouse, and all the equipment required to make it work is well in excess of $20 million. It's a good indication of the lengths to which growers are going in an effort to produce massive quantities of plants at the lowest possible production costs.

Figure 8-10. The one-of-a-kind crane system at Metrolina Greenhouses.

Computerized Wagons

At Emsflower, a giant bedding plant greenhouse combined with an open-to-the-public greenhouse tourist attraction in Emsbüren, Germany, they use large wagons pulled by a computer controlled in-ground chain system. Constructed by Dutch bedding plant grower Bennie Kuipers and his son, Tom (who designed the wagons and computer system to control them), the system is used to move millions of bedding plant flats throughout the 60 acre (24.3 ha) greenhouse.

The wagons are simple from a mechanical standpoint: four rubber tires and two pivoting axles with a steel and wooden flatbed top. The computer controls are housed in a box on the wagon's hitch; it talks with a central computer that activates the connection between the hitch and the chain that runs in channels buried in the floor. The computer can connect and disconnect the wagon from the chain at various "stations" in the facility. Overhead gantry-style cranes in each growing bay are used to load and unload the wagons.

Figure 8-11. Wagons at Emsflower in Germany combine simple wagons with computer controls.

Robots

One of the first attempts to design robotic plant transporters was at Hamer Bloemzaden, Zwindrecht, the Netherlands. This well-known plug producer wanted a machine that could automatically drive through the greenhouse and place and pick up bedding plant plugs without any human control at all. Beginning in the mid-1990s, they tried laser-guided systems but found the greenhouse actually expanded and contracted enough due to heat and cold that the system didn't remain accurate. They tried sound waves but found the water in the flood floors would soak into the concrete, affecting how the sound waves were reflected. Both systems left the robot driving through walls and closed doors. In the end, Hammer settled on having a human operator on the "robot."

People Still Required

Indeed, greenhouse technology still requires the input of humans. Every machine requires a human to make sure it's working properly—and often, a skilled technician to fix it when it isn't. As one grower once pointed out to us, it's easy to eliminate one or two people from a ten-person task. It's harder to eliminate three to six. Eliminating seven, eight, or nine gets tremendously expensive. And as for eliminating the tenth? Almost impossible, and incredibly expensive to even attempt. That is why most large growers in the United States still depend on human labor for most of their internal plant movement. They use electric or gasoline tow vehicles to pull trains of carts or racks in and out of the greenhouse, and hand labor to place plants on the floors.

Case Study: Bar Code Tracking in a Modern Plug Facility

Paul T. Karlovich

Bar code tracking continues to be an important means of maintaining business information at a modern high-level greenhouse operation. The emerging technology of RFID (radio frequency identification) will gradually replace bar codes, but cost barriers will continue to slow the use of this technology in the greenhouse industry.

For a greenhouse considering which technology to pursue, the first choice should be RFID, if no system is in place. C. Raker & Sons Inc., Litchfield, Michigan, continues to get high value from our bar code system, and this likely will continue for the foreseeable future.

There are two equally important components to the system we use at Raker. The first is the technology itself. This is the hardware and software necessary to do what needs to be done and includes computers, scanners, bar codes, RFID chips, antennae, and cabling hardware.

The second component is how we manage the system. This includes maintaining and upgrading the technology, monitoring the data accuracy, entering data into the system in a timely and consistent manner, retrieving and presenting data in a useful manner, and matching the technology system to the work process systems of the organization.

Figure 8-13. This scanner, manufactured by Sick Inc., Minneapolis, Minnesota, attaches to a computer serial port and is sensor-activated to read bar codes. The data recorded by the scan is in context to the activity being performed. This scanner is located on their sowing line.

Figure 8-12. Computer technology allows Raker to keep real-time track of thousands of plug trays—a competitive advantage in the fast-paced world of plug and cutting production.

Bar Codes: Beginning to End

At Raker, we place bar codes on every tray that is started in the system. We deal almost exclusively with flats, and our system lends itself well to putting a bar code on each one. The Vericell Vision software (The Corymb Group, Batavia, Illinois) generates unique bar codes. Since every bar code is a different number, we can attach all kinds of information to that number. Some of the information we track is the seed lot, sow date, tray status (i.e., dumped, in inventory, or shipped), ship date, customer, and greenhouse tray location. We can track any information we choose with this type of system.

Bar codes are very valuable because they can be scanned mechanically at the time the work is done, and the data is recorded instantaneously. Scanning is important because it eliminates human entry errors. For this reason we use scans to enter data in the computer wherever possible. In many cases, the ability to scan replaces human work. On the Raker sowing lines, an inline serial scanner reads the bar code at the end of the sowing process. As the bar code is scanned, the computer is updated with the information related to that activity. At sowing, the number of trays started is updated and the seed inventory is reduced at every scan. This information is immediately available to the rest of the company. In the good old days, a human would have done this on paper and it would not have been done as accurately or in as timely a manner as is possible with a computer. Does this sound familiar: How many trays did we *really* start last week? How much seed is *really* left? We have accurate, up-to-the-minute answers to those questions.

Bar codes are integral to our technology system. Once we have the tray coded, we can place that bar code in the greenhouse in a location. Raker uses moveable benches, each of which has its own unique bar code, so we "place" tray bar codes on the bench by scanning a bench bar code. The work done by the scan is always in context to the activity being done, so the same bar code is scanned to "move" trays to benches. We also use bench tags that are coded both by number and by ship week color to help the growers keep things organized visually in the greenhouse.

So we have a tray with a bar code, and we have information about when it was sown and the bench number it's on. Our benches move through our greenhouse, so the next step is to know where the bench is located (as we've grown and because benches move frequently, bench tracking is critical for knowing where a product is located). We employ an RFID system to track the movement of our benches through the greenhouse. Each bench has a permanently attached RFID button. These buttons can take many shapes, but ours are the size and thickness of a credit card. We place these cards in a high-density polyethylene block and attach the block to the underside of each bench. An RFID button is like our bar code in that each one is unique. When a button passes over an antenna, the antenna reads the information on the card and the information is sent back to the computer. Antennae are placed at all entry and exit points for benches into and out of our system. Like the bar codes and RFID buttons, each antenna has a unique position. Therefore, when a bench crosses an antenna, the computer knows exactly where the bench is in the greenhouse.

The fundamentals of bar code technology have changed little in recent years, but the products continue to improve. Bar code scan rates have increased significantly, which increases the chance of a good scan. Microscan scanners at Raker scan at 2,000 times per second. Older scanners scanned at much lower rates. Another area that has advanced greatly is wireless and Bluetooth technology. Wireless allows Raker to use portable, handheld computing devices to improve efficiency and to speed the work velocity. Updates are more closely tied to work in process in the greenhouse; efficiency is improved because work can be recorded immediately in digital format with no time spent transferring data from paper documentation. Finally, Bluetooth technology has eliminated wired, handheld scanners, which greatly increases the ease of scanning in the vicinity of a computer.

Figure 8-14. Benches are tracked through Raker facility by RFID buttons mounted on each bench. As the button passes over an antenna (the rectangular loop you see under the bench), the computer instantly knows that bench's location.

With access to the information from the tray bar code and the bench location, we're in a position to provide accurate and timely information as well as find the tray easily in a very large facility. We've accomplished two important goals. We have information that anyone at Raker with access to a computer can view, and we can find the trays quickly and efficiently. This is one huge advantage of computers: The information stored electronically can be widely and instantaneously accessible. This is a key point because in my experience, when information is kept solely on paper, it's rarely timely or widely available.

Beyond the internal data access, Raker is increasingly leveraging the Internet to make information available externally as well. Customers and brokers can quickly and easily view availability, place and review orders and order history, track shipments, and view images and rankings of items in the Raker Trial Garden. With information accurately stored in a database, B2B transactions are possible and are used between Raker and many of our brokers.

The Human Element

Having a computer system isn't enough. A very common mistake is to view the computer as the end of the system, when in reality it's only the beginning. A computer is a tool, and like any tool it's only useful if it's used effectively. Careful consideration and emphasis must be placed on the management of the system.

Figure 8-15. The biggest problem with bar codes is that humans can't read them. So Raker uses large color-coded tags on each bench as visual references. Color indicates the ship week.

At Raker, almost every employee is expected to use the computer. We've built systems that allow even novice computer users to become proficient very quickly. One of our goals is to make it as easy as possible for those doing the work to do it in the manner we expect. This means having enough computers and handheld devices and having them in convenient locations. This means making sure that when the technology breaks, someone is responsible for getting it fixed. This means investing in new technology continuously so the equipment doesn't become outdated.

Raker has several key philosophies in regards to people and technology. First, workers must be able to use the equipment easily in the day-to-day work they're expected to accomplish. Work systems and computer systems must align. If the systems are grossly mismatched, it's likely that one or the other will be mismanaged at the most critical time: when we're the busiest and the poor information affects the most people.

Second, the more workers who can accurately do the computer work we require, the more information we can collect and use. We expect everyone to use the computer, and it's built into the work process. Implementing technology is rarely perfect, so we work to listen to employees when they tell us why it's hard to use the computer. We eliminate as many issues as we can, and as a result we collect an amazing amount of information. This requires proper training, tools, and computer accessibility. This requires that the tools work and are repaired quickly when they break. With a functional system, we're then able to use the information in many ways to provide information both internally to our employees and management and externally to our customers, to assist in decision making.

A third critical management area is data validation. As part of the work process we build in steps to check the integrity of our data. We check continuously. This is essential. Without this we don't know if the information is accurate . . . and we all know about Murphy's Law.

Key places we check the data are at any starting point for a tray, any time the product moves, and any time the inventory changes (i.e., is dumped, shipped, transplanted, and so on). To do this effectively, employees are expected to check the data, and they're given the tools and computer access to do it easily and quickly. With handheld technology, this check can be incorporated into normal work activity with increased accuracy.

The final critical management consideration is support and investment. To maintain technology requires continuous maintenance and upgrade. This should be viewed as an investment—part of the cost of doing business. Raker is frequently asked what this investment should be. We answer that it should probably be 3–5% of your gross dollars on an annual basis. These dollars cover all costs, from information technology support staff to hardware and software maintenance.

A Cool Future

RFID is the long-term future of technology in the greenhouse. Prices have come down on RFID chips, and you can find prices of $0.12–0.25 per chip, but the chip quantity that must be purchased to get these prices are still high for many greenhouse applications. Raker has not invested fully in this system yet because bar codes still add high value, and the switch to RFID provides only an incremental increase in value, which is difficult to justify given the investment dollars necessary to switch. For those not yet using bar codes, the added value of RFID can be more easily justified.

Internet-based communication tools such as Facebook, Twitter, and smart tags are a new and intriguing development. These tools have added a new dimension to sales and marketing efforts. For better or worse, effective use of these tools requires dynamic content that draws customers back repeatedly. Bar code or RFID systems add the potential for a dynamic link to these media.

What's the Point?

The reason to implement a bar code or RFID system is that it makes good business sense. As society becomes increasing information- and Internet-based, growers need to make their business visible to their customer base. The investment pays for itself through increased employee efficiency and customer satisfaction. The marriage of technology and people is critical to making the system functional, efficient, and profitable. Building technology into a greenhouse requires a strategy and commitment; this is a significant business advantage to those who leverage the technology well.

* Published in *GrowerTalks* magazine, March 2008.

Bar Codes Stink*
Chris Beytes

Okay, so maybe that title is a bit strong. Bar codes have proven to be essential to our industry. But according to the guy who said the above phrase, Eric Claiborne, information systems manager for Knox Nursery in Winter Garden, Florida, bar codes have inherent weaknesses that can cause ineffective data gathering.

That's why, when it came to tracking plug trays through their 525,000 ft.^{2} (48,774 m^2) young plant facility, Eric convinced his bosses, brothers Bruce and Monty Knox, to invest in the next level of information-gathering technology: radio frequency identification (RFID). Knox began initial testing of the system in November 2006, and they went live with it Week 3 of 2008. The RFID system is combined with Knox's proprietary "Grower's Own" software.

How's it working? Eric says they were preventing dozens of shipping errors per week, on average, during the slow months of November and December. "If you take those mistakes into February and March, that number could go up five times," Eric projects. "I think we'll save tens of thousands of dollars a year in shipping mistakes."

"Not to mention the customer retention problem, if you have enough of those errors." Bruce adds.

Hello, Mr. Chip

Simply put, an RFID chip contains information about the product it's stuck to—in this case, a plug tray. Each chip has an antenna, and you read the contents of the chip using a scanner. The scanner "excites" the chip, which gets temporarily energized and reveals its content. This all happens instantaneously . . . and from a distance of many feet or yards away, depending on the scanner's power. It can happen even if foliage is blocking the tag or if the tray is already inside a cardboard box—all limitations of bar codes.

Another big benefit: speed. You can scan hundreds of RFID tags instantaneously. And maybe most important, you can scan product while maintaining your natural work flow. Employees carry or move the tray as they normally would, and if there's an antenna in close proximity, it will scan the tray. That's not to say Knox doesn't use bar codes. Each of their labels includes data in three forms: human readable, bar code, and RFID. That way they can choose to access the data however is most appropriate.

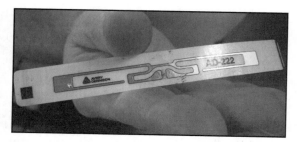

Figure 8-16. What an RFID label looks like from the back. From the front it resembles a regular plug tray label.

The downsides of RFID? It's hard to scan just one item unless you isolate it from others. And the tags won't scan reliably when surrounded by metal, such as on a shipping rack.

How Knox Uses RFID

Knox's system starts in the sowing room with empty plug trays. A worker instructs the in-house printer software how many labels to print of a particular variety and then uses an automatic printer to stick the polypropylene label, which has the RFID chip and antenna on the back, on the end of each tray. A second worker then passes each tray in front of a scanner to encode the chip with the same data that's on the printed label. (This tagging and coding process can and will be automated; Bruce didn't want to make the investment yet).

Next is filling and sowing. Trays move via conveyor past a scanner then through the tray filler. The tray gets sown and top-dressed with vermiculite, and then it's scanned again to confirm that what the first scan asked for is what was produced (both of these are currently bar code scans, but Eric will be changing these to RFID scans shortly). All of this is controlled by the seeder operator with a touch screen. If she hears a gentle beep, she knows the tray is correct. If she hears a car horn honk (the .wav file Eric chose to indicate mistakes), she knows something is wrong.

"Here's another reason why bar codes stink," Eric says. "You get soil stuck to that bar code constantly. [The seeder operator], as part of her job, has to wipe that bar code clean. She's getting distracted from her real job, which is putting seeds in a tray."

Also, the top coater spews vermiculite everywhere. "Because of different tray slope angles and dirty bar codes, we inevitably miss scans on dozens of trays per week that we know were sown. With RFID, I don't care how much soil or vermiculite is on there—it's going to get scanned."

Buffer: A Big Money-saver

Oversow or "buffer" is an important part of plug growing. If you have an order for twenty trays of a variety, you plant extra—say five additional trays—to make sure you have enough plugs to patch any empty cells and fill the order. However, with Knox's old system, they never knew how much buffer they were using and how much they were wasting. It was all guesswork until they did a manual inventory about two weeks before shipping.

Now, with Knox's Grower's Own software, they can scan empty trays (used for patching) out of the system immediately so they know their exact inventory up to three weeks sooner than before. They know if they have extra availability so they can sell it; they also know if they're short on a variety so they can notify customers. And thanks to this data, Knox is now analyzing and fine-tuning the exact amount of buffer they actually need. "We reduced our buffer substantially, and we have the solid data to continue to tweak the buffers based on yields for each lot sown," says Bruce. That's a big money-saver.

Shipping

Possibly the biggest money-saver of RFID comes in shipping. Before, workers would scan each tray by hand, probably having to move foliage out of the way so the scanner could see the bar code.

With RFID, trays are scanned automatically as they're dropped into a carton or loaded on a cart. The worker doesn't have to do anything other than listen for the beep that indicates all is well. That honking car horn sound means that the tray he just put in the box was wrong. That happened while we watched. A worker put a tray of 'Antigua Orange' marigolds into a box. The horn honked. Upon checking the label against the pick order, it turned out the order called for 'Antigua Yellow'. It took only a few seconds to find the right tray and complete the order correctly, saving untold time, money, labor, and customer complaints.

Figure 8-17. As Sunil Narain (right) and Bernard Nedd drop plug trays into boxes, the trays are automatically scanned by the RFID readers below the monitor.

Once the box is full, a tap of the touch screen generates a FedEx shipping label (which comes straight from the FedEx server in Memphis), a box contents sticker, and a packing list. If the order isn't correct, the computer won't let the worker make the labels, again preventing mistakes.

The Price of a Label . . . and the System

Why is Knox still the only grower using RFID on individual trays? Label cost might be the reason. Bruce says a regular tag costs 0.8 cents. An RFID tag costs 15 cents. That sounds like a deal-breaker to us. "But look at it compared to what we're paying for the plastic," Bruce reasons. "The tray is 60 cents, the soil is a quarter, vermiculite is 10 cents. Just to be able to capture that [information] and sell one more tray that you would have dumped, you paid for 100 of those labels."

Plus, there's the customer service aspect of earlier notification and fewer mistakes. "I thought all along that if we spent all this money but didn't get any payback, if we got more customers and more sales out of it, then that's the payback," Eric says.

9

Pest Control Equipment

The Basics of Greenhouse Pest Control

Raymond A. Cloyd

As we've said many times thus far, to produce a quality crop, greenhouse growers need to maintain proper irrigation and fertilization practices. But it's equally important to prevent the pests—the broad term for insects, mites, and diseases—that attack the diversity of plants grown in greenhouses, including bedding plants, potted plants, holiday crops, cut flowers, and specialty crops.

The major insect and mite pests that growers may encounter during crop production are primarily those with piercing-sucking mouthparts that remove plant fluids. These include aphids, whiteflies, thrips, mealybugs, and spider mites. Additional pests that you may encounter are fungus gnats, shore flies, and leaf miners.

Diseases that most commonly present problems during crop production include foliar or flower blights (i.e., botrytis), leaf spots (i.e., powdery mildew and several bacteria), crown rots (i.e., rhizoctonia), root rots (i.e., *Pythium*, *Phytophthora*, rhizoctonia, and *Thielaviopsis*), and viruses (i.e., impatiens necrotic spot virus [INSV]).

Where Do Pests Come From?

Pests are problems in greenhouses primarily because the environmental conditions, such as temperature and relative humidity, that are appropriate for plants are also conducive for pests. In fact, the higher temperatures that occur in greenhouses in spring and summer decrease the time required for insects and mites to complete their life cycle (egg to adult). In addition, plants, especially under propagation, are generally kept moist, which provides an ideal microclimate that promotes disease outbreaks. Poor sanitary practices—improper weed management, not removing plant and growing medium debris regularly, and reusing old

containers (without cleaning them) and old growing medium—will often lead to pest problems.

Figure 9-1. Because our products are primarily sold for their ornamental beauty, insects (such as these aphids), mites, and diseases aren't tolerated.

Pests of all kinds may enter greenhouses on contaminated plant material. Insects can also enter greenhouses through unscreened doors, sidewalls, and vents. Once insects are inside and the temperature is warm, populations can multiply rapidly. This can lead to the development of high populations that are difficult to control. Air currents or splashing water can spread fungal spores within a greenhouse. Plant material that is present year-round provides a continuous food supply for pests. These plants are usually well-watered and fertilized, which leads to the production of soft, succulent plant growth that insect and/or mite pests may easily feed upon. In addition, plants are generally spaced close together, which allows mites to disperse among crops. All these factors lead to more problems with pests.

Forms of Pest Control Products

To protect plants from the various pests and to produce a quality, salable crop, you can use a variety of pest control materials, including insecticides, miticides, fungicides, and bactericides, depending on the target pest or pests.

The primary methods of applying pest control materials are sprays, drenches, and granules.

Sprays

Sprays are normally applied to plant foliage to control aboveground pests, including aphids, whiteflies, mites, botrytis, and powdery mildew.

Drenches and Granules

Drenches are generally used to control belowground pests, including fungus gnats, shore flies, *Pythium*, and *Phytophthora*. Granules are applied to control both above- and below-ground pests. Before using any pest control material it is important that you read the label carefully in order to obtain information on specified rates and environmental concerns as well as directions on mixing, applying, handling, and storing the pest control material.

Methods of Pest Control Products

The pest control materials used to manage pests will work as contact, systemic, translaminar, protectant, or stomach poison.

Contact

Contact pest control materials kill pests when directly sprayed or when pests such as insects and mites come in contact with wet residues. Thorough coverage is essential in order to obtain adequate kill with contact pest control materials.

Systemic

Systemic pest control materials are those that are taken up by plants and transported (translocated) to other plant parts. They primarily kill pests that have piercing-sucking mouthparts, such as aphids and whiteflies, when these pests ingest the active ingredient during feeding. Systemics may be applied as a foliar spray, a drench, or a granule to the growing medium surface and then watered in. The drench and growing medium applications normally have longer residual activity than spray applications do.

Translaminar

Translaminar pest control materials are those in which the material penetrates leaf tissues and form a reservoir of active ingredient within the leaf. This provides

residual activity against insect and/or mite pests with piercing-sucking mouthparts even after spray residues dissipate (dry).

Protectant

Protectant pest control materials, which includes several fungicides, form a barrier on plant surfaces that prevents disease pathogens from penetrating plant tissues.

Stomach poison

Stomach poison pest control materials, such as the microbial insecticide *Bacillus thuringiensis* (Dipel and Gnatrol) and spinosad (Conserve), kill pests when they consume the active ingredient during feeding.

Product Availability

Pest control materials are available to greenhouse growers in various formulations, which are commonly abbreviated in the trade name. The formulation contains both the active ingredient and inert ingredients. The product is ready to use as packaged and sold or when diluted with water or another carrier. The main formulations are liquid, solid or dry, and ready-to-use. Liquid formulations include emulsifiable concentrates (EC), flowables (F), water-soluble concentrations or solutions (SC or S), and ultra-low volume concentrations (ULV). Solid or dry formulations include wettable powders (WP or W), water-soluble powders (WSP), soluble powders (SP), water-dispersible granules (WDG), dry flowables (DF), dusts (D), pellets (P), and granules (G). Ready-to-use formulations are those that require no mixing or loading. These include total release aerosols and fumigants or smokes.

Figure 9-2. Shown here is a sampling of the types of pest control products growers use.

Additional formulations are microencapsulation (ME) and water-soluble packets (WSP). Microencapsulated pest control materials are those in which liquid or dry particles are surrounded by a plastic coating. The active ingredient is released gradually as the plastic coating breaks down. Water-soluble packets are bags, which are placed into a spray tank filled with water; the packets dissolve and release their contents into the water. This type of formulation reduces worker exposure during mixing and loading. All formulations have their advantages and disadvantages; it's the responsibility of greenhouse growers to decide which ones to use based on application equipment.

Pesticide Application Equipment
Kurt Becker

Whether you're working in your yard, changing your truck's oil, or spraying your crop for thrips, the right tool often makes all the difference in the finished product. By thinking about the particulars of your spray program, choosing the right sprayer for the job is easy. Consider the logistics of when and where you're spraying. Do you have one gutter-connected range or numerous freestanding greenhouses? Do you have one center aisle or two end aisles? Are you a retail garden center open late on the weekends? All of these factors have an influence on how and when you spray. Keeping these points in mind when selecting a sprayer can help you make the best choice.

Types of Sprayers
Spray technology for the greenhouse can be classified in three categories: high volume, targeted low volume, and ultra low volume.

High volume
The high-volume category is the one growers are most familiar with. High-volume application, or hydraulic spraying, utilizes a spray pump with moderate to high pressure and a relatively high output. Characterized by spray pressures between 50 and 1,000 psi and flow rates between 0.5 and 4 gal. per minute (2–9 L/min.), hydraulic spraying is often referred to as "wet spraying." This type of application soaks the plants "to the point of runoff" (a term often used to describe an appropriate application amount). Droplet sizes vary from 100μ

(micron) to over 1000μ. A trained applicator can usually achieve very good results using this method, and it's typically the most trusted way to spray because the applicator can gauge his coverage of the plants by sight.

Hydraulic spray equipment can range from a hand-pressurized backpack sprayer to motorized sprayers utilizing high pressures and high flow rates. In general, higher pressures and lower flow rates result in finer droplets. Finer droplets usually result in better coverage using less solution. Larger droplets are good for soil penetration and sprays where the volume of water contributes to the product's efficacy, such as growth regulators and spray oils.

Commonly, growers will use a base volume of 100 gal. per acre (935 L/ha. Recent USDA/ARS trials have shown equal efficacy with half of the volume on bedding plants with no change to the equipment other than finer nozzles. Reduced flow rates and finer droplets result with finer nozzles leaving equal to better coverage but without the runoff.

Figure 9-3. High-volume spraying, or hydraulic spraying, is often referred to as "wet spraying." Shown here is a typical high-volume sprayer.

Low volume
The two remaining methods divide the technology referred to as low volume into two distinct groups. However, both share many characteristics. The term low volume refers to the amount of solution required. Low-volume application utilizes any one of a variety of mechanisms to atomize the spray solution into fine droplets. The smaller the droplet, the more droplets that can be produced from the same amount of solution. For example, one 100μ droplet will yield eight 50μ droplets and one-thousand-five 10μ droplets from the same volume of solution. This allows less solution

to go farther, cutting your chemical costs. Low-volume sprays produce little to no runoff and generally waste less solution than wet sprays do. Efficacy is generally very good but can vary with certain applications. Low volume isn't always recommended for growth regulator applications or sprays where higher water volumes are required for chemical efficacy.

Targeted low volume

This type of application refers to any method that uses low flow rates and smaller droplets but is still able to be directed toward specific targets or areas. Characterized by droplets between 40µ and 100µ in diameter, targeted low-volume sprayers create droplets that are small enough to cover more surface area with less solution than wet soaking sprays but large enough to be directed toward specific plants, benches, or areas without contaminating the remainder of the greenhouse. Targeted low volume is often very effective because it offers greater surface coverage while allowing the grower to aim the spray at specific problems or pests.

Equipment in this category includes high-pressure systems that utilize hydrostatic pumps and pressures

Figure 9-4. One advantage of low-volume sprays is that they produce little to no run off. Shown here is a typical low-volume sprayer.

of several thousand psi combined with lower flow rates and specialized nozzles; directed air atomizers, often with electrostatic induction of the droplets; and rotary disk atomizers that create small droplets by spinning them off a disk rotating at high revolutions per minute. Generally, the best of these systems offer spray velocities that will rustle the leaves and swirl the spray so that the solution penetrates the plant canopy. Some systems offer an air blast, either from a fan or a blower, that helps to achieve this penetration. A grower using one of these systems must learn to use it effectively and to trust that it is doing its job, as it's difficult to gauge coverage by sight. Some growers use commercially available hydrosensitive paper (a yellow card that turns blue when contacted by water or oil) placed throughout the crop to determine their coverage and train their applicators.

Ultra low volume (ULV)

Ultra-low-volume application is often the easiest and quickest method of chemical application. However, it's also the least selective–sort of a "shotgun" approach to chemical application. ULV systems create billions of very fine droplets that drift throughout the entire treatment area, covering all surfaces. ULV application, or "fogging" is a space treatment and needs to be used in sealed greenhouses to provide adequate coverage and to prevent contamination of other areas. ULV equipment creates particles that range from 1 to 25µ in diameter. Smaller particles are necessary to provide even, uniform drift and coverage throughout the treatment area. Uniformity of particle size is an important factor in the use of these systems. Equipment that produces a wide range of droplet sizes will often leave wet areas of spray with high concentrations of chemical in front of the machine.

The two most common systems available are stationary automatic aerosol generators, which use air atomization nozzles to create fine droplets, and thermal foggers, which use jet propulsion to throw a chemical fog a great distance very quickly. The automatic systems often have an attached fan to help distribute the chemicals throughout the greenhouse. These systems work on a timer and will start and stop without an applicator present. Placement of automatic foggers is very important, as there's no one directing the fog throughout the greenhouse. Often, additional horizontal airflow fans are needed to distribute the pesticide evenly over larger areas.

Thermal foggers are always attended and throw chemical fog distances up to 300' (91 m). Thermal foggers are also fast. The largest units can treat 100,000 ft.^{2} (9,290 m^2) in less than fifteen minutes. These machines typically use a carrier solution to help with the atomization of the solution. Carrier solutions are commonly dyed to make the fog more visible during application. This allows the user to see where they've fogged and avoid contact with the pesticide. Because thermal foggers are attended, sometimes better coverage can be achieved. By aiming the unit, a grower can ensure that the pesticide is evenly distributed throughout the entire greenhouse.

Recent trials with a newer design of ULV system that combines the best of both systems have been very successful. Utilizing high-volume air pumps, new PTO (power take off) driven systems can reach distances and application speeds similar to thermal foggers but without the heat. When mounted on a tractor, these systems, still under development, offer a fast application but with less limitations on the chemicals used in them.

Figure 9-5. Stationary aerosol generators run on a timer and do not require the presence of an operator.

Drenching Equipment

Another type of application that's gaining in popularity is precision drenching. With the advent of more systemic pesticides that are up taken by the roots, and with the increasing use of growth regulators applied as drenches, precision in applying these drenches is necessary. Until several years ago, growers either had to hand measure these products or carefully count as they drenched using regular watering equipment. Equipment has been introduced since then that allows for precise doses of chemical solutions to be applied directly to the pot. Typically, these machines control the flow from the wand by the use of a timed circuit. This allows for adjustable doses and variable intervals in between them. By offering different wand choices, including ones for hanging baskets, these machines greatly reduce the difficulty of applying precise chemical doses to plants and ensure accuracy when using volume-sensitive products, such as growth regulators.

Insect Screens
Paul Jacobson

The idea of stopping insect pests mechanically through the use of screening certainly isn't new. Most of our homes have had window screens to stop unwanted pests since the 1800s. However, the vast majority of commercial greenhouse growers in the United States still consider insect screening to be an untested, unconventional method of pest control, so they don't use them. Often, this comes as a surprise to growers in other parts of the world, who've been using insect screening technology for more than thirty years.

Crop, Climate, and Regulatory Differences

The primary crops grown in North American greenhouses are bedding plants in the spring and poinsettias in the fall. These aren't food crops, and therefore the United States has relatively low restrictions on the pesticides used on them to repel insects. Bedding plant growers largely reject screening because of its added cost and reputation for high maintenance. Greenhouse vegetable production, where there are fewer chemical pest control options, has been expanding in North America, but it still represents a smaller portion of overall U.S. greenhouse acreage.

Elsewhere in the world, the major greenhouse-grown crops, particularly in arid climates, tend to be vegetables. Pesticides options are greatly limited on food crops. In addition, some countries have more strict pesticide regulations than those in the United States, driving up the cost of legal chemicals, regardless of what crop they're used for.

Another factor that keeps some growers from considering insect screens: The humid climate found in many parts of North America necessitates a forced air-cooled environment via the use of exhaust fans. Growers who rely on fans often worry that screening over an intake vent will reduce airflow, burdening the fans and overheating the greenhouse. However, when properly installed and maintained, screening doesn't create a problem for fans.

In other, more arid parts of the world, greenhouses aren't as affected by humidity and frequently are passively or naturally cooled, meaning they rely on the prevailing wind currents to reduce the structure's heat gain. Except for possibly an occasional circulation fan, passively cooled structures don't use exhaust fans. Therefore, non-U.S. growers have much more financial and practical incentive to adapt to insect screen than do U.S. growers.

This isn't to say that you won't find insect screens in use in the States. Many research houses, plant breeders, and plug and cutting producers utilize screens as a matter of course. Additionally, a small but growing number of progressive bedding plant growers are using screen on traditional fan-cooled greenhouses, after they reach a comfort level with its compatibility to the exhaust fans.

Selecting and Using Insect Screen

The best way to think about insect screen is to recognize it for what it really is: a giant air filter. The market provides a wide variety of "filters" with varying mesh sizes, construction, warranties, and support service from which to choose. Of course, it would be ideal to screen out all pests, right down to tiny thrips, which, at just 265µ (0.01", 0.27mm) wide, are nearly microscopic. In fact, there are screens made with holes fine enough just for this purpose. The trade-off, however, is that the screen is so fine it will severely hamper airflow. Before you select the proper "filter," you have to determine the following key elements.

The type of crop to be grown

A research or breeding crop will require the tightest screens. Obviously, any edible crop is an excellent candidate for screening. A commercial bedding plant crop that will use screen as a supplement to chemical treatment can use a screen with larger holes that will permit more airflow while reducing the number of pest occurrences.

The type of insect to be screened

Whiteflies and aphids are much easier to screen than thrips due to their larger size. If they're the primary pest problem, a screen with larger holes can be used.

Relative damage

In many commercial applications, it's been found that thrips are sharply deterred by screens that were designed with bigger holes to screen out whiteflies. It's been theorized that, although technically small enough to make it through, most commercial whitefly screens present an acceptable barrier to thrips because they will move along seeking an easier target. If the crop can sustain damage from low levels of thrips that still may get through, a screen with larger holes may be the answer. This is particularly important for naturally ventilated greenhouses, as there will be no strong velocity of air drawing the thrips to the screen.

In these terms, you and your screen vendor must judge how your greenhouse will "breathe" by using this "filter." The smaller the target pest, the finer the screen must be.

Screening a Forced Air–Ventilated Greenhouse

Think about another air filter you may be familiar with: the air filter for an auto's engine, which requires many times the surface area of its intake vent. You can see this by the fact that the filter is pleated or folded many times. If the air filter were stretched out flat, it would be many feet long. If only a few inches of filter media was placed flat or flush across the throat of the engine's air intake, the velocity or speed of the air crossing through the filter would create too much chaotic turbulence, restricting the overall amount of air that the engine needs to "breathe" efficiently.

Greenhouse exhaust fans operate on the same principle. Exhaust fans are designed to draw outside air from an intake vent on one end of a greenhouse and vent it at the other end. As the air travels through the

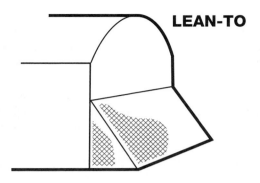

LEAN-TO

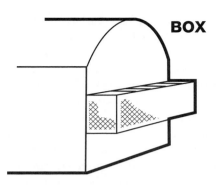

BOX

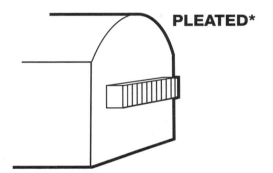

PLEATED*

Top View "Cut Away" of a Typical
Frame Holding Pleated Screen:

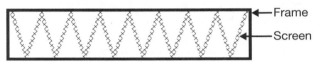

←Frame

←Screen

*Pleated insect screen installations with the
same total surface area as an unpleated piece
generate the same airflow characteristics, but
take up less space.

End of Glazing

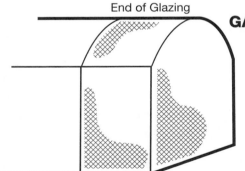

GABLE/END

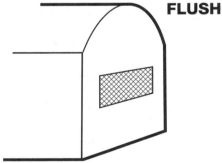

FLUSH

Figure 9-6. Common insect screen installations, shown on the intake vent end of the greenhouse. Growers
will often build a wood or metal frame to which they attach the insect screening, creating a large surface area
for good airflow.
Illustration courtesy of the National Greenhouse Manufacturers Association.

structure, it picks up heat generated from the solar gain in the greenhouse and upon reaching the other end this now-heated air is expelled to the atmosphere via the exhaust fans. Greenhouse designers take great care to ensure that the appropriate-sized fans are installed. The general rule has been to have fans achieve one complete exchange of air inside the greenhouse every minute.

The design, size, and horsepower rating of any given fan dictate how much air it will move in cubic feet per minute (cfm) at a given resistance. Whenever the resistance is increased, the cfm performance of the fan goes down. When resistance is decreased, the cfm performance of the fan goes up. There's an easy way to test this theory: Your lungs were built to efficiently move air through the natural resistance of the openings of your nose and mouth. If you try to breathe only through a small straw, you will quickly find that your lungs have encountered much more resistance. In principle, this is the same relationship that exhaust fans have to an intake vent. Naturally, the application of insect screen as an air filter over the intake vent of a greenhouse creates a concern about the ability of the fans to do their job efficiently.

This resistance can be scientifically measured, and is referred to as static pressure. (Any responsible vendor of insect screen will be able to supply a graph that charts the behavior of air as it passes through the screen at various speeds. This graph should have been created for the vendor by a reputable independent testing laboratory.) As the speed (face velocity) of the air hitting the screen increases, some of the air molecules bounce off the threads of the screen faster and more chaotically, creating more turbulence and increasing the static pressure of the screen. The more static pressure a screen creates, the harder it becomes for a fan to move air efficiently.

In other words, there's a relationship between the speed of air that meets the face of insect screen and the amount of resistance that's created: More face velocity (air speed) means more resistance of a given piece of insect screen. This leaves us with a dilemma: How can screen be effectively placed over an intake vent without disrupting the exhaust fan's ability to change the entire volume of the greenhouse's air in one minute?

The solution is found by increasing the amount of surface area of insect screen so that its resistance to the exhaust fans is minimized. Easy enough, one might say, but what about situations where the amount of surface area exceeds the surface area of the intake vent? It turns out that as long as the fans have enough surface area of insect screen, the shape of the insect screen installation does not affect them. Figure 9-6 shows various methods of increasing the surface area of insect screen in order to fit the constraints of any given greenhouse. The fans don't care what shape the screen structure takes, as long as there's enough overall surface area screen to allow the house to "breathe." You may notice that one acceptable method is to *pleat* the screen, just like the air filter on a car engine.

Calculating Surface Area

You are best served by allowing your insect screen vendor to perform the necessary calculations with the aid of an appropriate computer program, such as the one devised by North Carolina State University (http://ipm.ncsu.edu/ornamentals/airprogram.html), which compares a greenhouse's resistance, its fans' performance, the face velocity at the current intake vent, and the resistance of a given insect screen.

Quite often, the calculations show that the screen may be applied flush over the intake vent. This is especially true in cases where the greenhouse has a good-sized intake vent and the screen chosen has relatively larger holes designed to stop whiteflies and aphids.

Care, Maintenance, and Good Growing Practices

Sooner or later, any filter will get dirty, decreasing its effectiveness. Insect screening is no exception. It should be monitored frequently to ensure that dirt, dust, pollen, and debris aren't clogging it up. A good washing from behind with a hose is all it takes to clean it up, but be careful: Some screens have holes so fine that water fills up the holes by capillary action and can stop *all* airflow temporarily. Be sure you do this when the greenhouse doesn't need ventilation, such as during the morning hours.

Following are just some of the good growing practices to which you should adhere when using pest screen.

Keeping the greenhouse tight

Open doors and vents that aren't screened make screening worthless and a waste of money. Many growers build vestibules that create double entry doors or an "air lock" to prevent insects from following visitors in the door.

Eradicate weeds around the greenhouse

You must do this, especially around intake vents. Insects, particularly thrips, will use them as "temporary housing" until they're drawn into the greenhouse.

Keep an eye on other environmental conditions

Dusty service roads and the seeds from the notorious cottonwood tree can clog screens quickly.

Train your laborers

Teach your employees that screening is a valuable tool so they won't accidentally damage it through carelessness.

Regardless of where one grows, the trend is for government pesticide regulations to become more problematic and expensive to comply with. Insect screen will continue to increase in use due to its role as a cost-effective, chemical-free pest reduction solution. Just make sure you rely on a reputable, experienced vendor to help determine the proper quantity of screen you'll need to "filter" your greenhouse.

Chemical Storage Facilities

Jim Willmott

Growers often focus on pest control but neglect proper pesticide storage, which is a critical aspect of successful pest management. Improper storage presents human,

environmental, and economic risks. And, of course, it is a legal responsibility. Failure to adhere to federal, state, and local requirements may result in liability issues that could jeopardize your business.

Step number one for proper storage requires that pesticides be stored in their original containers along with their accompanying labels. Beyond this, thoughtful design and construction of your storage facilities, along with education of your workers and community officials, will minimize risks to your employees, the environment, and your profitability.

Designing a Storage Facility

Well-designed storage facilities reduce risks to people and the environment, including surface and groundwater supplies. Good design begins with a good plan. First, understand the federal, state, and local regulations. Next, assess the surrounding environment and understand the storage requirements for the pesticides that you'll be using. Federal law requires pesticide manufacturers to include storage requirements on pesticide labels and on material safety data sheets (MSDS). Review both the labels and MSDS to learn specific requirements for storage and also important environmental, health, and toxicology information. Much of this information is needed to satisfy community right-to-know regulations, which require you to provide information about the pesticides you store to emergency officials, including local fire departments.

Figure 9-7. Secure pesticide storage is safe, efficient—and the law.

Next, consider where to locate your storage area. It should be close to where the pesticides will be added to application equipment and where they will be applied. Minimizing the distance of transport minimizes the risk of a spill or leak. Water for filling sprayers and for cleaning equipment should be nearby. Storage areas should be separate from work or living areas.

Identify important environmental features both inside and outside the storage area. The pesticides you store will determine the inside conditions of your storage area. Generally, pesticides need to be kept cool, dry, and out of direct sunlight. Also, they must not be stored near human or animal food products, crop seed, or fertilizer.

To protect the environment surrounding your facility, avoid locations conducive to runoff into surface water such as streams, rivers, and lakes. Storage areas must be located where flooding is unlikely. If you're in an area with a high water table or soils that favor leaching, take steps to prevent leaching into groundwater. Impermeable floors with dikes to contain spills are best for all sites. Also, storage areas should be downwind and downhill from sensitive areas, such as homes, play areas, and ponds. Again, be sure to consult local officials for regulations that may prohibit building on certain sites or require construction features to minimize risks of environmental contamination.

Once you've decided on a location, you can begin to think of a design for your storage facility. Construction material choices are numerous, but avoid or minimize flammable materials, such as wood. Likewise, choose non-flammable insulation materials. Metal buildings with concrete floors are recommended. Some concretes may absorb pesticides that are spilled, so treating with a concrete sealer is a good idea.

Something that many growers fail to realize is that improper storage conditions reduce shelf life of pesticides, resulting in less than optimal or even no control of the target pests. The inside of storage areas should be cool, dry, and dark to preserve the shelf life of products. Also, there must be good ventilation. Fans should be installed to draw air away from the storage areas. Heat should be available, and temperatures should be controlled with thermostats. Extreme high or low temperatures will be detrimental to some pesticide formulations. For example, freezing often damages emulsifiable concentrates. Pesticides contained in cardboard, paper, or water-soluble packaging should never be stored directly on the floor where moisture, spills, or floods could damage the packaging.

Generally, wettable powder formulations have the longest potential shelf life. Liquid suspension and emulsifiable concentrates often have shorter shelf lives since the components are prone to separation. However, one should not assume how long a pesticide will be effective. It is necessary to check labels to be sure. Also keep in mind that many of the "newer" popular biological control pesticides have short shelf lives and should be used promptly.

Figure 9-8. Here is an example of improper storage. The coffee can has a duct-tape label indicating it contains Sevin dust, and the bag on the left has obviously gotten wet.

Storage areas must have lights. Install shelves and partitioning since different pesticides, especially herbicides, should be separated from other types of pesticides, such as insecticides and fungicides as well as from growth regulators. This helps to minimize any chance of cross contamination. Some states require that restricted-use pesticides be kept in structurally separate rooms within a storage facility. Measuring cups and scales should be available in the mixing and filling area. Accidental mixing of herbicides or even contamination through the use of measuring equipment may be disastrous, so carefully label any measuring or spray equipment especially when used for herbicides.

Decontamination facilities should be nearby, including showers, soap, and an eyewash station. Also, personal protective equipment (PPE), including spray suits, dust masks, respirators, and gloves, should be near but not in the storage facility. The required PPE for any pesticide is specified on the pesticide's label.

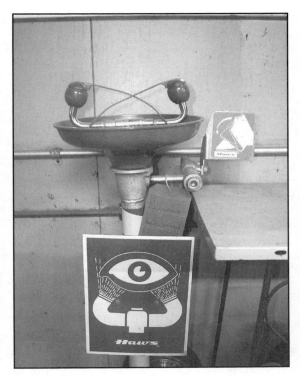

Figure 9-9. Decontamination facilities include an eyewash station.

Figure 9-10. Storage facilities should only be accessible to authorized employees.

In case of emergency spills, cleanup supplies should be readily accessible. Effective neutralizing chemicals, such as hydrated lime and sodium hypochlorite (bleach), should be available, along with absorptive clay, activated charcoal, vermiculite, pet litter, sawdust, or specialized pesticide-absorbent pillows to soak up spills and leaks. Other necessary tools include a shovel, brooms, dustpans, leak-proof containers to hold spilled pesticides, and a fire extinguisher that's appropriate for the products you store. Remember that specific steps must be taken to avoid fire risks. Local regulations may require installation of overhead sprinklers or other fire-containment systems. Fire alarms will warn employees and local fire and emergency officials. Emergency numbers for manufacturers should be readily accessible in case of emergency. Keep an up-to-date inventory of pesticides along with any emergency response information listed on labels or MSDS.

Finally, facilities should only be accessible to authorized employees who are trained in the principles of safe pesticide handling. Facilities should be locked to prevent intentional or accidental misuse or exposure. Some growers choose to secure windows with bars and use fencing with locked gates to offer additional protection. Weatherproof signs stating "Danger! Pesticides—Keep Out!" must be attached to all doors and windows.

Keep in mind some general considerations when storing pesticides:
• Always keep pesticides in their original containers—it's the law! Figure 9-8 shows irresponsible pesticide storage.
• Most pesticide products are dated, but marking them with dates of arrival in large, prominent print will help to ensure oldest products are used first.
• The best way to limit the risks associated with chemical storage is to limit the amount of pesticides that you store. Buy only what you plan to use in the near future.

Education

Under the federal Emergency Planning and Community Right-to-Know Act (EPCRA), employees must be educated about the risks of pesticides—including safe and proper pesticides storage. Be sure to understand this law, the Worker Protection Standard (WPS), and any state or local requirements. Furthermore, employees should understand safe and proper storage and handling procedures and what to do in case of an emergency, such as a spill or fire. Making a thorough effort to educate employees and to comply with all regulations will reduce your liability.

EPCRA requires that local police and fire officials must be notified and provided with a complete inventory of pesticides and other hazardous materials that are stored in your facilities. Be able to provide copies or labels and MSDS to emergency workers. These give specific directions regarding storage, spills, and firefighting. Keep phone numbers for the local fire department and state pesticide authorities accessible for help with emergencies involving spills, leaks, fires, or explosions. Additional emergency numbers now appear on pesticide labels.

If you need help or advice about chemical storage, contact your state cooperative extension specialists or agents. Also, state regulatory agencies as well as representatives for pesticide distributors, dealers, and manufacturers may be able to provide assistance.

Some Helpful References

- *A Virtual Tour of Pesticide Storage, An Online Learning Module.* Rutgers Cooperative Extension, Pest Management Program, Entomology Department, Blake Hall, Cook College, Rutgers University, New Brunswick, NJ 08903, http://www.recert.rutgers.edu/home/.
- *Pesticide Storage and Handling Practices on the Farm* explains proper handling and storage of pesticides on farmsteads. Provides a general overview of pesticide handling and storage, a risk assessment section, and recommendations for correcting problems related to pesticide storage. It was created in 1991 by G. Doerr and K. Embleton, and updated 1997, 2001. It is also available in Spanish, as *Practicas de Manejo y Almacenamiento de Pesticidas en la Granja,* created in 1992 by G. Doerr, K. Embleton, M. de Gortari, and G. Zywicki, and updated in 2001. You can download the software at http://www.epa.gov/seahome/farmpest.html.
- *How Safe is Your Pesticide Storage Facility* is a lesson plan with a set of jpg images you can copy and insert into a power point presentation. University of Delaware Cooperative Extension: http://www.udel.edu/pesticide/sanantonio.htm.
- "Proper Pesticide Storage," Colorado Environmental Pesticide Education Program Pesticide Fact Sheet #115, June 2006, http://wsprod.colostate.edu/cwis79/FactSheets/Sheets/115ProperStorage.pdf.

EPA Worker Protection Standards[1, 2]

Raymond A. Cloyd

The Environmental Protection Agency (EPA) has the responsibility under the Federal Insecticide, Fungicide, and Rodenticide Act (FIFRA) for managing worker protection programs when it comes to the use of pesticides. On January 1, 1995, the EPA implemented a standard called the Worker Protection Standards for Agricultural Pesticides, better known as WPS.

The main emphasis of WPS is to protect workers from exposure to pesticides. The rules were designed to limit handlers' (those individuals mixing and applying pesticides) and workers' (those individuals that may have potential contact with pesticide residues after application) exposure to pesticides, educate handlers and workers about the hazards associated with using pesticides, document applications, and provide specific precautions to reduce eliminate exposure. WPS applies to handlers and workers involved in the production of agricultural plants, including in greenhouses, nurseries, forestry, and farms.

Employees working in these designated industries are allowed to apply pesticides and re-enter into previously treated areas only after employers and employees have complied with WPS requirements. The general requirements may be found in the "Agricultural Use Requirement" box on each pesticide label covered by WPS. The details on how to comply with the label statements are found in the EPA publication *How to Comply with the Worker Protection Standard for Agricultural Pesticides: What Employers Need to Know,* http://www.epa.gov/oecaagct/htc.html.

The major requirements are:
- Training of handlers and workers
- A poster display
- Decontamination site
- Emergency assistance
- Application notification

---

[1] The information provided in this chapter is for educational purposes only and does not represent legal interpretations and opinions. Always read and follow label directions, as this represents how the product should be legally used.

[2] The author wishes to acknowledge Dr. Fred Whitford from the Purdue University Cooperative Extension Service, Purdue Pesticide Programs, for his comments and suggestions.

Training

All handlers and workers who *are not* certified pesticide applicators or licensed for pesticide application (e.g., private applicators) must be provided with pesticide safety training prior to applying, mixing, or working in treated areas. *Handlers* are employees who mix, load, or apply a pesticide or work on application equipment. Handlers must be trained before performing any handling task. *Workers* are those employees who perform labor such as harvesting, weeding, pruning, or any other task in a pesticide treated area within thirty days following an application. Workers must receive complete WPS safety training no more than five days after starting employment.

The content of the training is provided in the *How to Comply* manual and can be administered by having all workers and handlers view training tapes that have been approved by the EPA. EPA-approved training tapes are found at the North Dakota State University site "Worker Protection Standard Resources," http://www.ag.ndsu.nodak.edu/aginfo/pesticid/wps.htm. Example titles are *Pesticide Handlers and the Worker Protection Standard* and *Protecting Yourself from Pesticide Hazards in the Workplace*. In addition, EPA has produced training materials that can be used in place of the videos. To demonstrate compliance, employers should document all employees' training on WPS.

Poster Display

Employers must display the EPA pesticide safety poster that contains specific information on Worker Protection Standards and explains how workers can

Figure 9-11. All agricultural businesses, including green-houses, are required to post WPS information in a prominent, easily accessible place.

protect themselves from pesticides. This poster must be placed in a central location of the greenhouse operation that's easily accessible for employees. The poster requires that the name, address, and phone number of the nearest emergency medical facility be located at the bottom of the poster.

Decontamination Site

Employers must provide workers and handlers with a decontamination site or place to clean up. Materials and supplies including soap, water, and paper towels must be present at all times. In addition, employers are required to provide a change of clothes for employees after they've worked in a treated area.

Emergency Assistance

Employers are required to provide a means of transportation to the nearest emergency medical facility in case of an accident from pesticide exposure. In addition, employers must provide information on pesticide exposure to employees.

Application Notification

All pesticide labels that contain WPS information will provide restricted entry intervals (REI). This information is located in the "Agricultural Use Requirement" box on the pesticide label. The REI is the time period (in hours) that handlers and workers must remain out of the treated area after an application has been made. REIs for greenhouses may be four, twelve, twenty-four, or forty-eight hours. The REIs associated with greenhouses and nurseries are related to application methods, pesticide toxicity, and pesticide formulation. Information regarding each pesticide application must be posted with the following information: pesticide name, EPA registration number, active ingredient, location and description of treated area, time, date of application, and REI.

Rose growers need to enter greenhouses two to three times a day to harvest fresh cut rose flowers, so they applied for and were granted an exemption from the WPS that allows them to harvest greenhouse-grown roses before expiration of the REI. However, workers are still required to wear the appropriate personal protective equipment.

Personal Protective Equipment

Personal protective equipment (PPE) is listed on pesticide labels under the heading "Agricultural Use Requirements." PPE is the minimum protective equipment that must be worn when applying a designated pesticide. Personal protective equipment may include eyewear (goggles, face shield, or safety glasses with side shields and brow guards), respirator, chemical-resistant gloves, chemical-resistant footwear (and socks), chemical-resistant headgear, apron, chemical-resistant coveralls, long-sleeved shirt, and long pants. It's important for all handlers and workers to wear the appropriate PPE based on the label recommendations. All personal protective equipment should be cleaned immediately after use in order to avoid pesticide buildup on equipment and clothing.

Where to Get Publications

Information on WPS is available from the U.S. Government Printing Office (GPO). Employers may obtain the EPA manual *The Worker Protection Standard for Agricultural Pesticides—How to Comply: What Employees Need to Know*, which is also referred to as the *How to Comply* manual, by contacting either the GPO, Washington, DC 20402, Tel: (202) 783-3238; or the EPA, Office of Pesticide Programs, 401 M Street SW, Washington, DC 20460, Tel: (202) 382-2090. The publication number is 055-000-00442-1. In addition, they have a WPS quick-reference poster (publication number 055-000-00445-5). You can also access the EPA website at www.epa.gov/agriculture/awor.html. Many businesses now list the WPS training material for sale in their catalogs.

Questions about WPS should be directed to your state Department of Agriculture. They can be found at http://aapco.ceris.purdue.edu/htm/control.htm. In addition, many state Department of Agriculture offices make available free posters, signs, training videos, record-keeping sheets, *How to Comply* manuals, and worker/handler training books. Questions and training may also be provided by your state's Cooperative Extension Service. They can be found at http://www.ipmcenters.org/contacts/PSEPDirectory.cfm.

10

Greenhouse Sustainability

Figure 10-1. Most modern greenhouse have features built in, such as watersaving irrigation and energy-saving curtain systems, that help them be sustainable.

The Concept of Sustainability

Doug Cole

At the time of writing this chapter, much debate has taken place to determine the definition of sustainability and how it relates to the greenhouse industry. To some it means simply recycling. To others it means using biodegradable pots and labels, and to some it is a version of an organic program. To those working with actual sustainability certification, many additional factors are taken into account. But typically, when talking about sustainability in the greenhouse operation, the focus is in two areas: One

is the environmental side of greenhouse production, and the other is GAP, or good agricultural practices.

Environmental sustainability is concerned with all of our inputs, including items such as energy, fertilizer, and growing containers (pots, flats, and trays). The use of pesticides and the types of pesticides is a critical portion of being sustainable. Environmental sustainability is also concerned with recycling efforts and the waste that our companies produce. GAP, on the other hand, focuses on the workings of a company. For example, the main focus of GAP is on employees and the workplace. We will discuss this later in the chapter.

An oft-used acronym today is the three Rs: Reduce, Reuse, and Recycle. As positive as this phrase is, it doesn't cover the true meaning of sustainability in our industry. To address sustainability in this chapter, we will assume that it is better to view a sustainable business as one that does a good job supporting People, Planet, and Profit. When we neglect any one of these three topics, we are no longer sustainable. For example, if we do a fantastic job taking care of the people in our company and are very good to the environment, we can only continue in business if we are also making a profit.

Net Cost of Being Sustainable

Is there a net cost to being sustainable? Do we decide to carry out sustainable practices only because it "feels" right? These are tough questions. Another common question is whether we can command a higher price for our products if we show the consumer that they were produced in a sustainable way. The chances of charging more for our product are slim unless we create a way to market the concept effectively.

So why do it? Why be "sustainable"? The answer lies in the bigger picture. Let's look at some actions, employee buy-in, and what we can accomplish to be a "better" company.

Inputs

Energy

Conserving energy may not be as exciting as installing a biomass boiler, but conserving energy is where the first and most important focus should be. This not only cuts our fuel or electricity bill, but also cuts our carbon output.

Air infiltration is one of the highest areas of heat loss in a greenhouse. A poorly sealed facility is the easiest way to lose heat and one of the easiest to address. These can be old vents, poorly maintained doors, etc. Review the physical plant each year for air leakage and make the appropriate repairs.

Installing energy and/or shade curtains is standard today on greenhouse construction of any size other than double-poly Quonset houses. A double curtain is typical in northern climates, and even triple layer curtains are now being installed. An advantage of having more than one layer of curtain is that each layer can be of a different material so as to give the grower options based on the crop and the time of year. For example, one layer can be a clear material that is closed on cold winter days as well as nights. This clear material can be used to maintain humidity in a propagation area. The next layer could be a shade fabric that creates the right amount of light during the summer months. The third curtain could be a different percentage of shade or possibly a blackout curtain for the manipulation of day length. In southern climates, an exterior shade curtain over the entire structure can drop the demand on cooling systems drastically.

Natural ventilation has made a real comeback in recent years. Many growers have opted for rigid or semi-rigid glazing material on an open-roof structure. Materials such as glass, polycarbonate, and acrylic allow good light penetration while saving the labor of recovering on a regular basis as with polyethylene film, and they avoid the disposal problem that poly creates. Another bonus of having natural ventilation is the reduction of electrical use during warm weather.

Onsite power sources such as wind, solar, and geothermal can lower the need for offsite power, but for many growers the payback time is still too long to justify the considerable investment. One way to make the payback affordable is to apply for both state and federal grants.

Biofuel boilers can add much to the "profit" side of the sustainability triangle, and it can lessen our dependence on foreign fuels. What it does not do is lessen the carbon footprint of a greenhouse operation. Keep in mind that although biofuel can eliminate the use of fossil fuels, it does not eliminate the need for fuel of some kind. We are still making a similar carbon footprint.

Let's compare a wood chips to natural gas. We are using the same BTUs with both sources. With each source we are freeing sequestered carbon into the atmosphere. What is the difference? The largest difference is that with a biofuel we are also putting more byproducts into the atmosphere than we do using natural gas. In this case biofuels are not making us more sustainable. It could mean that we are pushing more profit to the bottom line, and in this may trump the concern over the additional byproducts.

Pesticides

Does one need to be organic to be sustainable? No. But as we learn more about the definitions of both organic and sustainable, we find that there are a number of similarities and differences. For example, a biodegradable pot could be considered organic, but a plastic pot could create less of a carbon footprint when we considering the production process. The same can be true of chemical pesticides versus other methods of pest control.

Some pesticide certification programs categorize products based on the long-term effects on the environment. This allows the grower to make decisions based on a range of factors and does not tie his hands.

Unlike an organic grower, who has to follow strict USDA organic standards, the sustainable grower can choose from a wide list of pesticides and can choose which pesticide is appropriate at a given time. These choices can include beneficial insects. The sustainable grower should be using products that are easy on the environment while still "getting the job done." On occasion it is more efficient to spray a stubborn pest with a more toxic (yet legal) chemical than to struggle with weekly sprays of a mild chemical and never get the problem under control. In the latter case, not only is the grower using much more chemical, he is also wasting staff time and creating more staff exposure to the pesticide.

The same is true for fungicides and plant growth regulators. Many of us might be surprised that although we dwell on insecticides, fungicides that have a larger problem breaking down in the environment.

Fertilizer

Fertilizer is an input that can easily be measured. Standards can be set for growers based on size of operation, seasonality, and crops grown. Not only is total use important, but type of fertilizer is also a factor. Phosphorous is one of the major elements that is typically monitored. Notice how we see the newer formulations of premixed fertilizer using less phosphorous. As important as phosphorous is, we have now realized that the amount we need is much less than what we used to apply.

One way to reduce the total use of fertilizer in a crop is by the use of slow-release fertilizers. For example, rather than applying soluble fertilizer with the irrigation water, we can use slow-release resin coated prills in our growing substrate. We may still need to use liquid feed, but hopefully at a reduced rate.

How we deliver fertilizer is of great importance. The old method of overhead watering and allowing runoff to enter the groundwater is used less and less. Many of the modern watering methods mentioned in chapter 5 and in the next paragraphs have helped us make great strides in fertilizer conservation.

Water

Of course, water very often goes hand-in-hand with fertilizer use. The importance of water conservation is quite different depending on where you are located. State water regulating agencies are looking into agricultural water usage much more than they did just a few years ago. Sustainability schemes are also looking at water usage more now than in the past. This will become the next big area of focus for sustainability.

We can reduce both our water and our fertilizer use by a number of methods. Ebb-and-flow benches, flood floors, trough watering, and drip irrigation are all good examples of methods to conserve fertilizer and water. It's great to install these systems, but the maintenance of them is crucial to making them run correctly.

Many growers have been able to recycle their irrigation water on large areas of land outdoors. This can be done by construction of drainage projects both on the ground surface and by installing below-ground drainage. The water is then channeled to a holding pond. From here the water is treated to eliminate pathogens, tested for salt content, and then used again on the crop.

Recycling

A plan should be put in place for the recycling of waste materials. Like the before mentioned topics, employee "buy-in" is critical in making a recycling program work. This can include plastics of all kind, office paper, paperboard, and metals, to name a few. Unlike a few years ago, today there are horticultural container manufacturers that actually want your used pots, flats, and trays. If you are working with a certification program, they will probably expect you keep your receipts of recycling when it is appropriate.

Substrate (growing media) is no different. Used potting substrate should be composted and used productively. That could mean mixing with topsoil for use in fields rather than putting in a Dumpster to end up in a landfill.

Bridging the GAP

Up until now we've focused on the environmental aspects of sustainability. The concept of "people" should also be addressed. For the most part we are referring to the employees of the company. Taking on this project can be done at the same time as our first topics, or it can be done separately. What is important is that action takes place. Rather than do nothing because the project is too large, I suggest that a grower starts with the environmental actions discussed earlier. These can make the biggest difference.

Many call this next step GAP, which stands for "good agriculture practices." If you are ready to work on GAP, there can be quite a long list of items to address. In some parts of the world this list can create quite a chore. For most of us the list is reasonable. Many of the topics that are needed to be satisfied are already in place due to our culture. For example, GAP sets workplace standards that to most of us are commonplace and expected, such as modern bathroom facilities, work breaks, running water, and a sheltered place to have lunch. However, some greenhouse owners neglect workplace issues that are considered a burden or unnecessary. For example, how many growers have fire extinguishers at all appropriate locations and have them professionally inspected each year? Are the full-time employees trained on how to use them? Do you have enough staff that is trained in CPR? If a fire or other emergency occurred, do you have an emergency plan in place? These are all things that hopefully get little actual use but are essential in an emergency situation. In terms of social responsibility, you can feel that you are doing "the right thing" for your employees. And just as importantly, in terms of lawsuits and OSHA compliance, being proactive in these areas can be quite cost-effective in the long run.

How to Get Started

Embracing sustainability can be done as one large project or it can be addressed in steps. What is important is that action takes place and you get buy-in from staff. One person or a committee should take on sustainability and address topics at a reasonable pace. There is no one definition of sustainability. Different certification organizations will have different criteria. The main certification organization currently serving North America is MPS (see Resources, below).

Figure 10-2. MPS helps guide growers in meeting sustainability guidelines, which are based on goals set and achieved by other growers.

Show Me the Money

If you ask "How much money will my company save by being sustainable?" there may not be an answer. Some will go down this road as a way to market their plants. Perhaps a retail buyer will decide to only purchase from certified growers. That alone could be the reason to start the process. Some may decide that this is the philosophically correct choice to make.

Let's go back to the phrase buy-in. When the concept of sustainability is engrained within the culture of a company, there are savings. Recycling saves money. Decreasing energy use saves money. Appropriate use of pesticides saves money. Having fewer accidents in the workplace saves money. If the concept is ingrained in the culture of the company, everyone takes a little more time thinking about what it is they are doing and if they can make a difference. That makes for a better business, overall. And that is, in the end, what sustainability is all about.

Resources

www.my-mps.com. MPS is an international sustainability implementation and certification organization founded in the Netherlands.

11

Specialized Facilities

Storing Seeds Successfully

Tim Raker

Successfully producing plants—and profits—depends on a multitude of events that need to happen inside and outside of your company. And how well you plan and execute any one of those events may affect your overall success. At C. Raker & Sons Inc., Litchfield, Michigan, nearly all our business is derived from producing and delivering plugs to finish growers. Like other companies, we have many tasks to perform well in order to ensure our success.

When we look only at the materials required to produce a plug trays, seed cost is our largest single expense. We depend on good seed quality, so providing an optimal storage environment for the seeds we purchase and then monitoring that environment are important examples of tasks that can ensure our success. In this section, I'll talk about factors affecting seed quality while being stored for future use. I'll also illustrate different methods for storing your seed so that you can ensure seed performance when it counts . . . when it's time to sow and propagate them.

Factors Affecting Seed Storage

Conditions essential for good seed storage are the opposite of conditions needed for good germination. Growers know that optimal germination for seeds begins when water and oxygen (and sometimes light) are present, with favorable (usually warm) temperatures. So to obtain good seed storage results, seeds need to be kept dry and cool. From information I've read, seed storage is best when the actual moisture content of the seed is kept at or below 8% and temperatures are kept as close to 40°F (4°C) as possible. When these two important conditions are met, studies indicate that the presence of oxygen is not a factor in seed longevity and seeds can be stored for long periods. To keep seeds from absorbing moisture while in storage, relative humidity (RH) within the storage chamber also needs to be controlled. If seed isn't kept in moisture-proof containers, the relative humidity within the chamber will influence the moisture content of the seed.

At Raker, we strive to maintain a 40°F (4°C) temperature in our seed storage. People entering the chamber during the day will cause the temperature to fluctuate some, but if your chamber has the appropriately sized refrigeration equipment, target temperatures can be quickly recovered. Just as temperatures fluctuate while accessing a chamber, relative humidity inside the chamber will also be affected. While temperature targets can be brought back down to your set point quite quickly, bringing the relative humidity back down to an acceptable level usually takes a bit more time. This, of course, depends on the type of equipment that you're using, which we'll discuss later.

To illustrate the effects of humidity on seed, let's revisit the ideal moisture content for seeds—8%. If you were to store seeds in non-moisture-proof containers at 40°F (4°C) and 90% RH for up to a year, the moisture content of the seed would eventually level off near 20%, greatly impairing your chances for good germination. If the RH is reduced to 15% and the temperature is kept at 40°F (4°C), then your seed would eventually dry down to 6% moisture content, thus allowing you to store your seed successfully for very long periods.

At Raker, we have adjusted our parameters since we installed our new seed storage cooler. Originally, we targeted 42°F air temperature along with a 25% relative humidity, giving us a total sum of the two numbers of 67. A rule of thumb for seed storage parameters is this: The sum of the ambient air temperature (measured in Fahrenheit) and the relative humidity should total a number between 80 and 90. You can surmise that if your sum total is higher (higher temperature and higher relative humidity), seed quality may be compromised over longer storage periods. If the sum total is lower (similar to our original parameters), this will mean that the energy used to cool and dry the chamber environment will increase, adding to the cost of storing seed products. What I'd recommend is targeting 40–42°F (4–5°C) and maintaining the relative humidity at 40–45%. At Raker, we find these parameters provide an optimal storage environment for most flowering seeds and at the same time minimize energy costs.

Environmental Equipment

A refrigerator is one of the simplest, most common items used to store seed. Some plug producers use refrigerators at their sowing stations to keep seed optimum while it's going through the seeding process. It also cuts down on the number of trips to the main seed storage chamber if it's not located close to the sow stations. For years, Raker used an old 60 ft.³ (1.7 m³) beverage cooler that we purchased from a convenience store. It was a convenient storage chamber, and because of its glass doors we were able to locate seed varieties even before we opened it, minimizing the time the doors were open and keeping temperature and humidity as close to optimum as possible. However, we discovered quickly that the relative humidity was difficult to control. Refrigeration, by design, does reduce humidity on its own, but at a slow pace compared to the way it controls temperature. We installed a dehumidifier that pulled the air out of the cooler, heated it to dry the air, and reintroduced it back into the chamber. In short, we made our cooler work harder to cool while bringing the relative humidity down to acceptable levels. It worked well, but as our seed storage needs expanded, we had to have better equipment to ensure a good storage environment.

Figure 11-1. These beverage coolers make good seed storage units, with the glass doors allowing you to locate the seed before opening the doors. However, humidity control can be challenging.

We purchased the chamber we now use from a company that builds custom walk-in coolers. We had the chamber designed around what the optimum environmental specifications for storing seed were and where we were going to locate the chamber. Our current seed storage chamber measures 18' long by 10' wide by 11' high (5.5 x 3 x 3.3 m), giving us 1,980 ft.³ (54.5 m³) of storage area, and it is large enough to handle all our future seed storage needs. The ceiling and walls are built out of 4" (10 cm) metal-clad foam panels that are tongue-and-grooved and lock together with cam locks to form a secure seal. This also makes for easy assembly and disassembly should we decide to relocate the chamber. We also designed an insulated floor into the chamber so that the concrete floor wouldn't let heat migrate inside the chamber. The cost came in at $65/ft.² ($699/m²) for the chamber structure itself. We then installed the cooling and dehumidifying units, along with some shelving to organize the seed. When the project was complete, we had invested nearly $100/ft.² ($1,076/m²) for our seed storage chamber, a large expense to be sure. But when storing hundreds of seed items worth hundreds of thousands of dollars that we rely on every day of the year, we felt the investment was justified.

We located the chamber inside the building and close to where the seeding operations take place for convenient access from the sow equipment lines. This building is adjacent to our greenhouse propagation area where high humidity from the greenhouse migrates into the seeding area during sow operations. This causes the relative humidity in the seed storage chamber to fluctuate widely during the day as the chamber is accessed. The action of opening and closing the door allows a rather large air exchange in the chamber, resulting in an instant increase of relative humidity. To counter this action, we have installed two dehumidifiers inside the chamber. By installing two, we have a redundant system that ensures some dehumidification in case one unit fails. We also use two refrigeration units to cool the chamber; again, redundancy in case one unit fails. We located temperature and humidity sensors inside the chamber that are connected to our greenhouse environmental control computer. This allows us to watch for fluctuations in temperature and humidity and create a history of our seed chamber environment throughout the year. Also, if environmental parameters fall outside the desired settings, an alarm will be triggered to alert us to check the equipment.

Figures 11-2, 11-3. Raker's custom-built seed storage chambers offer nearly 2,000 ft.^{3} (57 m^3) of optimum seed storage space.

A simple way to help restrict humidity from entering a chamber is to hang plastic stripping just inside the door opening. This provides a simple barrier to help control humidity fluctuations while still being easy to walk through. This method also helps reduce fluctuations in air temperature.

There are many companies that market compact dehumidifiers for small chambers that do a great job. We use two small units from Munters. An Internet search will reveal a multitude of dehumidification companies. The same goes for custom-built coolers/chambers. We purchased our chamber from a company called Norlake in Hudson, Wisconsin. They'll build a chamber to your specifications, no matter what size your business dictates. We've had good success with the products supplied by both companies.

In the end, if you store seeds, you need to analyze your seed storage needs. Stay simple if that's what you require; and no matter what, if you have seeds that you

would like to store for future use, it's best not to leave them on a shelf exposed to varying environmental conditions. Seal the packages as best you can and store them in a cool and dry area to ensure seed longevity.

Testing and Tracking

If you do resort to using a storage method such as a cool, dry area in your basement or if you use a storage facility where the environmental control isn't optimum, it would be wise to do some seed germination testing before sowing the stored seeds for a new season. For that matter, even if you're storing seed in an optimum environment, it's still a good idea to do spot germination testing on seeds that have been in storage for more than a year. It would be unwise to plan a new season using old seed that may have been exposed to conditions that would inhibit their performance.

This leads me to talk a little about tracking your seed from the time you receive it to the time that you finally use the last tray's worth of seed in a packet. At Raker, we offer a wide variety of annual, perennial, and florist products as seedlings—plugs. Anticipating our seed requirements becomes an important task. Of all the items on our product list, we usually have a certain amount of seed for each item on site, which, if necessary, allows us to schedule the sowing of a plug order the day we receive it. This list consists of hundreds of items of which we may inventory only one or two thousand seeds per item because we receive only a few orders for it, or several million seeds because it's a popular item. Knowing your needs in advance and having a good seed storage chamber gives you the option of purchasing your seed in advance and storing it until you need it.

We have one person dedicated to seed purchasing, monitoring seed requirements, and maintaining our item number database. If we add new seed varieties, we have to create a new item number for it so that we can track that item in our system. We track seed by count, so when seed items are received, the inventory is adjusted accordingly. We also attach a barcode to the seed package for verification and tracking of seed use at the sow stations. After this, the seed goes to the storage chamber to keep it in optimum condition. When the operators of a sow station have a sow requirement for an item, this person will scan the barcode on the seed package, which will display the seed's inventory information on the computer screen at that station. Here, the operator verifies that it's the right seed for

Figure 11-4. A clean, well-organized boiler room.

the order requirement and documents which seed lot status applies. Every time a new seed packet is opened, the current date is stamped on the packet, allowing the operators to know how long an opened package has been in storage.

As trays pass through the seeder, they're immediately and automatically scanned into production, and the amount of seed required for a specific tray is reduced in our seed inventory database. If it's a double-sow begonia in a 512 tray, then seed inventory for that item is reduced by 1,024 seeds for every tray of that item scanned into production. By being able to track seed this closely, we don't have to guess how much seed we have on hand for any item.

By employing this technology, and by knowing what our long- and short-term seed needs will be, we can avoid over-purchasing or coming up short on an item. Normally we purchase popular seed items by what our requirements are for a specific season or time of year and always rotate through our seed inventory to keep it fresh. Special orders are more of an at-once purchase, and we tend to purchase only the seed the order requires, taking into account the germination rates for those items. This eliminates storing a seed item that we may not have a future requirement for.

As I stated at the beginning, seed cost is the largest material expense in producing a tray of plugs, so take some guess work out of your germination results by giving it a good storage environment that will allow you to maximize performance with the seed you store.

The Proper Boiler Room

Jim Rearden

When it's cold outside, growers who enjoy the benefits hot water heat will tell you how imperative it is to have a reliable, well-engineered boiler room. To borrow a portion of a phrase, "a clean, well-lit place for boilers" is what it's really all about, especially when you consider that from its portals flow the lifeblood of the greenhouse operation—heat.

One thing to make clear right away in a discussion of what constitutes a boiler room is to clarify what a boiler room is *not*:

- It's not a place to store overflow supply items such as pots, flats, or growing media.
- It's not a chemical storage room. Chemicals or fertilizer dust could be pulled into combustion chambers and cause serious damage.
- It's not a proper storage place to park equipment such as sprayers or injectors.
- It's not a good place for tool storage or a workshop, as these areas tend to generate dust and debris, which clog up and damage boilers.
- It's not an all-purpose "mechanical room." Items such as air compressors and backup generators should have their own optimized space.

Interruptions to the critical mission of the boiler room seem to always occur at the most inopportune times: Christmas night, New Years' Eve—you get the picture. But most boiler room failures are due to a lack of attention to the poor, stoic denizens within: your boilers. They'll find a way to revenge poor maintenance, and their timing is seemingly impeccable. Hence, it should be the goal of a modern greenhouse operator to create and maintain a good location for them.

In my travels, I've seen boilers located in the most absurd places. I've found them located on top of office structures, in small closets, in mud-floored greenhouse lean-tos, and right inside the greenhouse with constant dousing from irrigation systems corroding the equipment to an early demise. I've even seen them in the middle of a headhouse, dotted with foil-wrapped food being heated for the day's lunch! These are not respectful environments in which to locate a humble and loyal servant that performs such a vital task.

Elements of a Proper Boiler Room

Use the following as a checklist (or just inspiration) to create the ideal boiler room for your facility. Each one is important; they are listed in no certain order.

Location

The boiler room can be either a separate structure or integrated into the greenhouse facility. In either case, it should be reasonably centrally located to the greenhouse facility or its contemplated future expansion areas.

Codes

The room or structure should comply with all local fire, structural, electrical, and construction codes.

Easy access

Plan to have easy access with adequate space on roads, paths, or lanes to move large equipment to and from the boiler room. Install doors that open wide enough and tall enough to accommodate removing, replacing, or adding equipment.

Utilities

All services and utilities must be brought to the boiler room and engineered and sized for the most expansion you envision. Paying to have proper gas, electric, and water lines installed now will be a great investment for the future.

Figure 11-5. Ductwork brings fresh combustion air to the boiler.

Combustion air

Boilers use a lot of fresh air in the combustion process (approximately 250 ft.^{3}/hour [7 m^3/hour] per 1 million BTUH of boiler input), and the boiler room needs to be set up to provide that in an adequate and controlled way. There are three ways to provide it: free air into the room, ducted air into the room, and ducted air to the boiler. The first two methods essentially "dump" outside air into the room. The last one feeds air directly to the boiler. However, "direct air" systems are relatively new and aren't available on all boilers. Combustion air is a bigger issue than this space allows for coverage in extreme detail, but typically, motorized louvers are installed in an exterior wall of the boiler room to provide combustion and ventilation air in a ratio of 1 in.^{2} (6.4 cm^2) per 1,000 BTUH boiler input for "atmospheric" units to 1 in.^{2} (6.4 cm^2) per 4,000–8,000 BTUH boiler input for "power" burner-equipped boilers. (A word about the newer "direct air" systems: They're nice because cold outside air is put directly into the inlet duct and not allowed to cool the boiler room. Also, you'll avoid the mess of all the dust, snow, and debris that accompany the combustion air.)

Heating

Yes, heating. It's important that you never let your boiler room freeze, and with some of the newer, higher efficiency boilers, they may not give off enough "jacket heat" to warm the room. Plan for a simple unit heater (at minimum) to take care of this.

Cooling

Some boilers rooms get brutally hot from the aforementioned jacket heat. A properly sized fan to move this heat from the boiler room to another area that can benefit from it makes sense and makes working in the boiler room bearable.

Lighting

Plan the same bright and adequate lighting as you would an office or any other workspace. This will help everyone do a better job during installation, operation, and maintenance. No one enjoys working with a flashlight in one hand and a screwdriver in the other when the boiler is down on a cold night.

Floor

The boiler room floor should be concrete with a minimum of a broom finish. The floor needs to be engineered to handle the loading of sometimes very heavy boilers. Also, the best boiler rooms I've seen include "housekeeping pads" for each floor-mounted piece of equipment. This is essentially a small slab, formed with 2 x 4s and poured on top of the floor in the dimension of the equipment to be installed. The housekeeping pad makes it easy to keep the boiler room floor clean.

Drains

The proper boiler room plan includes an engineered floor drain system with strategically placed grated inlets to accommodate water from pressure relief valves, drain or blow-down valves, condensate water from flue-gas condensing boilers (check environmental regulations), and floor clean-up runoff. It's vital that the floor drain system be integrated with the boiler system drain points before you start construction of the boiler room.

Figure 11-6. A "housekeeping pad" makes it easy to keep the area under the boiler clean and debris free.

Computer controls

While planning the layout of the electrical panels in the boiler room, remember to include space for any computer control panels that need to be located there as well. More boiler systems are being operated via the central environmental control system these days, and since these are the brains of the operation, it's smart to locate them strategically in an easy-access, well-lit space.

Fire safety

Depending on local code, you may need to have an automatic sprinkler system installed in your new boiler room. At minimum though, plan on a good-quality fire extinguisher.

Penetrations

The typical boiler room has vents, such as chimneys or "breaching," going out the top and heating water pipes going in and out of the sidewalls. Plan ahead where these penetrations will be made and follow proper procedures to seal them up. Depending on the style of construction, your roof may require "roof curbs" around the roof vents. Code may require that wall penetrations have a "fire-stop" or special sealant for safety wherever they go. If you have air inlets on the sidewalls, make sure they are above snow levels.

Venting

When boilers burn fuels such as oil, natural gas, and propane, they release exhaust in what is called the "products of combustion." One of the byproducts is water vapor. Depending on the fuel type, it will contain several other elements that give it acidity comparable to vinegar. Unless your boiler system is a "condensing" type or is equipped with a flue-gas condenser, this corrosive exhaust needs to be quickly carried up and out of the boiler room through an engineered venting system. A proper venting system is designed to remove the "exhaust steam" quickly, before it can cool down enough to form condensation droplets that can ruin expensive equipment in a short time. Usually the venting system is a metal duct that needs to terminate well above the boiler room and any surrounding buildings or obstacles. Depending on the height necessary, the venting may require an engineered guy-wire system to support it and will terminate with a windproof cap. Planning ahead here will make life much easier. I've seen many instances of trusses or other framing in the way of the venting. Make sure your construction plan includes clearances for the vents.

Central document storage and maintenance schedule

Set aside an area to keep a logbook and to file all maintenance records. Also, make a binder to store all product sheets, instruction manuals, and system drawings. The payoff to keeping this information organized comes back many times over the years. In this same area, I like to see a wall-mounted, laminated sheet with all service intervals planned for the next twenty years or more. Hang a grease pencil nearby to record the work for a quick visual reminder. Doing annual maintenance seems to be a struggle for almost all growers—how about putting your boilers on the same birthday party roster you set up for your staff? This most vigilant team member may not enjoy cake and punch, but an annual cleaning and adjusting will certainly be appreciated! I know of a boiler service company that actually sends cards that read, "Happy birthday, ya big galoot!"

Emergency numbers and procedures

Set up signs that readily identify the company you will turn to for service work on an annual and/or emergency basis. Also, if there are special procedures (such as backup fuel switchover) that must be done in emergencies, make them clear and train your staff.

Figure 11-7. A professionally planned and built boiler room shows attention to detail.

Spare parts and special tools

Set up an area for spare parts that are likely to fail occasionally. Pump motors and ignitors seem to quit when vendors and supply houses are closed and, in most cases, growers cannot afford to wait until they open to get the heat going again. Also, keep any special tools you need to work on your boilers in this area. Some growers need to be able to switch fuels on less than a few hours notice. If you'll need to change fuel orifices on the fly, you should keep all the parts and tools you'll possibly need handy. It also pays to rehearse the procedure occasionally.

Construction and installation

During construction and installation, keep all documents and packing lists in one place. Protect all materials and equipment from weather and theft. Use "good receiving practices" when shipments arrive. Construction is hectic, but being organized about this phase will pay off in reduced frustration down the line. Also, boilers are not good workbenches. Even though many of them offer a convenient horizontal surface, don't let them turn into a catch-all. They'll get scratched and worn, and you'll regret it later.

Finishing

The proper boiler room is finished with cleanly installed pipe insulation, painted exposed fittings and pipes, and labels indicating pipe contents (gas, hot water supply, etc.), and flow direction. Some regional codes require gas lines to be painted as well, usually safety yellow.

Get Professional Design Help

To get the best boiler room, turn to an industry-specific professional who knows the unique nature of our industry and will help you through all these areas. A professionally designed boiler room plan should include a complete piping plan showing all hot water, cold water, fuel, and drain lines as well as chimney vents. It should address equipment combustion and servicing clearances with a "footprint" drawing. It should include allowances for future expansion and incorporate emergency connections planned for a mobile boiler in the event of a catastrophic boiler room fire. Also, it should provide redundancy in all the vital equipment (i.e., boilers, pumps, and so on). Even one night without heat could be a catastrophe for your business.

Boilers (no matter how small) are not like unit heaters and should not be located in the greenhouse space. Because the energy they create can be delivered long distances, there's rarely a valid reason for not housing a boiler appropriately. Boilers offer a long economic life and if treated well will deliver many years of high-efficiency heating. Enjoy the fun and challenge of creating your own proper boiler room, and you'll be rewarded with higher net profits and less angst on those cold winter nights.

12

Putting It All Together

Figure 12-1. Careful consideration of your site before you build can save numerous headaches afterward.

Site Selection and Analysis

Sara Grosser

Selecting a site and developing the layout for your greenhouse operation can be an exciting, yet overwhelming, experience. Careful site selection and analysis, paired with a long-range site and structure plan, will result in a less stressful expansion process.

Site selection and analysis consist of the evaluation of community, infrastructure, utilities, environment, and terrain of a particular location. Included in the long-range structure and site plan is the layout and design for all greenhouse and headhouse structures, offices, parking and infrastructure, signage, and utilities. The outcome of each plan is influenced by the result of the other. For example, if utility access is limited, greenhouse layout is affected.

Site Selection

Identification of the market in which plant material will be sold is your first item of concern when selecting the greenhouse site. Select a parcel that will provide convenient access to your intended market. Should retailing be a part of your business plan, the importance of your location increases dramatically.

Once your target market is identified, determine the cost and availability of land in that area. Further consideration should be given to the potential growth of these markets to ensure that your greenhouse operation can develop and grow to meet any future demands.

Zoning

Zoning is an issue sometimes overlooked by property owners, who assume particular constraints don't exist. Zoning may require specific construction details; for instance, special engineering of the structure for local snow or wind loads. This often results in additional structural members, increasing your costs, which may exceed your budget. Additional zoning laws may prohibit greenhouse structures from being erected within a designated distance from a particular establishment. Investigate any forthcoming zoning regulations to determine if your future plans will be acceptable or if you should carry them out early in order to be grandfathered in.

Neighbors

Neighboring establishments, such as a major competitor, school, or shopping mall, have both positive and negative ramifications on a greenhouse location. Future construction of these or other attractions must also be evaluated when selecting your site.

Local residents can have a great influence on the construction of a greenhouse, with either eager support or aggressive opposition, depending on if they want you as a neighbor or not. Aside from how residents feel about the construction of a greenhouse operation, research the community to determine if local residents will satisfy your labor needs now and in the future. Availability of labor is critical, both for the present needs of your business as well as future growth.

Roads

A basic requirement for any greenhouse structure is an access roadway. When selecting a site, consider the simplicity or possible complexity of accessibility with existing and future byways. Will the existing streets accommodate semitrailers and other delivery and hauling vehicles? Will acceleration and deceleration lanes need to be added? Furthermore, does the site itself have an established driveway or access path? Consider the ease or difficulty of installing a private roadway. If a passageway exists, evaluate to determine if it suits your needs or requires alteration. Restructuring existing grade or modifying access roads can become quite expensive.

Water

Investigate the availability of water to the site. County and city water suppliers will set a meter virtually anywhere off the water main. Research the water service to determine if enough water pressure will be supplied. This may greatly affect the location of the greenhouse on the parcel as well as the equipment selected for installation in the greenhouse. Should water need to be hauled onto the site and stored in tanks or retention ponds, evaluate the costs incurred for additional equipment and/or services required, such as water trucks, tanks, pumps, and excavation of holding ponds. If current water service just meets the needs of the greenhouse operation, will availability increase to meet the forthcoming needs of the greenhouse operation? Another aspect of water assessment is water quality. Should conditions require treatment, investigate options in water alteration.

Electricity

Accessibility of electric service should be thoroughly explored. Large electric service providers usually ensure constant service, while smaller co-op services may experience occasional blackouts if energy use exceeds amount supplied. Discussing electrical needs with the local electric service provider is critical. Should electric service not be dependable, perhaps a generator is necessary to prevent loss of heat generation, ventilation, and other equipment relying on electric. As with water service, will electric requirements be satisfied with future expansion?

Heating fuel

The various equipment used in a greenhouse, particularly heating systems, utilize fuel for operation. Most equipment is manufactured to operate with natural gas, propane gas, or oil. Natural gas would be supplied via pipelines along the main road, while propane and oil are transported on trucks and contained in a tank on site. As with water and electric, discuss fuel requirements with local providers to determine the best solution as well as expected needs according to the long-range plan.

Environment

The surrounding environment will also affect greenhouse location. Air pollution is becoming an increasing concern and should be considered. Placement of a greenhouse operation on the windward side of the highway prevents the potentially intense exhaust fumes from entering the greenhouse environment. Light pollution in populated areas is another concern for many greenhouse managers, as this may affect the success of photoperiodic crops, such as poinsettias and mums. The availability of natural light is addressed later with orientation of the greenhouse. Noise pollution created by greenhouse equipment, such as exhaust fans, should also be taken into consideration, as local residents may express discontent when this noise occurs. Selection of natural ventilation will decrease this noise, keeping residents at ease.

Terrain

The terrain of the land should also be considered. Determine the amount of grading required to construct on level ground. Consider expansion needs as well. It's less costly to hire a bulldozer operator once rather than to require return trips.

Long-Range Site and Structure Planning

The ideal location for a production greenhouse on a particular parcel of land is where adequate light, drainage, and ventilation will occur. To achieve each of these goals, construction in a valley setting is least desirable, as cold air settles in the valley, resulting in increased utility costs. In addition, valley drainage is often times inadequate. Assess drainage capabilities prior to construction. Regardless of site, construct the greenhouse operation above the surrounding ground so rain and irrigation water will drain away.

Location and orientation of the greenhouse in terms of gutter direction becomes critical when the greenhouse is located above the 39th parallel (around Columbus, Ohio). Greenhouses constructed south of this mark are generally surrounded with an abundance of natural light, making house orientation less critical than those placed north of this mark. However, preferred orientation is with gutters running east/west. Greenhouses north of the 39th parallel have lower availability of natural light, resulting in increased vitality of greenhouse placement. These greenhouses should be erected with gutters running north/south. This orientation results in the shade created from the gutter line moving throughout the day, therefore not creating a constant dark area, which would result in a non-uniform crop.

Another consideration in regard to lighting is the location of the greenhouse in relation to obstructions. The greenhouse should be located a distance 2.5 times the height of the nearest obstruction that would block light. For example, if a structure 20' (6 m) tall exists, the greenhouse would ideally be placed 50' (15 m) from that structure to prevent shading the greenhouse. Other obstacles may include trees and large signage. When building around these obstacles, locate the greenhouse to the south or southeast. The next best locations in order of preference are: southwest, east, west, and north.

Wind is often a concern when constructing a greenhouse operation. For maximum ventilation, greenhouse roof vents should be placed on slope opposite that of the prevailing wind. On greenhouses with only one side or gable vent, place the vent on the windward side. If wind is not prevalent, installation of a double sidewall or gable vents helps to increase ventilation.

The placement of the headhouse and greenhouse structures depends greatly on the travel pattern of plant material from the time it is received to the time it is shipped. Map out this flow, including container filling, planting, watering, growing, packing, shipping, and any task in between. Include in this map the equipment used to perform each function, such as flat fillers, transplant machines, monorail system, watering booms, carts, shipping cartons, loading docks, etc. Determine space requirements for said equipment and design space to accommodate. Make provisions for future installation of equipment as part of the long-range site plan. The relation of the headhouse to the production greenhouse is a direct result of this process.

Figure 12-2. You can tell when a greenhouse has been designed with a master plan, because it is laid out neatly and efficiently.

Remaining considerations must be made for necessary office space. Although offices may be located within the headhouse initially, consider future expansion and office building location.

Roadway and site access require additional thought. Determine the types of vehicles to be accommodated by vendors and customers. Often times, material is delivered and shipped via semitrailers. Construction of a private drive and parking lot must accommodate this weight and size. In addition, consider traffic flow of deliveries and shipments, situating the greenhouse and headhouse effectively to avoid traffic jams and encourage traffic flow. Consider the area needed for delivery and shipping vehicles to turn around and move about on the property. Another item of consideration is parking for customers, employees, vendors, and visitors. Allow adequate space and remain within tolerable distance from operation.

Last but not least, plan for signage. Depending on the type of signage selected, electric may be required, or perhaps special provisions due to size or shape. This is especially critical for a retail operation.

Site analysis and long-range planning are vital to the success of a greenhouse operation. Improper site analysis in regard to any of the above topics can result in costly and inconvenient modifications later. How devastating and expensive it would be to demolish an existing building to make room for the new as a result of poor planning. It is imperative to determine if the selected site will accommodate operation needs in the present and for the next fifteen years.

Growing Your Business—For the Right Reasons

Mike Gooder

Are we growers who build . . . or builders who grow? Many of us within horticulture must continually ask ourselves that question. Unlike most other small businesses, success in horticulture drives huge capital investments into single-use, highly specialized facilities filled with unique equipment—just what every banker wants to finance . . . or better yet, foreclose on!

As an owner/manager, the complexity quadruples as you wear the hats of architect, engineer, developer, financier, general contractor, and even skilled (or in my case unskilled) laborer. Meanwhile, you're managing the day-to-day operations of your existing base of business while solidifying new markets for the additional production. How many hats must you wear?

In addition, the bigger your success and the bigger your investment, the bigger the demands on your management skills. Therefore, with so much capital, time, and energy being plowed into your growth, your first critically important objective is to determine that you're building for all the right reasons. That is, this is an expansion for sound business reasons, not an ego expansion. The next step is to develop the correct piece of property for your application. Finally, you have to make sure your plans not only reflect your needs today, but also take a strategic look at the future needs of the enterprise. Following is an evaluation of these three points.

Building for the Right Reasons

Are you completely convinced that it's time to step-up to the next level? Unsure? Your answers to the following questions and points may help you decide:

Will the expansion road lead to easy street or stressville? Will it bring greater opportunity for you and your staff without risking everyone's sanity and happiness? Have you maximized and optimized? Is your existing facility being utilized to its fullest potential?

The quickest and easiest way to crank up profits is by producing and/or marketing more from your existing facilities. For example, can you crank out another rotation by starting with rooted cuttings rather than unrooted cuttings?

Size is not relative to profitability. There exists no direct or indirect correlation. Many "big" growers will tell you they had more fun and took home more money

Figure 12-3. Unlike most other small businesses, success in horticulture requires huge capital investments in single-use, highly specialized facilities filled with unique equipment, such as this propagation facility at Plantpeddler in Cresco, Iowa.

when they were "small" growers. However, this is by no means a rule. Success and profitability are often the result of dedication, determination, and focus. Size is just one component of the formula.

Do you prefer to stay in your comfort zone or to attack the challenge of the unknown? If everything is "in sync" in your current business, are you ready to risk that success? Have you identified new markets, a new niche, untapped potential? Will the move put your existing customer base and cash stream in any form of jeopardy? Does this growth push you and your staff into situations that set you up for failure? Does your company feed on conquering the unknowns? Do you relish the opportunity to push yourself and those near you beyond your current plateau?

Beware of the "I'm bigger" ego trip. Don't become disillusioned by "squarefootitis." Be sincere in your reasons and objectives. Develop a complete business plan that proves to you and all those near and involved that your future growth is well founded.

You either go forward or backward. There is no standing still. Never has been, never will be. So what is the standardized answer for long-haul growth? Be aggres-

sively conservative or conservatively aggressive. What does that mean? It means build your business on a controlled growth curve and you build a business that lasts.

Are you sufficiently self-sufficient? Does your current size allow you to cover the varied aspects of your business? Or are you forced to spread your time and talents too thinly? Will you lose your freedom to do odd jobs out in the greenhouse? Does expanding allow you to attract more talent to secure your ability to weather adversity?

Eliminating Your Many Hats

So, you answered all the questions correctly *and* you've convinced everyone around you that the future involves growing. Now it's time to begin planning and logistics.

It starts with taking a strategic look at how to organize orderly, coordinated growth. One of the critical first steps is to eliminate some of the hats you wear. As the facilitator of growth, you need a clear desk and an uncluttered mind (or vice versa). Evaluate, delegate, and distribute your current list of duties. Farm out those things that bog you down. Build up critical staff early in the game . . . you'll need the help once you've completed the expansion. Remember, you can't do it all (even though you probably can). As much as you know you have the ability to do all the jobs, don't be selfish—share some of them with those around you. Don't be picky; give them the ones you abhor! Following are some keys to finding the help you need to grow your business.

Hire early, hire right

If you're going to grow your business, you'll need to grow your staff. Hire at least part of that crew early, before the craziness of the build engulfs you. Hiring early allows you to train and prepare the staff, and then put them to work during the project. An added bonus is that by being part of the construction, they take ownership in the project.

Challenge and nurture "insider" growth

Almost anyone can build buildings. What may make a business succeed or fail are the people who form the core. They are the business's heart and soul. They breathe life into the business. Don't overlook those who are closest to you! Some are clearly visible, while others prefer to hide in the shadows. Unless you're operating solo, inside your organization are people primed to help you grow the company into the future. If this weren't true, they probably would be working elsewhere.

In most circles, horticulture careers are at best demanding with average rewards. That means if you have dedicated staffers who've lingered with the company through good times and bad, they're ready for you to "build them" and "grow them" into the next phase of your company's growth.

Keep the "good sales guys" (and gals) coming by

You know the type, the true "road warriors." Looking and acting somewhat homeless, these folks always appear at your door with some bit of advice or information that can greatly condense your learning curve.

In the thirty years we've owned Plantpeddler, we've been blessed with a broad array of good salespeople who continue to greatly contribute to our success. Two of the first, Bob Whitman of Ball Seed Company and Skip Ruof of Yoder Brothers, took a couple of greenhorn college grads under their wings and helped us negotiate the obstacle course of those early years. Yes, without their insight, we may have made it, but they taught us a million lessons that we didn't have to learn through our usual trial-and-error method.

How do you keep them coming around? It really isn't that hard. Show them respect. Give them an honest chance for your business. And don't always make them buy lunch. In fact, we figure that anyone who makes it to "perfectly in the middle of nowhere" (i.e., Cresco, Iowa) deserves a free meal or a night out in the big city.

Develop "outsider expertise"

Now is the time to cash in your markers. Often working for free (or even less), put your suppliers to work on your development project. Throw a bone to those salespeople (see above) who are barking at your door. Put them to work chasing down answers to the challenges of your project. Then show your appreciation by supporting those who support you. As the customer, using support resources around you can save hundreds of hours and thousands of dollars. If you've picked your vendor partners correctly, now is the time to get the paybacks for your loyalty.

Another group of outsiders to develop are "moonlighters." Often working for considerably less than they earn on their day jobs, they bring bonus, bargain brainpower to your team. Likely, every facet of the project, from the most technical to the most mundane, has a part-time moonlighter who can bring expertise without capital waste. Explore this cost-effective method as you develop your expansion plan.

Believe in *you!*

I've probably saved the single-most important concept for last. It's about your corporation. Not the job you go to, but your personal company, "You Inc." At You Inc., you are the most important member. Your success, in a large part, will be determined by how much you believe in yourself and how you "manage" your company. Those near you must be overwhelmed with your confidence, energy, and enthusiasm. By believing totally in yourself, others can't help but believe in you, too. Prove to everyone just how much you believe and are committed to your life.

Build to Match Your Market

Expansion success starts with pre-marketing your new production. Determine your target market, then build to match. To be competitive today, you need to build facilities designed to meet the market you intend to serve. Every type of modern greenhouse structure, and the equipment within, can be tuned to maximize the profitability of the crops within—creating a crop-specific plant factory where agriculture, floriculture, and manufacturing meet to form the hybrid that represents today's "modern" greenhouse.

If your target is low-input, seasonal bedding plant production, then simple Quonsets may provide the best alternative. Economical and simple to construct and equip, they provide the ability to turn on and off houses (or zones) to accommodate production build-up cycles. On the flip side, the dollars expended per square foot traditionally are the most extreme when you're growing and marketing potted plants to a high-end retail trade.

Your answers to the following categories' questions will help you define how your marketing intentions will influence the facility requirements of your next project.

Sales driven or production driven

How will the product be marketed: retail, wholesale, or brokered? How will you determine your product mix—based on historical data and projected sales or what you are most efficient at producing? Does the crop fall within "comfort zone" of you, your staff, and your facilities? For new crops, it may be very difficult to find the necessary data to make reasonable business decisions.

Existing or new customer base

Do you clearly understand the expectations of your potential customers? Have you already served this market and understand it, or are you going to be prospecting for new customers? Will your customers commit to product or will it be produced on speculation?

Demands of customers

Are your customers driven by high quality or low price? I hope not both because they're on opposite ends of the spectrum. What's the seasonality of their demands? Do they keep your facilities full? Do they have defined order minimums, production standards, and stages that you have to meet? How about their service and support requirements? What are the terms of the sale? You may be thinking "2% 10, Net 30," and they're dragging it out to ninety days. This can have a huge impact on cash flow and the actual cost of the product.

Viability of market

Is the market alive and vibrant, or is it waning? What's the financial security of your customer base? Are you serving a stable market that's recession proof?

Growth potential (short- and long-term)

Are you riding the crest of the wave, or are you in the "tube" with it about to crash in on you? Are you focusing on the core products that form the basis of our industry or flashy fads that are sure to pass? Are you using new technology and genetics to bring competitive advantages? Are you discovering or developing new production efficiencies capable of separating you from the pack?

Competition and direction of market

Is the market already jammed full of low-cost producers or marketers who are losing money to stay in business? You know the types: "Lose money on every sale, and make it up on volume!" Is it a market that's undiscovered, where you can have free run? Can you create a seam in a mature market niche?

Entry costs

Does entry into the market require large capital injections to pump life into the business? Do barriers exist to keep amateurs out? Does the high entry fee hobble the competition?

Is it profitable?

The simple question that, unfortunately, a majority of us growers have the hardest time finding the answer to. Can we produce at a cost level that affords a fair return on our investment? Simply, is there profit in the production?

Can you take it to the bank?

Can you answer all of the above with positive responses? And can you write a reasonable business plan? If so, then this is the easy part!

Sorting Through the Maze

Everywhere you look you see potential products to grow, ways to sell, and places to go. This industry is blessed with unique markets and thousands of crops. From "commodity farming" of our "industrial genetics" (e.g., poinsettias, geraniums, mums) to ultra-specialized micro-production, and everything in between—millions of possible scenarios exist. No government intervention. No categorization. No restrictions. Here is a cottage industry with the only limitations being your imagination, intuition, and dedication.

Profitable, realistic opportunities

Focus on growth segments within the industry and then identify the products, suppliers, levels of consumer satisfaction, and market saturation. Is everyone involved in the niche healthy and happy? Are they growing? Look into your crystal ball to see where it may be headed. Pick the brains of those within the niche. Then start crunching some numbers.

Crops to fit niches

For every niche, there are perfect products. Put on your research hat and dig in. Build a list of options and start weeding them out. When your list is refined, focus on what you can do that separates your products within this niche. What opens the door? If possible, run production trials and test the market.

Crop-market match

Next, determine the cultural needs of the crops that fit your market, along with the level of quality and skill required. Run a cost analysis to ensure that you can find that delicate balance between input costs and perceived value.

Wish list

Your next task is to determine the requirements of your facility and equipment. From your crop culture and cost analysis, you should be able to build a wish list for the facility. From simple to sophisticated, you can have it all—for a price. This analysis will help you decide if you need to invest $5 or $50 per square foot.

Dreams, Crops, and Expansion Budgets

Now it all starts coming together. As you follow through the steps, the process identifies the needs and narrows your options. Put those crop-driven facility requirements on paper (a spreadsheet), then drop in budgetary numbers next to each item. The project scope becomes very real when you are building for the right reason: the crops.

Today, the greenhouse and equipment manufacturers can build precisely what we want. The newest industry "spin-o-nym" comes from my friend Jim Rearden of TrueLeaf Technologies, who coined the term "plantcentric engineering" to describe this holistic, functional design concept. By learning how to target the needs of a customer's crop, members of the National Greenhouse Manufacturers Association can turn dreams into reality. For owners and growers, the NGMA serves as a reservoir of free knowledge and advice. Use them to your advantage (visit www.ngma.com). Remember, they believe in the future of this industry too because they're gambling theirs on us!

Build for tomorrow

If you're in this business for the long haul, give your new construction effort the professional intensity it deserves. Quick fixes to resolve immediate capacity shortfalls will likely turn into a product flow and logistics nightmare that ends up costing you money from that day forward. You've seen those places: a lean-to on a lean-to on a lean-to! Where's the flow? How do you compete against the efficient facilities?

The same goes for price

Don't get caught in the cheaper-per-square-foot trap. While it's not necessarily true that higher cost equals better, use care not to underbuild for your climate. Greenhouses represent a harsh interior environment that's often located in an even harsher outdoor environment. A few extra dollars on the front end may make you considerably more secure as Mother Nature tests your investment.

Successful businesses plan

Develop a plan that allows your facility to grow as you follow through on your marketing plans. Simply stated, successful businesses plan. Often, those that fail have failed to plan. Think integration, automation, and flexibility in design. Considering the continued upward spiral of minimum wage, can you stay competitive against your automated competitors? At Plantpeddler, we invest every available dollar in labor efficiency (i.e., automation). We'll most likely never layoff staff because of a machine, but our income dollars per labor hour continues to grow. Our goal every year is to reduce labor cost as a percentage of sales.

Integration of the operation

The next step is to take leading-edge automation and develop a system specifically designed to bring it all together. Integration of automation, both existing and anticipated, will likely be the advantage that separates the leaders of this decade from those struggling to stay afloat. Though regional pockets of low-cost labor exist, we believe that having well-paid, technically inclined staff operating our robotics and automation will contribute to our enduring profitability.

Put Together Your "Dream Team"

The future is becoming clearer now. You've identified a niche (or several opportunities) within the industry. From your market study, you've defined a list of potential crops that fulfill the needs and desires of that niche. From the cultural needs of these crops, you've built a list of facility requirements and constructed a preliminary plan and budget. You're doing well, but now it's time to formalize all of your research and homework in the form a business plan that will help you sell the dream.

One of the most important steps in building that plan and accomplishing your goals is to develop your dream team—a group of peers and mentors that will help you clarify your vision of the future. Remember earlier when I spoke of keeping the good salespeople coming around, developing outsider expertise, and the value of supplier relations, including using the free sources of advice and expertise, such as the NGMA? Well, this is where you cash that in!

At Plantpeddler, we call them our "A-Team." They'll do just about anything for our company—including digging the holes for the columns! The A-Team brings us their experience from years of dealing with the other side of the industry, as suppliers of hardgoods and green goods. They are often much more in tune to the direction of our industry and where the future may deliver us than we are. Use your A-Team to bring you fresh ideas that aren't polluted by your biases or by preexisting paradigms. Sometimes the truth can be painful, but most often they'll deliver the opinions that help you see clearly into the future.

Here are some basic principles to being successful in building and utilizing the talents of your A-Team:

Start early

Bring in the team early! You want to get them involved at the very beginning of the project to ensure you don't waste time going down dead-end paths. Have them buy in to your dream early; let them have "ownership" of the dream.

Evaluate the roster

Identify those with positive impact *very early!* Evaluate what each team member can bring to the table. You need to strike a balance of personalities and philosophies. Can they coordinate with other vendors? Are they open to working within the team concept? Can

they let down their guard and lower their egos long enough to let all participate? Be careful here because personalities sometimes may surprise you. Don't be afraid to boot someone off the team to preserve a constructive core.

Two points for experience

Find out if they've worked on complex projects. Though your project may look simple on the outside, long-range planning requires complex thinking. Try to involve vendor partners that can visualize the results based on experiences. The ability to pull together multifaceted projects will help ensure the success of your growth. When in doubt, casually check references and visit recent projects. These will bring you up to speed in a hurry.

Huddle up

Bring the team together at project conception. Pull your team together and get everyone to sit at the same table. If possible, pass out a blank sheet of paper and start with a simple question such as, "What are your expectations of today's meeting," or "What are your expectations of this project?" Get an early read on every member's position. This might be the first time this group has sat down together, and that can make for an exciting event *or* a big disaster! Be prepared to deal with getting everyone headed in the same direction.

Pass the ball

Start passing out assignments. You didn't put this team together so that you could provide babysitter service. You're building a team to help you cost effectively conquer your goals and surpass your dreams. The job at hand is to take the knowledge base before you and put it to work for you. Make sure you're prepared with a chore list of what you really don't want to do. Give those jobs to the people you love . . . the characters sitting around that table.

The Business Plan

Now it all begins to come together. You've distributed the burden of legwork to the people who make a living within our industry finding answers to questions. They're fired up because you've challenged them. Meanwhile, you're able to focus on the business at hand, along with the critical overall management of the project—a perfect management balance.

Complex projects require sophisticated management. It still runs uphill. To be successful spending your money still requires your management skill. You need to keep focused on the direction of your project, steering the team down the path to your objectives. Whether you manage the project on paper, in a spreadsheet, or using project management software, it still comes back to your dedication, your expertise, and your tenacity if the job is to be done correctly.

A business plan directs business growth. A good plan looks at the past, the present, and the future. It's truly amazing what a thorough and well-thought-out business plan can do for you and your management team. The plan will help focus the team on a common direction. It gives you targets to shoot for. A good business plan serves as the key tool used in persuading your investors. You can have them begging to do business with you if you present yourself and your project correctly and professionally.

At Plantpeddler, business plan development is part of an overall growth strategy. The business plan formalizes goals and objectives in written form, reinforcing company direction. Along with looking ahead, it gives us the opportunity to reflect on our past performance, comparing our targets to the real numbers we achieved. Each draft of our business plan includes considerable text covering various aspect of the niche we've identified and how we're going to conquer that market. Our last business plan filled a 2"-thick three-ring binder.

You may be thinking this sounds like too much to handle, but it's really quite simple. Here is a list of the topics you will want to cover in your business plan: Where you have been? Where are you today? Where do you plan to go? How do you plan to get there? How will you finance it? How will you pay it back?

The Entrepreneurial Spirit

Quality is the end result of a quality approach. For any business, within floriculture or outside of it, success requires dedication that's driven by the entrepreneurial spirit. This spirit is the driving force behind our industry as well as the quality that determines the level you reach within our industry. By taking a proactive approach to business development, you can build into the future . . . for the right reasons.

13

Managing Your Business

Figure 13-1. Is your office an extension of your greenhouse, or is your greenhouse an extension of your office?

The Greenhouse Office

Bill Swanekamp

In the last chapter on greenhouse construction and expansion, Mike Gooder asked, "Are we growers who build . . . or builders who grow?" I can ask a similar question about how you manage your business: Is your office an extension of your greenhouse, or is your greenhouse an extension of your office? Why is this question so important? Because your answer will be an accurate indication of the future success of your business.

The Office Sets the Direction

Over the past forty years in the horticulture industry, I've watched many greenhouse businesses come and go. Without a doubt, the single common thread among businesses that fail is a poorly run office, or an office that's not directing the operations of the greenhouse. That's why it is imperative to establish, even from the conception of your business, a clearly defined business plan, which must include a clear chain of command.

The first step in this chain is to establish that the office sets the direction and tone for the rest of the company. For example, do the growers decide which crops will be grown and in what numbers? Or does the office solicit requests from your customers and then provide the greenhouse with a production schedule? It's obvious which method is superior and will result in the greatest demand for your products.

All too often this isn't how greenhouse businesses are run. Why is this? Well, at first, with small operations, the head grower, office manager, and principal owner are the same person. This is often unavoidable. However, as the business grows, it's essential to modify this arrangement and more clearly establish how decisions regarding the operation of the greenhouse will be made. The goal is to allow the office to be like "command central," where all the key information regarding the crops being grown and their availability is at the fingertips of the office staff. This means that good communication is essential between the office and the greenhouse.

For example, we constantly preach to the greenhouse staff to mentally connect how what they do in the greenhouse will affect the office. If, for some reason, a portion of the crop dies unexpectedly, the office should be the first to know, not the last. Why? Because if you're maintaining your inventory of growing crops on a computer system, and a portion of the crop isn't salable, it should be deducted from the inventory. If this doesn't happen because of a lack of communication on the part of the greenhouse staff, then products will be prebooked that don't exist. This can only lead to customer disappointment.

To provide an overview of an effectively run office, we'll discuss the following aspects of office management: computers, cost accounting, production, sales, accounts receivable (A/R), accounts payable (A/P), inventory control, and the general ledger (G/L).

Computers

Without a doubt, the most significant development affecting the efficiency of the greenhouse office is the modern computer system. I use the word "system" to emphasize the importance of software *and* hardware. Some think it's essential to purchase the fastest computer on the market; in reality, the quality of the software is far more important.

The size of your business will determine which software options you choose. You can spend as little as $500 for something such as QuickBooks by Quicken, or you can spend hundreds of thousands of dollars on a custom software package. The choice is yours, but it's essential to computerize as quickly as possible.

The advantages of computerizing are evident: (1) access information quickly and easily; (2) track inventory; (3) manage the collection of money and payment of bills; (4) keep accurate accounting records for payroll and taxes; and (5) manage your production. This last point is probably the most important, yet most difficult, part when choosing a software package.

Kube-Pak started the process of computerization thirty years ago. At that time, there was no off-the-shelf software package tailored for our industry. The task of selecting a software package was, at best, a compromise. We decided to run our business through an IBM mid-range computer due to the instability of PCs, which were still in their infancy. IBM had been serving the business community for years, and there were some off-the-shelf accounting packages developed to run on their hardware that offered complete integration of all the accounting functions: A/R, A/P, G/L, inventory, order entry, and sales analysis. The problem was that no one offered a production package that suited our needs as growers. This left us with no choice but to customize the production software to suit our needs.

In hindsight, this was a very good decision. Today, we have a package that's very stable and has had more than $1 million worth of custom programming. This sounds like a lot of money, but you must keep in mind this represents less than 1% of our gross sales over the past fifteen years. On average we spend about 0.8% per year on software and hardware, a very manageable figure. Keep in mind, over this same period of time our custom software program has saved us twice its cost in office and production labor.

One key point to remember about a computer system is this: It's only as good as the people who run it. Take the time to train yourself and your staff to properly run the computer system and then use it as much as possible. In the long run, your company will benefit from your computer system because you'll be able to provide your customers with better service and you will have key information at your fingertips.

Cost Accounting

Before we discuss production, it's important to introduce the concept of cost accounting. This is a subject that is avoided like the plague, but it's one of the most important functions of the office. Too often, pricing our products is based on what our competition is selling it for. In some cases this is fine, but without cost accounting there's a chance you are losing money on the sale of every plant. If that's the case, it won't be long before you are out of business.

Every greenhouse business is unique and has its own set of strengths and weaknesses. If your competition has a pot filling machine and you don't, don't you think their cost of production will be lower than yours? It would be illogical to think that your production costs are the same as your more-efficient competition. So you need to do cost accounting based on your business, not someone else's.

Overhead costs

The first step of cost accounting is determining what makes up your *overhead costs*. Overhead includes the following categories: electric, fuel for heating, fuel for trucks, chemicals, fertilizer, depreciation, repairs and maintenance, education, advertising, auto and truck expenses, bad debts, rental fees, health and business insurance, contributions, office supplies, office administration, postage, professional fees (accounting, legal, IT), taxes, telephone, travel, wages, and waste removal. There can be more categories than this, but it depends on how many different G/L accounts that you want to setup.

In addition to your overhead costs, each crop also has direct costs, such as the cost of the plant, pot, media, label, and sleeve or box. Your overhead costs plus your direct costs equal the total cost to produce any crop. We will talk about direct costs in more detail later.

The fundamental equation for doing cost accounting for a plant-production business is the concept of cost per square foot per week. This formula has been around for a long time and can be effective in predicting a crop's profitability, if it is used correctly. This number is determined by calculating your total number of square feet of covered and uncovered growing space. Next, you add up all your overhead costs. Finally, to determine your cost per square foot per week you divide the total overhead costs by the total number of growing square feet.

For example, if you have $820,000 in overhead costs and you use 80,000 ft.^{2}, then your cost per square foot per year is $10.25. If you divide the $10.00 by 52, then your cost per square foot per week is about $0.20.

$$800,000 / 80,000 = \$10.25 / 52 = \$.20/ft.^2/week$$

Variable costs

Some have concluded that once you have calculated this number, you are now in a position to accurately determine the cost of producing a crop. This is not actually the case. Over the past few years we have learned that there are other variables that have to be taken into consideration when calculating costs. These variables can be broken down into the three S's: Space Utilization, Shrinkage, and Seasonality.

Space utilization

First let's talk about space utilization. When you are calculating your cost per square foot per week, you are making the assumption that your greenhouse is full 100% of the time. This is not true. Our experience indicates that we are using only about 51% of the greenhouse over the spring season and about 50% of the space over the fall season. This means that the earlier calculation of $.20/ft.^{2}/ week is off by a factor of 2.

Your actual cost per square foot is:

$$\$820,000 / (80,000 \times 0.50) = \$20.50 / 52 = \$.40/ft.^2/week, \text{ or } \$0.20 / 0.50 = \$0.40.$$

Since you are using the greenhouse space only half of the time, the overhead costs must be allocated only to these crops. Remember, you are allocating your costs to growing crops, not empty floor space. If you do not have any crops on the floor at a given time, then you cannot allocate overhead costs to it. So the correct term of cost per square foot per week (CSFW) is really cost per used square foot per week. (CUSFW). Obviously, this has a dramatic impact on the true cost calculations since the CUSFW has just doubled!

Shrinkage

The second S is shrinkage. What is shrinkage? It is the difference between the total number of flats, pots, hanging baskets, seedlings, or rooted cuttings produced versus the total number sold. In some cases this difference can be very small, such as in the case of bedding plant flats, but it can be very large as in the case of seedling production.

How does shrinkage affect your application of overhead costs? Well, if you don't sell all the crops produced, then you must reallocate the overhead costs to the crops that did sell. If, for example, you lost flats by using them for patching other flats, to rot, to physical damage, or just to lack of sales and that amount equals

5% of your total crop, then you must add back that overhead to the crops that sold. The calculation would be as follows:

$$\$0.40 \times .05 = \$0.02 + \$0.40 = \$0.42$$

Now, let's say you are growing plugs that have to be fixed to 100% and typically you get about 85% viable germination. That means your shrinkage after fixing is 15%. The CUSFW would be as follows:

$$\$0.40 \times .15 = \$0.06 + \$0.40 = \$0.46$$

Again, you must allocate costs to not just greenhouse space or to crops grown, but to crops grown and sold. If you do not take shrinkage into account, you will be underestimating your true CUSFW and will be overestimating your profit. Remember to keep in mind that shrinkage also includes crops produced but not sold. This means you must keep track of all material dumped due to a lack of sales. There is also a hidden cost when crops are dumped, and that is the direct costs of the plant, pot, media, and label. These must also be added back to overhead since these costs were realized but not recouped through sales.

Seasonality

Finally, we come to the third variable S, seasonality. This is the most complicated and difficult of the three variables that affect costing. The basic premise of seasonality is that greenhouses do not generate their overhead costs evenly over the course of the year. Most greenhouse operations spend far more on overhead during the winter/spring (W/S) months versus the summer/fall (S/F). This is logical since a typical greenhouse will see its payroll reach its peak during the winter/spring period. Also, much more is spent on heating costs during the W/S than during the S/F.

Our experience indicates that an average greenhouse in the northeast U.S. will generate 75–80% of its revenue during the W/S period and 25–20% during the S/F. It is also reasonable that overhead costs will be generated in the same proportion. That being the case, it makes sense to allocate more of your overhead costs to the W/S period in proportion to the ratio of sales during this same period. The calculation would be as follows:

If gross sales equal \$1,300,000 and W/S sales total \$975,000, then \$975,000 / \$1,300,000 = 75%

Now you must define the length of the W/S period, which is usually January to May, or five months, or twenty-two weeks of the year. That means the S/F period is from June to December and is seven months in length, or thirty weeks. Now you take the total annual overhead of \$820,000 and multiply it by .75, which comes to \$615,000. This is the amount of overhead that will be allocated to the W/S period, and since this represents only twenty-two weeks, the calculation would be as follows:

$$\$615,000 / 80,000 \text{ ft.}^2 = \$7.69 / 22 =$$
$$\$0.35 \text{ cost per square foot per week.}$$

This is your new CSFW.

Now we have to apply the space utilization and shrinkage variables to our calculation. It would be as follows:

$$\$0.35 / .50 = \$0.70 \text{ CUSFW plus } \$0.70 \times .05 =$$
$$\$0.035 + \$0.70 = \$0.735 \text{ CUSFW.}$$

So, when we did our initial overhead calculation without any of the variables, it was \$0.20 CSFW. But after taking the proper variables into account our W/S overhead is now \$0.735 CUSFW. A dramatic difference!

The S/F calculation would be as follows:

$$\$820,000 \times .25 = \$205,000 / 80,000 \text{ ft.}^2 =$$
$$\$2.56 / 30 = \$0.085.$$

This is now your CSFW.

But we really want the CUSFW, so the calculation is:

$$\$0.085 / .50 = \$0.17 + \$0.17 \times .05 = \$0.0085 + \$0.17 =$$
$$\$0.1785 \text{ CUSFW.}$$

(For the sake of ease, you can round up to \$0.18 CUSFW.)

Now we have to use this information on a specific crop. Let's say you want to see if you are making money on your bedding plant crop. Table 13-1 is a typical Excel spreadsheet of how we do enterprise cost accounting. This is looking at a specific size flat and variety. All of the flats in this illustration are 804s (8

Table 13-1. Cost and Pricing for 804s, Spring 2010

(UPDATED: 10-6-10)	804 FLAT	804 FLAT	804 FLAT	804 FLAT	804 FLAT
MATERIALS	AGERATUM	BASIL	BEGONIA FROM 288	IMPATIENS FROM 512	IMPATIENS FROM 288
CUSFW: $0.50					
Growing Time--(wks)	6	5	6	6	4
# Plants per Flat	32	32	32	32	32
Cost of Plants per Cell	$0.030	$0.030	$0.053	$0.034	$0.053
Total Costs of Plants per Flat	$0.96	$0.96	$1.70	$1.08	$1.70
Cost of Insert	$0.24	$0.24	$0.24	$0.24	$0.24
Cost of Bottom Tray	$0.42	$0.42	$0.42	$0.42	$0.42
Cost of Label and Sticker	$0.09	$0.09	$0.09	$0.09	$0.09
Media @ 1.80/ft.^{3}	$0.45	$0.45	$0.45	$0.45	$0.45
Overhead - Delivery Inc in OH	$4.17	$3.47	$4.17	$3.82	$2.78
Total Costs per Flat	$6.33	$5.63	$7.07	$6.10	$5.68
2010 Selling Price per Flat	$8.00	$8.00	$8.00	$8.00	$8.00
Profit per Flat	$1.67	$2.37	$0.93	$1.90	$2.32
Gross Margin per Flat	20.9%	29.6%	11.7%	23.7%	29.0%

packs of 4 plants each, for 32 plants total) and have a footprint of 10" x 20" = 200 in.2 / 144 = 1.39 ft.². (There are 144 in.² in 1 ft.².) We have assumed a CUSFW of $0.50.

You will notice that the top of the spreadsheet listed the flat size and variety in columns. Then the crop time is noted along with the number of plants per flat. Next the direct costs of production are listed and finally the overhead is applied. This is then summed to show the total cost to produce each variety.

You will see from our example that the number of weeks that at flat is in the greenhouse has a large impact on its total costs. If you compare the impatiens grown from 512 plugs with those started from 288s, you will see that it costs less to grow the impatiens flats from 288s than the 512s because the amount of time to finish the crop is less. This demonstrates how much overhead can affect your profitability. The other point worth noting is the low amount of profit that bedding plant flats actually generate.

Let's take a look at another example of spring production: 10" hanging baskets. Many have wondered how to account for the hanging baskets that are grown over the crops that are on the floor. Some have assumed that no overhead should be applied to these crops since the space overhead is "free." On the surface this may seem reasonable, but when you take into account that overhead includes labor, fertilizer, pesticides, and administrative costs, you realize that this space is not free.

So how should you determine the amount of overhead to apply to hanging baskets grown overhead? We take the outside diameter of the hanging basket and imagine it is square in shape instead of round. So a 10" basket has an outside diameter of about 12" and therefore is: 12" x 12" = 144 in.² / 144 = 1 ft.². A 20" hanging basket has an outside diameter of about 22" x 22" = 484 in.² / 144 = 3.36 ft.². With this information you can now calculate your overhead costs to your hanging basket production. The example in table 13-2 will illustrate this.

In this illustration we used the overhead cost of $0.50 CUSFW, and after listing the variety name and crop time, noted the number of plants per hanging basket. After that, the spreadsheet details the direct costs of production and then applies the overhead. Again, this example shows that you may not be making as much money as you think on your hanging basket production.

The next illustration will show how overhead costs are calculated for crops grown in the S/F season. We will look at summer production of hardy mums.

Table 13-2. Cost and Pricing for 10" HBs, Spring 2010			
UPDATED 10-1-10	**10" HB**	**10" HB**	**10" HB**
MATERIALS	**BEGONIA 'DRAGON WING'**	**IMPATIENS**	**CALIBRACHOA 'MILLION BELLS'**
CUSFW: $0.50			
Crop Time (weeks)	10	12	15
# Plants per Basket	3	5	3
Cost of Plant	$0.33	$0.03	$0.46
Total Costs of Plants per HB	$1.00	$0.17	$1.39
Cost of Basket Setup	$0.52	$0.52	$0.52
Cost of Label and Sticker	$0.06	$0.06	$0.06
Media - 5/ft.³ @ 1.80/ft.³	$0.36	$0.36	$0.36
OH - # Wks x 1 ft.² x .50	$3.47	$3.99	$5.21
Total Costs per Basket	$5.42	$5.10	$7.53
Selling Price per Basket	$7.50	$7.50	$9.00
Profit per Basket	$2.08	$2.40	$1.47
Gross Margin per Basket	27.8%	32.0%	16.3%

The major difference between the overhead calculations for W/S and S/F is that the CUSFW is less for the S/F. We used a CUSFW of $0.50 for W/S and $0.18 for the S/F. By allocating more of our overhead to the W/S period where it is used, we get a more accurate picture of each crop's profitability versus allocating all costs equally over all twelve months.

With these examples and explanations, you are now in a position to calculate the profitability of your own crops. Keep in mind that this is a very valuable tool that will help you determine if you are making money on each crop and whether or not you should raise its price or discontinue growing it. It will take time to become proficient at using these tools, but it will pay rich dividends over time.

Production

A great dilemma most new businesses face is: What should I grow? (I'll discuss this point for just a minute before moving on to how the office should control the production process.)

Our human tendency is to grow whatever everyone else is growing. That makes sense, doesn't it? Well, it does if your competitors can't fill the demand in your area, or if they're doing a poor job and you're confident you can do a superior job at a competitive price.

But what about the situation where they're filling the demand and are doing a good job? What does this sound like? It's a prescription for disaster. If all you're doing is copying your neighbor, there's a strong likelihood you'll fail. Our industry is highly competitive and has a great capacity to overproduce almost every crop. So, if you're a small grower, you need to think carefully about what you'll grow and where you'll sell it.

A common mistake I've seen numerous small growers make is thinking they can compete with the largest growers by producing the same crops. Inevitably, this results in economic difficulties. It's better to discover some untapped niche market and become very good producing those crops. In addition to this, if you're a small grower with less than an acre (0.4 ha), it might be important to also sell your crops on a retail basis. With this setup—unique crops and a retail outlet in a great location—your chances for success increase dramatically.

Let's return to our discussion regarding the office controlling the production process. The office is the logical place where production decisions should be made. This means that numerous times throughout the year the office staff and the growing staff should sit down and map out next year's production. One suggestion is to review this year's production while the season is still in progress. That way it will be fresh in

Table 13-3. Cost and Pricing for 8", Fall 2010

UPDATED: 10-1-10	8" POT	8" POT	8" POT	8" POT
		CABBAGE &		
MATERIALS	MUM	KALE	DIANTHUS	MILLET
CUSFW: $0.18	URC	105	512	SED
Crop Time (weeks)	16	6	7	6
# Plants per Pot	1	1	5	6
Cost of Plant	$0.135	$0.15	$0.06	$0.08
Total Costs of Plants per Pot	$0.14	$0.15	$0.30	$0.46
Cost of Pot	$0.12	$0.12	$0.12	$0.12
Cost of Label and Sticker	$0.01	$0.01	$0.01	$0.01
Media @1.80/ft.^{3}	$0.17	$0.17	$0.17	$0.17
OH - # Wks x ft.^{2} x .18 (Pot Tight)	$0.38	$0.24	$0.24	$0.24
OH - # Wks x ft.^{2} x .18 (Spaced)	$1.38	$0.99	$1.32	$0.99
Total Costs per Pot	$2.21	$1.68	$2.17	$2.00
Selling Price per Pot	$2.70	$2.70	$2.80	$3.50
Profit per Pot	$0.49	$1.02	$0.63	$1.50
Gross Margin per Pot	18.2%	37.6%	22.7%	43.0%

your mind which crops are selling well and which are not. Often, if you wait till two or three months after the crops have shipped you'll have forgotten some of the finer points. The reason both should participate in the discussion is to ensure that the greenhouse is growing crops the growers are comfortable with and that the office can sell them because they match the customers' needs. This may sound elementary, but you don't want to grow things just because you can or grow plants that the office can't sell. Both teams must be in sync.

Once these growing decisions are made, it's imperative to organize all purchasing decisions to ensure that the proper hardgoods are on hand when necessary and that the greenhouse facility can handle the quantities projected. Oh, you forgot about that! Yes, every greenhouse has a finite capacity. I'm amazed each year by the number of plug customers who want to cancel their last shipment of plugs because they ran out of room. Did someone steal some greenhouse space over the winter? Not likely; they just didn't properly calculate their space allocation.

As you can see, by having the greenhouse staff working closely with the office staff, many production issues can be avoided and a relatively smooth and profitable season will ensue.

Sales

I've already mentioned the connection between production and sales, but let's focus on sales for a minute. To whom will you sell your product? Independent garden centers? Grocery chains? Big boxes? Landscapers? Wholesalers? Retailers? There are many choices, but it's important to keep one thing in mind: Sell your products where you can make the most profit. This sounds like fun, doesn't it? Who of us wants to sell to the lowest bidder? No one! Yet without a clear marketing plan, that's exactly what you'll do.

The real challenge is finding the customers who'll pay you the price you want for your products. It can be done, but you must examine your strengths and weaknesses. For example, if you're a small grower, it's unlikely you can produce your crops for the same cost as a large grower. Therefore, don't try to compete directly against him. Instead, find crops he's not producing and learn how to grow them well. If all the large growers are producing bedding in jumbo 606 packs, then it might be a good idea to specialize in potted bedding or maybe even perennials. If the large growers are selling to the mass merchandisers, focus your business on selling retail directly or to independent garden centers that want to distinguish themselves from the large chains. Give them what they want, but give them something different. That way you're not directly competing with the Goliaths of our industry.

One of the best arrangements for making profits is to grow your own material and then sell it retail. In this scenario, the importance of location can't be stressed enough. What sense does it make to build a greenhouse on some old country road that no one travels and then try to sell retail? That's another prescription for disaster. Yet, year after year, I've watched good-intentioned growers do exactly that. Yes, they work hard, but hard work usually doesn't overcome poor decision-making. Establish your business where it has the greatest potential to succeed.

Accounts Receivable

Now we're talking nuts and bolts. When it comes to managing your business successfully, one key area is collecting money. Surprised? You shouldn't be. Look at all the commercials on TV offering to assist you with paying off your debts. Wonder why? Because in America, not paying your bills is very common. This includes the greenhouse industry. So, the question you need to ask yourself is, "How am I going to collect my money?"

At first, it might be best to make all your sales on a cash basis. That way you don't have to worry about collecting. Eventually though, your business will grow and it will be necessary to offer credit terms. Ideally, you'll be running your business through a computer system that records A/R information with each transaction. Then, once an invoice is paid, you can easily record the transaction and update the customer's account. Additionally, at the end of each month, you'll be able to generate a statement for each customer that indicates if any late charges are due.

Prior to all of this, you must first determine which customers are going to receive credit. This is not an easy process, and it needs to be well documented. In order for a customer to establish credit, there are a number of steps that must be completed. First, the customer must sign a credit application, which gives you permission to contact the vendors he's listed as references. It's imperative that one of the owners signs the application, not a bookkeeper. The application should clearly outline your terms, such as net thirty days, and what interest rate you'll charge per month if the invoice isn't paid on time. If you don't specify this information on your credit application, you won't receive any late charge payments if you ever have to turn the account over to collection.

Next, you need to contact the vendors listed on the application and ask them to provide you with a credit history. Usually, three vendors must respond in order for a new customer to receive credit. Some key points to ask these vendors are if there's any history of bad checks or long delays in payment. If there are, then it might be best to postpone granting credit. If all of the vendors reply that the customer is a COD (cash on delivery) customer that has not established credit, then you must make a decision whether or not to grant credit based on your past history with this customer. It might be possible to grant him limited credit so that your exposure is minimal.

At Kube-Pak, we've come up with another method of reducing our exposure, called PPI, or Pay Previous Invoice. It means we deliver the first shipment on credit, but when the second delivery is made the customer must pay for the first delivery, and so forth. That way you give the customer an opportunity to sell some of the first delivery before he must pay for it. This keeps new customers on a tight leash but allows you to find out if they're good-paying customers.

What do you do if a customer doesn't pay his bill on time? Unfortunately, it's very common in the horticultural business for this to happen. Since we're an industry of small companies, often your customer uses you as his bank. If this happens, you must first decide if you can handle this arrangement. Without sufficient cash coming in, you may need to borrow from your bank to meet your financial obligations and pay interest on this loan because of unpaid receivables. If this occurs, then the question arises: Will you charge interest on late payments? To help you answer this question, I'll ask you another one: Do you know of any banks that lend money interest free? Hardly! So there's your answer: If banks charge interest on borrowed money, so should you.

Now here comes the difficult part. Will you stick to your guns and insist that your customers pay those late charges? Our experience has shown us that you must insist that all late charges be paid in order for a customer to maintain his credit standing. If they don't appreciate that it costs you money to carry them past their credit terms, then you don't want them as a customer, plain and simple. If you adopt this policy, there is one caveat: Be prepared to lose some customers. Somehow our industry has been lead to believe that late charges are evil and it's not necessary to pay them. Don't contribute to this misconception. Establish your credit policy and stick to it. In the long run, you'll weed out poor-paying customers and maintain a positive cash flow for your business.

Accounts Payable

Paying your vendors in an orderly and timely fashion is one of the most important aspects of acquiring good prices on your hardgoods purchases. At Kube-Pak, we've established the policy that we will *not* use our vendors as a bank. Each year, we negotiate with our bank to get the lowest possible interest rate on borrowed money. This gives us the necessary credit to pay our vendors prior to selling each crop.

There are many methods for tracking A/P, but the easiest I've found is one I learned in college almost forty years ago: Pay your bills once a week. In our case, we pay our bills every Wednesday. As each bill comes in, we carefully review its terms and determine the date it's due. Then we assign the payment date to that invoice based on the closest Wednesday prior to its due date. We've set up thirty-one file folders, marked from 1 to 31. If the third Wednesday in January is the 21st, for instance, we'll file the bill in the file marked 21. Each bill that comes in is assigned to a Wednesday and is filed appropriately. When January 21 comes around, all the bills due on that date will be in the file marked 21 and will be organized for payment. If you're paying your bills by computer, many systems offer this option of payment.

Inventory Control

I won't spend a lot of time on this subject because it's very basic, and there's little question about how important it is to know what plants you have available to sell at any given time. In this day and age, it's essential to keep track of your inventory with a computer system. The best arrangement is if you can enter a starting inventory prior to the season. Then, as orders are placed, they're automatically deducted from the live inventory. With this method, your office staff will know exactly how much of each item is sold and how much is still available for sale. Meanwhile, your customers will highly value the fact that you can immediately inform them of your current availability. As mentioned earlier, you must make sure the greenhouse updates the office of any losses so the inventory stays current.

General Ledger

This is the last step of the accounting process. It's here that all the sales, expenses, assets, and liabilities are recorded and balanced. If you haven't studied accounting at the college level, it might be difficult to master the intricacies of the G/L. But don't despair. Most software packages incorporate a G/L program, and it's just a matter of defining the various G/L categories to get it running. If you lack experience in this area, ask your accountant to help you. Once the files are set up, the computer will do the rest of the work. If you're still having a problem with this aspect of the office, take an evening course at your local community college to get more experience.

It's through the G/L that you'll be able to determine your profitability because the G/L will feed the sales information and the expenses to a trial balance or an income statement. You won't have to guess whether or not you're making a profit because this information will be in your computer. Also, as you purchase new equipment, the assets can be properly recorded on the G/L and set up for depreciation. If you have a loan with the bank, this will be shown on the G/L as a liability. The computer will then calculate your retained earnings and give you a good indication of your net worth. Sounds easy, doesn't it? Well, it's not. As with all things though, once you master the variables and become familiar with the various roles of the ledger sheet, you'll be more comfortable with it.

Need Help? Find a Partner

Running an efficient business is possible, but it takes a great deal of effort and experience. If as a small grower you lack these skills, consider partnering with someone else who has business experience. Take advantage of all the industry opportunities to learn from the "experts," and, if possible, get some schooling.

It's been said that "knowledge is a powerful thing." Never doubt the truthfulness of this statement. Equip yourself with the best tools that you can and take advantage of all the educational opportunities available. If you do, your business will clearly be on the road to success.

14

Marketing Your Business and Your Products

Building Your Business's Image

Mike Gooder

It surrounds us, envelops us, and brainwashes us. Today, our world revolves around it: image marketing.

Historically, image was immaterial to greenhouse producers. We were "indoor farmers." It was all about growing a "good crop," and each year growing more of the same. The market was local. Quality on the truck today set the price for tomorrow. "Street value" had little or nothing to do with cost of production. Healthy margins allowed sloppy pricing. Winners made up for losers. Colorful catalogs, logos, point of purchase (POP) sales tools, and slick marketing pieces weren't required . . . actually, they didn't exist. Wow, it's a different world we market in today!

As with almost every dynamic industry in our economy, growth dictates complexity and sophistication during the maturation process. Granted, simple marketing methods may still work for the simplest of producers, but as you climb up the ladder in ornamentals, the more intense, dynamic, and critical image building becomes.

Maybe you're saying, "Why does that matter? What can business marketing do for my greenhouse, nursery, or garden center?"

Cresco, Iowa?

When you're located "perfectly in the middle of nowhere," marketing your business and creating an image is critical to building your success. Most individuals within our industry have heard of Plantpeddler even though we are a small, young producer located in an obscure corner of Iowa. But through image building and the marketing of the business, Plantpeddler has developed international partnerships, ships internationally, has been featured in many forms of press, is respected as an industry innovator, and has thousands of loyal customers at all levels within our industry. Goals that seemed to be crazy dreams when we started marketing our business became reality by following a defined marketing plan. Through marketing, you, too, can make your crazy goals become reality.

Image building is something that successful entrepreneurs and enterprises work at every day. It emanates from everything they do and becomes a part of everything they are. It radiates the message that you're a serious professional. There's no rule that says just because you're small, you have to act like it!

To see the value of image marketing, take time to analyze the giants in the corporate world. Businesses such as Coca-Cola, Apple, Ford, and Nike spend millions to create, build, and maintain their corporate images, trademarks, and brand positioning. Most likely you can sketch their trademarks, sing their jingles, and tell us which of their products you last purchased. The marketing of their businesses involves every venue and juncture to build a positive brand identity in the marketplace.

Is Coke the best pop? Does Apple build the best computer and smart phone? Does Ford build the best cars and trucks? Is Nike swooshing its way down the court, track, and field with the only brand of footgear (and now every sporting accessory known to mankind)? Not necessarily. But millions of customers are loyal to these brands. One of the biggest debates ever at Plantpeddler revolved around the decision to have a pop machine on site, and whether it should be Pepsi or Coke. I witnessed brand identity, loyalty, and business marketing first hand.

Marketing Your Business

How does all this relate to the green industry or, more specifically, to your business? In simple terms, you can either sell commodities at commodity prices, or you can establish a plan to separate yourself. As today's production potential intensifies and margins evaporate, separating yourself from the pack may be the one thing that grows your profits, expands your opportunities, and brings quality of life to you and your staff. It's not as easy as it appears, however. Success involves hundreds of steps. Following are a few key ones.

Commitment

It takes total commitment. Marketing starts the first day you open for business or, by default, it starts today. Business marketing campaigns aren't created on a whim. You and all those around you need to buy in from the start and be ready for the long haul. Successful business marketing requires commitment from beginning to end. And the end is when you are no longer in business.

Do your homework

Study those around us. Look inside our industry, beside us, and outside of horticulture. Go back and review Marketing 101 again (or for the first time). With a million titles to pick from, read a book or two on marketing (make this tip a habit). A few great titles are *Outsmarting Goliath* by Debra Koontz Traverso, *Discipline of Market Leaders* by Michael Treacy and Fred Wiersema, and *Guerrilla Marketing* by Jay Conrad Levinson, and finally, a personal favorite, *The Tipping Point* penned by Malcolm Gladwell.

Look at the ads

Look at all advertising in a different way. Ask, "What's the message, and how is it packaged?" Pick up any form of print media and tear out ads that grab your attention. Collect them, categorize them, find common themes, and build from there. Listen to radio ads with an ear tuned to concepts and ideas. Chitchat with friends and staff about TV ad campaigns. Which ones keep you watching, laughing, replaying, and remarking? TV may not be in your immediate plans, but marketing is marketing no matter what the medium.

Consider principles from every business of any size that appears to be successful, effective, and having fun! Sometimes the smallest fish create the biggest splash. Just think of a few tiny examples that started in car trunks, garages, and dorm rooms—Nike, Apple, and Facebook. They may involve running shoes and computers, not greenhouses, but these guys never thought small. What's truly important is don't reinvent the wheel. Use concepts from successful campaigns to pick and fit the puzzle pieces together. This will ensure success while taking advantage of huge shortcuts.

Email and social media

With the recent evolution in marketing avenues, tap the low-cost and often no-cost alternatives of e-mail, Internet, and social media. Harvest e-mail addresses of present and perspective customers to develop your e-mail list to electronically distribute your "propaganda" at basically no cost (however, be well aware of e-mail anti-spam laws and regulations!). Develop your own website using low-cost software packages or search out a web developer (who oftentimes can be hired as a moonlighter). Don't overlook the growing power of Facebook, Twitter, and other new and emerging social media to reach customers in ways that were not even a marketing concept the last time the *Redbook* was published. Provide useful information and update it regularly to give your customers reasons to come back to your website or your social media feed and keep engaged.

Plan to succeed

Planning makes perfect. The commitment to marketing is dependent on a commitment to plan and that requires time. It's a simple truism: "We never plan to fail, but we often fail to plan."

A team effort

Form a marketing team. Depending on how small your company is, your team may be a team of one: you! Larger organizations need a cross-sectional representation of the business. Include all divisions and operations. Remember, the entire operation has to buy in—not only sales, but also the production crew, the accounting department, and the maintenance staff.

At the outset of the team meetings, start with a blank sheet of paper. With an open mind, write down and reinforce your business objectives. Is it to sell X units of product? Generate X amount or percentage of net profit? Expand to X many square feet? Or to gather X amount of market share? These are just a few examples. It's important to first define what you want to accomplish. What is the niche you are chasing? Where is your future market, and how do you hit the target—or, more precisely, the bull's eye? Then set some goals. Without goals, how can you measure success?

Start writing down concepts, proven and unproven, that may help you reach each objective. Put your team to work. Provide a marketing concepts notepad on every desk or in their pockets. You, however, should sleep with yours under your pillow. From the raw lists created, you'll formulate the plan of attack.

Build it

Think of marketing as building. Greenhouse owners love to invest in infrastructure. My recommendation is that you treat marketing the same way you treat infrastructure. Or better yet, consider it the gateway to infrastructure investment. You must realize going in that much of your investment in marketing will go without visible results. But you're in it for the long haul, remember? Think continuity, and there will be rewards.

That's the core philosophy at Plantpeddler. We are first a marketing company, then a sales company, and lastly a production company. Remember, the first two make the third option viable. As our industry surges forward, being successful in horticulture will be measured more by the marketing splash you make than the production ripple you create.

Enhance your niche

Develop "niche unique" products. Think about the products and how they match the niche you're defining. Turn that standard 6" (13 cm) poinsettia into something that distinguishes your products to your customers. Stand out in the crowd. It's not about how easy your product is to sell. It's about how easy your product is to buy.

Be recognizable

Standardize your look. Copy the big guys here. Company logo, font style, and colors are simple starting points. Use them everywhere and consistently. Where haven't you seen the Nike swoosh? Why has Heineken trademarked its green color? Why has Ford trademarked the font used for its name? Someone, someday will create the "swoosh" of horticulture.

It's all about coordinating your efforts and developing a look and feel for your company. Marketing is all encompassing. From the boardroom to the bathroom, from the copy in your ads to the words of your staff, from vehicle graphics to ballpoint pens—link every part and parcel into a common theme. It has to become brainwash—for you, for your staff, and, most important, for your customers.

Pulling It All Together

Way back in 1985, Plantpeddler purchased its first computers, not for accounting or environmental control, but to use as tools in marketing our business. It is truly incredible how our business grew because of this simple commitment to technology. Since then, we have invested and developed the information technology side of the business to include a full array of capabilities, allowing at-once and flexible marketing to match all forms of media. Is it perfect? No, but computers have wormed their way into every element of what we are about, continuing to help us grow more than just plants. No matter your size or level of sophistication, today there are numerous cost-effective methods for building marketing campaigns. Technology offers tremendous opportunities to "be small but act big."

We're firm believers in using moonlighters and marketing interns to help with marketing. Yet, as we have grown, we can justify retaining the talents of professional marketers to coordinate our common theme and strategic planning. Today, as our company continues to grow through a defined marketing objective, we're building a complete in-house marketing department.

But often it's the little things that reap the biggest rewards. You never know who your next ally may be, or when or where you'll meet. Your best strategy is to turn everyone into believers. Take the extra steps. Say thanks to everyone around you, including people whom you pay for their services. Formalize it in a note with your logo emblazoned upon it. Whether customer, supplier, or even competitor, never discount the value of believers. Some of the best customers of our wholesale division are competitors of our retail division. They believe in us, and we enjoy their business. And the favors go both ways. Win-win! We all need to remember that our competition is not within our industry; it's the world outside that steals away the consumers' discretionary income that we survive on.

Stay alert to no-cost and low-cost opportunities to be visible. Go out of your way to support a community project or event. Get involved—and include green goods. Get to know an insider at your local newspapers, radio stations, and television stations. Get them interested in what you're up to, and be an expert to whom they can turn. You'll never be able to measure the value of tours of your greenhouse by schools and community civic groups, but rest assured that you'll be rewarded tenfold, at least.

There will be days when you'll navigate troubled waters. The goal must be to turn all negatives into positives. Do that, and you'll win believers for life. Don't burn bridges; build them instead.

Networking is often an overused buzzword, but bridge building goes back to a game that my buddy Jim

Rearden (president of TrueLeaf) and I have been playing since back in the early 1980s. "Never miss the chance to rub elbows, it'll pay dividends." Through elbow rubbing we've gained the insights of lifetimes by swapping stories with Vic Ball at the very first GrowerExpo and at the Ohio Short Course "hanging" with the late Marc Cathey of the U.S. Department of Agriculture and later head of the American Horticulture Society (arguably the single-most influential researcher in our industry), as well as the likes of Anna Ball, Dr. Dave Koranski, Paul Ecke II, Norm White, Margery Daughtrey, and Michael Danziger. This is a tiny sampling of individuals who form the foundation upon which our industry is built . . . yet because of the intimate nature of our industry, they're approachable and real. Take advantage of the opportunities to network for a moment and build bridges for a lifetime of future possibilities.

The next, simplest, and often overlooked marketing rule: Never run out of business cards. It's amazing that people treat something so simple, so cheap, and yet so basic as a precious commodity. Be liberal! Spread them around like a bad cold. You'll never believe the places they'll show up or the impact and payback that an embossed 2 x 3.5" piece of card stock can create. Pack them at all times. Pass them out like they're free. Because not only are they free, they can be your meal ticket.

Somewhere along this path of business marketing you need to define or reinforce your marketing strategy. This can be accomplished through a number of methods, but two of the most effective are surveying (or polling) your audience, and using focus groups.

Surveys are most effective when you can hit your potential target as closely as possible. The more highly refined your database or mailing list, the closer your results will match the niche you're targeting. Response rate can be a major factor in accuracy. Adding an incentive for replying, follow-up phone calls, and other "push" methods can improve reply rate and accuracy. The survey results only provide value if you a committed to summarizing and analyzing the data.

Focus groups bring a relatively newer dimension to marketing, especially within our historically "unsophisticated" industry. This can be easily accomplished without complication. Bring together a defined cross-section of your customer base for a discussion of the elements within your marketing plan. This can be structured and formal or unstructured and casual. To prevent bias, you may wish to employ the services of an independent third party to facilitate the discussions.

Stay Dedicated

Now you have it all coming together—clearly defined target, a great marketing plan, standardized imagery, and several methods with which to measure results. You're out there building your business, rubbing those elbows, and establishing your brand. As you move forward, keep redefining your goals and analyzing the focus of your marketing plan. Keep adjusting, adapting, and trying new techniques. Some will fail; many will work. Stay dedicated and you will succeed. And when you do, you'll have that feeling of accomplishment you deserve—and a balance sheet that proves it was worth the commitment.

Ten Laws of Niche Marketing
Bob Frye

Niche marketing isn't for everyone. As with any enterprise, it has its limitations and its proper place. It may or may not be for you. You have to measure its merits respective to your own individual perspective.

I feel our industry is evolving to where niche marketing may become more viable than ever before. Much of my vision in this transition may be out of raw necessity, especially for smaller growers.

At The Plantation, we had nearly twenty years of experience striving to perfect our geranium market. Along the way, we learned from our stupidity and our brilliance. In retrospect, one overwhelming fact exists: As newcomers to the industry, we didn't have the luxury of knowing what couldn't be done. Most would have said, "No way can you sell a $15 geranium!" My point here is, don't be limited by what others say. True niche marketing in this industry is still a new game with different rules. The following "laws" are only part of the rules we obey.

If niche marketing is one of your interests, read on. I wrote this not to pass judgment, but to share what we learned and what worked for us at The Plantation.

Law 1: Product Differentiation through Modification and Specialization

This law is the first of ten laws because all niche marketing revolves around a specific product. Without a *legitimate* niche product, none of your niche marketing efforts will work.

You're probably not a good candidate for niche marketing if you can't or won't produce a novel product with significant differences compared with industry standards. Your customer must, at first glance, recognize unique product with extraordinary differences. These differences also must include a significant cost/benefit advantage for the customer. Short-term perception of added value isn't enough. It has to prove itself over time in the customer's environment to gain full niche credibility.

Some crops lend themselves easily to such value-added modifications, and some don't. Shy away from those crops that are only partial nominees—differences won't be significant enough. Niche products almost always require more expensive, detailed production techniques in combination with longer production schedules. Your best niche opportunities will be found with those species where substantial base markets already exist. Consider those where specialization in the above value-added concepts haven't yet been demonstrated or offered. Annuals often offer the best niche opportunities, as they have built-in obsolescence and yearly repeat sales.

Law 2: Demand Must Always Exceed Supply

This is our industry's most difficult discipline. Once you've selected a niche product, you must control production and build demand so that demand always exceeds supply. This precept should be unconditionally accepted and trusted as a cornerstone of the essential strategy for optimized niche marketing. This law is the heartbeat of most monopolies and oligopolies. Failure to trust this law is destructive to the efforts and objectives of most successful niche markets.

Sell year round based on finite, limited production inventories. You should always sell out, but selling out "early" is a misguided goal that may indicate that you've priced too low. The objective is to use the whole season at the highest prices. In a perfect world, the *last* unit of production is sold to the last customer of the season at the highest possible price.

Law 3: Prices Must Increase through the Season

At the beginning of the selling season, you might offer lower prices for early orders and payments in exchange for early cash flow and planning benefits. This early-order program significantly extends the sales season in a very compressed seasonal business. The date of your first incremental price increase should become

traditional and known by your customer base to allow them low-price options. After the early order interval, prices should go up incrementally through the growing and selling season. In addition to increased revenues, it promotes and reinforces the options offered by the early order program.

Early sales (resulting in the reduction of supply) become the barometer to timing-specific incremental price increases to maximize future revenue per unit of production. Price increases become a race against disappearing inventories. Incremental price increases become a sales tool to further promote sales and customer decision making. If for some reason it's obvious you'll have excess inventories, long inventories must be dumped or wholesaled *well outside* your defined market area so as not to affect or destroy your pre-existing market development and strategies. Prices should never go down. You should never hold "sales." Such inventory-reducing measures are counter to true niche marketing as stated in Law 2 and will more than negate the value of your early order program.

Law 4: Use the "250 Rule" to Qualify a Product and Enterprise

This method of niche marketing has no middlemen by design. If the product you choose to produce and retail can't be sold realistically at 250% above total production and marketing costs (all fixed and variable costs included), the production and marketing model is inferior. You can find better options for your money in direct-from-production-to-consumer markets. The message with this law is to analyze cost, cash flow, and market before the fact. An essential part of any marketing system is to eliminate the unknowns and variables.

Law 5: Define and Target a Specific Customer

Become a *buyer's* destination, not a shopper's destination. If your business is a true niche, you'll eventually have few shoppers. You don't want shoppers. You want buyers. Make a list. Identify and specifically define the customer profile you want and the factors that motivate this sector as buyers. This will define your advertising and promotion, which are extensions of your product and marketing objectives. Never advertise price. If you need to use price to attract customers or describe your product, you don't have a niche product and you're not a niche marketer. If (after established in the niche) you don't close a sale on at least 95% of the people who walk through the door, your niche marketing model is flawed.

Law 6: Ensure Your Customer's Success with Your Product

Your customer's success with your product is the weld that holds the whole machine together. It's where word-of-mouth referrals originate. Your product has to stand the test of time in different environments under an almost infinite number of variables. The customer has to experience long-term added value from your product. It has to be worth the price. Throw traditional perceived-value concepts out the window. Superior performance is what will bring the customer back year after year.

To ensure this type of success with your product, you need to become an expert in its extended culture and care. You need to transfer this knowledge to your customers. It needs to become a mandatory part of each sale because your success depends upon it. The customer isn't only the caretaker of your product, but the caretaker of your reputation, as well. The satisfied customer is the critical link to future success. Every customer counts, not just the big spenders. This law involves more than action; it involves an attitude of servitude. Without this attitude, this law becomes the weak link in the niche model.

Law 7: Look for Opposites

By definition, niche markets deviate from the norm. These deviations will identify you in the marketplace as different. Being nontraditional and different is an ally, especially when you're on the right side of Law 6. Study and list the compromises your competitors make to turn a quick buck at the expense of their product and/or their customer's success. Then do the opposite. Don't just be different—be right. Customers will reward you with their loyalty. This law, while short, is probably one of the most appreciated and impactful.

Law 8: Don't Devalue Your Product

Niche markets are not variety stores. If you have a true niche product, it is special and targeted and commands your full attention. Trying to do too much will dilute your efforts and devalue your product. Lamborghini dealers don't want Chevy buyers in their showrooms. You need to commit completely to niche concepts and laws, or the niche will be the first to suffer. You need to have the patience, vision, time, and capital to allow the niche to mature. Don't devalue it by offering something for everyone. It simply won't promote your niche as effectively. Niche marketing is the opposite of "me too" marketing (see Law 7).

Law 9: Be Comprehensively Superior

One of the most significant similarities between all successful niche marketers is the ability of the proprietor to be superior in all aspects of the production and sales process. This is your objective, and it's a never-ending journey. This is hard to do if you prefer production to marketing or vice versa. Niche markets are market leaders and market makers by definition. Their products become the standard of excellence and largely define value guidelines for the industry. You haven't achieved niche status if a competitor or other outside influences dictate your price.

Law 10: Discipline Must Prevail

A predominate enemy of niche marketing is compromise. Niche products and associated processes are seldom, if ever, compromised. Guard against rationalizing compromise as flexibility at the expense of your product and processes. The detail and discipline you exercise in protecting the integrity of your niche is likely to determine your success.

Obey the Laws

To sum up, building a solid niche market is (1) a continuous, long-term process; (2) perfected over several seasons of disciplined marketing and production expertise; combined with (3) the proper niche attitude.

None of this will work without discipline and adherence to all the laws of niche marketing. Breaking one law may put the entire process at risk. These laws all operate in concert to form a highly organized, reliable marketing system. Once this system is established, organized, fine-tuned, and maintained, it becomes a stand-alone asset of great value.

15

Retail Facilities

Retail Greenhouse Design

Jeff Warschauer

Retail greenhouse design is just not about greenhouse structures anymore. In this 18th edition of the *Ball Red-Book,* garden center retailers are focused on serving the consumer, no matter what the age and gender. Today's garden center is faced with a complex set of challenges, such as flat homes sales, a struggling economy, varying age and gender groups, new and ever-changing trends, and new demographics, as well as venturing into new sales opportunities in areas never imagined and much different from the traditional garden center employees' skill sets.

So why are retailers of all sizes building new greenhouses, well as specialty structures such as covered walkways, canopies, and a vast selection of utility structures?

As we mentioned in the previous edition of the *RedBook,* those of you who have traveled the world may have noticed that flowers are almost everywhere. For example, the homes and cities of Europe are filled with flowers. It's common to purchase flowers from the local sidewalk market and bring them home for no special reason or occasion.

The United States has been behind this level of consumption, but about thirty years ago the demand started to increase. This was partly fueled by the marketing efforts of independent garden center owners, growers, brokers, and breeders, not to mention new market opportunities using nationally recognizable branded plants. The U.S. had been doing a better job growing and marketing flowers and plants to homeowners and commercial landscapers.

Then the really big explosion hit! The large mass-market home centers, grocery stores, and discount stores started to build retail greenhouses. And as the larger corporate stores expanded, the independent retailers followed.

But in Europe the market is different. In much of Europe they don't have shopping malls like we do in the United States, so independent garden centers there tend to be more of a "destination lifestyle center," or a "one-stop shop," selling not just plants but also gifts, furniture, hardware, lumber, landscape services, pet, and bird supplies. Many Euro garden centers are property developers or landlords leasing a portion of the property to other retailers, such as grocery and clothing stores. Grocery stores are a favorite; they see customers several times a month and even weekly, giving the garden center more opportunities to sell to that shopper.

Theme areas also add to the destination appeal, including haunted houses during Halloween, family fun centers, on-the-farm experiences in agri-tourism, fish farms, cafés, bakeries, and much more.

The key here is that the European garden center, like the American big box store, is visited by the customer many more times in a year than the typical independent garden center that only sells green goods and gifts.

Today's trend in independent garden centers is toward an upscale look, with more warmth and that stay-awhile-and-shop look and feel. This is contrary to the big boxes, which offer low price and convenient physical locations. Instead, most independent garden centers provide a pleasurable shopping experience, customer service, specialty products, and a broader green goods inventory.

Figure 15-1. The trend in independent garden centers is upscale and impressive.

What's Different about a Retail Greenhouse?

In production greenhouses you're providing an environment for efficient plant growth. A typical environment would be high light, high humidity, and high temperatures. Commercial production greenhouses produce a wide range and a large volume of plants, so maximizing the space for volume production is essential. One way commercial growers do this is to use narrow aisles, leaving as much of the interior space as possible for plant production, not for employee and customer convenience and comfort. Equipment such as cooling fans, heaters, and lighting systems must be efficient and provide accurate conditions to the plants. Plant transport, order pulling, and shipping are the functions that must take place in the production greenhouse.

When we look at the requirements for a garden center, we find that what's good for plants isn't necessarily very good for a retail customer. The retail environment should be as dry as possible.

Often overlooked or understated in your budget, lighting fixtures are very important and must provide quality light for customers to shop by, as well as look attractive—after all, they're part of the overall interior decor scheme.

Placement of clear or shaded roof coverings must be considered based on what's underneath. You certainly wouldn't want a glass roof over the bagged-goods, gift, and checkout areas. Clear coverings allow too much sunlight to enter, bleaching out the packaging of the retail hard goods inside, sunlight shining into the cash register's LCD screens, and making it difficult to read. And that magnified sunlight makes it very hot for your customers.

Space is always at a premium, but aisles must be wide enough for two shoppers with carts to pass by each other easily. Think about your local supermarket on a busy day and how it's possible for you to shop while others are next to you.

Heating, cooling, and irrigation equipment must be out of sight and quiet.

Another important issue is maintenance. Unlike commercial growers who seem to have the tools and labor available to handle repairs and maintenance, the retail operator in many cases doesn't have these available but must account for how he will handle problems efficiently when they arise with minimal interruption to retail shopping.

Design Considerations

This falls into four categories: your personal needs and likes, the aesthetics of the finished facility, practical considerations (this is a greenhouse, after all), and your budget.

The retail garden center must incorporate a place and environment for many uses, including annuals, perennials, floral, gifts, toys, Rx (a place for fertilizers and chemicals), hardware items, lawn and garden equipment, outdoor furniture, outdoor pottery and statuary, leisure goods, grills, spas, lighting, specialty and seasonal sales area for product(s) such as fresh and artificial Christmas trees and wreath area, food items, restaurant/café/bakery, nursery products, landscape services, aquatic offerings, pet sales, pet and animal food, birding accessories, books and magazines, seasonal goods, offices, restroom facilities, customer service desk, re-potting area, classroom or seminar area, a themed event area, a shopping cart holding area, a fixed checkout area as well as satellite checkouts.

Many of the above items may require a different environment, such as temperature, humidity, lighting, and spacing within the structures. In some cases, some of these items can share environments. The use of beams to reduce the number of interior columns will provide more practical space for merchandise. When using multiple structures, such as several gutter-connected structures, you have the ability to place these items in areas that have different coverings, spacing, cooling, and heating options.

Alternative structures are equally important. Consider using covered canopies and walkways to merchandise your bagged goods as well as outdoor nursery and perennial materials. These structures allow your customers and products to stay dry during inclement weather and are a great place to hold plant basket inventories overhead.

Utility locations both inside and outside require careful planning. Be sure you have a master plan for all your electrical and water needs. Develop a master plan for today as well as the future. This should include future support buildings, loading and unloading areas, warehousing, drainage, and overflow parking. Work with design experts experienced in retail garden center design rather than production greenhouse design.

Retail Fixtures

Concrete blocks and boards have for years been the rule of thumb for merchandising in a retail garden center greenhouse. Pegboard and metal racks were commonplace in the hardgoods retail area. Today attractive, high-quality fixtures are important for both your indoor and outside sales areas. You can choose decorative shelves with aluminum and wood trim, beautiful aluminum benches with color-coordinated trim, or solid wood benches, all of which give the shopper a feeling of comfort, warmth, and confidence. Many retail suppliers also offer their own product-specific displays.

Other options that are gaining popularity, and are common in Europe, are automatic flood irrigation benches and manual self-watering benches and displays, as described in chapter 5. Instead of an open-weave wire bench bottom, these benches have a solid bottom that contains the run-off as well as dirt and leaf drop—no more dirty floors. These benches can be automatically flooded from a built-in plumbing and containment system or simply by a hose and drained into a tank or drain that was planned for during the design phase.

Speaking of design, fixture layout by qualified individuals is important to maximize the space you have to work with. These individuals can also play a key role in assisting you with changes in themes as the seasons and holidays change. In other industries, retail businesses wouldn't dream of planning a commercial building design without the help of a professional design person, and you shouldn't either.

Can You Grow and Retail in the Same House?

Most greenhouses used strictly for growing have higher levels of light and humidity than do retail greenhouses. Also, production greenhouses need to turn over higher volumes of plants in a short time during the plant production cycle. In order to maximize space utilization, a production greenhouse needs as much growing space as possible in order to produce as many plants as possible within that structure.

A retail greenhouse must also inventory many plants while leaving room for customers to shop comfortably. Wider aisles, lower humidity, and less light are consistent with a retail-friendly shopping experience.

There are ways to compromise and design a commercial greenhouse that works as a retail-friendly greenhouse. The following options work well for both growing and retailing.

- Tall structures with high sidewalls tend to provide a cooler, more consistent climate.
- Wide structures are more cost effective when purchased in multiples and have fewer interior columns to interfere with growing space, customer aisles, and merchandising space.
- Glass, acrylic, and polycarbonate glazing can provide a high level of light for growing and higher light levels during overcast days.
- Energy curtains can be used to control light and heat within the greenhouse environment, blocking out high light to keep customers comfortable.
- Concrete floors allow clean, dry shopping and easy movement for shopping carts. For the growing greenhouse, a cleaner environment means less risk of disease, easy cart maneuvering, and more uniform humidity, which can be controlled using mechanical equipment.
- Irrigation can be accomplished using a watering boom that can be parked out of the way at the end of the greenhouse when customers are present.

Employees can hand water during business hours when the boom would interfere with retail customers. Flood and self-watering benches and displays are gaining popularity to avoid the inconvenience to customers and provide uniform watering.

- Checkout and customer service areas need to be shaded and cool and can incorporate mechanical lighting. Steel roof covering over this area is an option but would provide too much shade for growing a crop. One alternative that works very well is using a translucent covering that still allows some light for growing. This covering can be added to any portion of the roof. Another option would be to hang some sort of canopy over the areas that you want to shield from full sun. Some retailers suspend large fabric umbrellas over their cash registers using heavy nylon lines. It's inexpensive and attractive.

Typical Costs

As with the structures discussed in chapter 1, a retail greenhouse's price depends on myriad factors, including the type and style of structure, glazing, frame options, doors, heating equipment, cooling equipment, construction labor, floor options, plumbing, foundation, and its overall width and length.

A rough average price for a retail-style, gutter-connected greenhouse equipped with a double-poly roof and 8-mm twin-wall polycarbonate sides and ends, with wall unit heaters, fans, and manual doors is $12–15/ft.^{2} ($129–162/m^2). This doesn't include installation labor or labor for basic electric and plumbing or a concrete floor. Adding these other items can run the price up to $20–23 per ft.^{2} ($215–248/m^2).

Changing specifications to a hard-covered structure (i.e., glass, acrylic, or polycarbonate) with hot water heat, positive pressure cooling, and automatic doors along with upgraded painted extrusions will average $25–35 per ft.^{2} ($269–377/m^2) and approximately $35–40 per ft.^{2} ($377–431/m^2) with options. Prices in the retail industry can range even higher ($50–65 per ft.^{2} [$550–701/m^2]) when special requirements are needed, such as custom frame designs or engineering requirements to meet specific building codes.

A rule of thumb for expansion is that gutter-connected greenhouses are more cost effective than freestanding structures when adding the subsequent structures to the first structure. You save by not having to purchase both sets of columns and gutters; you simply add each new building to the existing common wall.

Zoning Considerations

Zoning ordinances vary from location to location. In some cases, zoning laws may not allow for a retail garden center business because the location may be zoned for residential and agricultural use only. Your community may allow you to petition the local government to allow you to operate your retail center under an agricultural, commercial variance.

In the past years, many parts of the country allowed individual building departments to govern the design, strength, and safety of building construction. Today, many of these local government agencies are being replaced by organizations such as the IBC (International Building Code). When choosing a greenhouse manufacturer, be sure they can engineer a structure that will not only meet your own needs but also that of your local building codes. One important way of qualifying your supplier and protecting yourself is to make sure your greenhouse company's engineer is licensed as a registered engineer in your state and that he or she can affix a state seal to the blueprints and prepare all the necessary structural calculations.

Steel Retail Buildings

Many greenhouse manufacturers specialize in steel buildings. Most greenhouses are manufactured and installed using a steel frame. The basic component of retail steel buildings is also a steel frame. The common factor that you find on most retail steel buildings is that they make use of a solid steel skin roof.

However, most greenhouse manufacturers deal with single-story construction and don't offer added necessities, such as plumbing, electric, and drywall. One option is to purchase your steel structure from your greenhouse supplier and then subcontract the other work to a local general contractor. The advantage of using your greenhouse manufacturer as your steel building supplier is that in many cases his structure can be added or gutter-connected to your new or existing greenhouse. This can be a real cost savings to you.

If you're looking for multiple floors and custom engineering, it may pay to seek out a steel building supplier that specializes in that type of construction. When using another type of building, both building manufacturers should work together to tie the two buildings together if this is to be the design.

Seek out the Experts

Many greenhouse manufacturers and consulting firms offer services related to building greenhouses and utility buildings. Several manufacturers operate separate divisions within their company that specialize in retail garden centers. Consultants offer services that include:

- Building design (both structural and architectural)
- Demographics
- Traffic flow (both vehicular and human)
- Business planning and management
- Marketing
- Merchandizing and signage
- Infrastructure and mechanicals, such as heating, cooling, electric, plumbing, lighting, flooring, door placement, and permitting
- Employee training (customer service)
- Human resources
- Product inventory
- Permitting
- POS systems

What's most important is that you choose a company that has retail experience. As they say, "Retail is detail." So many issues, from permitting to aesthetics to greenhouse environment, are different in the retail business compared with the commercial greenhouse. That's why it's important you seek out a retail expert.

A Retailer's Biggest Challenge

An independent retailer's biggest challenge is finding ways to increase the frequency of customer visits to their store, as well as increasing sales during inclement weather. Here are a few ideas that have had a positive impact on many of our country's leading independent garden centers. Keep in mind that you must analyze your situation both from a monetary and a physical facilities standpoint. And you must do careful research, discussing your project with industry consultants and professional planners such as architects, engineers, and building and zoning codes officials. Federal, state and local municipality laws may apply.

- Greenhouses today can be covered with metal insulated roofs that meet new energy codes, and many are air conditioned. Traditional concrete floors are now treated in various ways, such as acid staining, to make them more aesthetically pleasing and easier to clean.
- Visit other garden centers and nurseries that have made change and increased customer visits and, of course, sales to see what ideas you can incorporate.

- Covered walkways improve sales during inclement weather.
- Open-walled greenhouse canopies built along with more expensive "year-round" enclosed greenhouses reduce your per-square-foot cost for a new garden center build.
- Ad a café that serves prepared food items that require little to no kitchen preparation other than unwrapping and serving, and in some cases minor assembly of foods or simple "bake-off" items, as well as salads and premade sandwiches and wraps that food purveyors describe as ready to serve. Food cost and labor ratios are typically lower and more predictable. The impact on major kitchen equipment is minimal compared with a facility that prepares foods onsite.
- Install a café that serves food items that require kitchen preparation. The typical impact of food preparation and service is greater, as most health departments have regulations that are more stringent. Also, the kitchen equipment is more extensive, such as a dishwasher versus a three-bay sink. If using open fryers and griddles, it's typical that a fire suppression system must be added.
- Fudge sales are a relatively a low-risk investment, as you can start out by purchasing fudge "slabs" from vendors or by making the fudge from packaged ingredients that make the preparation relatively foolproof. The display of fudge is very important to the success of any fudge sales program. The most impressive method is kettle-cooking the fudge and cooling it on a marble slab for display in glass cases. Vendors such as Calico (www.calicofudge.com) offer all the equipment and supplies. The alternative is to buy in premade fudge for display in dedicated cases.
- Produce fruits and vegetables for seasonal or year-round sales. For seasonal sales, you can buy in local fruits and vegetables, displaying them in your current fixtures. After a relatively short season, you're out of the produce business till the next year.
- Cheeses require a small inventory and little space, but you need to have knowledge of the best cheeses for your demographics, as well as availability. They go well with other items that you may be selling, such as crackers and condiments.
- Local/regional wines can distinguish your garden center. Typically, state liquor licenses are available and affordable compared with much more expen-

sive liquor licenses that allow you to sell alcohol products from around the world. Like cheeses, some expertise is required, but it's easy to build events around wine.

- A bakery is one of the best opportunities to increase traffic and keep them coming back. Pies are available from many vendors and rival your best homemade pie recipe. Most pies are pre-packaged and you simply remove from box, thaw for cream and meringue pies, and bake for fruit pies. Many garden centers only sell bakery items during the fall and holiday seasons.
- Ice cream and smoothies are high-margin food items. Soft ice cream seems to be the current trend and requires only a machine and nearby three-bay sink for cleanup. Hard ice cream is another option, but this category will require more refrigerated display space as well as increased labor and inventories.
- Other food options can include condiments such as jams, jellies, and sauces; pickled fruits and vegetables; dry goods such as chips, crackers and pastas; coffee and teas; and more.

The goal is to find product to sell that will bring the customer into your store more often, not only providing a product and service but offering your customer a shopping experience they can't find down the street.

Be advised that preparing and serving food has many risks as well as benefits. Consider the impact food may have on your parking if you seat patrons versus just selling takeaway. Serving food on premises can also impact your physical facilities, such as restrooms and the need for air-conditioned space. Remember the food costs and labor associated with these different food kiosks. Incremental sales departments need to be a profit center, not just another overhead expense. You must analyze your situation both from a monetary and physical facilities standpoint as well as your willingness to venture into areas of the unknown.

Key Design Structure Summary Checklist

___ Integrate your team with your outside design team (greenhouse architects, consultants, greenhouse manufacturer's engineers and sales personnel that are experienced in retail applications).

___ Each structure's use will dictate many of the design choices (for single and multiple structures), including aesthetics, costs, and structure options.

___ Covering choices are based on use of the retail space under cover, as well as costs and codes associated with each type of covering.

___ Doors are available in aluminum or steel, operated manually as well as automatically. Factor in customer-use doors as well as doors used for servicing your business, such as overhead doors. Americans with Disabilities Act (ADA) hardware should be part of your door design.

___ Carefully think through your design plans for water runoff. Consider downspout options for gutter runoff as well as runoff from floor drains, irrigation, parking, and property. Water flowing to retention ponds and into the municipal system must be taken into account by your design team.

Structure options:

___ Structure styles. Many structure styles/shapes lend themselves better to certain coverings and vents, as well as the overall aesthetics of your facility design. Certain structure styles are better suited for greenhouses only, such as gothic- and Quonset-style roofs. Other structure styles, such as Venlo and A-frame greenhouses, also work well as utility buildings (storage, sales areas, cafes, checkout areas, and so on). They more readily accommodate solid metal insulated roofing, and can be built with wide column spacing for open floor area.

___ Column spacing. Certain greenhouse designs allow for more of an open area with fewer columns to deal with when planning your aisles and merchandising your store. Column eliminators (beams) can eliminate even more columns.

___ Frame. For aesthetics and durability, you can powder-coated or anodized the greenhouse structure and its components. Be aware of extended lead times to have this done. If you are powder coating or anodizing the structure, you may want to consider the same for the doors for a consistent look.

___ Heat. There are different types of "retail friendly" heating, including radiant floor heat and upper hot water heat, such as fin tube. This heat is efficient and quiet compared with less expensive unit heaters.

___ Shading systems. Available in many different colors and design styles, make sure they meet both your customers' and your plants' needs.

___ Mechanical cooling. Many options are more effective in different climates, so what would work well in a humid climate might not be ideal in dry parts of the country.

___ Natural ventilation cooling. Decide locations for vents such as roof and side vents and if both are needed. Keep in mind that vents may allow light, condensation, direct sun/heat, harmful UV, and potential drips in an area where you do not want to have the risks.

___ Width and length. Many choices are available. Note that fewer gutters are better in most retail applications. That's because you want as much wide open floor space as possible for creating displays, merchandising product, and managing customer flow through your facility. Plus, gutters are not necessarily attractive to look at, and each gutter requires a downspout to take away rainwater.

___ Sidewall height.

___ Custom frame design. Many greenhouse manufactures can work with your design team to provide you with a custom look that is truly yours.

___ Partition walls on multiple gutter-connected buildings. This will allow you to have multiple zones/climates within one large building. Partitions will also allow you to shut down certain buildings when not in use, such as in winter.

Considerations for buildings:

___ Retail and production greenhouses covered with plastic, glass, polycarbonate, or acrylic; with a multitude of options.

___ Retail greenhouse styles based on different uses and environmental requirements.

___ Outdoor covered canopy. Popular widths are from 15 to 52' (4.6–15.8 m). A canopy is an excellent structure for annuals, nursery stock, and perennials, and it provides an overhead structure for extra hanging basket inventory.

___ Outdoor covered customer walkways. At widths of 8–15' (2.4–4.6 m), they keep shoppers dry during foul weather and allow for the overhead inventorying of hanging baskets.

___ Retractable shade houses and greenhouses. These are for three- to four-season use. Check with your manufacturer to ensure that these structures will handle the environmental challenges in your area (such as wind and snow).

___ Outdoor fixed shade houses. For non-winter use, these low-cost, popular specialty structures can be used for for annuals, nursery, and perennials sales areas.

___ Outdoor covered area for protecting bagged goods and other hardgoods.

Preliminary design and schedules to include:

___ Design process to include your business plan

___ Proposal presentation and review

___ Bid period

___ Permitting and approvals

___ Refer results to inside team for selection among options and decisions to proceed

___ Utility requirements

___ Fire sprinkler requirements as well as firewall requirements

___ Wetlands issues

___ Scheduling, including weather allowances

___ Solicitation of bids based on approved specifications

___ Construction contracts

___ Full document review established with consultant, architect, and greenhouse manufacturer

___ Legal consultation

___ Handicap access considerations: aisles, accessibility, egress

___ Excavation, demolition, existing conditions

___ Mobilization and manufacturing

___ Construction documents (drawing and specifications), site plan, services plan

___ Financial, legal, and insurance documents

___ Material specs and named suppliers preferred over performance specifications (ensure level of detail is enough to answer all your questions and that the scope, extent, and expected quality of work is clear to you without need for interpretation and explanation)

___ Construction (consider weather factors, labor availability)

___ Commissioning and training

___ Occupancy and first product

___ Ensure security issues relating to the business operation are adequately covered

___ OSHA and union construction issues

Temporary facilities during construction:

__ Restrooms for staff and construction crew
__ Trailer or other temporary building for office staff to conduct day-to-day business such as receiving inventory and doing interviews
__ Space for secure storage of equipment during and after construction
__ Utilities
__ Security
__ Temporary storage of early plant deliveries, if required
__ Office, staff, storage, mechanical, and electrical areas
__ Receiving, packing, and shipping areas
__ Secure area with cover if a new site, to eliminate lost days of work due to rain or snow

Caution: *Do not* **proceed with ordering materials and services without having a guarantee of permit acquisitions. This includes all approval from federal, state, and local sources.**

Examples of the Kinds of Garden Center Facilities Being Built Today

Figure 15-2. Plymouth Nursery, Plymouth, Michigan

Figure 15-4. Stauffers of Kissel Hill, Lancaster, Pennsylvania

Figure 15-3. Linvilla Orchards and Garden Center, Media, Pennsylvania

Figure 15-5. The Farm at Green Village, Green Village, New Jersey

Examples of the Kinds of Garden Center Facilities Being Built Today

Figure 15-6. Green Roof at Briggs Garden & Home, North Attleboro, Massachusetts

Figure 15-8. Mariani Gardens, Armonk, New York

Figure 15-7. Cactus & Tropicals, Draper, Utah

Figure 15-9. Wilson's Garden Center, Newark, Ohio

Index

purlins, 6
push-pull drives, 14, 16, 48, **48**
Pythium, 102, 184

Q

quality of life, 162
quality of product, 161
quaternary ammonium chloride salts, 38
Quonset-type houses, 3, 8

R

radiant heat, 64–65
radiation, 116
  diffuse, **25,** 25–26
  direct, **25,** 25–26
  long-wave, 2
  solar, 1
  ultraviolet, 24, 30
radio frequency identification (RFID), 177, 179–80,
    180
  shipping and, 180–81, **181**
  tags for, 172
Raker, C., & Sons Inc. (Litchfield, MI), **176,**
    176–79, **177, 178,** 201–4, **203**
Rearden, Jim, 216, 231–32
reciprocating seeders, 145, **145**
recirculation fan, 110–11
recycled water, treating, 100–102, **105**
recycling, 200
  sustainability and, 199
Reduce, Reuse, and Recycle, 197–98
reflective shade fabrics, 17
refrigeration, seed storage in, 202, **202**
relative humidity, seed storage and, 201–2
restricted entry intervals (REI), 195
retail facilities, 235–40
  challenges in, 239–40
  costs and, 238
  design considerations, 236–37
  experts and, 239
  fixtures, 237
  popularity of open-roof greenhouse for, 12
  shadehouses in, 17
  steel buildings, 238

theme areas in, 235
trends in, 235, **236**
zoning, 238
retractable-roof greenhouses, 6, 11, **11,** 12–13, **13,**
    18–19, **19, 108**
  natural ventilation in, 107
  open-roof greenhouse versus, 14–15
  wind and, 14
ribbon blenders in batch mixing, 140
ridge-vent greenhouses, **108**
rigid-frame system, 18
rigid-plastic glazing, 32–35
  acrylic, 32–33
  fiberglass, **31,** 32
  polycarbonate, **33,** 33–34
  pros and cons, 34–35
roads, site selection and analysis and, 210
robotic cars, **172**
robotics in horticulture, 159, **159**
robots, 175
Rollerbahn, 172
roller conveyors, 155, **155,** 170, **170**
rolling benches, 57–58, **58,** 80–81
rolling-roof greenhouses, 11, **11**
roll-media filters, 79
roof glazing, 6
  for sawtooth design, 7
  See also open-roof greenhouses; retractable-roof
    greenhouses; rolling-roof greenhouses
  hinged, 12, **13,** 14
  pitched, 6
  retractable, 11, **11, 13**
roof skylights, 22
root medium, pores at container capacity, 69
Rough Brothers, 10, 15, 16
Rovero rolling-roof greenhouse, 14
Rovero Systems, 11
Runkle, Erik, 131
runoff water
  capturing, 99–100
  constituents of, 98
  filtration of, 101
  for headhouse, 21